msdn training

2640A: Upgrading Web Development Skills from ASP to Microsoft® ASP.NET

Microsoft®

Course Number: 2640A
Part Number: X10-28235
Released: 01/2003

END-USER LICENSE AGREEMENT FOR MICROSOFT OFFICIAL CURRICULUM COURSEWARE –STUDENT EDITION

PLEASE READ THIS END-USER LICENSE AGREEMENT ("EULA") CAREFULLY. BY USING THE MATERIALS AND/OR USING OR INSTALLING THE SOFTWARE THAT ACCOMPANIES THIS EULA (COLLECTIVELY, THE "LICENSED CONTENT"), YOU AGREE TO THE TERMS OF THIS EULA. IF YOU DO NOT AGREE, DO NOT USE THE LICENSED CONTENT.

1. **GENERAL.** This EULA is a legal agreement between you (either an individual or a single entity) and Microsoft Corporation ("Microsoft"). This EULA governs the Licensed Content, which includes computer software (including online and electronic documentation), training materials, and any other associated media and printed materials. This EULA applies to updates, supplements, add-on components, and Internet-based services components of the Licensed Content that Microsoft may provide or make available to you unless Microsoft provides other terms with the update, supplement, add-on component, or Internet-based services component. Microsoft reserves the right to discontinue any Internet-based services provided to you or made available to you through the use of the Licensed Content. This EULA also governs any product support services relating to the Licensed Content except as may be included in another agreement between you and Microsoft. An amendment or addendum to this EULA may accompany the Licensed Content.

2. **GENERAL GRANT OF LICENSE.** Microsoft grants you the following rights, conditioned on your compliance with all the terms and conditions of this EULA. Microsoft grants you a limited, non-exclusive, royalty-free license to install and use the Licensed Content solely in conjunction with your participation as a student in an Authorized Training Session (as defined below). You may install and use one copy of the software on a single computer, device, workstation, terminal, or other digital electronic or analog device ("Device"). You may make a second copy of the software and install it on a portable Device for the exclusive use of the person who is the primary user of the first copy of the software. A license for the software may not be shared for use by multiple end users. An "Authorized Training Session" means a training session conducted at a Microsoft Certified Technical Education Center, an IT Academy, via a Microsoft Certified Partner, or such other entity as Microsoft may designate from time to time in writing, by a Microsoft Certified Trainer (for more information on these entities, please visit www.microsoft.com). WITHOUT LIMITING THE FOREGOING, COPYING OR REPRODUCTION OF THE LICENSED CONTENT TO ANY SERVER OR LOCATION FOR FURTHER REPRODUCTION OR REDISTRIBUTION IS EXPRESSLY PROHIBITED.

3. **DESCRIPTION OF OTHER RIGHTS AND LICENSE LIMITATIONS**

   3.1   *Use of Documentation and Printed Training Materials.*

      3.1.1   The documents and related graphics included in the Licensed Content may include technical inaccuracies or typographical errors. Changes are periodically made to the content. Microsoft may make improvements and/or changes in any of the components of the Licensed Content at any time without notice. The names of companies, products, people, characters and/or data mentioned in the Licensed Content may be fictitious and are in no way intended to represent any real individual, company, product or event, unless otherwise noted.

      3.1.2   Microsoft grants you the right to reproduce portions of documents (such as student workbooks, white papers, press releases, datasheets and FAQs) (the "Documents") provided with the Licensed Content. You may not print any book (either electronic or print version) in its entirety. If you choose to reproduce Documents, you agree that: (a) use of such printed Documents will be solely in conjunction with your personal training use; (b) the Documents will not republished or posted on any network computer or broadcast in any media; (c) any reproduction will include either the Document's original copyright notice or a copyright notice to Microsoft's benefit substantially in the format provided below; and (d) to comply with all terms and conditions of this EULA. In addition, no modifications may made to any Document.

      Form of Notice:

      © 2003. Reprinted with permission by Microsoft Corporation. All rights reserved.

      Microsoft and Windows are either registered trademarks or trademarks of Microsoft Corporation in the US and/or other countries. Other product and company names mentioned herein may be the trademarks of their respective owners.

   3.2   *Use of Media Elements.* The Licensed Content may include certain photographs, clip art, animations, sounds, music, and video clips (together "Media Elements"). You may not modify these Media Elements.

   3.3   *Use of Sample Code.* In the event that the Licensed Content includes sample code in source or object format ("Sample Code"), Microsoft grants you a limited, non-exclusive, royalty-free license to use, copy and modify the Sample Code; if you elect to exercise the foregoing rights, you agree to comply with all other terms and conditions of this EULA, including without limitation Sections 3.4, 3.5, and 6.

   3.4   *Permitted Modifications.* In the event that you exercise any rights provided under this EULA to create modifications of the Licensed Content, you agree that any such modifications: (a) will not be used for providing training where a fee is charged in public or private classes; (b) indemnify, hold harmless, and defend Microsoft from and against any claims or lawsuits, including attorneys' fees, which arise from or result from your use of any modified version of the Licensed Content; and (c) not to transfer or assign any rights to any modified version of the Licensed Content to any third party without the express written permission of Microsoft.

3.5   *Reproduction/Redistribution Licensed Content.* Except as expressly provided in this EULA, you may not reproduce or distribute the Licensed Content or any portion thereof (including any permitted modifications) to any third parties without the express written permission of Microsoft.

4.   **RESERVATION OF RIGHTS AND OWNERSHIP.** Microsoft reserves all rights not expressly granted to you in this EULA. The Licensed Content is protected by copyright and other intellectual property laws and treaties. Microsoft or its suppliers own the title, copyright, and other intellectual property rights in the Licensed Content. You may not remove or obscure any copyright, trademark or patent notices that appear on the Licensed Content, or any components thereof, as delivered to you. **The Licensed Content is licensed, not sold.**

5.   **LIMITATIONS ON REVERSE ENGINEERING, DECOMPILATION, AND DISASSEMBLY.** You may not reverse engineer, decompile, or disassemble the Software or Media Elements, except and only to the extent that such activity is expressly permitted by applicable law notwithstanding this limitation.

6.   **LIMITATIONS ON SALE, RENTAL, ETC. AND CERTAIN ASSIGNMENTS.** You may not provide commercial hosting services with, sell, rent, lease, lend, sublicense, or assign copies of the Licensed Content, or any portion thereof (including any permitted modifications thereof) on a stand-alone basis or as part of any collection, product or service.

7.   **CONSENT TO USE OF DATA.** You agree that Microsoft and its affiliates may collect and use technical information gathered as part of the product support services provided to you, if any, related to the Licensed Content. Microsoft may use this information solely to improve our products or to provide customized services or technologies to you and will not disclose this information in a form that personally identifies you.

8.   **LINKS TO THIRD PARTY SITES.** You may link to third party sites through the use of the Licensed Content. The third party sites are not under the control of Microsoft, and Microsoft is not responsible for the contents of any third party sites, any links contained in third party sites, or any changes or updates to third party sites. Microsoft is not responsible for webcasting or any other form of transmission received from any third party sites. Microsoft is providing these links to third party sites to you only as a convenience, and the inclusion of any link does not imply an endorsement by Microsoft of the third party site.

9.   **ADDITIONAL LICENSED CONTENT/SERVICES.** This EULA applies to updates, supplements, add-on components, or Internet-based services components, of the Licensed Content that Microsoft may provide to you or make available to you after the date you obtain your initial copy of the Licensed Content, unless we provide other terms along with the update, supplement, add-on component, or Internet-based services component. Microsoft reserves the right to discontinue any Internet-based services provided to you or made available to you through the use of the Licensed Content.

10.   **U.S. GOVERNMENT LICENSE RIGHTS**. All software provided to the U.S. Government pursuant to solicitations issued on or after December 1, 1995 is provided with the commercial license rights and restrictions described elsewhere herein. All software provided to the U.S. Government pursuant to solicitations issued prior to December 1, 1995 is provided with "Restricted Rights" as provided for in FAR, 48 CFR 52.227-14 (JUNE 1987) or DFAR, 48 CFR 252.227-7013 (OCT 1988), as applicable.

11.   **EXPORT RESTRICTIONS.** You acknowledge that the Licensed Content is subject to U.S. export jurisdiction. You agree to comply with all applicable international and national laws that apply to the Licensed Content, including the U.S. Export Administration Regulations, as well as end-user, end-use, and destination restrictions issued by U.S. and other governments. For additional information see <http://www.microsoft.com/exporting/>.

12.   **TRANSFER.** The initial user of the Licensed Content may make a one-time permanent transfer of this EULA and Licensed Content to another end user, provided the initial user retains no copies of the Licensed Content. The transfer may not be an indirect transfer, such as a consignment. Prior to the transfer, the end user receiving the Licensed Content must agree to all the EULA terms.

13.   **"NOT FOR RESALE" LICENSED CONTENT.** Licensed Content identified as "Not For Resale" or "NFR," may not be sold or otherwise transferred for value, or used for any purpose other than demonstration, test or evaluation.

14.   **TERMINATION.** Without prejudice to any other rights, Microsoft may terminate this EULA if you fail to comply with the terms and conditions of this EULA. In such event, you must destroy all copies of the Licensed Content and all of its component parts.

15.   <u>DISCLAIMER OF WARRANTIES.</u> **TO THE MAXIMUM EXTENT PERMITTED BY APPLICABLE LAW, MICROSOFT AND ITS SUPPLIERS PROVIDE THE LICENSED CONTENT AND SUPPORT SERVICES (IF ANY)** *AS IS AND WITH ALL FAULTS,* **AND MICROSOFT AND ITS SUPPLIERS HEREBY DISCLAIM ALL OTHER WARRANTIES AND CONDITIONS, WHETHER EXPRESS, IMPLIED OR STATUTORY, INCLUDING, BUT NOT LIMITED TO, ANY (IF ANY) IMPLIED WARRANTIES, DUTIES OR CONDITIONS OF MERCHANTABILITY, OF FITNESS FOR A PARTICULAR PURPOSE, OF RELIABILITY OR AVAILABILITY, OF ACCURACY OR COMPLETENESS OF RESPONSES, OF RESULTS, OF WORKMANLIKE EFFORT, OF LACK OF VIRUSES, AND OF LACK OF NEGLIGENCE, ALL WITH REGARD TO THE LICENSED CONTENT, AND THE PROVISION OF OR FAILURE TO PROVIDE SUPPORT OR OTHER SERVICES, INFORMATION, SOFTWARE, AND RELATED CONTENT THROUGH THE LICENSED CONTENT, OR OTHERWISE ARISING OUT OF THE USE OF THE LICENSED CONTENT. ALSO, THERE IS NO WARRANTY OR CONDITION OF TITLE, QUIET ENJOYMENT, QUIET POSSESSION, CORRESPONDENCE TO DESCRIPTION OR NON-INFRINGEMENT WITH REGARD TO THE LICENSED CONTENT. THE ENTIRE RISK AS TO THE QUALITY, OR ARISING OUT OF THE USE OR PERFORMANCE OF THE LICENSED CONTENT, AND ANY SUPPORT SERVICES, REMAINS WITH YOU.**

16.   <u>EXCLUSION OF INCIDENTAL, CONSEQUENTIAL AND CERTAIN OTHER DAMAGES.</u> **TO THE MAXIMUM EXTENT PERMITTED BY APPLICABLE LAW, IN NO EVENT SHALL MICROSOFT OR ITS SUPPLIERS BE LIABLE FOR ANY SPECIAL, INCIDENTAL, PUNITIVE, INDIRECT, OR CONSEQUENTIAL DAMAGES WHATSOEVER (INCLUDING, BUT NOT**

LIMITED TO, DAMAGES FOR LOSS OF PROFITS OR CONFIDENTIAL OR OTHER INFORMATION, FOR BUSINESS INTERRUPTION, FOR PERSONAL INJURY, FOR LOSS OF PRIVACY, FOR FAILURE TO MEET ANY DUTY INCLUDING OF GOOD FAITH OR OF REASONABLE CARE, FOR NEGLIGENCE, AND FOR ANY OTHER PECUNIARY OR OTHER LOSS WHATSOEVER) ARISING OUT OF OR IN ANY WAY RELATED TO THE USE OF OR INABILITY TO USE THE LICENSED CONTENT, THE PROVISION OF OR FAILURE TO PROVIDE SUPPORT OR OTHER SERVICES, INFORMATION, SOFTWARE, AND RELATED CONTENT THROUGH THE LICENSED CONTENT, OR OTHERWISE ARISING OUT OF THE USE OF THE LICENSED CONTENT, OR OTHERWISE UNDER OR IN CONNECTION WITH ANY PROVISION OF THIS EULA, EVEN IN THE EVENT OF THE FAULT, TORT (INCLUDING NEGLIGENCE), MISREPRESENTATION, STRICT LIABILITY, BREACH OF CONTRACT OR BREACH OF WARRANTY OF MICROSOFT OR ANY SUPPLIER, AND EVEN IF MICROSOFT OR ANY SUPPLIER HAS BEEN ADVISED OF THE POSSIBILITY OF SUCH DAMAGES. BECAUSE SOME STATES/JURISDICTIONS DO NOT ALLOW THE EXCLUSION OR LIMITATION OF LIABILITY FOR CONSEQUENTIAL OR INCIDENTAL DAMAGES, THE ABOVE LIMITATION MAY NOT APPLY TO YOU.

17. <u>LIMITATION OF LIABILITY AND REMEDIES</u>. NOTWITHSTANDING ANY DAMAGES THAT YOU MIGHT INCUR FOR ANY REASON WHATSOEVER (INCLUDING, WITHOUT LIMITATION, ALL DAMAGES REFERENCED HEREIN AND ALL DIRECT OR GENERAL DAMAGES IN CONTRACT OR ANYTHING ELSE), THE ENTIRE LIABILITY OF MICROSOFT AND ANY OF ITS SUPPLIERS UNDER ANY PROVISION OF THIS EULA AND YOUR EXCLUSIVE REMEDY HEREUNDER SHALL BE LIMITED TO THE GREATER OF THE ACTUAL DAMAGES YOU INCUR IN REASONABLE RELIANCE ON THE LICENSED CONTENT UP TO THE AMOUNT ACTUALLY PAID BY YOU FOR THE LICENSED CONTENT OR US$5.00. THE FOREGOING LIMITATIONS, EXCLUSIONS AND DISCLAIMERS SHALL APPLY TO THE MAXIMUM EXTENT PERMITTED BY APPLICABLE LAW, EVEN IF ANY REMEDY FAILS ITS ESSENTIAL PURPOSE.

18. **APPLICABLE LAW.** If you acquired this Licensed Content in the United States, this EULA is governed by the laws of the State of Washington. If you acquired this Licensed Content in Canada, unless expressly prohibited by local law, this EULA is governed by the laws in force in the Province of Ontario, Canada; and, in respect of any dispute which may arise hereunder, you consent to the jurisdiction of the federal and provincial courts sitting in Toronto, Ontario. If you acquired this Licensed Content in the European Union, Iceland, Norway, or Switzerland, then local law applies. If you acquired this Licensed Content in any other country, then local law may apply.

19. **ENTIRE AGREEMENT; SEVERABILITY.** This EULA (including any addendum or amendment to this EULA which is included with the Licensed Content) are the entire agreement between you and Microsoft relating to the Licensed Content and the support services (if any) and they supersede all prior or contemporaneous oral or written communications, proposals and representations with respect to the Licensed Content or any other subject matter covered by this EULA. To the extent the terms of any Microsoft policies or programs for support services conflict with the terms of this EULA, the terms of this EULA shall control. If any provision of this EULA is held to be void, invalid, unenforceable or illegal, the other provisions shall continue in full force and effect.

Should you have any questions concerning this EULA, or if you desire to contact Microsoft for any reason, please use the address information enclosed in this Licensed Content to contact the Microsoft subsidiary serving your country or visit Microsoft on the World Wide Web at http://www.microsoft.com.

Si vous avez acquis votre Contenu Sous Licence Microsoft au CANADA :

DÉNI DE GARANTIES. Dans la mesure maximale permise par les lois applicables, le Contenu Sous Licence et les services de soutien technique (le cas échéant) sont fournis *TELS QUELS ET AVEC TOUS LES DÉFAUTS* par Microsoft et ses fournisseurs, lesquels par les présentes dénient toutes autres garanties et conditions expresses, implicites ou en vertu de la loi, notamment, mais sans limitation, (le cas échéant) les garanties, devoirs ou conditions implicites de qualité marchande, d'adaptation à une fin usage particulière, de fiabilité ou de disponibilité, d'exactitude ou d'exhaustivité des réponses, des résultats, des efforts déployés selon les règles de l'art, d'absence de virus et d'absence de négligence, le tout à l'égard du Contenu Sous Licence et de la prestation des services de soutien technique ou de l'omission de la 'une telle prestation des services de soutien technique ou à l'égard de la fourniture ou de l'omission de la fourniture de tous autres services, renseignements, Contenus Sous Licence, et contenu qui s'y rapporte grâce au Contenu Sous Licence ou provenant autrement de l'utilisation du Contenu Sous Licence. PAR AILLEURS, IL N'Y A AUCUNE GARANTIE OU CONDITION QUANT AU TITRE DE PROPRIÉTÉ, À LA JOUISSANCE OU LA POSSESSION PAISIBLE, À LA CONCORDANCE À UNE DESCRIPTION NI QUANT À UNE ABSENCE DE CONTREFAÇON CONCERNANT LE CONTENU SOUS LICENCE.

EXCLUSION DES DOMMAGES ACCESSOIRES, INDIRECTS ET DE CERTAINS AUTRES DOMMAGES. DANS LA MESURE MAXIMALE PERMISE PAR LES LOIS APPLICABLES, EN AUCUN CAS MICROSOFT OU SES FOURNISSEURS NE SERONT RESPONSABLES DES DOMMAGES SPÉCIAUX, CONSÉCUTIFS, ACCESSOIRES OU INDIRECTS DE QUELQUE NATURE QUE CE SOIT (NOTAMMENT, LES DOMMAGES À L'ÉGARD DU MANQUE À GAGNER OU DE LA DIVULGATION DE RENSEIGNEMENTS CONFIDENTIELS OU AUTRES, DE LA PERTE D'EXPLOITATION, DE BLESSURES CORPORELLES, DE LA VIOLATION DE LA VIE PRIVÉE, DE L'OMISSION DE REMPLIR TOUT DEVOIR, Y COMPRIS D'AGIR DE BONNE FOI OU D'EXERCER UN SOIN RAISONNABLE, DE LA NÉGLIGENCE ET DE TOUTE AUTRE PERTE PÉCUNIAIRE OU AUTRE PERTE

DE QUELQUE NATURE QUE CE SOIT) SE RAPPORTANT DE QUELQUE MANIÈRE QUE CE SOIT À L'UTILISATION DU CONTENU SOUS LICENCE OU À L'INCAPACITÉ DE S'EN SERVIR, À LA PRESTATION OU À L'OMISSION DE LA 'UNE TELLE PRESTATION DE SERVICES DE SOUTIEN TECHNIQUE OU À LA FOURNITURE OU À L'OMISSION DE LA FOURNITURE DE TOUS AUTRES SERVICES, RENSEIGNEMENTS, CONTENUS SOUS LICENCE, ET CONTENU QUI S'Y RAPPORTE GRÂCE AU CONTENU SOUS LICENCE OU PROVENANT AUTREMENT DE L'UTILISATION DU CONTENU SOUS LICENCE OU AUTREMENT AUX TERMES DE TOUTE DISPOSITION DE LA U PRÉSENTE CONVENTION EULA OU RELATIVEMENT À UNE TELLE DISPOSITION, MÊME EN CAS DE FAUTE, DE DÉLIT CIVIL (Y COMPRIS LA NÉGLIGENCE), DE RESPONSABILITÉ STRICTE, DE VIOLATION DE CONTRAT OU DE VIOLATION DE GARANTIE DE MICROSOFT OU DE TOUT FOURNISSEUR ET MÊME SI MICROSOFT OU TOUT FOURNISSEUR A ÉTÉ AVISÉ DE LA POSSIBILITÉ DE TELS DOMMAGES.

LIMITATION DE RESPONSABILITÉ ET RECOURS. MALGRÉ LES DOMMAGES QUE VOUS PUISSIEZ SUBIR POUR QUELQUE MOTIF QUE CE SOIT (NOTAMMENT, MAIS SANS LIMITATION, TOUS LES DOMMAGES SUSMENTIONNÉS ET TOUS LES DOMMAGES DIRECTS OU GÉNÉRAUX OU AUTRES), LA SEULE RESPONSABILITÉ 'OBLIGATION INTÉGRALE DE MICROSOFT ET DE L'UN OU L'AUTRE DE SES FOURNISSEURS AUX TERMES DE TOUTE DISPOSITION DEU LA PRÉSENTE CONVENTION EULA ET VOTRE RECOURS EXCLUSIF À L'ÉGARD DE TOUT CE QUI PRÉCÈDE SE LIMITE AU PLUS ÉLEVÉ ENTRE LES MONTANTS SUIVANTS : LE MONTANT QUE VOUS AVEZ RÉELLEMENT PAYÉ POUR LE CONTENU SOUS LICENCE OU 5,00 $US. LES LIMITES, EXCLUSIONS ET DÉNIS QUI PRÉCÈDENT (Y COMPRIS LES CLAUSES CI-DESSUS), S'APPLIQUENT DANS LA MESURE MAXIMALE PERMISE PAR LES LOIS APPLICABLES, MÊME SI TOUT RECOURS N'ATTEINT PAS SON BUT ESSENTIEL.

À moins que cela ne soit prohibé par le droit local applicable, la présente Convention est régie par les lois de la province d'Ontario, Canada. Vous consentez Chacune des parties à la présente reconnaît irrévocablement à la compétence des tribunaux fédéraux et provinciaux siégeant à Toronto, dans de la province d'Ontario et consent à instituer tout litige qui pourrait découler de la présente auprès des tribunaux situés dans le district judiciaire de York, province d'Ontario.

Au cas où vous auriez des questions concernant cette licence ou que vous désiriez vous mettre en rapport avec Microsoft pour quelque raison que ce soit, veuillez utiliser l'information contenue dans le Contenu Sous Licence pour contacter la filiale de succursale Microsoft desservant votre pays, dont l'adresse est fournie dans ce produit, ou visitez écrivez à : Microsoft sur le World Wide Web à http://www.microsoft.com

Contents

About This Course

This section provides you with a brief description of the course, audience, suggested prerequisites, and course objectives.

Description

The course provides the information that developers need to know to successfully upgrade their Web development skills from being able to create Active Server Pages (ASP) to Microsoft® ASP.NET. The material that comprises this course explains the differences in ASP versus ASP.NET, thereby creating an understanding of the efforts that are involved in getting an existing ASP Web application functioning in an ASP.NET environment. This course also reveals the new features of ASP.NET that can be used to improve an existing ASP Web application.

Finally, this course provides students with several strategies for migrating ASP Web applications to ASP.NET, as well as a corresponding list of tasks that must be completed for successful migration.

Audience

This course is intended for existing Web developers who are currently writing ASP Web applications.

Student prerequisites

This course requires that students meet the following prerequisites:

- Ability to create Hypertext Markup Language (HTML) pages with tables, images, and forms.

- Experience using a scripting language, such as Microsoft Visual Basic® Scripting Edition or JavaScript.

- Experience using ASP to create Web applications.

- Ability to retrieve data from a relational database by using ActiveX® Data Objects (ADO).

- Familiarity with a Microsoft .NET-based programming language.

Course objectives

After completing this course, students will be able to:

- Explain the main differences between ASP and ASP.NET, the main .NET-based programming language features, and the .NET application just-in-time (JIT) compiling and execution model.

- Create Web Forms by using HTML controls, Web controls, and third-party controls.

- Use the trace feature of ASP.NET and the Microsoft Visual Studio® .NET debugger to debug ASP.NET Web applications.

- Use Microsoft ADO.NET to access data from a database.

- Manage state in an ASP.NET Web application.

- Implement Microsoft Windows®–based and Forms-based authentication in an ASP.NET Web application.

- Create and consume XML Web services from an ASP.NET Web application.

- Access existing Component Object Model (COM) components by using .NET COM interop from an ASP.NET Web application.

- Develop and apply strategies for migrating ASP Web applications to ASP.NET, and to port ASP pages to ASP.NET.

- Prepare an ASP.NET Web application for deployment.

Optional course objectives

This course includes four appendixes that may be included at the instructor's discretion:

- Appendix A, "Accessing XML Data"

  This teachable appendix explains how to work with Extensible Markup Language (XML) data in an ASP.NET Web application by using **System.Xml** objects.

- Appendix B, "Improving Microsoft ASP.NET Web Application Performance Using Caching"

  This teachable appendix explains how to improve the performance of an ASP.NET Web application by using the ASP.NET caching features.

- Appendix C, "Job Aid: Migrating ASP Web Applications to Microsoft ASP.NET"

  This Job Aid provides a list of the actions that need to be taken when migrating an ASP Web application to ASP.NET.

- Appendix D, "Review Game"

  This interactive game provides an opportunity to apply the knowledge gained in this course.

Student Materials Compact Disc Contents

The Student Materials compact disc contains the following files and folders:

- *Autorun.exe.* When the compact disc is inserted into the CD-ROM drive, or when you double-click the **Autorun.exe** file, this file opens the compact disc and allows you to browse the Student Materials compact disc.

- *Autorun.inf.* When the compact disc is inserted into the compact disc drive, this file opens Autorun.exe.

- *Default.htm.* This file opens the Student Materials Web page. It provides you with resources pertaining to this course, including additional reading, review and lab answers, lab files, multimedia presentations, and course-related Web sites.

- *Readme.txt.* This file explains how to install the software for viewing the Student Materials compact disc and its contents and how to open the Student Materials Web page.

- *2640A_ms.doc.* This file is the Manual Classroom Setup Guide. It contains a description of classroom requirements, classroom setup instructions, and the classroom configuration.

- *Settings.xml.* This file is used to display the course materials on this compact disc.

- *Viewer.htm.* This file is used to display the course materials on this compact disc.

- *Democode.* This folder contains demonstration code.

- *Flash.* This folder contains the installer for the Macromedia Flash 6.0 browser plug-in.

- *Fonts.* This folder contains fonts that may be required to view the Microsoft Word documents that are included with this course.

- *Labfiles.* This folder contains files that are used in the hands-on labs. These files may be used to prepare the student computers for the hands-on labs.

- *Media.* This folder contains files that are used in multimedia presentations for this course.

- *Mplayer.* This folder contains the setup file to install Microsoft Windows Media™ Player.

- *Practices.* This folder contains files that are used in the hands-on practices.

- *Viewer.* This folder contains files that are used to display the course materials on this compact disc.

- *Webfiles.* This folder contains the files that are required to view the course Web page. To open the Web page, open Windows Explorer, and in the root directory of the compact disc, double-click **Default.htm** or **Autorun.exe**.

- *Wordview.* This folder contains the Word Viewer that is used to view any Word document (.doc) files that are included on the compact disc.

Document Conventions

The following conventions are used in course materials to distinguish elements of the text.

Convention	Use
Bold	Represents commands, command options, and syntax that must be typed exactly as shown. It also indicates commands on menus and buttons, dialog box titles and options, and icon and menu names.
Italic	In syntax statements or descriptive text, indicates argument names or placeholders for variable information. Italic is also used for introducing new terms, for book titles, and for emphasis in the text.
Title Capitals	Indicate domain names, user names, computer names, directory names, and folder and file names, except when specifically referring to case-sensitive names. Unless otherwise indicated, you can use lowercase letters when you type a directory name or file name in a dialog box or at a command prompt.
ALL CAPITALS	Indicate the names of keys, key sequences, and key combinations—for example, ALT+SPACEBAR.
`monospace`	Represents code samples or examples of screen text.
[ ]	In syntax statements, enclose optional items. For example, [*filename*] in command syntax indicates that you can choose to type a file name with the command. Type only the information within the brackets, not the brackets themselves.
{ }	In syntax statements, enclose required items. Type only the information within the braces, not the braces themselves.
|	In syntax statements, separates an either/or choice.
▶	Indicates a procedure with sequential steps.
...	In syntax statements, specifies that the preceding item may be repeated.
...	Represents an omitted portion of a code sample.

msdn training

Introduction

Contents

Introduction

- Name
- Company affiliation
- Title/function
- Job responsibility
- Programming, networking, and database experience
- Visual Studio .NET experience
- Expectations for the course

Course Materials

- **Name card**
- **Student workbook**
- **Student Materials compact disc**
- **Course evaluation**

The following materials are included with your kit:

- *Name card.* Write your name on both sides of the name card.

- *Student workbook.* The student workbook contains the material that is covered in class, in addition to the hands-on lab exercises.

- *Student Materials compact disc.* The Student Materials compact disc contains the Web page that provides you with links to resources pertaining to this course, including additional readings, practice and lab answers, lab files, multimedia presentations, and course-related Web sites.

Note To open the Web page, insert the Student Materials compact disc into the CD-ROM drive, and then in the root directory of the compact disc, double-click **Autorun.exe** or **Default.htm**.

- *Course evaluation.* To provide feedback on the course, training facility, and instructor, you will have the opportunity to complete an online evaluation near the end of the course.

  To provide additional comments or inquire about the Microsoft Certified Professional (MCP) program, send e-mail to mcphelp@microsoft.com.

Prerequisites

- Ability to create HTML pages including tables, images, and forms
- Experience using a scripting language, such as Visual Basic Scripting Edition or JavaScript
- Experience using ASP to create Web applications
- Ability to retrieve data from a relational database using ADO
- Familiarity with a .NET-based programming language

This course requires that you meet the following prerequisites:

- Ability to create Hypertext Markup Language (HTML) pages including tables, images, and forms.

- Experience using a scripting language, such as Microsoft Visual Basic® Scripting Edition or JavaScript.

- Experience using Active Server Pages (ASP) to create Web applications.

- Ability to retrieve data from a relational database by using Microsoft ActiveX® Data Objects (ADO).

- Familiarity with a Microsoft .NET-based programming language.

Course Outline

- Module 1: Introduction to Microsoft ASP.NET Web Application Development
- Module 2: Developing a Microsoft ASP.NET Web Application User Interface
- Module 3: Debugging Microsoft ASP.NET Web Applications
- Module 4: Accessing Data Using Microsoft ADO.NET
- Module 5: Managing State in a Microsoft ASP.NET Web Application
- Module 6: Authenticating Users
- Module 7: Creating and Consuming XML Web Services

Course outline

Module 1, "Introduction to Microsoft ASP.NET Web Application Development," describes ASP.NET architecture and explains how it relates to the Microsoft .NET Framework. This module also explains how to use the Microsoft Visual Studio® .NET object-oriented programming languages to develop ASP.NET Web applications.

Module 2, "Developing a Microsoft ASP.NET Web Application User Interface," explains how to create an ASP.NET Web application user interface (UI) by using Web Forms, ASP.NET server controls, and event handlers. This module also explains how to validate user input by using validation controls and explains how the Web page postback process works.

Module 3, "Debugging Microsoft ASP.NET Web Applications," explains how to analyze the cause of logic errors in your ASP.NET Web application by using ASP.NET trace functionality and the Visual Studio .NET debugger.

Module 4, "Accessing Data Using Microsoft ADO.NET," explains how to use Microsoft ADO.NET to access data. This module also explains how to use the Visual Studio .NET built-in tools to access data by using ADO.NET, and how to programmatically access data with ADO.NET.

Module 5, "Managing State in a Microsoft ASP.NET Web Application," explains how to manage state in an ASP.NET Web application, including server-side and client-side state management.

Module 6, "Authenticating Users," introduces the different types of authentication methods that are supported by ASP.NET and explains how to implement Microsoft Windows®-based and forms-based authentication in an ASP.NET Web application.

Module 7, "Creating and Consuming XML Web Services," explains how to call an XML Web service directly, by using a browser, and by proxy from a Web Form. This module also covers how to create and publish XML Web services by using Visual Studio .NET.

Course Outline *(continued)*

- **Module 8: Calling COM Components**
- **Module 9: Migrating ASP Web Applications to Microsoft ASP.NET**
- **Module 10: Deploying Microsoft ASP.NET Web Applications**
- **Appendix A: Accessing XML Data**
- **Appendix B: Improving Microsoft ASP.NET Web Application Performance Using Caching**
- **Appendix C: Job Aid: Migrating ASP Web Applications to Microsoft ASP.NET**
- **Appendix D: Review Game**

Module 8, "Calling COM Components," explains how to access existing Component Object Model (COM) components by using .NET COM interop. This module also covers how to create a COM object and call methods on that object, and how to use the type library importer to import COM component type information into your ASP.NET Web Form. Finally, you will learn how to manage the errors that may be generated from a call to a COM object.

Module 9, "Migrating ASP Web Applications to Microsoft ASP.NET," examines the various strategies that can be used to migrating ASP Web applications to ASP.NET. This module also covers the main issues to consider when migrating ASP Web applications to ASP.NET. Finally, you will learn the steps that are required to port an .asp page to an .aspx page.

Module 10, "Deploying Microsoft ASP.NET Web Applications," explains how to determine which files are needed to deploy an ASP.NET Web application, and then explains how to deploy an ASP.NET Web application manually or by using Windows Installer files.

Appendices

Appendix A, "Accessing XML Data," explains how to read, write, and display Extensible Markup Language (XML) data in an ASP.NET Web application by using the XML classes that are contained in the .NET Framework. This appendix also covers using the XML Web server control to display XML data, either with or without Extensible Stylesheet Language Transformation (XSLT) style sheets, and the reading and writing of XML data by using a **Dataset** object.

Appendix B, "Improving Microsoft ASP.NET Web Application Performance Using Caching," explains how to improve the performance of an ASP.NET Web application by using the caching features of ASP.NET.

Appendix C, "Job Aid: Migrating ASP Web Applications to Microsoft ASP.NET," provides a list of the actions that need to be taken when migrating an ASP Web application to ASP.NET.

Appendix D, "Review Game," provides an opportunity to apply your new knowledge in an interactive game.

Initial Logon Procedure

* Passwords in MOC courses must be complex
* You must perform your initial logon by using P@ssw0rd

Complex passwords

To meet the complexity requirements for the password that you will use in this course, you must include characters in your password from at least three of the following four categories:

- Uppercase letters (A to Z)
- Lowercase letters (a to z)
- Numbers (0 to 9)
- Symbols (! @ # $)

To create the password that you will use in this course, you must log on either as **Student**xx, where xx is your student number, or as **Student**, depending on the classroom setup.

Tasks

▶ **Log on to your account**

1. Press CTRL+ALT+DEL to open the **Log On to Windows** dialog box.

2. In the **User name** box, type **Student**xx or **Student**

3. In the **Password** box, type **P@ssw0rd**

4. In the **Log on to** box, select the name of the domain that is used in the course or the name of your computer, and then click **OK**.

   The **Logon Message** dialog box appears, stating that your password must be changed at initial logon.

Microsoft Official Curriculum

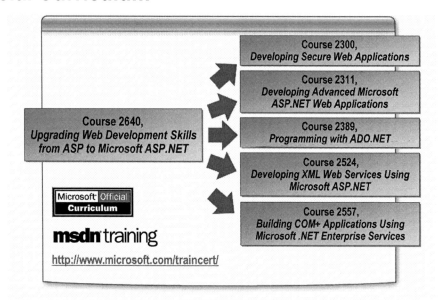

Introduction

Microsoft Training and Certification develops Microsoft Official Curriculum (MOC), including Microsoft MSDN® Training, for computer professionals who design, develop, support, implement, or manage solutions by using Microsoft products and technologies. These courses provide comprehensive skills-based training in instructor-led and online formats.

Additional recommended courses

After taking Course 2640, *Upgrading Web Development Skills from ASP to Microsoft ASP.NET*, you may be interested in taking one of the following courses to further develop your skills.

Course	Title and description
2300	*Developing Secure Web Applications* This three-day course teaches Web developers the knowledge and skills that are required to build Web applications by using secure coding techniques.
2311	*Developing Advanced Microsoft ASP.NET Web Applications* This three-day course will teach advanced Web developers how to build and deploy sophisticated object-oriented ASP.NET Web Applications by using C# and Visual Basic .NET.
2389	*Programming with ADO.NET* This three-day course will teach developers to build data-centric applications and Web services with ADO.NET, Microsoft SQL Server™ 2000, and the .NET Framework.
2524	*Developing XML Web Services Using Microsoft ASP.NET* This three-day course teaches experienced software developers how XML Web Services can be used to solve common problems that occur in the distributed application domain.
2557	*Building COM+ Applications Using Microsoft .NET Enterprise Services* This five-day course teaches students how to build scalable, distributed applications that use .NET Enterprise Services and the .NET Framework.

Other similar courses may become available in the future; therefore, for up-to-date information about recommended courses, visit the Microsoft Training and Certification Web site.

Microsoft Training and Certification information

For more information, visit the Microsoft Training and Certification Web site at http://www.microsoft.com/traincert/.

Microsoft Certified Professional Program

Exam number and title	Core exam for the following track
Exam 70-305: *Developing and Implementing Web Applications with Microsoft Visual Basic .NET and Microsoft Visual Studio .NET*	MCAD/MCSD
Exam 70-315: *Developing and Implementing Web Applications with Microsoft Visual C# .NET and Microsoft Visual Studio .NET*	MCAD/MCSD

Microsoft
CERTIFIED
Professional

http://www.microsoft.com/traincert/

Introduction

Microsoft Training and Certification offers a variety of certification credentials for developers and Information Technology (IT) professionals. The Microsoft Certified Professional program is the leading certification program for validating your experience and skills, and for keeping you competitive in today's changing business environment.

Related certification exams

This course helps students to prepare for Exam 70-305: *Developing and Implementing Web Applications with Microsoft Visual Basic .NET and Microsoft Visual Studio .NET.*

This course also helps students to prepare for Exam 70-315: *Developing and Implementing Web Applications with Microsoft Visual C#™ .NET and Microsoft Visual Studio .NET.*

Exam 70-315 and 70-305 are core exams for the Microsoft Certified Application Developer (MCAD) the Microsoft Certified Solution Developer (MCSD) certification.

MCP certifications

The Microsoft Certified Professional program includes the following certifications:

- MCAD

  The MCAD for Microsoft .NET credential is appropriate for professionals who use Microsoft technologies to develop and maintain department-level applications, components, Web or desktop clients, or back-end data services, or for those professionals who work in teams that develop enterprise applications. The credential covers job tasks ranging from developing to deploying, to maintaining these solutions.

- MCSD

  The MCSD credential is the premier certification for professionals who design and develop leading-edge business solutions by using Microsoft development tools, technologies, platforms, and the Microsoft Windows DNA architecture. The types of applications MCSDs can develop include desktop applications and multiuser, Web-based, N-tier, and transaction-based applications. The MCSD credential covers job tasks ranging from analyzing business requirements to maintaining solutions.

Certification requirements

The certification requirements differ for each certification category and are specific to the products and job functions that are addressed by the certification. To become a Microsoft Certified Professional, you must pass rigorous certification exams that provide a valid and reliable measure of technical proficiency and expertise.

For More Information   See the Microsoft Training and Certification Web site at http://www.microsoft.com/traincert/.

You can also send e-mail to mcphelp@microsoft.com if you have specific certification questions.

Acquiring the skills tested by an MCP exam

MOC and MSDN Training can help you develop the skills that you need to do your job. They also complement the experience that you gain while working with Microsoft products and technologies. However, no one-to-one correlation exists between MOC and MSDN Training courses and MCP exams. Microsoft does not expect or intend for the courses to be the sole preparation method for passing MCP exams. Practical product knowledge and experience is also necessary to pass the MCP exams.

To help prepare for the MCP exams, use the preparation guides that are available for each exam. Each Exam Preparation Guide contains exam-specific information, such as a list of the topics on which you will be tested. These guides are available on the Microsoft Training and Certification Web site at http://www.microsoft.com/traincert/.

Facilities

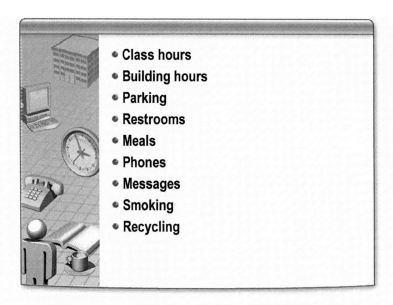

msdn training

Module 1: Introduction to Microsoft ASP.NET Web Application Development

Contents

Overview

- **Introduction to ASP.NET**
- **Developing an ASP.NET Web Application Using Visual Studio .NET**
- **.NET Programming Model Changes**

Introduction

Microsoft® ASP.NET is more than the next version of Active Server Pages (ASP); ASP.NET is a unified Web development platform that provides the services that are necessary for developers to build enterprise-class Web applications. Although ASP.NET is largely syntactically compatible with ASP, it also provides a new programming model and infrastructure for more secure, scalable, and stable Web applications. ASP.NET is not backwards compatible with ASP, but you can augment your existing ASP applications by incrementally adding ASP.NET functionality to them.

This module describes the ASP.NET architecture and how it relates to the Microsoft .NET Framework. This module also explains how to use the Microsoft Visual Studio® .NET object-oriented programming languages to develop ASP.NET Web applications.

Note The code samples in this module are provided in both Microsoft Visual Basic® .NET and C#.

Objectives

This module provides you with the skills and knowledge that are needed to develop an ASP.NET Web application by using Visual Studio .NET and a .NET-based programming language.

After completing this module, you will be able to:

- Explain ASP.NET Web application elements and the ASP.NET Web application process model.
- Create an ASP.NET Web application by using Visual Studio .NET, and be able to explain the component parts of the Web Application.
- Implement the major programming model changes between ASP and ASP.NET.

Lesson: Introduction to ASP.NET

- ASP Web Application Architecture
- ASP.NET Web Application Architecture
- Overview of ASP.NET
- Multimedia: The ASP.NET Process Model

Introduction

This lesson provides an overview of ASP.NET Web application elements and describes the ASP.NET Web application process model.

Lesson objectives

After completing this lesson, you will be able to:

- Explain the general architecture of an ASP Web application.
- Explain the general architecture of an ASP.NET Web application.
- Explain the key elements that comprise ASP.NET.
- Explain the ASP.NET Web application process model.

ASP Web Application Architecture

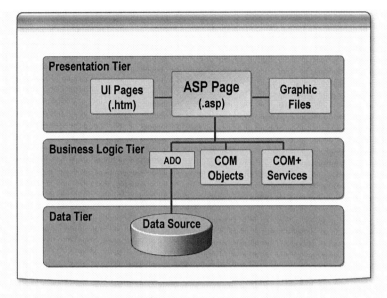

Introduction	ASP Web applications can be developed in a multiple-tier architecture. This type of modular programming can isolate the Web application from changes that are made to any part of the system.
Presentation tier	The presentation tier includes everything specific to the user interface (UI) technology. The .asp page typically contains only presentation-tier content and the supporting logic. .html UI pages are used for static content.
Business logic tier	The business logic tier includes business services, state management, and business rules logic.
	In ASP Web applications, most business logic is contained in component object model (COM) objects and COM+ services.
Data tier	The data tier includes data and data store software, including relational databases, e-mail stores, message queues, and directory services.
	In ASP Web applications, Microsoft ActiveX® Data Objects (ADO) is the method that is used to access data sources.

ASP.NET Web Application Architecture

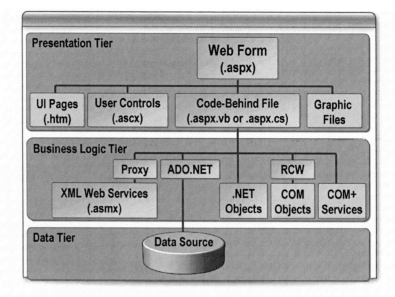

Introduction

ASP.NET Web applications are intended to be created by using a multiple-tier architecture. This type of modular programming can improve maintainability by isolating the rest of the Web application from changes that are made to any part of the system.

Presentation tier

The presentation tier includes everything specific to the UI technology. In ASP.NET Web applications, the Web Form (.aspx file) typically contains the presentation layout. The code-behind file (.aspx.vb or .aspx.cs file) contains the logic supporting the presentation.

When building Web Forms and code-behind files, you can use ASP.NET user controls (.ascx files) to create common UI elements. You can then program these UI elements for specific tasks. ASP.NET user controls also allow you to build a Web Form rapidly out of reusable components.

Note For more information about creating Web Forms, see Module 2, "Developing a Microsoft ASP.NET Web Application User Interface," in Course 2640, *Upgrading Web Development Skills from ASP to Microsoft ASP.NET.*

Business logic tier

The business logic tier includes business services, state management, and business rules logic.

ASP.NET Web applications can connect to a number of business services including:

- COM objects

   A proxy that is known as the runtime callable wrapper (RCW) handles the interface between ASP.NET code and the unmanaged COM object.

   > **Note** For more information about accessing COM objects, see Module 8, "Calling COM Components," in Course 2640, *Upgrading Web Development Skills from ASP to Microsoft ASP.NET.*

- COM+ services

   You use the **EnterpriseServices** namespace to access unmanaged COM+ services from ASP.NET.

   > **Note** For more information about accessing COM+ services, see the Visual Studio .NET online Help files or Course 2557, *Building COM+ Applications Using Microsoft .NET Enterprise Services.*

- XML Web Services

   In ASP.NET, XML Web services are accessed through a proxy that manages the connection to the XML Web service.

   XML Web services are used to provide programmatic access to remote applications. XML Web services enable the exchange of data, in either client-server or server-server scenarios by using Internet data transfer standards. Applications that are written in any language, using any component model, and running on any operating system can provide or access XML Web services.

   > **Note** For more information about XML Web services, see Module 7, "Creating and Consuming XML Web Services," in Course 2640, *Upgrading Web Development Skills from ASP to Microsoft ASP.NET.*

- .NET objects

   Local .NET objects run in the .NET managed code environment. These objects are the .NET replacement for COM objects.

   In ASP.NET, local .NET objects can be accessed directly.

Data tier

The data tier includes data and data store software, including relational databases, e-mail stores, message queues, and directory services.

In ASP.NET Web applications, Microsoft ADO.NET is the preferred method used to access data sources. However, ADO can also be used to access data sources.

> **Note** For more information about data access, see Module 4, "Accessing Data using Microsoft ADO.NET," in Course 2640, *Upgrading Web Development Skills from ASP to Microsoft ASP.NET.*

Overview of ASP.NET

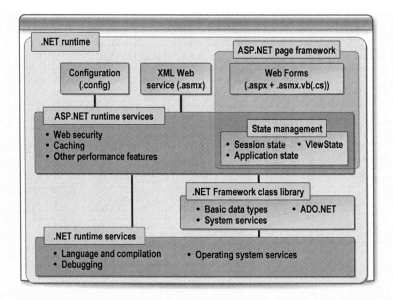

Introduction

The .NET Framework is a new computing platform that simplifies Web application development in the highly distributed environment of the Internet. ASP.NET is part of the .NET Framework.

ASP.NET has been designed to offer significant performance improvements over ASP and other Web application development platforms. ASP.NET takes advantage of performance enhancements that are found in the .NET Framework and the common language runtime. All ASP.NET code is compiled, rather than interpreted, thereby allowing early binding, strong typing, and just-in-time (JIT) compilation to native code. ASP.NET is also easily factorable, meaning that developers can remove modules (a session module, for example) that are not relevant to the application that they are developing. Finally, ASP.NET includes performance counters that developers and system administrators can monitor to test new applications and to gather metrics on existing applications.

.NET runtime services

All of the code that you write for ASP.NET Web applications is hosted and run in the common language runtime. Code that is written for the common language runtime is called managed code because the code runs in an environment in which many tasks, such as type checking, are managed for you.

.NET common language runtime services provide a number of services and resources including:

■ Type Management

The common language runtime enforces strict type management so that all of the code uses clearly defined types. This strict type management is a departure from ASP code, which was essentially typeless. The strict definition of types for all of the data allows for better control and security of data. For example, a method call can not inadvertently pass an integer parameter when a string is expected.

■ JIT Compilation

ASP.NET Web pages are compiled to Microsoft intermediate language (MSIL), which is a CPU-independent set of instructions that can be efficiently converted to native code. At runtime, the MSIL is JIT-compiled to native code. The common language runtime supplies a JIT compiler for each supported CPU architecture; therefore, the same MSIL can be JIT-compiled and run on multiple computers that feature different architectures. This native language independence allows ASP.NET Web applications to compile and run at the most advantageous state for the given architecture.

■ Memory Management

Memory management is handled automatically in the common language runtime. You allocate memory by using the **new** keyword, and the common language runtime handles the actual memory allocation for the new object. You do not need to de-allocate objects explicitly from memory. A garbage collection process runs periodically to remove unused objects and to clean up memory.

The object code that you write for ASP.NET Web applications is very similar to ASP code, because ASP also provides automatic memory management.

■ Exception Manager

The common language runtime provides true structured exception handling, which was not available in ASP Web applications. When a runtime error occurs in an ASP.NET Web application, an exception is generated. You can write **Try...Catch...Finally** blocks to handle exceptions.

The .NET Framework class library

The .NET Framework class library includes classes, interfaces, and value types that expedite and optimize the ASP.NET Web application development process and provide access to system functionality. To facilitate interoperability between programming languages, the .NET Framework classes, interfaces, and value types comply with the Common Language Specification (CLS). As a result of this CLS compliance, classes, interfaces, and value types can be used from any programming language whose compiler conforms to the CLS.

The .NET Framework classes, interfaces, and value types are the foundation on which .NET applications, components, and controls are built. The .NET Framework includes types that perform the following functions:

- Represent base data types and exceptions.

- Encapsulate data structures.

- Perform input/output (I/O).

- Access information about loaded types.

- Invoke .NET Framework security checks.

- Provide data access, rich client-side graphical user interface (GUI), and server-controlled, client-side GUI.

The .NET Framework class library also contains the ADO.NET classes that are used for accessing databases. ADO.NET offers better performance than ADO, and it is designed to support disconnected data and XML data.

Note For more information about data access, see Module 4, "Accessing Data Using Microsoft ADO.NET," in Course 2640, *Upgrading Web Development Skills from ASP to Microsoft ASP.NET*.

Configuration

ASP.NET configuration settings are stored in XML-based files, which are human readable and writable. Each Web application can have a distinct configuration file, and you can extend the default configuration scheme to meet your requirements.

Machine-level configuration settings are stored in the machine.config file. There is only one machine.config file on each Web server. The machine.config file can then be used to store the settings that apply to all of the ASP.NET Web applications that are residing on that Web server.

Application and directory-level settings are stored in Web.config files. Each Web application has at least one Web.config file. Virtual directories can also have their own Web.config files that contain settings that are specific to that directory.

ASP.NET run-time services

ASP.NET provides a variety of run-time services that can be used to manage security, state, caching, and performance in your Web applications. For example, ASP.NET provides a service called Forms-based authentication to secure access to your Web application.

Note For more information about Forms-based authentication, see Module 6, "Authenticating Users," in Course 2640, *Upgrading Web Development Skills from ASP to Microsoft ASP.NET*.

ASP.NET also provides easy-to-use application and session-state functionality, which will be familiar to ASP developers, and which are readily compatible with all of the other .NET Framework application programming interfaces (APIs).

Note For more information about ASP.NET State Management, see Module 5, "Managing State in a Microsoft ASP.NET Web Application," in Course 2640, *Upgrading Web Development Skills from ASP to Microsoft ASP.NET*.

Code access security

To help protect computer systems from malicious code, to allow code from unknown origins to run safely, and to protect trusted code from intentionally or accidentally compromising security, the .NET Framework provides a security mechanism called code access security. Code access security allows code to be trusted to varying degrees, depending on the code's origin and on other aspects of the code's identity. Code access security enforces the varying levels of trust on code, which minimizes the amount of code that must be fully trusted to run. Using code access security can reduce the likelihood that your code can be misused by malicious or error-filled code.

Code access security can also reduce the risks that will arise from the security vulnerabilities in your code. You can specify the set of operations that your code should be allowed to perform, as well as specify the operations that your code should never be allowed to perform.

Note For more information on code access security, see the Visual Studio .NET online Help files or Course 2350, *Developing and Deploying Secure Microsoft .NET Framework Applications*.

Multimedia: The ASP.NET Process Model

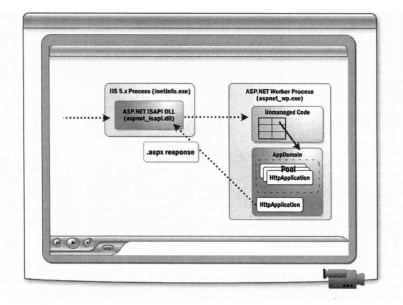

Introduction

In ASP, the Internet Server Application Programming Interface (ISAPI) ASP extension that processes .asp pages is typically an integrated part of Internet Information Services (IIS). As a result of this integration, failures in ASP also cause IIS to fail. In addition, when you change the configuration of ASP, you must restart ASP and may need to also restart IIS.

ASP.NET uses its own ISAPI dynamic-link library (DLL) and a separate worker process to handle incoming ASP.NET Web requests. As a result of this separation, failures in ASP.NET should not affect IIS, and ASP.NET can also be updated or rebooted without affecting IIS.

ASP.NET ISAPI DLL

When ASP.NET is installed on IIS 5.0 or 5.1, it registers an ISAPI DLL named aspnet_isapi.dll with IIS. When IIS receives a request for any ASP.NET resource, such as an .aspx file or an .asmx file, it routes the request directly to the ASP.NET ISAPI DLL.

Note Requests for resources such as .htm files are not routed to the ASP.NET ISAPI DLL. These resources are returned to the caller in accordance with the IIS application settings for those resources.

ASP.NET worker process

When the ASP.NET ISAPI DLL receives a request, it starts a worker process, if one is not already running. The name of the worker process is aspnet_wp.exe. In a default installation of the .NET Framework, there will only be one instance of this worker process running on a computer.

Note You can configure multiple instances of a worker process to run; for example, one instance per CPU for higher throughput. Configuring multiple instances of a worker process is beyond the scope of this course.

The worker process contains an unmanaged code section that examines the Uniform Resource Locator (URL) of the Web request. The URL determines which ASP.NET Web application should process the Web request. The worker process uses a lookup table to find the appropriate ASP.NET Web application to process the Web request. If an appropriate ASP.NET Web application is not found, the worker process creates a new application domain to handle the request.

Application domains are synonymous with ASP.NET Web applications. Application domains are also known as AppDomains. Each AppDomain contains a pool of HttpApplication instances. An HttpApplication instance is pulled from the pool and assigned the Web request. The pool allows multiple Web requests to be processed simultaneously; however, each Web request is single-threaded.

When the HttpApplication instance completes the request, it returns to the pool, and a response is then returned to the client.

Shutting down an application

There are several conditions that will cause an application domain to shut down and restart. When ASP.NET must restart an AppDomain, it simply removes the entry in the table that points to the AppDomain. When a new request arrives, the table does not have an entry; therefore, ASP.NET creates a new AppDomain that handles all of the future requests. The old AppDomain continues running until it completes all of its current requests. Finally, the old AppDomain shuts down.

The following changes will cause an AppDomain to restart:

- Configuration change

  If the machine.config or Web.config files are changed, ASP.NET detects the change and restarts the affected AppDomain.

- Global.asax change

  If the global.asax file is changed, ASP.NET detects the change and restarts the affected AppDomain.

- Bin directory change

  If an assembly in the bin directory is changed, ASP.NET restarts the AppDomain that corresponds to that bin directory.

- Compilation count change

  When an ASP.NET Web page is changed, it is recompiled. You can set a compilation element in the Web.config file that specifies how many times a Web page can be recompiled before ASP.NET restarts the AppDomain. Each Web page recompile degrades an application domain's performance; establishing a recompiling limit therefore helps control the overall performance of the Web application.

Note For more information on the compilation element, see the Visual Studio .NET online Help files.

Lesson: Developing an ASP.NET Web Application Using Visual Studio .NET

* **Instructor-led Practice: Developing an ASP.NET Web Application**
* **ASP.NET Web Application Project Files and References**
* **The .aspx Page and the Page Class**
* **Code-Behind Files**
* **Multimedia: ASP.NET Execution Model**

Introduction

ASP.NET has been designed to work seamlessly with Visual Studio .NET. The Visual Studio .NET tools that are available for developing ASP.NET Web applications include:

- Visual designers for Web pages with drag-and-drop controls and code views with syntax checking.
- Code-aware editors that include statement completion, syntax checking, and other Microsoft IntelliSense® features.
- Integrated compilation and debugging.
- Project management tools that can be used for creating and managing application files, including the deployment of application files to local or remote servers.

Lesson objectives

In this lesson, you will learn how to create an ASP.NET Web application by using Visual Studio .NET. You will also learn about the component parts of an ASP.NET Web application.

After completing this lesson, you will be able to:

- Create an ASP.NET Web application by using Visual Studio .NET.
- List the project files and references that are created by the ASP.NET Web application project.
- Describe the .aspx page and Page class.
- Describe the purpose of code-behind files.
- Explain the ASP.NET Web page generation process.

Instructor-led Practice: Developing an ASP.NET Web Application

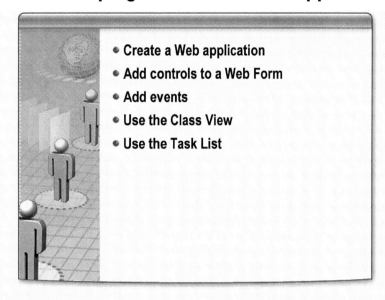

- Create a Web application
- Add controls to a Web Form
- Add events
- Use the Class View
- Use the Task List

Introduction

In this practice you will create an ASP.NET Web application project by using Visual Studio .NET. Then, you will add Web controls to a Web Form by using the Visual Studio .NET Toolbox. Finally, you will use the Visual Studio .NET task list and the Web Forms designer.

Note The solution code for this practice is located in the *install_folder*\Practice\Mod01*language*\Hello\Solution folder. The URL for the solution is http://localhost/upg/mod01-*language*-Hello-solution/default.aspx

Dynamic Help

In Visual Studio .NET, Dynamic Help tracks the exposed screens and location of the cursor in the of Web application code. Dynamic Help then changes the displayed help items based on an analysis of the topics that are most likely to be needed by the programmer.

1. Start Visual Studio .NET.

2. On the **Help** menu, click **Dynamic Help**.

   Show how the help topics relate to tasks that would be performed from the **Start Page**.

   Explain how the **Contents**, **Index**, and **Search** icons can be used as different means to locate help.

3. Click the **Index** icon.

4. In the **Look for** drop-down list box, type **Page class**

5. In the index list, locate the **Page class**, and click **properties**. The Page Properties help page is displayed.

6. Click the **IsPostBack** property on the Page Properties help page. The Page.IsPostBack Property help page is displayed.

7. Click the **Language Filter** icon in the upper-left corner of the Page.IsPostBack Property help page and select **C#**.

   Explain how the IsPostBack code sample on the help page changes as you select the different language filter options.

8. Click the **Language Filter** icon and select **Show All**.

   Explain how **Show All** (no filter) results in seeing all language samples on the help page.

Create a Web application

In the following steps you will create a new ASP.NET Web application, including a single default Web Form with a related code-behind file.

9. From the **File** menu, point to **New**, and then click **Project**.

10. In the **New Project** dialog box, perform the following steps:

    a. Select the **Visual Basic Projects** or **Visual C# Projects** folder, depending on which language you are using.

    b. Select the **ASP.NET Web Application** template.

    c. Set the location to http://localhost/upg/mod01-cs-Hello or http://localhost/upg/mod01-vb-Hello, depending on which language you are using.

    d. Click **OK**.

11. Right-click the **WebForm1.aspx** file in Solution Explorer and click **Rename**.

12. Enter **default.aspx** as the new file name, and then press ENTER.

Add controls to a Web Form

In the following steps you will add **TextBox**, **Button** and **Label** controls to the default Web Form.

13. Right-click the Web Form in Design view and select **Properties**.

14. In the **DOCUMENT Property Pages** dialog box, perform the following steps:

    a. Change the **title** property to **Hello World**.

    b. Change the **pageLayout** property to **FlowLayout**.

    c. Click **OK**.

Note   You can also use the Properties window to change the properties for the Web Form and the other elements in the Visual Studio .NET project.

---

15. On the Web Form, type the following text:

```
Hello
Please enter your name:
```

16. In the Toolbox, select the **Web Forms** tab and double-click **TextBox**.

17. In Design view, move the **TextBox** so that it is located to the right of the text that asks for the user's name.

18. In the Toolbox, double-click **Button**.

19. In Design view, move the **Button** so that it is located underneath the **TextBox**.

20. In the Toolbox, double-click **Label**.

21. In Design view, move the **Label** so that it is located to the right of the Hello text.

22. In the Properties window, select **TextBox1** from the drop-down list box and set the following properties.

Property	Value
ID	txtUserName

23. In the Properties window, select **Button1** from the drop-down list box and set the following properties.

Property	Value
ID	cmdEnterName
Text	Enter Name

24. In the Properties window, select **Label1** from the drop-down list box and set the following properties.

Property	Value
ID	lblUserName
Text	*Blank*

25. Right-click the **default.aspx** page in Solution Explorer, and select **Build and Browse**.

The form is displayed in a browser, inside Visual Studio .NET. You can enter text in the text box and click the button, but there is currently no functionality.

26. Close the browser window.

Add events

In the following steps you will add an event handler to the **Button** control to link the **TextBox** and **Label** controls.

27. Double-click the **Enter Name** button on the Web Form.

This action will create a **Click** event handler for the **Button** control.

28. Add the following code to the **cmdEnterName_Click** event handler:

Visual Basic .NET

```
lblUserName.Text = txtUserName.Text
```

C#

```
lblUserName.Text = txtUserName.Text;
```

Use Class View

In the following steps you will use **Class View** to review the methods and properties of a class.

29. From the **View** menu, select **Class View**.

    The **Class View** allows you to display all of the properties and methods of a class.

30. In the Class View window, expand **mod01-**_language_**-Hello**, **Hello**, and **WebForm1**.

    This action will display all of the properties and methods for the **WebForm1** class.

31. Right-click the **Page_Load** method, and select **Go To Definition**.

    This action will take you to the **Page_Load** event handler source code.

Use the Task List

In the following steps you will use the **Task List** to track TODO comments in your code.

32. From the **View** menu, select **Other Windows**, and then click **Task List**.

    The **Task List** allows you to collect and jump to errors and TODO comments in your code.

33. Right-click the **Task List** window, point to **Show Tasks**, and then click **Comment**.

34. Inside the **Page_Load** event handler, modify the comment to have a TODO:

```
Visual Basic .NET

'TODO Put user code to initialize the page here
```

```
C#

//TODO Put user code to initialize the page here
```

Notice that when you move the caret to another line of code, the TODO comment appears in the Task List window. You can also customize the task list to use keywords, other than TODO, to track source code tasks.

35. Click the Solution Explorer tab to view Solution Explorer.

36. Right-click the **default.aspx** page in Solution Explorer, and then click **Build and Browse**.

37. Enter your name and click the **Enter Name** button.

    The Web Form should refresh, and display your name.

ASP.NET Web Application Project Files and References

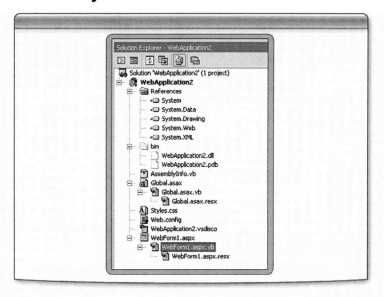

Introduction

When you create a new Web application project or open existing projects, Visual Studio .NET creates a number of files that support the project and the projects development in Visual Studio .NET.

Solution files

When you create a new ASP.NET Web applications project, a solution is also created. Each solution can hold one or more projects.

A folder is created for each solution in the \My Documents\Visual Studio Projects folder; this folder contains one or more of the following Visual Studio .NET settings files:

- Solution files (.sln)

    The *SolutionName*.sln file extension is used for the solution files that link one or more projects together. .sln files are similar to Visual Basic group (.vbg) files, which appear in previous versions of Visual Basic.

- Solution User Options (.suo)

    The *SolutionName*.suo file extension is used for the Solution User Options files that accompany any solution records and customizations that you add to your solution. This file saves your settings, such as breakpoints and task items, so that they are retrieved each time you open the solution.

Project files

Each Web application project consists of a single Web application that is stored in its own folder. Web application projects are created in a new folder in the \Inetpub\wwwroot folder. Within the project folder are the project configuration file and the code files that comprise the project. In addition to these files, a virtual directory that points to the project folder is created in IIS.

The Project Configuration file is an XML document that contains references to all of the project items, such as forms and classes, in addition to containing project references and compilation options. Visual Basic .NET project files use a .vbproj extension, while C# project files use a .csproj extension. These extensions enable you to differentiate between the files that are written in other .NET-compatible languages, thereby making it easier to include multiple projects that are based on different languages within the same solution.

ASP.NET Web application project files

The following list describes the file types and extensions that are included in an ASP.NET Web application project:

- ASP.NET Web Forms (.aspx)

    ASP.NET Web Forms are used when you need to build dynamic Web sites that will be accessed directly by users.

    ASP.NET Web Forms are supported by a code-behind file that is designated by the extension *WebForm*.aspx.vb or *WebForm*.aspx.cs.

- ASP.NET Web services (.asmx)

    ASP.NET Web services are used when you want to create dynamic Web sites that will only be accessed by other programs.

    ASP.NET Web services are supported by a code-behind file that is designated by the extension *WebService*.asmx.vb or *WebService*.asmx.cs.

- Classes and code-behind files (.vb or .cs)

    Code-behind files carry two extensions, the page type (.aspx or .asmx), and the Visual Basic extension (.vb) or the C# extension (.cs). For example, the full file name for the code-behind file for a default ASP.NET Web Form is WebForm1.aspx.vb for a Visual Basic .NET project, and for a C# project it is WebForm1.aspx.cs.

- Discovery files (.disco and .vsdisco)

    Discovery files are XML-based files that contain links (in the form of URLs) to resources that provide discovery information for an XML Web service. These files enable programmatic discovery of XML Web services.

- Global application classes (Global.asax)

    The Global.asax file, also known as the ASP.NET application file, is an optional file that contains the code that can be used to respond to application-level events that are raised by ASP.NET or raised by HttpModules. At runtime, Global.asax is parsed and compiled into a dynamically generated .NET Framework class that is derived from the **HttpApplication** base class.

- Resource files (.resx)

    A resource file is any nonexecutable data that is logically deployed with an application. A resource might be displayed in an application as error messages or as part of the UI. Resources can contain data in a number of forms, including strings, images, and persisted objects. Storing your data in a resource file allows you to change the data without recompiling your entire application.

- Styles.css

  The Styles.css file is the default style sheet file for the ASP.NET Web application.

- Web.config file

  The Web.config file contains configuration settings, such as assembly binding policy, remoting objects, and so on, that the common language runtime reads, along with settings that the application can read. Web.config files also contain the global application classes that support a project.

Other files

Any files that are not based on a programming language will have their own extensions. For example, a Crystal Report file uses the .rpt extension, and a text files uses the .txt extension.

Project assembly

When a Web application project is compiled, two additional types of files are created:

- Project Assembly files (.dll)

  All of the code-behind files (.aspx.vb and .aspx.cs) in a project are compiled into a single assembly file that is stored as *ProjectName*.dll. This project assembly file is placed in the /bin directory of the Web application.

- AssemblyInfo.vb or AssemblyInfo.cs

  The AssemblyInfo file is used to write the general information, specifically assembly version and assembly attributes, about the assembly.

Note For more information on files that support ASP.NET Web applications, see the Visual Studio .NET online Help files.

Project references

The ASP.NET Web Application project automatically adds the essential project references to the following .NET Framework assemblies:

- **System**

  The **System** assembly contains the fundamental classes and base classes that define commonly used values and reference data types, events and event handlers, interfaces, attributes, and processing exceptions.

- **System.Data**

  The **System.Data** assembly contains the classes that constitute the ADO.NET architecture, which is the primary data access method for managed applications.

- **System.Drawing**

  The **System.Drawing** assembly contains the classes that provide access to GDI+ basic graphics functionality.

- **System.Web**

  The **System.Web** assembly contains the classes and interfaces that enable communication between browser and server.

- **System.Xml**

  The **System.Xml** assembly contains the classes that provide standards-based support for processing XML.

The .aspx Page and the Page Class

ASP.NET Web Form (.aspx file)

- Derived from the Page class
- May have a related code-behind file (.aspx.vb file or .aspx.cs file)
- Objects available through the Page class
  - Application
  - Session
  - Request
  - Response
  - Server
  - Context
  - Controls collection

Introduction

In ASP.NET Web applications, the Web Form (.aspx file) typically contains the presentation layout.

Derived from the Page class

Every .aspx page derives from the **Page** class and inherits all of the methods and properties that the **Page** class exposes. The @ **Page** directive defines the page-specific attributed that is used by the ASP.NET page parser and compiler when you build a page. When Visual Studio .NET creates the .aspx page file and the code-behind file for a Web Form, it generates a new class that inherits from the **Page** class. For example, if you create a new Web Forms page and name it **WebForm1**, a new class named **WebForm1** is derived from the **Page** class, as shown in the following code example:

Visual Basic .NET

```
Public Class WebForm1
    Inherits System.Web.UI.Page
```

C#

```
public class WebForm1 : System.Web.UI.Page
```

Inheriting from the **Page** class not only makes all of the members of the **Page** class available to the code-behind file; it also allows ASP.NET to combine the code in the .aspx page file with the code in the code-behind file into a single compiled class at compile time. This single compiled class contains all of the methods and properties that are exposed by the **Page** class, as well as the methods and properties that are implemented by your code.

Code-behind files

.aspx Web Forms can be stand-alone files that combine the UI with the supporting logic. When Visual Studio .NET creates a new Web Form, it creates two files, the .aspx file and the .aspx.vb or .aspx.cs code-behind file. In this model, the .aspx page is intended to contain only the UI code and controls. A second code-behind file is created to contain the supporting logic.

The Page class members

The **Page** class includes the ASP **Intrinsic** objects (**Application, Session, Request, Response, Server,** and **Context**) that are implemented in ASP.NET as class instances. The class instances are exposed as properties of the **Page** object. For example, the **Server** functionality is provided by a class called **HttpServerUtility**. Because the instance of **HttpServerUtility** is exposed as the **Server** property of the **Page** class, you can call its methods (the **Server.Transfer** method, for example) just as you can in ASP.

Note For more information on **Page** class members, see the Visual Studio .NET online Help files.

Code-Behind Files

Code-Behind files (.aspx.vb file or .aspx.cs file)

- **Contain the ASP.NET Web application programming logic**
- **One per .aspx page file**
- **Cannot use multiple programming languages in a code-behind file**
- **Associated with the .aspx page file by using the Inherits attribute of the @ Page directive**

Introduction

When Visual Studio .NET creates an .aspx Web Form, the programming logic resides in a separate file, which is called the code-behind file. The code-behind file has an .aspx.vb extension when the programming logic that is written in Visual Basic .NET, and an .aspx.cs extension when written in C#.

Code-behind files

Each Web Form in an ASP.NET Web application has its own code-behind file. By default, a code-behind file has the same name as the page with which it is associated. For example, the Web Form page Form1.aspx will have a Visual Basic .NET code-behind file named Form1.aspx.vb or a C# code-behind file named Form1.aspx.cs.

Each code-behind file is associated with its corresponding .aspx page by using the **Inherits** attribute of the **@ Page** directive. A typical .aspx Web Form directive looks like the following code example:

Visual Basic .NET

```
<%@ Page Language="VB" AutoEventWireup="false"
Codebehind="WebForm1.aspx.vb"
Inherits="WebApplication1.WebForm1"%>
```

C#

```
<%@ Page Language="c#" AutoEventWireup="false"
Codebehind="WebForm1.aspx.cs"
Inherits="WebApplication1.WebForm1"%>
```

Although ASP.NET allows you to place programming logic in the .aspx page file, it is recommended that the event handlers and all of the programming logic be placed in the code-behind files. Separating the programming logic from the UI design allows developers to work on the code-behind files while UI designers work on the .aspx file.

The following code example illustrates the contents of a code-behind file:

```
Visual Basic .NET

Public Class WebForm1
    Inherits System.Web.UI.Page

#Region " Web Form Designer Generated Code "

    'This call is required by the Web Form Designer.
    <System.Diagnostics.DebuggerStepThrough()> Private Sub
InitializeComponent()

    End Sub

    Private Sub Page_Init(ByVal sender As System.Object, ByVal
e As System.EventArgs) Handles MyBase.Init
        'CODEGEN: This method call is required by the Web Form
Designer
        'Do not modify it using the code editor.
        InitializeComponent()
    End Sub

#End Region

    Private Sub Page_Load(ByVal sender As System.Object, ByVal
e As System.EventArgs) Handles MyBase.Load
        'Put user code to initialize the page here
    End Sub

End Class
```

```csharp
C#
using System;
using System.Collections;
using System.ComponentModel;
using System.Data;
using System.Drawing;
using System.Web;
using System.Web.SessionState;
using System.Web.UI;
using System.Web.UI.WebControls;
using System.Web.UI.HtmlControls;

namespace namespace
{
  /// <summary>
  /// Summary description for WebForm1.
  /// </summary>
  public class WebForm1 : System.Web.UI.Page
  {
      private void Page_Load(object sender, System.EventArgs
e)
      {
          // Put user code to initialize the page here
      }

      #region Web Form Designer generated code
      override protected void OnInit(EventArgs e)
      {
          //
          // CODEGEN: This call is required by the ASP.NET Web
Form Designer.
          //
          InitializeComponent();
          base.OnInit(e);
      }

      /// <summary>
      /// Required method for Designer support - do not modify
      /// the contents of this method with the code editor.
      /// </summary>
      private void InitializeComponent()
      {
          this.Load += new
System.EventHandler(this.Page_Load);
      }
      #endregion
  }
}
```

Multimedia: ASP.NET Execution Model

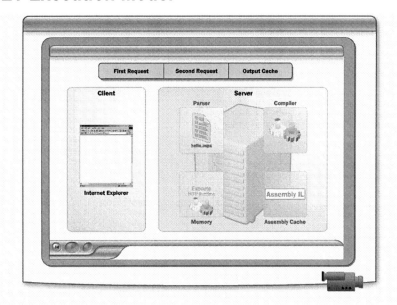

Introduction

In ASP.NET, the individual language compilers compile the code that is written by developers into an intermediate language called MSIL. The MSIL is then either compiled to native code by the runtime at install time or JIT-compiled at first execution. This model improves the performance of the Web applications because the Web pages are not newly generated each time a client requests a Web page.

In this animation, you will see how ASP.NET generates a Web page that is requested by a client.

First request

When the client requests a Web page for the first time, the following actions occur:

1. The client browser issues a GET HTTP request to the server.

2. The ASP.NET parser compiles the source code in the ASP.NET Web application.

3. If the code was not already compiled into a DLL, ASP.NET invokes the compiler.

4. Runtime loads and executes the MSIL code.

Second request

When the client requests the same Web page for the second time, the following actions occur:

1. The client browser issues a GET HTTP request to the server.

2. Runtime loads and immediately executes the MSIL code that was already compiled during the user's first attempt at accessing the Web page.

Output cache

When the output cache is enabled, identical repeated Web page requests are not processed by the Web application. Instead, a cached copy of the Web page is returned to the client:

1. The client browser issues a GET HTTP request to the server.

2. The server finds the requested Web page in the output cache and returns it to the client.

Lesson: .NET Programming Model Changes

* ASP.NET Coding Changes
* Structured Exception Handling
* Memory Management

Introduction

The programming model for ASP.NET Web applications is different from the ASP Web application programming model. Whereas ASP allowed convoluted coding, ASP.NET is designed to support structured, object-oriented programming. In this lesson, you will learn about the major programming model changes between ASP and ASP.NET.

Lesson objectives

After completing this lesson, you will be able to:

- Create ASP.NET pages that conform to the ASP.NET programming model.

- Use structured exception handling to handle runtime errors.

- Use the **Dispose** method to release memory for unmanaged resources.

ASP.NET Coding Changes

- **Page directives**
  - **Language** directive must be in the **@ Page** directive
- **Structural changes**
  - All functions variables must be declared within a **<script>** block
  - Only one language per page
  - Render Functions are no longer supported; use **Response.Write**
- **Design-Time controls are no longer supported**
  - Replace with Web controls

Introduction

There are a number of coding changes between ASP and ASP.NET. The primary changes that will affect you as a developer are the shift of code to <script> blocks and the replacement of "Render Functions" with **Response.Write** and the replacement of Design-time controls with Web controls.

Note For a more detailed listing of the code and programming model changes between ASP and ASP.NET, see Module 9, "Migrating ASP Web Applications to Microsoft ASP.NET," and Appendix C, "Job Aid: Migrating ASP Web Applications to Microsoft ASP.NET," in Course 2640, *Upgrading Web Development Skills from ASP to Microsoft ASP.NET*.

Page directives

In ASP, you must place all of the directives on the first line of a page, within the same block, as shown in the following code example:

Visual Basic Scripting Edition

```
<% LANGUAGE="VBSCRIPT" %>
```

In ASP.NET, you will be required to place the **Language** directive with a **Page** directive, as shown in the following code example:

Visual Basic .NET

```
<% @Page Language="VB" %>
```

C#

```
<% @Page Language="c#"%>
```

You can have as many lines of directives as you need, and the directives can be located anywhere in your .aspx file. However, a best practice is to place all of the directives at the beginning of the file.

Structural changes

Structural changes are those that affect the layout and coding style of a Web page. You need to be aware of several structure changes, from ASP to ASP.NET, to ensure that your code will work in ASP.NET:

- Declaring functions and variables in code blocks.

    In ASP, you can declare subroutines and variables in **<%...%>** render blocks, as shown in the following code example:

```
Visual Basic Scripting Edition

<%
   Dim X
   Dim Y
   Dim str
   Sub MySub()
      Response.Write "This is a string."
   End Sub
%>
```

In ASP.NET, declaring subroutines and functions in render blocks is not allowed. Variables are allowed in render blocks, but they are accessible only within the render block.

In ASP.NET, a best practice is to declare all subroutines, functions, and variables within **<script runat=server>** blocks, as shown in the following code example:

```
Visual Basic .NET

<script language = "vb" runat = "server">
   Dim str As String
   Dim x, y As Integer

   Function Add(I As Integer, J As Integer) As Integer
      Return (I + J)
   End Function
</script>
```

```
C#

<script language="c#" runat="server">

string str;
int x, y;
int Add(int I, int J)
{
   return (I + J);
}
</script>
```

■ Only one language per page.

In ASP, you basically have two choices for your programming language: Visual Basic Scripting Edition or Microsoft JScript®. You are able to mix and match blocks of script in either language on the same page.

In ASP.NET, you can code in any common language runtime-compliant language. The languages that are currently provided by Microsoft include: C#, Visual Basic .NET, and JScript. Visual Basic Scripting Edition does not exist in .NET, as it has been fully subsumed by Visual Basic .NET.

In ASP.NET, each page may be in a different language; however, you cannot mix languages on the same Web page as you could in ASP.

■ Render Functions are no longer supported.

A Render Function is a subroutine that contains sections of Hypertext Markup Language (HTML) that are embedded throughout the body of the function, as shown in the following code example:

Visual Basic Scripting Edition

```
<% Sub RenderMe() %>
<H3> This is HTML text being rendered. </H3>
<% End Sub  %>
```

Render Functions are difficult to read and maintain, and are no longer allowed in ASP.NET. The simplest way to replace a "Render Function" in ASP.NET is to replace your HTML outputs with calls to **Response.Write**, as shown in the following code example:

Visual Basic .NET

```
<script language="vb" runat="server">
   Sub RenderMe()
      Response.Write("<H3> This is HTML text being
            rendered. </H3>")
   End Sub
</script>

<% Call RenderMe() %>
```

C#

```
<script language="c#" runat="server">
void RenderMe()
{
   Response.Write("<H3> This is HTML text being rendered.
      </H3>");
}
</script>
```

Depending on the complexity and amount of your rendering code, consider using custom Web controls instead of **Response.Write**. The custom Web controls allow you to programmatically set your **HTML** attributes and separate your code from the text on the Web page.

Design-time controls are no longer supported

In ASP, Microsoft Visual InterDev® supported the use of design-time controls, such as the **Grid** control, which created server-side script that generated an HTML table. These design-time controls do not function in ASP.NET; therefore, they must be replaced with Web controls. For example, you can replace the **Grid** design-time control with the **DataGrid** Web control.

Structured Exception Handling

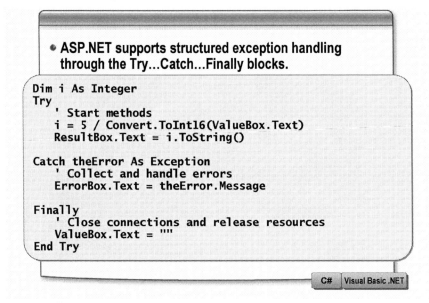

* ASP.NET supports structured exception handling through the Try...Catch...Finally blocks.

```
Dim i As Integer
Try
    ' Start methods
    i = 5 / Convert.ToInt16(ValueBox.Text)
    ResultBox.Text = i.ToString()

Catch theError As Exception
    ' Collect and handle errors
    ErrorBox.Text = theError.Message

Finally
    ' Close connections and release resources
    ValueBox.Text = ""
End Try
```

C#   Visual Basic .NET

Introduction

ASP did not support structured exception handling. After any section of code that could cause an error, you had to check the value of the **Err** object to determine whether an error occurred. The following code example shows how you could structure ASP code to detect and handle an error:

Visual Basic Scripting Edition

```
<%
  On Error Resume Next
  input1 = 5
  input2 = 0
  result = input1/input2
  If Err.Number <> 0 then
      Response.Write("An input is invalid.")
  Else
      Response.Write(result)
  End If
%>
```

With ASP.NET, you can use structured exception handling to route and handle errors more easily.

Structured exception handling syntax

Structured exception handling assists you in creating and maintaining Web applications by using robust, comprehensive error handlers. Structured exception handling is code that is designed to detect and respond to errors during execution. Using the **Try...Catch...Finally** statement, you can protect blocks of code that have the potential to raise errors.

The syntax of **Try...Catch...Finally** statement is shown in the followed code example:

```
Visual Basic .NET

Dim i As Integer
Try
  ' Start methods
  i = 5 / Convert.ToInt16(ValueBox.Text)
  ResultBox.Text = i.ToString()

Catch theError As Exception
  ' Collect and handle errors
  ErrorBox.Text = theError.Message

Finally
  ' Close connections and release resources
  ValueBox.Text = ""
End Try
```

```
C#

int i;
try
{
  // Start methods
  i = 5 / Convert.ToInt16(ValueBox.Text);
  ResultBox.Text = i.ToString();
}
catch (Exception theError)
{
  // Collect and handle errors
  ErrorBox.Text = theError.Message;
}
finally
{
  // Close connections and release resources
  ValueBox.Text = "";
}
```

Notice that you declare variables outside of the **Try** block so that even if the **Try** block fails, the **Finally** block can still close and release resources.

The Try block

The **Try** block contains the section of code that you want your error handler to monitor.

The Catch block

The **Catch** block contains the code that will manage any error that does occur. If an error occurs in the **Try** block, program control is passed to the appropriate **Catch** statement for disposition.

Catch blocks allow for specific error filtering. Errors can be filtered based on the class of the exception or on any conditional expression. You can define **Catch** blocks for as many specific errors as you want to handle.

The **Catch** block may be omitted for methods where errors are either not raised or do not need to be handled.

The Finally block

The code in the **Finally** block always executes last, just before the error-handling block loses scope, regardless of whether the code in the **Catch** blocks has executed. Therefore, you will need to place all of the cleanup code, such as the code that is used for closing files and releasing objects, in the **Finally** block, where it will execute last.

Memory Management

- **Unused managed resources are removed by the garbage collector**

- **To release unmanaged resources explicitly call the Close and Dispose methods**

```
Dim myLog As EventLog = Nothing
Try
    myLog = New EventLog()
    myLog.Source = "MyWebApp"
    If Not EventLog.SourceExists("MyWebApp") Then
        EventLog.CreateEventSource("MyWebApp", "MyLog")
    End If
    myLog.WriteEntry("Event has occurred.")
Finally
    If Not (myLog Is Nothing) Then
        myLog.Close()
    End If
End Try
```

C#   Visual Basic .NET

Introduction

Automatic memory management is one of the services that the common language runtime provides during managed execution. The common language runtime manages the allocation of memory for a Web application. A garbage collection algorithm is used to reclaim memory when active applications no longer need the resource.

Scarce resources, such as database and network connections, must be managed properly to maximize the scalability of ASP.NET Web applications. A best practice in both ASP and ASP.NET is to immediately close a resource, after it is no longer needed, to maximize scalability.

The .NET memory management process

Each time you use the **new** operator to create an object the runtime allocates memory for that object. So long as space is available, the runtime continues to allocate space for new objects.

The garbage collector's optimizing engine determines the best time to perform a collection, thereby freeing some memory. When the garbage collector performs a collection, it checks for objects that are no longer being used by the Web application and performs the necessary operations to reclaim their memory.

Because garbage collection and object de-allocation is not determinable, you cannot control when memory is freed for objects. However, you can assist the garbage collector by explicitly closing .NET objects.

Unmanaged resources

For the majority of the objects that your managed Web application creates, you can rely on the garbage collector to perform the necessary memory management tasks automatically. However, unmanaged resources objects usually require explicit cleanup.

An unmanaged resource is any resource outside of the common language runtime, such as a file handle, window handle, network connection, or database connection. Because these unmanaged resources are often shared with other applications, you will want to release them as soon as possible.

When a managed object uses unmanaged resources, you need to use a **Dispose** method and implement the **IDisposable** interface, which can be explicitly called to release resources. You can implement a **Close** method, which is more semantically compatible with releasing database connections, files, or similar resources. Most .NET Framework classes that use unmanaged resources implement both a **Close** and **Dispose** method.

The Close, Dispose model of releasing resources requires the client to explicitly call the **Close** or **Dispose** methods. If these methods are not explicitly called, the object will remain in memory, holding an open resource until garbage collection occurs.

The following example code illustrates how to call the **Close** method on an **EventLog** object, after logging an entry to the system event log. The **EventLog** class is located in the **System.Diagnostics** namespace:

```
Visual Basic .NET

Imports System.Diagnostics
...
Dim myLog As EventLog = Nothing
Try
  ' Create an EventLog instance and assign its source.
  myLog = New EventLog()
  myLog.Source = "MyWebApp"

  ' Create the source, if it does not already exist.
  If Not EventLog.SourceExists("MyWebApp") Then
      EventLog.CreateEventSource("MyWebApp", "MyLog")
  End If
  ' Write an informational entry to the event log.
  myLog.WriteEntry("Event has occurred.")

Finally
  If Not (myLog Is Nothing) Then
      myLog.Close()
  End If
End Try
```

<u>C#</u>

```csharp
using System.Diagnostics;
...
EventLog myLog=null;
try
{
  // Create an EventLog instance and assign its source.
  myLog = new EventLog();
  myLog.Source = "MyWebApp";

  // Create the source, if it does not already exist.
  if (!EventLog.SourceExists("MyWebApp"))
      EventLog.CreateEventSource("MyWebApp", "MyLog");

  // Write an informational entry to the event log.
  myLog.WriteEntry("Event has occurred.");
}
finally
{
  if (myLog!=null) myLog.Close();
}
```

Lab 1: Developing an ASP.NET Web Application Using Visual Studio .NET

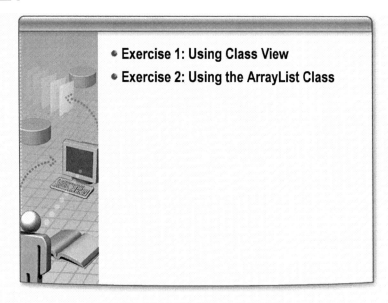

Objectives

After completing this lab, you will be able to:

- Use the Class View window to locate classes and their associated implementation code.

- Create an **ArrayList** collection class, add items to that collection, and then iterate the collection.

Note This lab focuses on the concepts in this module and as a result may not comply with Microsoft security recommendations.

Scenario

In this lab, you will create a single Web Form that uses an **ArrayList** class to store a list of flower names. You will write code that, when the Web Form is loaded, iterates the **ArrayList** and copies the flower names into a **ListBox** control on the Web Form. Your completed Web Form should resemble the following illustration.

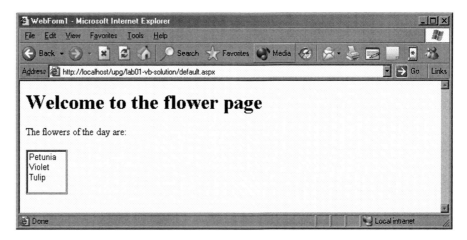

Solution

The solution project for this lab is located in the *install_folder*\Labfiles\Lab01\ *language*\Solution folder, where *language* is CS or VB. You can also view the solution Web Form, which is available at http://localhost/upg/ lab01-*language*-solution/default.aspx.

Estimated time to complete this lab: 30 minutes

Exercise 1
Using Class View

In this exercise, you will use the Class View window to locate the implementation code for the **Page_Load** event handler. You will work with Microsoft Visual C#™ or Visual Basic .NET.

▶ **Open the Lab01 Solution**

This solution file contains a Web application project named Flowers.

1. In Visual Studio .NET, from the **File** menu, click **Open Solution**.

2. In the Open Solution window, click the **My Projects** shortcut.

3. Open the **Labfiles**, **Lab01**, *language*, and **Starter** folders.

4. Select **Lab01.sln**, and then click **Open**.

   The Flowers project has not been modified from its default creation state.

▶ **Change the Web Form name**

It is a best practice to always rename Projects and Web Forms from their default names so that you can easily find and identify them later.

1. Use Solution Explorer to find the WebForm1.aspx page.

2. Rename WebForm1.aspx to default.aspx.

Class view

▶ **Locate the Page_Load event handler**

The **Page_Load** event handler runs whenever the page is requested.

1. Use the Class View window to view the Flowers project.

2. Expand the **Flowers**, **Flowers**, and **WebForm1** folders.

3. Right-click the **Page_Load** event handler and select **Go To Definition**.

4. Scroll up to the **WebForm1** class definition, and change the class name from **WebForm1** to **Default_Form**.

Exercise 2
Using the ArrayList Class

▶ **Create and populate an ArrayList object**

This Array list will display the types of flowers.

1. In the **Default_Form** class, create a protected field of type **System.Collections.ArrayList**:

Visual Basic .NET

```
Protected flowers As System.Collections.ArrayList
```

C#
```
protected System.Collections.ArrayList flowers;
```

2. In the **Page_Load** event handler, add the following code:

Visual Basic .NET

```
flowers = New System.Collections.ArrayList()
flowers.Add("Petunia")
flowers.Add("Violet")
flowers.Add("Tulip")
```

C#

```
flowers = new System.Collections.ArrayList();
flowers.Add("Petunia");
flowers.Add("Violet");
flowers.Add("Tulip");
```

3. Open the default.aspx page in Design view.

4. In the Properties window, change the **pageLayout** property to **FlowLayout**.

5. Enter the following text on the default.aspx page.

```
Welcome to the flower page
The flowers of the day are:
```

6. Format the first line of text, "Welcome to the flower page," as Heading 1 style by selecting the text and choosing **Heading 1** from the block format drop-down list in the toolbar.

7. Drag a **Listbox** control from the toolbox onto the Web Form.

8. Using the Properties window, locate the **ID** property, and change the **ID** to **lstFlowers**.

9. Return to the window containing the default.aspx.vb or default.aspx.cs code-behind file.

10. Locate the code that you entered in Step 2 to populate the **flowers** object.

11. After that code, enter the needed code to populate **lstFlowers** with the flower names, as shown in the following code example:

Visual Basic .NET

```
Dim flower As String
For Each flower In flowers
    lstFlowers.Items.Add(flower)
Next
```

C#

```
foreach (string flower in flowers)
{
    lstFlowers.Items.Add(flower);
}
```

12. In Solution Explorer, right-click default.aspx and click **Build and Browse**.

The Web Form should display the list of flowers from the **ArrayList** object that you created.

**msdn**®training

Module 2: Developing a Microsoft ASP.NET Web Application User Interface

Contents

Microsoft®

Overview

- **Creating an ASP.NET Web Application User Interface**
- **Validating User Input**
- **Creating and Using User Controls in an ASP.NET Web Form**
- **Processing ASP.NET Web Forms**

Introduction

In this module, you will learn how to create a Microsoft® ASP.NET Web application user interface (UI) by using Web Forms, ASP.NET server controls, and event handlers. You will also learn how to validate user input by using validation controls and how the page postback process works.

Note   The code samples in this module are provided in both Microsoft Visual Basic® .NET and C#.

Objectives

After completing this module, you will be able to:

- Create an ASP.NET Web application UI.
- Implement event handlers by using code-behind files.
- Validate user input by using validation controls.
- Create and use user controls.
- Explain how ASP.NET Web Forms are processed.

Lesson: Creating an ASP.NET Web Application User Interface

- **ASP.NET Server Controls**
- **Creating an ASP.NET Web Application User Interface Using ASP.NET Server Controls**
- **Customizing the Appearance of ASP.NET Server Controls**
- **Creating Event Handlers for ASP.NET Server Controls Using Web Forms Designer**
- **Instructor-led Practice: Creating a Web Application User Interface**

Introduction

In this lesson, you will learn how to create a Web application UI by building a Web Form that includes ASP.NET server controls and event handlers.

Lesson objectives

After completing this lesson, you will be able to:

- Explain the difference between Web server controls and HTML server controls.
- Create an ASP.NET Web application UI by using ASP.NET server controls.
- Customize the appearance of ASP.NET server controls.
- Implement event handling by using the Web Forms Designer.

ASP.NET Server Controls

- **HTML Server Controls and Web Server controls**

Feature	HTML Server controls	Web Server controls
How the ASP.NET server controls relate to HTML elements	Each HTML server control corresponds to a HTML element	Web server controls render as HTML
Namespace	System.Web.UI.Html Controls	System.Web.UI.WebControls
Events supported	Client-side and server-side	Typically server-side only

- **All ASP.NET server controls use the runat=server attribute**
- **Web server controls start with the asp: prefix**

```
<asp:Button id="btnSubmit" runat="server"
    Text="Submit"></asp:Button>
```

Introduction

Developing a Web application UI involves the adding of visual elements that provide information, such as a text label, to users, and adding elements that solicit input, such as buttons and drop-down lists from users.

In traditional ASP development, the UI is built by using HTML elements and Microsoft ActiveX® controls. When developing an ASP.NET UI, you use ASP.NET server controls, as well as the HTML elements and ActiveX controls.

There are two types of ASP.NET server controls: HTML server controls and Web server controls.

HTML server controls

The HTML server controls correspond to the standard HTML elements. The HTML server controls reside in the **System.Web.UI.HtmlControls** namespace. HTML server controls can handle both server-side and client-side events.

Web server controls

Web server controls are defined as abstract controls in which the actual HTML that is rendered by the control can be quite different from the model against which you program. For example, a **RadioButtonList** Web server control might be rendered in a table or as inline text with other HTML. The Web server controls reside in the **System.Web.UI.WebControls** namespace. Web server controls can detect browser capabilities and then create the appropriate output for both basic and rich (HTML 4.0) browsers. Web server controls typically handle server-side events.

HTML code for ASP.NET server controls

The HTML code that is used for HTML server controls appears very similar to the HTML code that is used for standard HTML elements. However, all of the ASP.NET server controls include a **runat=server** attribute that differentiates the ASP.NET server control from a standard HTML element. Web server controls also include an **asp:** prefix in the HTML tag, as shown in the following code example:

```
<asp:Button id="btnSubmit" runat="server"
    Text="Submit"></asp:Button>
```

Creating an ASP.NET Web Application User Interface Using ASP.NET Server Controls

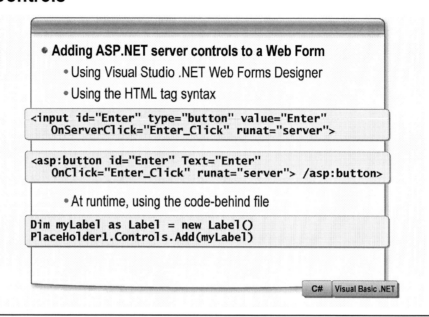

- **Adding ASP.NET server controls to a Web Form**
  - Using Visual Studio .NET Web Forms Designer
  - Using the HTML tag syntax

```
<input id="Enter" type="button" value="Enter"
    OnServerClick="Enter_Click" runat="server">
```

```
<asp:button id="Enter" Text="Enter"
    OnClick="Enter_Click" runat="server"> /asp:button>
```

  - At runtime, using the code-behind file

```
Dim myLabel as Label = new Label()
PlaceHolder1.Controls.Add(myLabel)
```

C#   Visual Basic .NET

Introduction

There are three ways to add ASP.NET server controls to an ASP.NET Web Form:

- Using Microsoft Visual Studio® .NET Web Forms Designer.
- Using the HTML tag syntax.
- Using the code-behind file.

Adding ASP.NET server controls using Visual Studio .NET

The most common method for adding ASP.NET server controls to a Web Form is by using the Visual Studio .NET Web Forms Designer. By using the Visual Studio .NET Web Forms Designer, you can place ASP.NET server controls accurately on the Web Form and immediately see their location and properties.

You add ASP.NET server controls to a Web Form by using the Visual Studio .NET Toolbox. The following steps add an ASP.NET server control to a Web Form in Visual Studio .NET:

1. Open Visual Studio .NET, and then open the solution that contains the Web Form that you want to edit.

2. Open the Web Form to which you want to add an ASP.NET server control by double-clicking that page in Solution Explorer.

3. Verify that the page is displayed in Design mode by clicking the **Design** button that appears directly below the text/design editor pane.

4. Open the Toolbox window by moving the mouse pointer over the **Toolbox** tab.

5. To add Web server controls, click the **Web Forms** tab of the Toolbox. To add HTML server controls, click the **HTML** tab of the Toolbox.

6. Drag the control from the Toolbox and place it on the Web Form in the preferred location.

   If the **pageLayout** setting of the Web Form is set to **GridLayout**, you can place the form anywhere on the page. If the **pageLayout** setting for the Web Form is set to **FlowLayout**, the control is placed at the cursor location or at the top-left corner of the page.

7. Save the Web Form.

Positioning ASP.NET Server Controls on an ASP.NET Web Form

In Design view of the Visual Studio .NET Web Forms Designer, there are two ways to position ASP.NET server controls on your Web Form: **Flow Layout** and **Grid Layout**.

When the **pageLayout** property is set to **FlowLayout**, the client Web browser positions the HTML elements one after the other, in the order that they appear in the HTML code that is generated by the Web server. The HTML elements flow from left to right within a line, and from bottom to top within the Web Form.

When the **pageLayout** property is set to **GridLayout**, the HTML elements are displayed at the locations that are specified by you on the Web Form. An **MS POSITIONING="GridLayout"** attribute is added to the opening **<BODY>** HTML tag, and the positioning grid is activated in Design view.

Adding ASP.NET Server controls to a Web Form using the tag syntax

ASP.NET server controls can also be added to a Web Form by using the HTML tag syntax. If you are familiar with creating HTML elements by using standard HTML code, then this process of using the HTML tag syntax is very similar. Remember that when creating ASP.NET server controls, you must include the **runat=server** attribute. If you are creating a Web server control, you must also include the **asp:** prefix.

The following example code shows how to add the **HtmlInputButton** HTML server control to a Web Form:

```
<input id="Enter" type="button" value="Enter"
  OnServerClick="Enter_Click" runat="server">
```

The following example code shows how to add the **Button** Web server control to a Web Form:

```
<asp:button id="Enter" Text="Enter" OnClick="Enter_Click"
  runat="server"> </asp:button>
```

Adding ASP.NET Server controls to a Web Form at runtime

To add ASP.NET server controls to a Web Form at runtime you must first add a **PlaceHolder** control to the Web Form, and then add one or more ASP.NET server controls to the **PlaceHolder** control.

Adding an ASP.NET server control to the Web Form at runtime involves the following steps:

1. Add a **PlaceHolder** control to the Web Form.

2. Declare a new instance of the ASP.NET server control in the code-behind file.

3. Add the ASP.NET server control instance, which you created in Step 2, to the **PlaceHolder's Controls** collection.

The following example code illustrates how to add a **Label** Web server control to a Web Form at runtime:

Visual Basic .NET

```
Dim myLabel as Label = new Label()
PlaceHolder1.Controls.Add(myLabel)
```

C#

```
Label myLabel = new Label();
PlaceHolder1.Controls.Add(myLabel);
```

Note   The **PlaceHolder** control is designed to be used on pages that are using **Flow Layout**, and as such, the control cannot be positioned absolutely. The control cannot be positioned absolutely because controls added during runtime may require other controls on the page to shift position. **Flow Layout** allows controls to shift dynamically. The **Grid Layout** option does not allow ASP.NET server controls to shift dynamically.

Customizing the Appearance of ASP.NET Server Controls

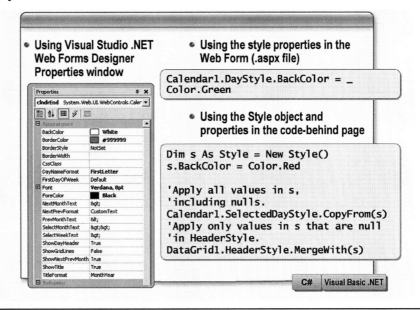

Introduction

When designing your ASP.NET Web Form, you will typically want to customize the appearance of ASP.NET server controls. For example, in the **Calendar** Web server control, you may want to display the day that is selected by a user in a color that is different from the color that is used for the rest of the days. You can customize the appearance of ASP.NET server controls in one of the following ways:

- Using the Visual Studio .NET Web Forms Designer Properties window.
- Using the style properties in the Web Form (.aspx file).
- Using the **Style** object and the properties that are in the code-behind file.

Customizing the appearance of an ASP.NET server control using the Properties window

To customize the appearance of ASP.NET server controls by using the Web Forms Designer Properties window, you need to do the following:

1. If the Properties window is not visible, choose **Properties Window** from the **View** menu or press F4.

2. If the ASP.NET server control that you want to modify is not selected, use the **Object** drop-down list to select it.

   Alternatively, in Design view, select the ASP.NET server control for which you want to customize the appearance.

3. In the Properties window, select the property that you want to modify.

4. Specify a value for that property.

   Depending on the property, you might be required to type a text or numerical value, select a value from a list of property values, or set the value in a custom editor.

When you make changes by using the Properties window, Visual Studio .NET automatically updates the HTML code for that page. You can also customize the appearance of ASP.NET server controls by directly editing the HTML in HTML view. Because of the number of possible settings and the possibility of typing mistakes when directly editing the HTML in HTML view, you should use the Properties window to customize the appearance of ASP.NET server controls whenever possible.

Customizing the appearance of an ASP.NET server control using the style objects and its properties in the .aspx file

You may customize the appearance of an ASP.NET server control programmatically. The ASP.NET server controls expose one or more style objects that encapsulate additional appearance properties. An example style object is the **Font** style property, which exposes a style object of type **FontInfo**, which contains individual properties pertaining to the font, such as **Size**, **Name**, **Bold**, and so on. You can customize the appearance of ASP.NET server controls by using the exposed style objects and their properties.

To customize the appearance of ASP.NET server controls programmatically, use the following hierarchical convention for specifying the style object and the property that you want to set:

```
Control.StyleObject.Property = value
```

The following example code shows how you might set the **BackColor** property for the **DayStyle** object of a **Calendar** Web server control:

Visual Basic .NET

```
Calendar1.DayStyle.BackColor = Color.Green
```

C#

```
Calendar1.DayStyle.BackColor = Color.Green;
```

Customizing the appearance of an ASP.NET server control using the Style object in the code-behind file

You can also create an object of type **Style** and copy or merge the values of a **Style** object's properties to one of the styles of an ASP.NET server control. By using a **Style** object, you can apply the same styles to several different ASP.NET server controls that are in your ASP.NET Web application. In effect, you can create a virtual style sheet as a **Style** object and then apply that style sheet to a series of ASP.NET server controls.

To create a **Style** object and apply it to ASP.NET server controls:

1. Create an instance of the **Style** object and set its properties:

```
Visual Basic .NET

Dim s As Style = New Style()
s.BackColor = Color.Red
```

```
C#

Style s = new Style();
s.BackColor = Color.Red;
```

2. Assign the **Style** object to a control by using one of the following methods:

- The **CopyFrom** method, which applies all of the settings from a **Style** object, including null settings.

- The **MergeWith** method, which copies only the properties that are already set on the **Style** object, omitting the **Style** properties that have not been set.

  The **MergeWith** method will not overwrite any of the existing style elements.

The following example code shows how to create a **Style** object, set one of its properties, and then apply the **Style** object to two different control **Style** objects, using the **CopyFrom** and **MergeWith** methods:

```
Visual Basic .NET

'Apply all values in s, including nulls.
Calendar1.SelectedDayStyle.CopyFrom(s)
'Apply only values in s that are null in HeaderStyle.
DataGrid1.HeaderStyle.MergeWith(s)
```

```
C#

//Apply all values in s, including nulls.
Calendar1.SelectedDayStyle.CopyFrom(s);
//Apply only values in s that are null in HeaderStyle.
DataGrid1.HeaderStyle.MergeWith(s);
```

Creating Event Handlers for ASP.NET Server Controls Using Web Forms Designer

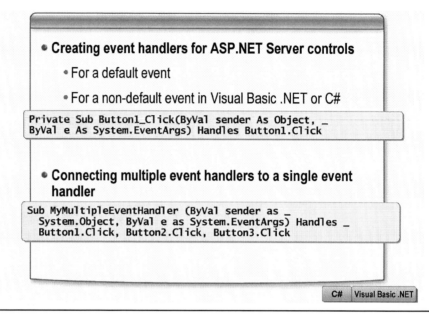

Introduction

ASP.NET replaces the linear processing model of ASP by emulating the performance of an event-driven model. The ASP.NET page framework is used to make the associations of an event to an event handler implicitly.

Creating event handlers for ASP.NET server controls

ASP.NET server controls have a default event, which is the event that is most commonly associated with a specific ASP.NET server control. For example, the default event for a **Button** Web server control is the **Click** event. You can create event handlers for both the default event and other events:

- To create the event handler for a default event

  In Design view of the Web Forms Designer, double-click the ASP.NET server control or page. The Code Editor opens the code-behind file with the insertion point in the event handler.

- To create an event handler for non-default events in Visual Basic .NET

  a. Open the code-behind file or switch to the Code Editor for the page.

  b. At the top of the Code Editor window, select the control from the left-hand drop-down list, and then select the event from the right-hand drop-down list.

- To create an event handler for non-default events in C#

    a. In Design view, select the control, and then press F4 to display the Properties window.

    b. In the Properties window, click the **Events** ⚡ button.

        The Properties window displays a list of the events for that control, with boxes to the right that display the names of event handlers that are bound to those events.

    c. Locate the event for which you want to create a handler and then, in the event name box, type the name of an event handler.

        Alternatively, you can double-click the event name box to create a handler whose name follows the convention *controlID_eventname*.

        The new event handler is created in the code-behind file with the name that you typed or with the generated name.

    The following example code shows the new event handler that has been generated for a **Button** control:

```
private void Button1_Click(object sender, _
System.EventArgs e)
```

Connecting multiple events to a single event handler

Although each event typically has its own event handler, you can also bind multiple events to a single event handler. These multiple events can be triggered from the same ASP.NET server control or from several different ASP.NET server controls. For example, you may want to bind the **Click** events of several **Button** Web server controls in a Web Form to a single event handler.

For both Visual Basic .NET and C#, you must add specific code to the event-handler method signature that resides in the code-behind file:

- To connect multiple events to a single event handler in Visual Basic .NET

    Modify the Handles clause of a method by adding the names of the events that the method should handle. Separate the event names with commas. The following example code shows how you can bind the method **MyMultipleEventHandler** to events that are associated with three controls:

```
Sub MyMultipleEventHandler (ByVal sender as Object, _
    ByVal e as EventArgs) Handles Button1.Click, _
        Button2.Click, Button3.Click
```

Note When connecting multiple controls to a single event handler, all of the controls must have the same method signature.

- To connect multiple events to a single event handler in C#:

  a. In Design view, select a control whose event you want to bind to a method.

  b. In the Properties window, click the **Events** button (). The Properties window displays a list of the events for that control, with boxes to the right that display the names of the event handlers that are bound to those events.

  c. From the drop-down list, select the method to which you want to bind the event. The methods that are displayed in the list are those that have the correct signature for the event that you want to handle. The Code Editor opens, showing the method that you selected. In addition, a line is added to the page's **InitializeComponent** method to perform the binding. The following is an example of the code that performs the binding:

```
this.Button1.Click += new
    System.EventHandler(this.myEventHandler);
this.Button2.Click += new
    System.EventHandler(this.MyMultipleEventHandler);
this.Button3.Click += new
    System.EventHandler(this.MyMultipleEventHandler);

Private void MyMultipleEventHandler(object sender,
System.EventArgs e
```

  d. Repeat Steps a through c for the next control whose event you want to bind to the method.

Instructor-led Practice: Creating a Web Application User Interface

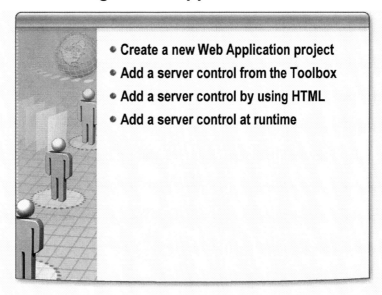

- **Create a new Web Application project**
- **Add a server control from the Toolbox**
- **Add a server control by using HTML**
- **Add a server control at runtime**

Introduction

In this practice, you will create a Web Form with HTML server controls and Web server controls. You will see how to add ASP.NET server controls by using the following:

- The Visual Studio .NET Toolbox
- HTML
- The code-behind file and the **PlaceHolder** control.

Create a new Web Application project

In the following steps you will create a new Web application project.

1. In Visual Studio .NET, create a new ASP.NET Web Application project. Name this project **UIPractice**.

2. In Solution Explorer, notice the files that are created automatically when a new ASP.NET Web Application project is created.

   By default, the first Web Form in the project, named **WebForm1.aspx**, is displayed in the Design window.

Add a server control from the Toolbox

In the following steps you will add a server control from the Toolbox.

3. In the Toolbox window, if it is not already selected, select the **Web Forms** tab, and view the Web server controls that are available for designing the Web Form.

4. Drag a **TextBox** control from the **Toolbox** and drop it on the Web Form.

5. Change to HTML view and show the HTML code that is added by Visual Studio .NET to place the **TextBox** control on the Web Form.

Add a server control by using HTML

In the following steps you will add a server control by using HTML.

6. Add a **Button** control to the page by adding the following line of code between the <form> and </form> tags:

```
<asp:Button id="btnGo" runat="server"></asp:Button>
```

7. Switch back to Design view and drag the newly created button down beneath the **TextBox** control.

8. In the Properties window for the button, change the **Text** property to Go!

9. From the Toolbox, drag a **PlaceHolder** control to the Web Form.

   Note that the **PlaceHolder** control cannot be positioned on the page similar to other controls. The **PlaceHolder** control does not have a style attribute, which is required for placing controls in a specific location on the page.

10. To reflect the changes that you made in Design view, switch to HTML view.

    Notice the changes that have been made to the HTML.

Add a server control at runtime

In the following steps you will add a server control at runtime.

11. Switch to Design view.

12. Double-click the page to open the code-behind file.

    The cursor is automatically placed in the **Page_Load** event handler on the page.

13. Add a **Label** control to the page by creating a new **Label** object, setting its **Text** property to **My runtime label**, and add the **Label** control to the **PlaceHolder** that is named PlaceHolder1.

    Your code should look like the following:

```
Visual Basic .NET

Dim myLabel as Label = new Label()
myLabel.Text = "My runtime label"
PlaceHolder1.Controls.Add(mylabel)
```

```
C#

Label myLabel = new Label();
myLabel.Text = "My runtime label";
PlaceHolder1.Controls.Add(myLabel);
```

14. Build and browse the Web Form to test the changes.

Lesson: Validating User Input

- ASP.NET Validation Controls
- Adding ASP.NET Validation Controls to a Web Form
- Demonstration: Validating User Input Using ASP.NET Validation Controls

Introduction

In this lesson, you will learn how to validate user input by using ASP.NET validation controls.

Lesson objectives

After completing this lesson, you will be able to:

- Describe the purpose of the various ASP.NET validation controls.
- Add validation controls to a Web Form.

ASP.NET Validation Controls

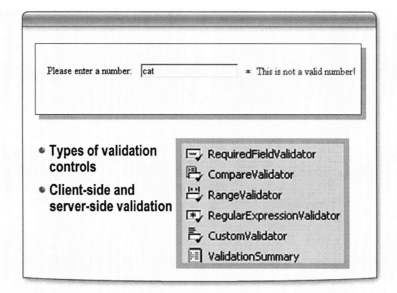

Introduction

Many Web Forms request user input, which is then typically submitted to the Web server for processing. To prevent processing errors and unnecessary posts to the Web server, you can use ASP.NET validation controls to verify the correctness of the user input before the posting of the page to the Web server.

Types of ASP.NET validation controls

The following table lists the types of validation controls that are available in Visual Studio .NET for ASP.NET Web applications, how you can use them, and a description of each.

Type of validation	Control to use	Description
Required entry	**RequiredFieldValidator**	Ensures that the user does not leave an entry empty.
Comparison to a value	**CompareValidator**	Compares a user entry to a constant, or to the value of another control.
Range checking	**RangeValidator**	Ensures that an entry is within a specified range.
Pattern matching	**RegularExpressionValidator**	Matches the entry to a defined pattern, such as an e-mail address.
User-defined	**CustomValidator**	Ensures that an entry matches logic that you specify.

You can associate more than one validation control to an ASP.NET server control. For example, you might specify that a field is required by using the **RequiredFieldValidator** control and that it contain a specific range of values by using the **RangeValidator** control.

The **ValidationSummary** control does not perform validation, but it is used in conjunction with the preceding listed controls. The purpose of the **ValidationSummary** control is to display the error messages from all the validation controls on the Web page in a single location.

Server-side and client-side validation

Input validation can take place on both the server and the client. Server-side validation is always required by ASP.NET whereas client-side validation is optional. If the user is working with a browser that supports dynamic HTML (DHTML), the validation controls can also perform validation by using client script. Using client scripts can substantially improve response time of a Web application because the user does not have to wait for the page to be sent to, and returned from, the Web server. If the browser supports DHTML, you have greater control over the layout of error messages and can display an error summary in a message box.

Adding ASP.NET Validation Controls to a Web Form

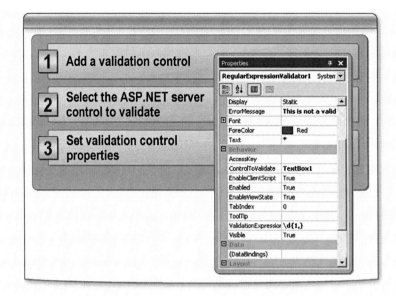

Introduction

Because all of the validation controls share a common object model, the process of adding validation controls to a Web Form is the same for all of the controls. In Visual Studio .NET, you simply drag the validation control onto the Web Form, select the ASP.NET server control to validate, and then set the properties of the validation control.

Add a validation control

To add a validation control to a Web Form, open the **Web Forms** toolbox, select one of the available validation controls, and then drag the validation control next to the ASP.NET server control that you want to validate.

Select the ASP.NET server control to validate

You select the ASP.NET server control to validate by opening the Properties window and selecting the appropriate ASP.NET server control ID from the drop-down list that is next to the **ControlToValidate** property. You can add multiple validation controls to a single ASP.NET server control. All the validation controls that are added to the ASP.NET server control must evaluate as **True** before that ASP.NET server control is accepted and the Web Form can be processed.

Set validation control properties

After the validation control is placed on the page, use the Properties window to enter the control-specific properties, such as the validation expression, error message, text message, and display.

Demonstration: Validating User Input Using ASP.NET Validation Controls

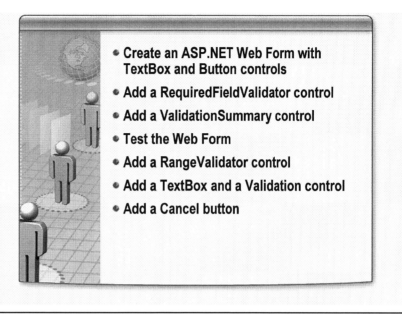

* Create an ASP.NET Web Form with TextBox and Button controls
* Add a RequiredFieldValidator control
* Add a ValidationSummary control
* Test the Web Form
* Add a RangeValidator control
* Add a TextBox and a Validation control
* Add a Cancel button

Introduction

In this demonstration, you will see how a **RequiredFieldValidator** control can be used to verify that a **TextBox** control is correctly filled in before a Web Form is processed.

▶ **To run this demonstration**

Create an ASP.NET Web Form with TextBox and Button controls

In the following steps you will create an ASP.NET Web Form with **TextBox** and **Button** controls.

1. Create a new ASP.NET Web Application project named ValidationTst1.

2. The project opens with WebForm1 in the Design view.

3. Switch to **FlowLayout**.

4. Drag the following Web controls from the Toolbox to WebForm1: a **TextBox** and a **Button**.

Add a RequiredFieldValidator control

In the following steps you will add a **RequiredFieldValidator** control to the Web Form.

5. Add a **RequiredFieldValidator** control next to the **TextBox** control.

6. Set the properties of the **RequiredFieldValidator** control in the Properties window, as shown in the following table.

Property	Value
ControlToValidate	TextBox1
ErrorMessage	An input is required
Text	*

7. Show that the property **Display** of the **RequiredFieldValidator** is set to **Static** by default.

Add a ValidationSummary control

In the following step you will add a **ValidationSummary** control to the Web Form.

8. Add a **ValidationSummary** control to the bottom of WebForm1.

Test the Web Form

In the following steps you will test the Web Form.

9. Save, build and browse the Web Form.

10. Leave the **TextBox** control blank and click the **Button** control.

    Notice that the **Text** property, an asterisk (*), is displayed where you placed the **RequiredFieldValidator** control, and that the **ErrorMessage** text is displayed in the **ValidationSummary** control.

Add a RangeValidator control

11. Switch back to WebForm1.aspx.

12. Add a **RangeValidator** control to the Web Form, next to the **RequiredFieldValidator** control.

13. Set the properties of the **RangeValidator** control in the Properties window, as shown in the following table.

Property	Value
ControlToValidate	TextBox1
ErrorMessage	Out of range
Text	<
MaximumValue	100
MinimumValue	16
Type	Integer

14. Save, build and browse the page.

15. Leave **TextBox1** blank and then click the **Button** control.

    You should see the message **An input is required** in the **ValidationSummary** control.

16. Type a value greater than 100 or less than 16, and then click the **Button** control.

    You should get the text message **Out of range** from the **RangeValidator** control.

17. Reopen WebForm1.aspx, select the **RequiredFieldValidator** control, and change the property **Display** to **Dynamic**.

18. Save, build and browse the page.

19. Enter a value greater than 100 or less than 16, and then click the **Button**.

    You should get the text message **Out of range** from the **RangeValidator** control. Notice that this time the text message **Out of range** is directly next to the input control because the **RequiredFieldValidator** does not hold the space for its text message (dynamic display mode).

Add a TextBox and a Validation control

20. Reopen WebForm1.aspx, add a second **TextBox** control, and then add a **RegularExpressionValidator** control next to the **TextBox** control.

21. Right-click the **RegularExpressionValidator** control and click **Properties**, or click the **RegularExpressionValidator** control, if the Properties window is still open, and enter the following properties:

    a. In the **ErrorMessage** property, type **Invalid E-mail address!**

    b. In the **ControlToValidate** property, select **TextBox2**.

    c. In the **ValidationExpression** property, select **Internet E-mail Address**.

22. Save, build and browse the page.

23. Type an incorrect e-mail address in the second text box and then click the **Button**.

You should get the message Invalid E-mail address! from the RegularExpressionValidator control.

24. Select **View Source** and show the client-side validation HTML code.

Add a Cancel button

25. Add a second button to WebForm1.

26. Set the **Text** property to **Cancel**, and then change the **CausesValidation** property for the **Cancel** button to **False**.

27. Build and browse the page.

28. Click **Cancel**.

The button posts back to the server although no information was entered in the **TextBox** control.

Lesson: Creating and Using User Controls in an ASP.NET Web Form

- **What Is a User Control?**
- **Why Use User Controls?**
- **Creating a User Control**
- **Demonstration: Creating a User Control**
- **Using a User Control on a Web Form**
- **Demonstration: Using a User Control on a Web Form**

Introduction

A user control is an ASP.NET page that can be imported as a server control by other ASP.NET Web Forms. Similar to Web server controls, which are components that run on the server, user controls provide UI and other related functionality. After you have created a user control, it can then be used by other pages in the same Web application.

In this lesson, you will learn what user controls are, why you should consider using them in your Web applications, how to reference a user control from an ASP.NET Web Form, and finally, learn how to access the properties that are in a user control.

Lesson objectives

After completing this lesson, you will be able to:

- Explain what a user control is and why you might use one.
- Create a user control.
- Use a user control on a Web Form.

What Is a User Control?

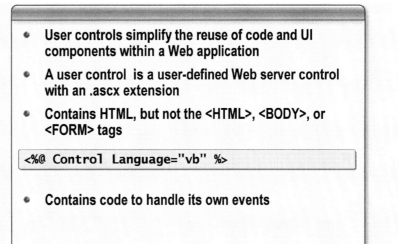

* **User controls simplify the reuse of code and UI components within a Web application**
* **A user control is a user-defined Web server control with an .ascx extension**
* **Contains HTML, but not the <HTML>, <BODY>, or <FORM> tags**

```
<%@ Control Language="vb" %>
```

* **Contains code to handle its own events**

C#   Visual Basic .NET

Introduction

Because user controls can simplify the reuse of code and common UI components, understanding what they are and how they work is an important part of learning about ASP.NET Web application development.

Definition

User controls are ASP.NET pages with an .ascx file extension. User controls offer an easy way to partition and reuse common UI functionality across your ASP.NET Web applications. Similar to a Web Form, you can write these controls with any text editor, or develop them by using classes. Also, similar to a Web Form, user controls are compiled when first requested and then stored in server memory to reduce the response time for subsequent requests. Unlike Web Forms, however, user controls cannot be requested independently; user controls must be included in a Web Form to work.

> **Note** The Microsoft .NET Framework prevents files with the .ascx file extension from being viewed in a Web browser. This is a security measure that ensures that the user control cannot be viewed as a stand-alone ASP.NET page.

What is in a user control?

A user control consists of HTML and code, but because user controls are used by Web Forms, they do not contain the **<HEAD>**, **<BODY>**, or **<FORM>** HTML tags. Instead, these HTML tags are included in each Web Form that uses the user control.

When a user control is used by a Web Form, the user control participates in the event life cycle for that Web Form. Also, because a user control is an ASP.NET page, it has its own page logic. For example, a user control can handle its own post-back in its **Page_Load** event handler.

> **Note** User controls are different from custom server controls. To learn more about creating custom server controls, see "Developing ASP.NET Server Controls" in the Visual Studio .NET documentation.

User controls and their associated code-behind files

Just as Web Forms have code-behind files, user controls also have an associated code-behind file. The **@ Page** directive is used in Web Forms to associate a code-behind file, whereas the **@ Control** directive is used to reference a code-behind file from a user control page. The **@ Control** directive can only be used with user controls, and you can only include one **@ Control** directive per .ascx file.

For example, to reference a code-behind file for a user control that is named **WebUserControl1**, in a Web application project named **test**, you use the following **@ Control** directive:

Visual Basic .NET

```
<%@ Control Language="vb" Codebehind="WebUserControl1.ascx.vb"
Inherits="test.WebUserControl1" %>
```

C#

```
<%@ Control Language="c#" Codebehind="WebUserControl1.ascx.cs"
Inherits="test.WebUserControl1" %>
```

Note   The **@ Control** directive supports the same attributes as the **@ Page** directive, except for the **AspCompat** and **Trace** attributes. Because the **@ Control** directive does not use the **Trace** attribute, you must add the **Trace** attribute to the **@ Page** directive for the .aspx page that calls the user control, if you want to enable tracing for that user control.

User control vs. Web server control

A user control is not the same as a Web server control. Web server controls include not only form-type controls, such as buttons and text boxes, but also include specific controls, such as a calendar.

Why Use User Controls?

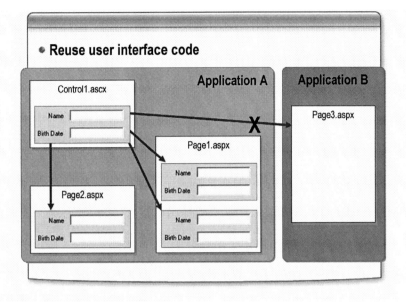

Introduction

There are several advantages to using user controls in your ASP.NET Web applications. User controls are self-contained, can be used multiple times, and can be written in a different language from the main hosting Web page.

Advantages to using user controls

User controls are used for numerous purposes, such as creating headers and navigation bars, and for repeating blocks of code in a Web application project.

Note In traditional ASP Web pages, **include** files are used for code and UI reuse. In ASP.NET, user control pages replace the functionality of **include** files.

User controls offers many advantages when developing a Web application, including:

- User controls are self-contained. User controls provide separate variable namespaces, which means that none of the methods and properties of the user control conflicts with any of the existing methods or properties of the hosting Web page.

- User controls can be used more than once within a hosting Web page without causing property and method conflicts.

- User controls can be written in a language different from that of the main hosting Web page. For example, a user control that is written in C# can be used on a Web Form that is written in Visual Basic .NET.

Sharing user controls

A single user control can be shared among all the pages within a Web application. However, the .aspx pages in one Web application cannot host a user control from another Web application. To use a user control in multiple Web applications, the user control must be copied to the virtual root folder of each Web application.

To share controls amongst multiple Web applications, you can also create a Web custom control, which behaves similarly to a shareable user control. Web custom controls are more difficult to create than user controls because, unlike user controls, Web custom controls cannot be created by using the visual tools that are provided by Visual Studio .NET; therefore, all development is done by code only.

Note For more information about user controls and Web custom controls, see "Web User Controls and Web Custom Controls" in the Visual Studio .NET documentation.

Creating a User Control

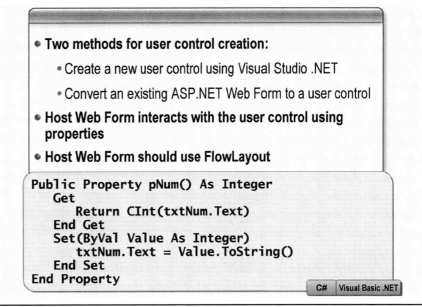

- **Two methods for user control creation:**
  - Create a new user control using Visual Studio .NET
  - Convert an existing ASP.NET Web Form to a user control
- **Host Web Form interacts with the user control using properties**
- **Host Web Form should use FlowLayout**

```
Public Property pNum() As Integer
    Get
        Return CInt(txtNum.Text)
    End Get
    Set(ByVal Value As Integer)
        txtNum.Text = Value.ToString()
    End Set
End Property
```

C#   Visual Basic .NET

Introduction

You can create a new user control or convert an existing ASP.NET Web Form to a user control.

Creating a new user control

To create a new user control:

1. Right-click a Web application project in Solution Explorer in Visual Studio .NET, point to **Add**, and then click **Add Web User Control**.

2. Give the control a name and then click **Open**.

   A file with an .ascx extension is created.

Note The user control is created with the page layout set to the **FlowLayout** mode, and with an **@ Control** directive on the page. When you build the UI portion of a user control in Visual Studio .NET, you must use **FlowLayout** rather than **GridLayout** However, you can drag a **Grid Layout Panel** control from the HTML section of the toolbox, if you need to build the parts of the user control by using grid layout instead of using flow layout.

---

3. Add the UI elements.

   You build the user control just as you would build an ASP.NET Web Form, adding UI elements from the Toolbox in Visual Studio .NET or by writing the HTML.

Note When you build the UI portion of a user control in Visual Studio .NET, you must use flow layout rather than grid layout.

---

4. Add event procedures for UI elements and **Page** events. Similar to building any other ASP.NET Web Form, you add event handlers to the code-behind file.

5. Create properties for interacting with the host Web Form.

    Properties allow the hosting Web Form to read and write values into the UI elements on the user control. Properties on the user control hide the implementation of the control.

Converting an existing Web Form to a user control

To convert an existing Web Form to a user control:

1. Remove all **<HTML>**, **<BODY>,** and **<FORM>** tags.

2. If there is an existing @ **Page** directive on the Web Form, change it to an @ **Control** directive.

    Although most @ **Page** attributes are also supported by the @ **Control** directive, ensure that there are no unsupported attributes.

    Note For more information on the attributes that are supported by the @ **Page** and @ **Control** directives, see "Directive Syntax" in the Visual Studio .NET documentation.

    ---

3. Add a **className** attribute to the @ **Control** directive.

    The **className** attribute allows the user control to be strongly typed when it is added to a Web Form.

4. Rename the file to a name that reflects its purpose, and then change the file extension from .aspx to .ascx.

Using properties to provide access

The host Web Form is the Web Form that will include the user control. The host Web Form does not have direct access to the UI elements that are on a user control. Therefore, you use public properties in a user control to expose the UI elements that are in the control so that the host can then use the UI elements.

For example, if a user control is composed of two text boxes, you would need a property for each text box so that the host page can read and write the value in each text box.

The following code is the HTML part of a very simple Visual Basic .NET user control that includes a single text box:

```
<%@ Control Language="vb" Codebehind="WebUserControl1.ascx.vb"
    Inherits="WUCproject.WebUserControl1" %>
<asp:textbox id="txtNum" runat="server" />
```

To expose the values of the text box to the host Web Form, you must create a public property. The following code, which is in the code-behind file for the user control, creates a property named **pNum**. The **pNum** property exposes the **Text** property of the user control's text box control.

Visual Basic .NET

```
Public Property pNum() As Integer
  Get
      Return CInt(txtNum.Text)
  End Get
  Set(ByVal Value As Integer)
      txtNum.Text = Value.ToString()
  End Set
End Property
```

C#

```
public int pNum
{
  get
  {
      return Convert.ToInt32(txtNum.Text);
  }
  set
  {
      txtNum.Text = Convert.ToString(value);
  }
}
```

By using properties on the user control, all public variables, properties, and methods of the user control become the properties and methods of the control that is in the host page. For example, if the user control shown in the preceding code is named userText1 on the host page, you can read from and write to the **userText1.pNum** property. Likewise, if you create a public function in the user control, it becomes a method that can be used from the host page.

Demonstration: Creating a User Control

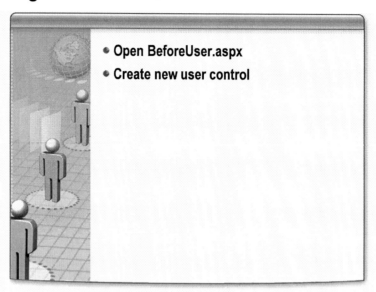

Introduction

In this demonstration, you will see how to create a user control by using Visual Studio .NET. In the next demonstration in this lesson, "Demonstration: Using a User Control on a Web Form," you will use the newly created user control in a Web Form.

The completed code for this demonstration is in the numberbox.ascx file in the *install_folder*\Democode\Mod02\VB folder or *install_folder*\Democode\Mod02\CS folder.

▶ **To run this demonstration**

Open BeforeUser.aspx

1. Create a new Web application project.

2. Add the beforeuser.aspx page to the Web application project.

   This file can be found in *install_folder*\Democode\Mod02*language*\.

   Important If you are using C# for this demonstration, you must change the namespace of the beforeuser.aspx page to match the namespace of the project. If you are using Visual Basic .NET, the namespace is changed automatically when you add the beforeuser.aspx page to the project.

   ---

3. Open the page and show the source HTML.

   The HTML creates the same combination of controls (a text box and two validation controls) in two places on the page.

4. In Design view, group select and copy the first set of text box and validation controls from the page.

Create a new user control

5. Create a new user control by adding a new user control to the project, and Name the user control **numberbox.ascx**.

6. Show the HTML for the page and point out the **@ Control** directive that was created by Visual Studio .NET.

7. In Design view, paste in the text box and validation controls.

8. Open the code-behind file for the new user control.

9. In the code-behind file, create a public property for the value of the text box, as shown in the following code example:

Point out that when you enter the header for the **pNum** property, Visual Studio .NET creates a template for the **Get** and **Set** properties.

```
Visual Basic .NET

Public Property pNum() As Integer
    Get
        Return CInt(txtNum1.Text)
    End Get
    Set(ByVal Value As Integer)
        txtNum1.Text = Value.ToString()
    End Set
End Property
```

```
C#

public int pNum
{
    get
    {
        return Convert.ToInt32(txtNum1.Text);
    }
    set
    {
        txtNum1.Text = Convert.ToString(value);
    }
}
```

Point out that the **Set** property does not take any arguments. The value being passed is automatically placed into a variable called **value**, which is accessible to the **Set** property.

10. Save your changes to the numberbox.ascx page.

11. Leave Visual Studio .NET open.

You will continue with this demonstration in "Demonstration: Using a User Control on a Web Form," which appears after the next topic in this lesson.

Using a User Control on a Web Form

- **Use the @ Register directive to include a user control in an ASP.NET page**

```
<%@ Register TagPrefix="demo" TagName="validNum"
    Src="numberbox.ascx" %>
```

- **Insert the user control in a Web Form**

```
<demo:validNum id="num1" runat="server"/>
```

- **Use the Get and Set properties of the user control**

```
'Get properties of the user control
lblSum.Text = (num1.pNum + num2.pNum).ToString()

'Set properties of the user control
num1.pNum = 5
num2.pNum = 7
```

| C# | Visual Basic .NET |

Introduction

You can place a user control in any ASP.NET Web Form. The page that references the user control is called a host, and the user control is then included in that host.

Including user controls

User controls are included in an ASP.NET Web Form by using the @ **Register** directive, as shown in the following code example:

```
<%@ Register TagPrefix="demo" TagName="validNum"
    Src="numberbox.ascx" %>
```

The **TagPrefix** attribute determines a unique namespace for the user control so that multiple user controls with the same name can be differentiated from each other. The **TagName** attribute is the unique name for the user control. The **Src** attribute is the virtual path to the user control file.

Using the user control

After registering the user control with the @ **Register** directive, you can place the user control tag in the Web Form, just as you would place an ordinary Web server control, including using the **runat="server"** attribute. The following code example adds two user controls to a Web Form:

```
<demo:validNum id="num1" runat="server"/>
<demo:validNum id="num2" runat="server"/>
```

When the primary Web Form is requested, the runtime compiles the user control file and makes it available to the page.

Using the Get and Set properties

In event handlers on the host page, you can access the properties of the user control by adding declarations for the user control. The following code example shows declarations for two **numberbox** user controls:

Visual Basic .NET

```
Protected num1 As numberbox
Protected num2 As numberbox
```

C#

```
protected numberbox num1;
protected numberbox num2;
```

In the preceding code examples, **numberBox** is the name of the class that implements the user control. The variable name (**num1** or **num2**) must be the same as the **id** attribute that is used when adding the user control to the Web Form.

The following code example calls the **Get** property of the **num1** and **num2** user controls:

Visual Basic .NET

```
lblSum.Text = (num1.pNum + num2.pNum).ToString()
```

C#

```
lblSum.Text = (num1.pNum + num2.pNum).ToString();
```

The following code example calls the **Set** property of the **num1** and **num2** user controls to display the constants 5 and 7 in the user control:

Visual Basic .NET

```
num1.pNum = 5
num2.pNum = 7
```

C#

```
num1.pNum = 5;
num2.pNum = 7;
```

Demonstration: Using a User Control on a Web Form

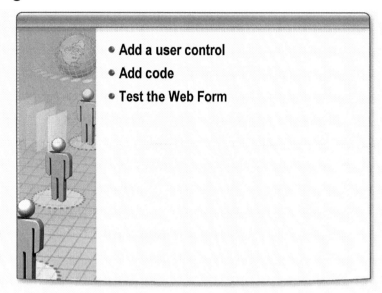

Introduction

In this demonstration, you will see how to use a user control on a host Web Form.

The completed code for the Visual Basic .NET demonstration is in the *install_folder*\Democode\Mod02\VB\afteruser.aspx file.

The completed code for the Visual C# demonstration is in the *install_folder*\Democode\Mod02\CS\afteruser.aspx file.

Note   This demonstration builds on the preceding demonstration in this lesson, "Demonstration: Creating a User Control."

▶ **To run this demonstration**

Add a user control

In the following steps you will add a user control to a Web Form.

1. Edit the beforeuser.aspx Web Form.

2. Delete the two sets of text boxes and validation controls (six controls in all).

3. Using a drag-and-drop operation, place the numberbox.ascx user control from Solution Explorer onto the Web Form, at the location of the first set of controls that you just deleted.

4. View the HTML for the page; the @ **Register** directive was added by Visual Studio .NET, along with the tag for the user control, as shown in the following code example:

```
<%@ Register TagPrefix="uc1" TagName="numberbox"
Src="numberbox.ascx" %>
...
<uc1:numberbox id=Numberbox1 runat="server">
</uc1:numberbox>
...
```

5. Place a second numberbox.ascx user control onto the beforeuser.aspx Web Form, at the location of the second set of controls that you just deleted.

   Visual Studio .NET adds the following HTML to create the user control:

```
<uc1:numberbox id=Numberbox2 runat="server">
</uc1:numberbox>
```

Add code

In the following steps you will add code in the code-behind file of the beforeuser.aspx code-behind file.

6. In the code-behind file for the file beforeuser.aspx, add declarations for the two new user controls:

Visual Basic .NET

```
Protected Numberbox1 As numberbox
Protected Numberbox2 As numberbox
```

C#

```
protected numberbox Numberbox1;
protected numberbox Numberbox2;
```

7. Change the **Compute** button's event handler to read the values from the user controls:

Visual Basic .NET

```
Private Sub Button1_Click(ByVal sender As Object, _
        ByVal e As EventArgs) Handles Button1.Click
    If Page.IsValid Then
        lblSum.Text = _
            CStr(Numberbox1.pNum + Numberbox2.pNum)
    End If
End Sub
```

C#

```
private void Button1_Click(object sender,
        System.EventArgs e)
{
    if (Page.IsValid)
        lblSum.Text = Convert.ToString(Numberbox1.pNum +
            Numberbox2.pNum);
}
```

Test the Web Form

In the following steps you test the Web Form.

8. Build and browse the beforeuser.aspx Web Form.

9. View the HTML source in the browser.

10. Point out how the user controls are rendered in HTML.

11. In the numberbox.ascx user control, add initialization code to the **Page_Load** event handler:

Visual Basic .NET

```
If Not Page.IsPostBack Then
    txtNum1.Text = "0"
End If
```

C#

```
if (!Page.IsPostBack)
    txtNum1.Text = "0";
```

12. Build and browse the beforeuser.aspx Web Form.

Point out that the user control now has an initial value of 0.

Lesson: Processing ASP.NET Web Forms

- **Events in the Web Page Generation Process**
- **Multimedia: Page Event Life Cycle Process**
- **Maintaining the State of ASP.NET Server Controls**

Introduction

In this lesson, you will learn how a Web Form is processed and how ASP.NET maintains the state of ASP.NET server controls.

Lesson objectives

After completing this lesson, you will be able to:

- Describe the events in the ASP.NET Web page generation process.
- Explain how ASP.NET maintains the state of ASP.NET server controls.

Events in the Web Page Generation Process

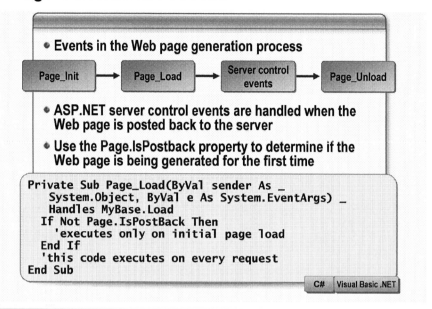

- **Events in the Web page generation process**

  Page_Init → Page_Load → Server control events → Page_Unload

- **ASP.NET server control events are handled when the Web page is posted back to the server**

- **Use the Page.IsPostback property to determine if the Web page is being generated for the first time**

```
Private Sub Page_Load(ByVal sender As _
    System.Object, ByVal e As System.EventArgs) _
    Handles MyBase.Load
  If Not Page.IsPostBack Then
    'executes only on initial page load
  End If
  'this code executes on every request
End Sub
```

C# | Visual Basic .NET

Introduction

It is important to understand the sequence of events that occur when a Web page is processed. This understanding will help you to program your Web Forms and Web applications more effectively.

Web page processing stages

ASP.NET Web applications are event-driven. The **Page** class and the ASP.NET server controls that have been added to the Web Form fire several events when a server requests a Web page. At runtime, the code in a Web Form and any code in the code-behind file that is associated with the Web Form, are compiled into an assembly. When executed, the code in the assembly fires events that you can handle.

Web page processing consists of the following events, which occur in the following order:

1. **Page_Init**. This event initializes the page by creating and initializing the Web server controls on the page.

2. **Page_Load**. This event runs every time that the page is requested.

3. **Server control events**. This event includes change events (for example, **Textbox1_Changed**) and action events (for example, **Button1_Click**).

4. **Page_Unload**. This event occurs when the page is closed or when the control is passed to another page.

Events that are associated with the ASP.NET server controls, such as the user clicking the button, are triggered on the client-side but are fired and handled on the server-side when the Web page is posted back to the server.

The end of Web page processing includes the disposal of the Web page from memory.

Using the Page.IsPostback property

The **Page_Load** event runs on every request for a Web page, whether it is the first request of the Web page or a postback. Because the **Page_Load** event runs with every request for a Web page, all of the code that is within the **Page_Load** event will execute each time that the Web page is requested. You can use the **Page.IsPostBack** property to control the code that executes, when the Web page is requested, as shown in the following code example:

```vb
Visual Basic .NET

Private Sub Page_Load(ByVal sender As System.Object, _
  ByVal e As System.EventArgs) _
  Handles MyBase.Load
  If Not Page.IsPostBack Then
    'executes only on initial page load
  End If
  'this code executes on every request
End Sub
```

```csharp
C#
private void Page_Load(object sender,
  System.EventArgs e)
{
  if (!Page.IsPostBack)
  {
      // executes only on initial page load
  }
  //this code executes on every request
}
```

Multimedia: Page Event Life Cycle Process

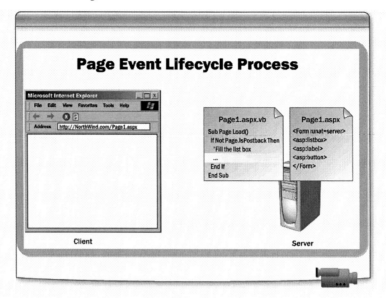

Introduction

In this animation, you will see how Web Forms work in ASP.NET and how the **Page_Load** event can be coded to only run the first time that a page is displayed. You will also see how controls can be made to post immediately to the server.

Maintaining the State of ASP.NET Server Controls

- Server control state is stored in _VIEWSTATE, a hidden control on the .aspx page
- _VIEWSTATE stores state in a string value of name-value pairs

```
<form name="Form1" method="post" action="WebForm1.aspx"
    id="Form1" runat="server">
    <input type="hidden" name="__VIEWSTATE"
    value="dDw3NzE0MTExODQ70z4=" />
    'HTML here
</form>
```

- Maintain the state of select ASP.NET server controls vs. maintaining the state of all the ASP.NET server controls on a Web Form

```
<%@ Page EnableViewState="False" %>
```

```
<asp:ListBox id="ListName" EnableViewState="true"
runat="server"></asp:ListBox>
```

Introduction

Web applications are stateless, which means that the server does not retain any of the information on prior client requests.

ASP.NET Web Forms manage the problem of storing the ASP.NET server control state by adding a hidden control named **_VIEWSTATE**, which records the state of the controls on the Web Form. Specifically, the **_VIEWSTATE** control is added to the Web Form, denoted by the tag **<Form ... runat**="server">. The **_VIEWSTATE** control records the state of the controls that are included between the **<Form>** tags on a Web Form.

As the Web page travels back and forth between the client to the server, ASP.NET server control state is kept with the Web page and it can be updated at either end of the transaction (at the client or the server).

Because the state of the Web application is kept inside the Web Form, the Web page request can be randomly routed in a Web server farm, and it does not need to keep returning to the same server. The advantage of the **_VIEWSTATE** control is that the programmer can concentrate on the page design and do not need to build the infrastructure that is necessary to maintain the Web page state.

Guideline for maintaining the state of ASP.NET server controls

By default, a Web Form saves the state of the ASP.NET server controls on the Web Form. However, for Web Forms with multiple controls, the size of the _VIEWSTATE control can slow the Web application performance. To maximize Web application performance, you may want to maintain the state of select ASP.NET server controls vs. maintaining the state of all ASP.NET server controls on a Web Form. To disable maintaining the state of all ASP.NET server controls on a Web Form, set the **EnableViewState** attribute of the **@ Page** directive to **false**, as shown in the following code example:

```
<%@ Page EnableViewState="False" %>
```

To enable saving state for a specific control, set the **EnableViewState** attribute of that control, as shown in the following code example:

```
<asp:ListBox id="ListName" EnableViewState="true"
    runat="server"></asp:ListBox>
```

Lab 2: Developing an ASP.NET Web Application User Interface

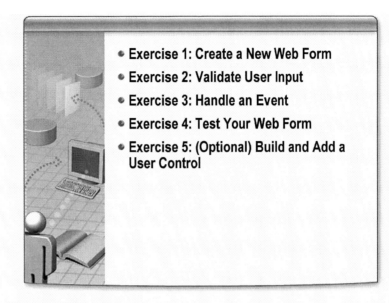

- Exercise 1: Create a New Web Form
- Exercise 2: Validate User Input
- Exercise 3: Handle an Event
- Exercise 4: Test Your Web Form
- Exercise 5: (Optional) Build and Add a User Control

Objectives

After completing this lab, you will be able to:

- Add ASP.NET server controls to an ASP.NET Web Form.
- Validate user input.
- Handle events on a Web Form.

Note This lab focuses on the concepts in this module and as a result may not comply with Microsoft security recommendations.

Prerequisites

Before working on this lab, you must have:

- Knowledge of Visual Studio.
- Knowledge of a.NET-based programming language.

Scenario

You are creating a Web Form that accepts user input, validates the information that is provided by the user, and then performs some calculations on the input that is provided by the user.

Estimated time to complete this lab: 45 minutes

Exercise 1
Create a New Web Form

In this exercise, you will build a new ASP.NET Web Form that accepts user input.

Scenario

You need to build a Web Form that prompts the user to provide the following information:

- Two numbers.
- An operand.
- Two dates.

You should use **TextBox** controls to allow the user to provide the two numbers and one of the dates. Use a **Calendar** control to provide the selection of the second date. Use a **DropDownList** control to allow a user to select an operand.

The following illustration provides one example of how the Web Form may look at the end of this exercise. Your Web Form may look very different, but should have a similar number of controls.

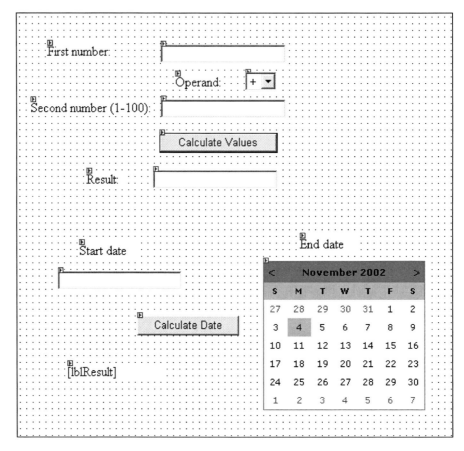

▶ **Open the Lab02 Solution**

1. In Visual Studio .NET, from the **File** menu, click **Open Solution**.

2. In the Open Solution window, click the **My Projects** shortcut.

3. Double-click the **Labfiles** folder, and then double-click the **Lab02** folder.

4. Double-click the folder that represents the language you are using (either **CS** to complete this lab by using C# or **VB** to complete the lab by using Visual Basic .NET).

5. Double-click **Starter**, select **Lab02.sln**, and then click **Open**.

6. In the project, double-click **WebForm1.aspx** to display the Web Form in Design view.

▶ **Add the TextBox controls to the Web Form**

The Web Form that you are creating will require at least three **TextBox** controls. Two of these controls will accept numbers from user input; the third control will allow a user to input a date. You may want to add an additional **TextBox** control that will display the results of the calculations. You may also use a **Label** control or some other method for displaying the results.

1. Using the Toolbox, drag the **TextBox** controls to the form and arrange them according to your page design.

2. Using the Properties window for each **TextBox** control, change the **ID** of each control to an appropriate name.

   In the solution for this lab, the controls that accept numbers are named **txtNum1** and **txtNum2**. The control that accepts a date is named **txtDate1**. The fourth **TextBox** control, which will display the results of the calculations, is named **txtResult**.

▶ **Add a Calendar control**

For one of the calculations that the **WebForm1.aspx** page will perform, users need to provide two dates. For demonstration purposes, you will have users enter a date in a **TextBox** control and then select a second date from a **Calendar** control:

1. From the Toolbox, drag a **Calendar** control to the page.

2. Using the Properties window for the **Calendar** control, rename the control.

3. In the solution for this lab, the control is named **clndrEnd**.

4. At the bottom of the Properties page, click **Auto Format**.

5. Select a scheme for the calendar, and then click **OK**.

▶ **Add a DropDownList control**

Your Web Form should allow users to choose the type of calculation that the page will perform between the two numbers. One way to allow users to choose the type of calculation is to add a **DropDownList** control that provides the common operands.

1. From the Toolbox, drag a **DropDownList** control to the Web Form.

2. In the Properties window, change the name of the **DropDownList** control.

3. In the solution for this lab, the control is named **listOperand**.

4. In the Properties window for the control, click **Items**.

5. Click the ellipsis icon ▦ that is to the right of **Items** to edit the item list.

6. Click **Add**, click the box that is to the right of the **Text** property, and then type one of the following operands:

   - +

   - −

   - *

   - /

   - %

7. Repeat Step 5 until all five of the operands have been added to the list.

   Your ListItem Collection Editor window should look like the following illustration.

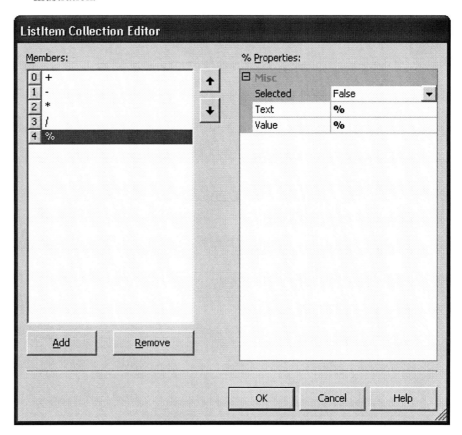

8. Click **OK** to save your changes and to return to the Web Form design window.

▶ **Add Button controls**

The Web Form that you are building will perform two separate calculations. You need to add two buttons to the Web Form to allow the user to start the calculations.

1. From the Toolbox, add two **Button** controls to the Web Form.

   Place one button below the **txtNum2** control, and the other **TextBox** control below the **txtDate1** control.

2. For the first **Button** control, change the **Text** property to **Calculate Values**.

3. Change the **Text** property of the second **Button** control to **Calculate Date**.

4. Give each **Button** control an appropriate name.

   In the solution for this lab, the controls are named **btnCalculateValues** and **btnCalculateDate**.

▶ Add Label controls

To make the Web Form readable to users, you should add **Label** controls that will provide the following instructions to the user:

1. Each **TextBox** control should have a label describing the type of input that is expected from the user.

2. The **Calendar** control should have a label describing the **Calendar** control's purpose.

3. Add an additional label that will be used programmatically to display the results of the calendar calculation.

4. In the Properties window for this label, change the name to **lblDateResult** and delete the word **Label** in the **Text** property, so that the **Text** property is blank.

   Refer to the illustration at the beginning of this exercise to ensure that your Web Form has all of the necessary controls.

Exercise 2
Validate User Input

In this exercise, you will add validation controls to the Web Form.

Scenario

You want to ensure that the information that is provided on the Web page is in the correct format. Specifically, you must verify that the two values supplied by the user are truly numbers, that the second value is a **Double** between 1 and 100, and that the date that is entered is in the proper **Date** format.

▶ **Add RequiredFieldValidator controls**

1. Add a **RequiredFieldValidator** control to the Web Form, so that the **RequiredFieldValidator** control is just to the right of the **txtNum1** control.

2. In the Properties window, set the **ControlToValidate** property to the **txtNum1** control.

3. Set the **Text** property to an asterisk (*) or a similar symbol.

4. Set the **ErrorMessage** property to **The first number is a required field**.

5. Add a second **RequiredFieldValidator** control to the Web Form, placing the **RequiredFieldValidator** control to the right of the **txtNum2** control.

6. Set the second **RequiredFieldValidator** control's properties to match the first **RequiredFieldValidator** control, except that this second control should validate the **txtNum2** control and the **ErrorMessage** property should refer to the second number.

▶ **Add a RegularExpressionValidator control**

You want to ensure that the two values that are entered on the page are valid numbers. For the **txtNum1** control, you will use a **RegularExpressionValidator** control to ensure that the value in the text box contains only numeric characters:

1. From the Toolbox, add a **RegularExpressionValidator** control to the Web Form, just to the right of the first **RequiredFieldValidator** control.

2. Set the properties for this control according to the information in the following table.

Property	Setting
ErrorMessage	The first number is not a valid number
Text	<
ControlToValidate	txtNum1 (or the name that you assigned to the first **TextBox** control)

3. Change the **ValidationExpression** property to allow any number of numeric characters, but to not allow non-numeric characters:

    a. Click the ellipsis icon ⊞ that is to the right of the **ValidationExpression** property.

    b. In the Regular Expression Editor window, select **(Custom)**.

    c. In the **ValidationExpression** property, type an appropriate expression.

        Use the Help link to find more information on the validation syntax, and then write an expression that allows only numeric characters.

        There are several correct expressions. For example, one of the possible correct expression is **\d{1,}**

    d. Click **OK** to save your changes.

▶ **Add a RangeValidator control**

For the second **TextBox** control, you want users to only enter a number of type **Double** that has a value between 1 and 100 by using a **RangeValidator** control.

1. From the Toolbox, add a **RangeValidator** control to the right of the **txtNum2** control.

2. Set the properties for the **RangeValidator** control according to the following table.

Property	Setting
ErrorMessage	The second number must be between 1 and 100.
Text	*
MaximumValue	100
MinimumValue	1
Type	Double
ControlToValidate	txtNum2 (or the name that you assigned to the second **TextBox** control)

▶ **Add a CompareValidator control**

You will use a **CompareValidator** control to ensure that the **txtDate1** control contains a valid date. When using a **CompareValidator** control, you set a minimum date for that control, and then use the **GreaterThan** operator to compare the entered date to the minimum date.

1. From the Toolbox, add a **CompareValidator** control to the Web Form, to the right of the third **TextBox** control.

2. Set the properties for the **CompareValidator** control according to the information in the following table.

Property	Setting
ErrorMessage	This is not a valid date.
Text	*
Operator	GreaterThan
Type	Date
ValueToCompare	01/01/1900 (or any minimum date)
ControlToValidate	txtDate1 (or the name that you assigned to the third **TextBox** control)

▶ **Add a ValidationSummary control**

When the validation controls respond to an invalid entry, it is useful for the user to have a summary of the errors on the page. A **ValidationSummary** control lists all of the validation control errors on the page:

1. From the Toolbox, add a **ValidationSummary** control to the page.

2. Change the **HeaderText** property for the **ValidationSummary** control to **The following errors were found:**

3. Save the Web Form.

Exercise 3
Handle an Event

In this exercise, you will add the code that is needed to handle the **Click** event for each button that is on the Web Form. The code for each button will perform some basic calculations and then return values to the Web Form.

Scenario

After users have entered information in the Web Form, and this information has been validated, you want the Web Form to perform the basic calculations. The first button's **Click** event handler will perform the calculation that was specified by the operand in the **DropDownList** control; the second button's **Click** event handler will calculate the difference between the two dates that the user has provided on the Web Form.

▶ **Calculate a value**

1. In the Web Form Design view, double-click the **Calculate Values** button.

   You are redirected to the code-behind file for the Web Form, and the button's **Click** event handler is created by Visual Studio .NET.

2. In this event handler, the following tasks must be completed:

   • Convert the text in the first two **TextBox** controls to decimal values.

   • Determine which operand is selected in the **DropDownList** control.

   • Perform a calculation on the two numbers by using the selected operand.

   • Return the result of the calculation to the **TextBox** control that is on the Web Form.

   One possible solution to handling these calculations is shown in the following example code:

```
Visual Basic .NET

Dim x As Decimal = Convert.ToDecimal(txtNum1.Text)
Dim y As Decimal = Convert.ToDecimal(txtNum2.Text)

Select Case (listOperand.SelectedItem.Text)
   Case "+"
      txtResult.Text = (x + y).ToString()
   Case "-"
      txtResult.Text = (x - y).ToString()
   Case "*"
      txtResult.Text = (x * y).ToString()
   Case "/"
      txtResult.Text = (x / y).ToString()
   Case "%"
      txtResult.Text = (x Mod y).ToString()
End Select
```

```
C#

decimal x = Convert.ToDecimal(txtNum1.Text);
decimal y = Convert.ToDecimal(txtNum2.Text);

switch (listOperand.SelectedItem.Text)
{
    case "+":
        txtResult.Text=(x+y).ToString();
        break;
    case "-":
        txtResult.Text=(x-y).ToString();
        break;
    case "*":
        txtResult.Text=(x*y).ToString();
        break;
    case "/":
        txtResult.Text=(x/y).ToString();
        break;
    case "%":
        txtResult.Text=(x%y).ToString();
        break;
    default:
        break;
}
```

▶ **Calculate a TimeSpan**

In the **Click** event for the **Calculate Date** button, you will calculate the difference in time between the date that is entered in the **txtDate1** control and the date that is selected on the **Calendar** control.

1. On the Web Form, double-click the **Calculate Date** button.

   You are redirected to the **Click** event for the button in the code-behind file.

2. In this event handler, the following tasks must be completed:

   • Convert the text in the **TextBox** control to a **DateTime** variable.

   • Assign a second **DateTime** variable to the **Calendar** control's **SelectedDate**.

   • Create a **TimeSpan** variable.

   • Determine which **DateTime** variable is lower (that which is representing an earlier date) and subtract it from the other **DateTime** variable.

   • Assign the result to the **TimeSpan** variable.

   • Return the **TimeSpan** variable as the **Text** property of the lblDateResult **Label** control.

One possible solution to handing these calculations is shown in the following code example:

Visual Basic .NET

```
Dim dt1 As DateTime = Convert.ToDateTime(txtDate1.Text)
Dim dt2 As DateTime = clndrEnd.SelectedDate
Dim dtResult As TimeSpan
If (dt2 > dt1) Then
    dtResult = dt2.Subtract(dt1)
    lblDateResult.Text = "The first date is " & _
        dtResult.Days & " days before the second date."
Else
    dtResult = dt1.Subtract(dt2)
    lblDateResult.Text = "The first date is " & _
        dtResult.Days & " days after the second date."
End If
```

C#

```
DateTime dt1 = Convert.ToDateTime(txtDate1.Text);
DateTime dt2 = clndrEnd.SelectedDate;
TimeSpan dtResult;

if (dt2>dt1)
{
    dtResult = dt2-dt1;
    lblDateResult.Text="The first date is " +
        dtResult.Days + " days before the second date.";
}

else
{
    dtResult = dt1-dt2;
    lblDateResult.Text="The first date is " +
        dtResult.Days + " days after the second date.";
}
```

▶ Using the Page_Load event

A **Calendar** control has no default selected date. If you try to use the **SelectedDate** property of the calendar and a user has not yet selected a date, the calendar does not use the date that is highlighted in the UI; instead, the calendar uses a minimum date. For this ASP.NET Web application, the default selected date should match the UI (which always defaults to the current date) when the page loads; however, the **Calendar** control should retain the user-selected date for subsequent post backs.

1. Using the **Page.IsPostBack** method in the **Page_Load** event handler for the Web Form, add code that sets the **Calendar** control's **SelectedDate** property equal to today's date, but only when the page is loading for the first time.

2. Your code should look like the following:

```
Visual Basic .NET

If Not (Page.IsPostBack) Then
    clndrEnd.SelectedDate = DateTime.Today
End If
```

```
C#

if (!Page.IsPostBack)
    {
        clndrEnd.SelectedDate=DateTime.Today;
    }
```

Exercise 4
Test Your Web Form

In this exercise, you will test your Web Form.

▶ **Build and browse**

In Solution Explorer, right-click the **Web Form** and choose **Build and Browse**.

▶ **Test the validation controls**

1. Without entering any values in the form, click the **Calculate Values** button.

   Rather than sending information to the server, the two **RequiredFieldValidator** controls should appear on the Web page, along with the **ValidationSummary** list.

2. In the first text box, type your name and then click the **Calculate Values** button.

   The **RequiredFieldValidator** control disappears, but the **RegularExpressionValidator** control appears because your name is not a valid number.

3. Change the text in the first text box to a valid number, enter 150 in the second text box, and then click **Calculate Values**.

   The first **TextBox** is now valid, but the **RangeValidator** for the second **TextBox** appears because the value is greater than 100.

4. Enter a valid value in the second text box, choose an operand in the **DropDownList**, and then click **Calculate Values**

   The Result **TextBox** changes to show the calculated result.

5. In the Date **TextBox** control, enter some text, and then click the **Calculate Date** button.

   The **CompareValidator** control displays, indicating that you did not enter a valid date.

▶ **Test the calendar calculations**

1. Enter a valid date in the **TextBox** control. For example, you can enter **04/02/1970**.

2. Click **Calculate Date**.

3. The **lblDateResult** control displays the difference (in days) between today's date and the date that you entered.

4. Select a different date in the **Calendar** control, and then click **Calculate Date** again.

5. The **lblDateResult** label changes to reflect the new **TimeSpan** difference.

Exercise 5 (Optional)
Build and Add a User Control

In this exercise, you will build a simple user control and add it to your Web Form. This user control will be used as a header or footer for your Web Form. You can design this user control to display any information that you want; the solution for this lab displays a label and two hyperlinks, one for each of the language solutions to this lab.

The following illustration provides one example of how the Web Form may look at the end of this exercise, with the user control added to the top of the page.

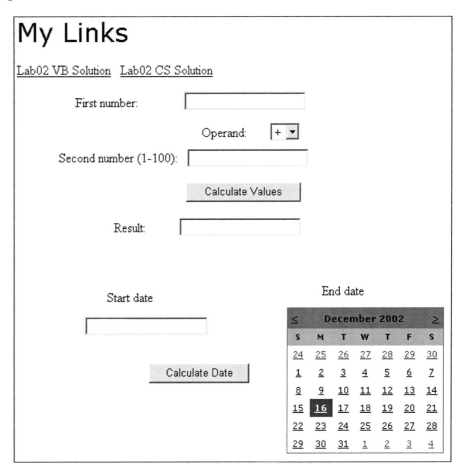

▶ **Create the Web user control**

1. In Solution Explorer, right-click the **Lab02** project, point to **Add**, and then click **Add Web User Control**.

2. In the **Name** text box in the Add New Item - Lab02 window, type **Links.ascx** and then click **Open**.

3. In the designer for Links.ascx, drag the UI components that you want to use from the Toolbox to the page, and then arrange them.

   In the solution for this lab, a label and two hyperlink controls are added. The hyperlinks point to the following two Uniform Resource Locators (URLs):

   ```
   http://localhost/upg/Lab02-VB-Solution/WebForm1.aspx

   http://localhost/upg/Lab02-CS-Solution/WebForm1.aspx
   ```

4. Save your changes, and then build the project.

▶ **Add the user control to the Web Form**

1. In Solution Explorer, double-click **WebForm1.aspx** to open the page in the designer.

2. From Solution Explorer, drag **Links.ascx** to the designer surface of WebForm1.aspx.

   A grey box appears in the upper left corner that is labeled **UserControl - Links1**.

3. Switch to HTML view.

   What HTML code was added to WebForm1.aspx?

   _____

   _____

4. Build and browse WebForm1.aspx.

5. Verify that the user control displays.

msdn® training

Module 3: Debugging Microsoft ASP.NET Web Applications

Contents

Overview

- **Tracing in ASP.NET Web Applications**
- **Debugging ASP.NET Web Applications**

Introduction

On occasion, your Microsoft® ASP.NET Web application will not function because of logic errors. Logic errors, which occur while the Web application is running, result in unexpected values or output in response to user actions. To fix logic errors, you must analyze their cause.

To analyze the cause of logic errors in your ASP.NET Web application, you can use the ASP.NET trace functionality and the Microsoft Visual Studio® .NET debugger.

Note The code samples in this module are provided in both Microsoft Visual Basic® .NET and C#.

Objectives

After completing this module, you will be able to:

- Use the trace functionality of ASP.NET to obtain the execution details of Web page requests.

- Use the Visual Studio .NET debugger to debug ASP.NET Web applications.

Lesson: Tracing in ASP.NET Web Applications

* Tracing in ASP Web Applications
* The Tracing Process in ASP.NET Web Applications
* Enabling Tracing in ASP.NET Web Applications
* Adding Custom Trace Messages to ASP.NET Web Applications
* Viewing and Analyzing ASP.NET Web Application Trace Information
* Demonstration: Tracing in ASP.NET Web Applications

Introduction

This lesson introduces the trace functionality of ASP.NET. The ASP.NET trace functionality can be used for analyzing the cause of logic errors in ASP.NET Web applications. This lesson explains how to use the ASP.NET trace functionality to analyze the cause of logic errors in an ASP.NET Web application.

Lesson objectives

After completing this lesson, you will be able to:

* Explain the tracing process in Active Server Pages (ASP) Web Applications.
* Explain the tracing process in ASP.NET Web applications.
* Enable tracing in an ASP.NET Web application.
* Add custom trace messages to ASP.NET Web applications.
* View and analyze the ASP.NET Web application trace.

Tracing in ASP Web Applications

* **Tracing in ASP Web Applications was done Using:**
  * **Response.Write** statements
  * **<% %>** syntax
* **Disadvantages of Response.Write statements in ASP Web applications**
  * Time consuming to add and remove
  * May forget to remove unnecessary statements which may confuse users

Introduction

Tracing is used to obtain the execution details for a Web page request. Tracing can be used for analyzing the cause of logic errors in ASP.NET Web applications. After you find the cause of the logic errors you can then fix them.

Tracing in ASP Web applications

In ASP Web applications, one of the preferred methods of tracing was to use **Response.Write** statements or the **<%= %>** syntax to output the value of the variables to the client browser. Although it is easy to trace ASP Web applications by using **Response.Write** statements, there are also disadvantages, including:

- It is time-consuming to add multiple **Response.Write** statements, and to then remove them from a Web page.

- You may forget to remove an inappropriate **Response.Write** statement, which may then confuse users.

The Tracing Process in ASP.NET Web Applications

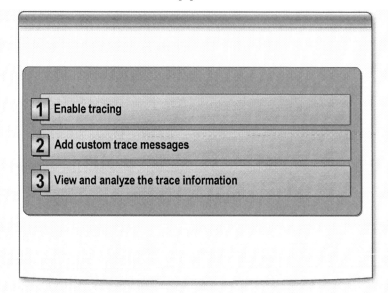

Introduction

Although ASP.NET supports the **Response.Write** statement, tracing is a better method for viewing the page-execution process. One advantage of using the ASP.NET tracing features is that you do not need to remove the trace messages from the code. You can disable tracing in ASP.NET Web applications, thereby preventing the users from seeing unnecessary information.

Enabling tracing

Tracing in ASP.NET Web applications can be done at the ASP.NET Web application level or at the ASP.NET Web Form level. You can enable tracing in ASP.NET Web applications by using one of the following options:

- The **<trace>** element in the Web.config file or machine.config file.
- The attributes of the @ **Page** directive in ASP.NET Web Forms.

Note In Visual Studio .NET, ASP.NET Web Application projects, tracing is enabled by default.

Add custom trace messages

To display information that is specific to the requested Web page, you can add custom trace messages by using members of the **Trace.Write** statements or the **Trace.Warn** statements.

View and analyze the trace information

ASP.NET trace information can be displayed as part of the Web page output or collected in a log file. You set the location for trace information by using the **<trace>** element in the Web.config file or the machine.config file. If the **<trace>** element is configured to display the trace information, the trace information then displays at the bottom of the ASP.NET Web Form. If the **<trace>** element is configured to log the trace information, the information is then stored in an .axd file, which can then be viewed in a Web browser.

Enabling Tracing in ASP.NET Web Applications

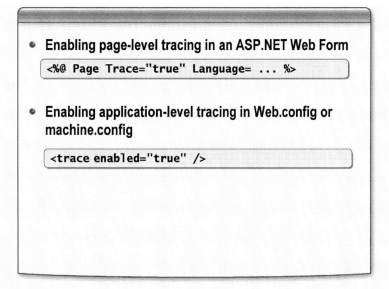

- **Enabling page-level tracing in an ASP.NET Web Form**

  ```
  <%@ Page Trace="true" Language= ... %>
  ```

- **Enabling application-level tracing in Web.config or machine.config**

  ```
  <trace enabled="true" />
  ```

Introduction

Enabling tracing in an ASP.NET Web application involves setting the trace level. You can set the trace level by using the attributes of the @ **Page** directive and the **<trace>** element of the Web.config file or the machine.config file.

To enable page-level tracing

To enable page-level tracing, set the **Trace** attribute of the @ **Page** directive to **true**. For example, the following example code demonstrates how to set the **Trace** attribute of the @ **Page** directive:

```
<%@ Page Trace="true" Language= … %>
```

To enable application-level tracing

To enable application-level tracing, set the **enabled** attribute of the **<trace>** element, in the Web.config or machine.config file, to **true**. For example, the following example code demonstrates how to set the **enabled** attribute in the Web.config or the machine.config file:

```
<trace enabled="true" />
```

Adding Custom Trace Messages in ASP.NET Web Applications

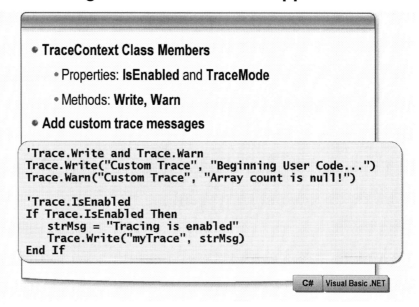

* **TraceContext Class Members**
  * Properties: **IsEnabled** and **TraceMode**
  * Methods: **Write, Warn**
* **Add custom trace messages**

```
'Trace.Write and Trace.Warn
Trace.Write("Custom Trace", "Beginning User Code...")
Trace.Warn("Custom Trace", "Array count is null!")

'Trace.IsEnabled
If Trace.IsEnabled Then
    strMsg = "Tracing is enabled"
    Trace.Write("myTrace", strMsg)
End If
```

C#   Visual Basic .NET

Introduction

To add custom trace messages to ASP.NET Web applications you need to use the **TraceContext** class and its members.

The TraceContext class

The **TraceContext** class is available in the **System.Web** namespace. The main properties and methods of the **TraceContext** class are:

- Properties:

  - **IsEnabled**. This property indicates whether tracing is enabled for the current Web request.

  - **TraceMode**. This property gets or sets the sorted order in which trace messages should be output to a requesting browser.

- Methods:

  - **Warn** (*category, message*). This method writes trace information to the trace log. Unlike the **Write** method, all warnings for the **Warn** method appear in the log as red text. The *category* parameter is a string containing a description of the trace *message,* and it is used to classify and group trace messages. The *message* parameter is a string containing the trace message to be written to the trace output.

  - **Write** (*category, message*). This method writes trace information to the trace log. The *category* parameter is a string containing a description of the trace *message,* and it is used to classify and group trace messages. The *message* parameter is a string containing the message to be written to the trace output.

Note For a complete list of the **TraceContext** class members and their corresponding syntax, see the **TraceContext** Class topic in the Microsoft .NET Framework Class Library Reference in the Visual Studio .NET product documentation.

Adding custom trace messages

The **TraceContext** class is available to you by using the **Trace** property of the **Page** class. The **Trace** property stores a pointer to the **TraceContext** object for the current Web page request.

The following example code demonstrates how to use the **TraceContext** class to write trace messages:

Visual Basic .NET

```
Trace.Write("Custom Trace", "Beginning User Code…")
Trace.Warn("Custom Trace", "Array count is null!")
```

C#

```
Trace.Write("Custom Trace", "Beginning User Code…");
Trace.Warn("Custom Trace", "Array count is null!");
```

The resulting trace messages appear as shown in the following illustration. The trace message, Array count is null!, has been written by using the **Warn** method, and it will appear as red text in the trace information.

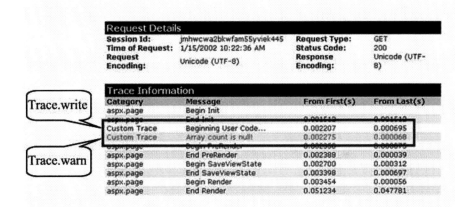

The following example code demonstrates checks to see if tracing is enabled for the requested Web page:

Visual Basic .NET

```
If Trace.IsEnabled Then
  strMsg = "Tracing is enabled"
  Trace.Write("myTrace", strMsg)
End If
```

C#

```
if (Trace.IsEnabled)
{
  strMsg = "Tracing is enabled";
  Trace.Write("myTrace", strMsg);
}
```

Viewing and Analyzing ASP.NET Web Application Trace Information

- **Trace information:**
  - Request Details, Trace Information, Control Tree, Cookies Collection, Headers Collection, Form Collection, QueryString Collection, Server Variables
- **Specifying trace information display location**

  ```
  <trace enabled="true" pageOutput="true | false" />
  ```

- **Viewing trace information on a Web page output**
  - View the Web page in a Web browser

- **Viewing trace information stored in a log file**

  ```
  http://ServerName/ApplicationName/trace.axd
  ```

Introduction

You can use the ASP.NET trace functionality to obtain the execution details about a Web page request.

ASP.NET Web application trace information

In ASP.NET, the execution details about a Web page request are referred to as the trace information or trace output.

The ASP.NET Web application trace information consists of several categories. The following table lists the trace information categories and the description of the type of information that each trace information category contains.

Trace Information Categories	Description
Request Details	Information about the request, including session identification (ID), time of request, type of request, and request status.
Trace Information	Output from the standard and custom trace statements. The "From First(s)" column contains the total time since execution until the trace is executed, and the "From Last(s)" column displays the increment duration.
Control Tree	List of all of the items that are on the Web page, along with the size of each item.
Cookies Collection	List of the cookies that are being used.
Headers Collection	List of all of the items in the Hypertext Transfer Protocol (HTTP) header.

(continued)

Trace Information Categories	Description
Form Collection	List of the controls, and their values, on the Web form that is being posted.
QueryString Collection	List of the variables and their values that are appended to the Uniform Resource Locator (URL).
Server Variables	List of all of the server variables and their values.

Note For more information about trace information, see "Reading Trace Information" in the Visual Studio .NET documentation.

Viewing the ASP.NET Web application trace information

Before you view the trace information, you must specify where to display the trace information:

■ To specify the trace information display location.

Set the **pageOutput** attribute of the **<trace>** element in the Web.config or machine.config file. To display the trace information on the Web page output, set the **pageOutput** attribute to **true**. Rather than having the trace information displayed at the bottom of each Web page, you can have ASP.NET save the trace information in a separate log, named trace.axd. This log file can then be viewed in a Web browser. To display the trace information in a separate Web browser window, set the **pageOutput** attribute to **false**. For example, the following example code demonstrates the syntax of the **pageOutput** attribute of the **<trace>** element:

```
<trace enabled="true" pageOutput="true | false" />
```

■ To view the trace information.

To view the trace information on a Web page, view the ASP.NET Web page in a Web browser. To view the trace information that is stored in the log file, browse to the trace.axd file, which is in the Web application's virtual directory:

```
http://ServerName/ApplicationName/trace.axd
```

Demonstration: Tracing in ASP.NET Web Applications

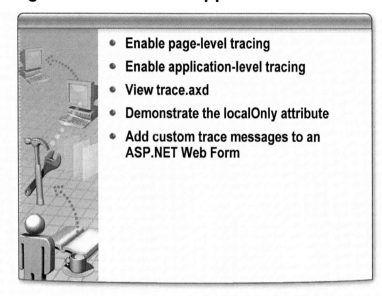

- Enable page-level tracing
- Enable application-level tracing
- View trace.axd
- Demonstrate the localOnly attribute
- Add custom trace messages to an ASP.NET Web Form

In this demonstration, you will enable page-level and application-level tracing, and add custom trace statements to a Web Form. The files for this demonstration are in the *install_folder*\Democode\Mod03*Language* folder.

Enable page-level tracing

1. In Visual Studio .NET, open the Mod03-vb-Benefits or Mod03-cs-Benefits project.

2. In the open Web application project, enable tracing in the ShowBenefits.aspx page by including the **trace** attribute in the @ **Page** directive, as shown in the following code example:

```
<%@ Page Trace="true" ... %>
```

3. Build and browse the ShowBenefits.aspx page.

4. Select some of the benefit check boxes and then click **Submit**.

   The selection values that are sent to the Web server are displayed in the trace information.

5. Click a benefit hyperlink.

Enable application-level tracing

6. Open the Web.config file for the Mod03-vb-Benefits or Mod03-cs-Benefits project and locate the **trace** element.

7. Show and explain the attributes that are set for the **trace** element.

8. Enable application-level tracing by setting the **enabled** attribute of the **trace** element to **true**.

9. Save the changes to the Web.config file.

10. View the BenefitsDetails.aspx page in the browser.

View trace.axd

Rather than writing the trace information to the page, ASP.NET wrote the information to the trace.axd page.

11. View the trace.axd page at the following URL:

```
http://localhost/upg/mod03-vb-Benefits/trace.axd
or
http://localhost/upg/mod03-cs-Benefits/trace.axd
```

12. Click the **View Details** hyperlink to see the trace statements that were saved to memory.

Demonstrate the localOnly attribute

Have students browse to the BenefitDetails.aspx page on the Instructor's computer by typing the following URL where *XY* is either vb or cs depending on which project the instructor is using:

```
http://london/upg/mod03-XY-Benefits/BenefitDetails.aspx
```

Add custom trace messages to an ASP.NET Web Form

13. In the ShowBenefits.aspx page, locate the **Page_Load** event handler in the code-behind file, and then add a custom trace message that displays the message **Beginning of Page_Load** in a category that is named **ShowBenefits**.

    Your code should look like the following:

    Visual Basic .NET

    ```
    Trace.Warn("ShowBenefits", "Beginning of Page_Load")
    ```

    C#

    ```
    Trace.Warn("ShowBenefits", "Beginning of Page_Load");
    ```

14. In the **Page_Load** event handler, add another custom trace message that displays the value of the **Page.IsPostBack** property.

    Your code should look like the following:

    Visual Basic .NET

    ```
    Trace.Warn("ShowBenefits", "IsPostBack=" & Page.IsPostBack)
    ```

    C#

    ```
    Trace.Warn("ShowBenefits","IsPostBack=" + Page.IsPostBack);
    ```

15. Build and browse the ShowBenefits.aspx page.

    Locate the custom trace messages in the trace information.

16. Disable tracing for the ShowBenefits.aspx page by setting the **Trace** attribute to **false**.

17. Save the ShowBenefits.aspx page, and then view the page in the browser.

    Note   You do not have to rebuild the project because you did not change any code.

    No trace messages are shown on the page even though application-level tracing is enabled.

Lesson: Debugging ASP.NET Web Applications

- **The Visual Studio .NET Debugger**
- **Demonstration: Debugging ASP.NET Web Applications in Visual Studio .NET**
- **How to Enable Remote Debugging for ASP.NET Web Applications**

Introduction

In this lesson, you will learn how to debug ASP.NET Web applications by using the Visual Studio .NET debugger.

Lesson objectives

After completing this lesson, you will be able to:

- Debug ASP.NET Web applications in Visual Studio .NET by using the Visual Studio .NET debugger.

- Explain the process of enabling remote debugging for an ASP.NET Web application.

The Visual Studio .NET Debugger

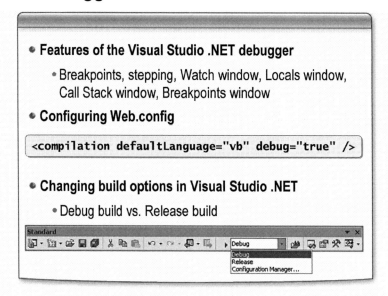

Introduction

You can analyze the cause of logic errors in ASP.NET Web applications by using the Visual Studio .NET debugger. The Visual Studio .NET debugger allows you to stop at procedure locations, inspect memory and register values, and change variables, thereby allowing you to look at how your code does or does not work.

Before you can debug ASP.NET Web applications, you must enable debugging for ASP.NET Web applications. To enable debugging for an ASP.NET Web application, configure the Web.config file for the ASP.NET Web application and then change the ASP.NET Web application project build options in Visual Studio .NET.

The Visual Studio .NET debugger features

The following table lists the features of the Visual Studio .NET debugger and provides a correspondingly brief description for each feature.

Feature	Description
Breakpoints	A breakpoint tells the debugger that a Web application should pause execution, either at a certain point in the code or when a certain condition occurs.
	The Visual Studio debugger has four types of breakpoints:
	• A function breakpoint that causes the Web application to break when execution reaches a specified location within a specified function.
	• A file breakpoint that causes the Web application to break when execution reaches a specified location within a specified file.
	• An address breakpoint that causes the Web application to break when execution reaches a specified memory address.

(*continued*)

Feature	Description
Stepping	Stepping is one of the most common debugging procedures. Stepping consists of executing code one line at a time.
	The **Debug** menu provides three commands for stepping through code:
	• Step Into
	• Step Over
	• Step Out
	Step Into and Step Over differ in only one respect, and that is in the way that they handle function calls. Either command instructs the debugger to execute the next line of code. If the line contains a function call, Step Into executes only the call itself, then halts at the first line of code inside of the function. Step Over executes the entire function and then halts at the first line of code outside of the function.
	Use Step Into if you want to look inside the function call. Use Step Over if you want to avoid stepping into functions.
Watch window	The Watch window can be used to evaluate variables and expressions, and to store the results.
	You can also use the Watch window to edit the value of a variable or register. (You cannot edit the value of const variables.) You can edit and display register values for native-code applications only.
Locals window	The Locals window displays variables that are local to the current context.
Call Stack window	The Call Stack window can be used to view the function or the procedure calls that are currently on the stack.
Breakpoints window	The Breakpoints window lists all of the breakpoints that are currently set in your Web application, and it displays the breakpoint properties. In the Breakpoints window, you can set breakpoints, delete breakpoints, enable or disable breakpoints, edit a breakpoint's properties, or go to the source or disassembly code that is corresponding to a specific breakpoint.

Enabling debugging for an ASP.NET Web application

To enable debugging for an ASP.NET Web application, in the Web.config file, you need to set the **debug** attribute of the **compilation** element to **true**, as shown in the following code example:

```
<compilation defaultLanguage="vb" debug="true" />
```

Note For more information on the **compilation** element, see "<compilation> Element" in the Visual Studio .NET documentation.

Visual Studio .NET build options

Within Visual Studio .NET, you can build ASP.NET Web applications in either debug mode or release mode. Debug mode adds more processing requirements to the ASP.NET Web application, thereby reducing performance. However, Debug mode does allow you to use the features of the Visual Studio .NET debugger. Release mode builds a more streamlined version of the ASP.NET Web application, but it does not allow for debugging. In Release mode, you set the build mode from the tool bar, as shown in the following illustration.

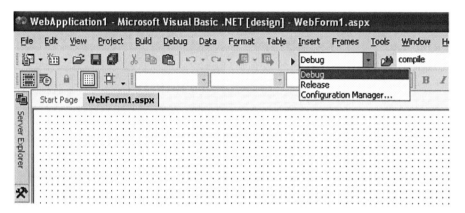

You can also choose to run the Web application in Debug or Release mode, which is set on the **Debug** menu. To run an ASP.NET Web application in debug mode, you must first select a Startup Project and Startup Page from Solution Explorer. In Solution Explorer, right-click on a project, choose **Set as Startup Project**, and then right-click a page and choose **Set As Start Page**.

In the **Debug** menu, you have two options available for running the Web application: **Start** or **Start Without Debugging**. These options are shown in the following illustration.

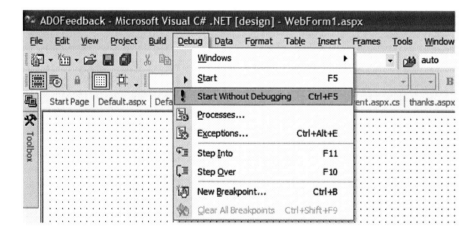

To debug an ASP.NET Web application, you need to build in debug mode and then select **Start** from the **Debug** menu or from the toolbar. When you run the ASP.NET Web application by selecting **Build and Browse** from the Solution Explorer or **View in Browser** from Solution Explorer, the Visual Studio .NET debugger will not start, and you will not be able to debug the ASP.NET Web application.

Demonstration: Debugging ASP.NET Web Applications in Visual Studio .NET

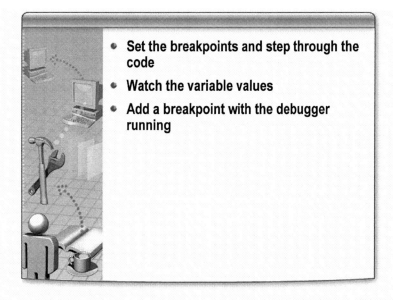

- **Set the breakpoints and step through the code**
- **Watch the variable values**
- **Add a breakpoint with the debugger running**

In this demonstration, you will use the Visual Studio .NET debugger to set breakpoints, step through the code, and view the values of the variables. The files for this demonstration are in the *install_folder*\Democode\Mod03\ *Language* folder.

Set breakpoints and step through the code

1. In Visual Studio .NET, open the Mod03-vb-Benefits or Mod03-cs-Benefits ASP.NET Web application project.

2. Open the code-behind file for the ShowBenefits.aspx page.

3. Set a breakpoint in the **cmdSubmit_Click** event handler by clicking in the left margin next to the event handler declaration.

4. Build and browse the ShowBenefits.aspx page.

5. In the browser, select a couple of the benefits check boxes and then click **Submit**.

6. In Solution Explorer, right-click **ShowBenefits.aspx** and then choose **Set As Start Page**.

7. Run the ASP.NET Web application project in debug mode by clicking the **Start** button ▶ on the toolbar.

8. In the browser, select the **Medical** and **Retirement Account** check boxes, and then click **Submit**.

9. Notice the information that is displayed in the Call Stack window, the Autos window, and the Locals window:

   - The Call Stack window displays the names of the functions on the call stack.

   - The Autos window displays the names and the values of the variables in the current and previous code statements.

   - The Locals window displays the names and the values of all of the local variables that are in the current scope.

10. Pause the mouse on the **lblSelections.Text** property to show that its current value displays in the ToolTip.

11. Step into the first two statements in the **Click** event handler by clicking **Step Into** on the Debug toolbar as shown in the following illustration or pressing F11, stopping when the **For Each** line is highlighted.

Watch the variable values

12. Highlight the **li.Selected** code, right-click on the highlighted **li.Selected** code, and then click **Add Watch**.

    Clicking **Add Watch** adds a **Watch** statement for that value and opens the Watch window.

13. Repeat Step 12 to add a **Watch** statement for the **li.Value** property.

14. Slowly step through the **For Each** loop twice, and watch the value of the **li.Selected** variable and **li.Value** variable change. Stop when the value of **li.Selected** is **False**.

15. At this point, **li.Selected** is equal to **False** and **li.Value** includes the string "Life Insurance." Change the **li.Selected** value to **True** in the Watch window.

16. Step through a few more lines of code.

17. Click **Continue** on the toolbar, as shown in the following illustration, to let the **Click** event handler run.

    Control returns to the browser.

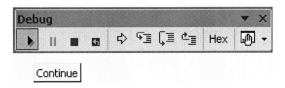

Add a breakpoint with the debugger running

In the following steps, you will add a breakpoint to a different Web Form while the debugger is still running.

18. In Visual Studio .NET, switch to the BenefitDetails.aspx code-behind file.

19. Set a breakpoint in the **Page_Load** event handler in the code-behind file for the BenefitDetails.aspx page.

Note You are adding this breakpoint while the debugger is running.

---

20. In the browser, click one of the benefits hyperlinks.

21. Click **Stop Debugging** on the toolbar to stop debugging, as shown in the following illustration.

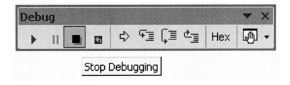

22. Disable the breakpoints by right-clicking on them and clicking **Disable Breakpoint**.

    This action keeps the breakpoint, but the debugger will not stop on them.

23. Clear all of the breakpoints in the ASP.NET Web application project by clicking **Clear All Breakpoints** on the **Debug** menu.

How to Enable Remote Debugging for ASP.NET Web Applications

* **Remote debugging:**
  * Simplifies team development
  * Simplifies Web development
* **Requirements for remote debugging:**
  * Visual Studio .NET or remote components installed on Web server
  * Visual Studio .NET installed on the client
  * Administrative access to the Web server
  * Access for the user who is performing the debugging

Introduction

Debugging is generally used to catch errors during the creation of a Web application. As such, most debugging occurs locally; that is, you are running the Visual Studio .NET debugger on the same computer that hosts the Web application. Sometimes you may need to debug Web applications that are on numerous disparate servers from a single computer. Remote debugging allows you to debug a Web application that is running at a remote location.

Requirements for remote debugging

For remote debugging to work, the following conditions must be met:

* Either Visual Studio .NET or the remote components of Visual Studio .NET must be installed on the Web server that hosts the Web application that you want to debug.

* Visual Studio .NET must be installed on the client computer, which is the computer from which the debugging will occur.

* The user who is performing the debugging must have access permissions on the remote Web. To grant access to a user, you add the user to the **Debugger Users** group on the server. This permission is required even if the user is an administrator on the remote server.

Procedure: remote debugging

To debug remotely:

1. On the client computer, start Visual Studio .NET.

2. On the **File** menu, click **Open**, and then click **Project From Web**.

3. In the **Open Project From Web** dialog box, enter the URL of the server from which you want to open the ASP.NET Web Application project, and then click **OK**.

4. In the **Open Project** dialog box, navigate to the ASP.NET Web Application project on the remote server, and then click **Open**.

5. After the ASP.NET Web Application project is open, you can set breakpoints and run the Web application in debug mode exactly as you would run a local application.

Note   For more information about remote debugging, see "Debugging Web Applications on a Remote Server" and "Setting Up Remote Debugging" in the Microsoft .NET Framework software development kit (SDK) Documentation.

Lab 3: Debugging ASP.NET Web Applications

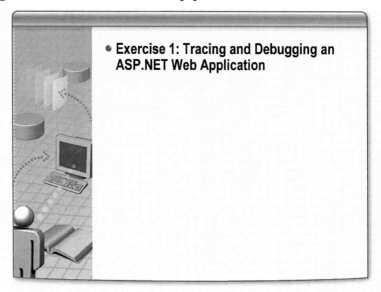

* Exercise 1: Tracing and Debugging an
  ASP.NET Web Application

Objectives

After completing this lab, you will be able to:

- Create a debug build of an ASP.NET Web application.
- Add breakpoints to an ASP.NET Web Form.
- Find and correct errors by using debugging.

Note This lab focuses on the concepts in this module and as a result may not comply with Microsoft security recommendations.

Prerequisites

Before working on this lab, you must have:

- Knowledge of Visual Basic .NET or C#.
- Knowledge of how to use the Visual Studio .NET debugger.

Scenario

In this lab, you will find and fix errors in a Web application by using the Visual Studio .NET debugger.

**Estimated time to
complete this lab:
30 minutes**

Exercise 1
Tracing and Debugging an ASP.NET Web Application

In this exercise, you will fix bugs that have been found in an ASP.NET Web application.

Scenario

The Web application is a simple shopping basket that uses session state to store a user's book selections. A **ListBox** control is populated with books from a Microsoft SQL Server™ database. The Web Form displays the book titles and prices in the **ListBox** control, and displays the total number of items and the total price for the books in **TextBox** controls. The user can select an item from the list and then click the **Remove** button to remove the selected item. The item should be removed from the list (and session state) and the totals in the shopping basket should be updated to reflect this change.

The following bug has been filed against the Web application. Read the bug and the steps the tester used to reproduce the error, and then fix the Web application so that it works as expected.

Bug: 12458	**Project**: Shopping Cart application	**Tester**: test4
Priority: 1	**Severity**: 1	Not applicable
In the Cart.aspx page, the **Remove** button does not work as expected. Instead of just removing the selected item from the list, the item is removed and then the list is doubled in size. This error happens with every click of the **Remove** button. If you try to remove the same item twice, an error is generated. Also, the totals do not seem to be calculated properly.		
Repro steps:		
1. Browse the Cart.aspx page. 2. Select any item from the list, and then click **Remove**. 3. Note that initial item is removed, but the list is now twice as long. 4. Select a different item in the list, and then click **Remove** again. 5. The list is now three times as long as the original list.		

▶ **Open the Lab03 solution**

1. In Visual Studio .NET, from the **File** menu, click **Open Solution**.

2. In the Open Solution window, in the shortcut list, click **My Projects**.

3. Expand the **Labfiles**, **Lab03**, *language*, and **Starter** folders.

4. Select **Debug.sln**, and then click **Open**.

▶ **Run the Web application**

1. In Solution Explorer, right-click **Cart.aspx**, and then click **Set As Start Page**.

2. Click the **Start** button ▶ to run the Web application in debugging mode.

3. Select an item in the **ListBox** control, and then click **Remove**.

   Is the item removed from the list? What happens?

   _____

4. Close Microsoft Internet Explorer.

▶ **Add a breakpoint to the Page_Load event handler**

1. In Solution Explorer, open the code-behind file for the **Cart.aspx** page.

2. In the **Page_Load** event handler, set a breakpoint at the first line of code.

3. Click the **Start** button to run the Web application in debugging mode.

   Internet Explorer opens, and then control is returned to Visual Studio .NET.

4. Step through the code to see how the Web Form populates the **ListBox** control.

   The **Page_Load** event handler calls three methods: **GetArray**, **PopulateList**, and **GetTotals**. What does each of these methods do?

   The **GetArray** method:

   _____

   _____

   The **PopulateList** method:

   _____

   _____

The **GetTotals** method:

_____

_____

5. Continue to step through the code until control is returned to Internet Explorer and the Web Form has loaded.

6. Close Internet Explorer to stop debugging and return to Visual Studio .NET.

▶ **Add a breakpoint to the cmdRemove_Click event handler**

1. In the code-behind file for the **Cart.aspx** page, remove the breakpoint in the **Page_Load** event handler.

2. Set a breakpoint at the first line of code in the **cmdRemove_Click** event handler.

   Because the error on this page occurs during the process of removing an item from the **ListBox** control, the cause of the error may be within the **cmdRemove_Click** event handler or the code that the handler calls.

3. Click the **Start** button to run the Web application in debugging mode.

   Internet Explorer opens, and the page loads normally.

4. Select an item in the **ListBox** control, and then click **Remove**.

   Control is returned to Visual Studio .NET.

5. Step into the code to see how the code removes an item from the **ListBox** control.

6. Close Internet Explorer and return to Visual Studio .NET.

▶ **Enable tracing**

1. In Visual Studio .NET, open the Cart.aspx page, and then switch to HTML view.

2. In the **@ Page** directive, enable tracing for the page.

   When complete, the **@ Page** directive should look like the following code example:

```
Visual Basic .NET

<%@ Page trace="true" Language="vb" AutoEventWireup="false"
Codebehind="Cart.aspx.vb" Inherits="Debug.WebForm1" %>
```

```
C#

<%@ Page trace="true" language="c#"
Codebehind="Cart.aspx.cs" AutoEventWireup="false"
Inherits="Debug.WebForm1" %>
```

3. Open the code-behind file for the Cart.aspx page.

4. Remove the existing breakpoints from the code-behind file.

5. At the beginning of each of the following event handlers and methods, add a **Trace** statement that displays when the event handler or method is fired:

   Page_Load, **GetArray**, **PopulateList**, **GetTotals**, and **cmdRemove_Click**.

Tip   To make the trace messages easier to detect on the page, you may want to use the **Warn** method, rather than the **Write** method, of the **Trace** object.

For example, the code that you add to the **Page_Load** event handler may look like the following code example:

Visual Basic .NET

```
Trace.Warn("MyTrace", "Start of Page_Load")
```

C#

```
Trace.Warn("MyTrace", "Start of Page_Load");
```

6. Click the **Start** button to run the Web application in debugging mode.

   Internet Explorer opens, and the page loads and displays the trace information at the bottom of the page.

   List the events that are displayed in the trace information, in the order in which they fire:

   _____

   _____

7. Select an item in the **ListBox** control, and then click **Remove**.

   List the events that are now displayed in the trace information, in the order in which they fire:

   _____

   _____

Important   Note that when the page is posted back to the server, the **Page_Load** event handler, and the methods that it calls, fire before the **cmdRemove_Click** event fires.

What happens in the **Page_Load** event handler that might cause the **ListBox** control to display the list of items more than once?

_____

_____

_____

8. Close Internet Explorer.

9. In the **Page_Load** event handler, what code can you add to prevent the **GetArray**, **PopulateList**, and **GetTotals** methods from running when the form is posted back during a **Click** event?

_____

_____

▶ **Fix the bug**

1. In the **Page_Load** event handler, add the **Page.IsPostback** property so that the **GetArray**, **PopulateList**, and **GetTotals** method calls only occur when the page is initially loaded.

   When complete, your **Page_Load** event handler should look similar to the following code example:

```
Visual Basic .NET

If Not Page.IsPostBack Then
    GetArray()
    PopulateList()
    GetTotals(arCart.GetValueList())
End If
```

```
C#

if (!Page.IsPostBack)
{
    GetArray();
    PopulateList();
    GetTotals(arCart.GetValueList());
}
```

2. Remove any existing breakpoints from the code.

3. Click the **Start** button to run the Web application in debugging mode.

4. Select an item from the **ListBox** control, and then click **Remove**.

   What happens?

   _____

   _____

   This error is caused when you try to access the methods of an object before an instance of the object has been created.

   Based on the information that is displayed in Internet Explorer, what object has not been instantiated?

   _____

▶ **Find the new bug**

1. Close Internet Explorer.

2. In the code-behind file, add a breakpoint to the first line of code in the **cmdRemove_Click** event handler.

3. Click the **Start** button to run the Web application in debugging mode.

4. Select an item in the **ListBox** control, and then click **Remove**.

   Control is returned to Visual Studio .NET.

5. Step into the code.

   On which line of code is the exception thrown?

   _____

   _____

   Why is the exception being thrown, when it wasn't thrown before you added the **Page.IsPostBack** code to the **Page_Load** event handler?

   _____

   _____

6. Stop debugging and return to Visual Studio .NET.

7. Remove the breakpoint.

► **Fix the second bug**

There are several ways to correct this error. The following solution provides one method for fixing the error.

1. In the **RemoveItem** method, add code that creates an instance of the **arCart SortedList** object and assigns it a value equal to the **array** Session variable.

    You code should look similar to the following:

    Visual Basic .NET

    ```
    arCart = New SortedList()
    arCart = Session("array")
    ```

    C#

    ```
    arCart = new SortedList();
    arCart = (SortedList)Session["array"];
    ```

2. Click the **Start** button to run the Web application in debugging mode.

3. Select an item in the **ListBox** control, and then click **Remove**.

    The Web form should remove the item from the list and the totals should be updated as expected.

► **Disable tracing**

Before resolving the Cart.aspx bugs, you want to ensure that the Web application testers do not see the trace messages when they retest the Cart.aspx page. Rather than removing all of the **Trace.Warn** calls in your code, you will disable tracing at the page level:

1. In Visual Studio .NET, open Cart.aspx.

2. Switch to HTML view.

3. Remove the **trace=true** attribute from the @ **Page** directive.

4. Save Cart.aspx, and then view the page in a browser.

msdn training

Module 4: Accessing Data Using Microsoft ADO.NET

Contents

Microsoft

Overview

- Overview of ADO.NET
- Reading Data Using DataReaders
- Programmatically Accessing Data Using DataSets
- Visually Generating DataSets
- Data-Bound Controls
- Best Practices for Secure and Reliable Data Access

Introduction

In Active Server Pages (ASP) Web applications, you use Microsoft® ActiveX® Direct Objects (ADOs) to access data. In Microsoft ASP.NET Web applications, you will use Microsoft ADO.NET to access data. In this module, you will learn how to use Microsoft Visual Studio® .NET built-in tools to access data by using ADO.NET. You will also learn how to access data programmatically with ADO.NET.

Note The code samples in this module are provided in both Microsoft Visual Basic® .NET and C#.

Objectives

After completing this module, you will be able to:

- Explain how ADO.NET provides data access for ASP.NET Web applications.

- Retrieve data from a data source by using the **DataReader** class.

- Programmatically use **Connection**, **Command**, and **DataAdapter** objects to create and work with **DataSet** objects.

- Visually use **Connection**, **Command**, and **DataAdapter** objects to create and work with **DataSet** objects.

- Display the data from an ADO.NET data source on an ASP.NET Web Form.

- Explain several techniques that can be used to ensure that ADO.NET is secure and reliable.

Lesson: Overview of ADO.NET

* What Is ADO.NET?
* The ADO.NET Object Model
* Multimedia: Using ADO.NET to Access Data
* Comparing DataSets and DataReaders
* Practice: The ADO.NET Architecture

Introduction

Efficient and effective data access is an important feature for highly interactive Web applications. In this lesson, you will learn how ADO.NET provides high quality data access to ASP.NET Web applications.

Lesson objectives

After completing this lesson, you will be able to:

- Compare ADO and ADO.NET.
- Explain the ADO.NET object model.
- Explain the process that ADO.NET uses to access data.
- Compare **DataSet** and **DataReader** objects.

What Is ADO.NET?

ADO	ADO.NET
Designed for connected environments	Designed for disconnected environments
COM-based	.NET-based
Uses OLE DB to access data	Uses .NET Framework Data Provider for SQL Server and .NET Framework Data Provider for OLE DB
ADO XML format only	Advanced XML support
Recordset	DataSet

Introduction

ADO.NET is a set of classes that you can use to access data sources and manipulate data within your ASP.NET Web application. ADO.NET is a new technology that is based on the usefulness of ADO; however, ADO.NET is not a revision of ADO. ADO.NET is a completely new way to manipulate data. ADO.NET contains numerous improvements over ADO, and it greatly simplifies the process of connecting your ASP.NET Web application to a database.

ADO.NET coexists with ADO. As a result, although most of the new Microsoft .NET-based Web applications will be written by using ADO.NET, ADO remains available to the .NET programmer through the .NET COM interoperability services.

Note For more information about using ADO in ASP.NET Web applications, see Module 9, "Migrating ASP Web Applications to Microsoft ASP.NET," in Course 2640, *Upgrading Web Development Skills from ASP to Microsoft ASP.NET.*

ADO, ADO.NET comparison

ADO.NET contains a number of improvements over ADO including:

- Connections

   Unlike ADO, which relies on long-term connections, ADO.NET is specifically designed for data-related operations that use intermittent connections in a normally disconnected environment.

- Programming model

   ADO is based on the Component Object Model (COM), while ADO.NET is based on the Microsoft .NET Framework. As a result of being based on the .NET Framework, ADO.NET has a more flexible data access model.

- Data access

  ADO uses OLE DB to access data. ADO.NET can use the.NET Framework Data Provider for OLE DB or the .NET Framework Data Provider for Microsoft SQL Server™. The .NET Framework Data Provider for SQL Server is designed to take advantage of the advanced features of SQL Server 7.0.

- XML support

  ADO can save and open data in Extensible Markup Language (XML), but only by using the default ADO XML format. ADO.NET is based on XML, and it offers almost unlimited XML data-formatting options.

- Local data storage

  ADO uses **Recordset** to store data locally. ADO.NET uses **DataSet** objects to store data locally. The **DataSet** object is designed to work in a disconnected mode and then reconnect to return data to a data source.

The ADO.NET Object Model

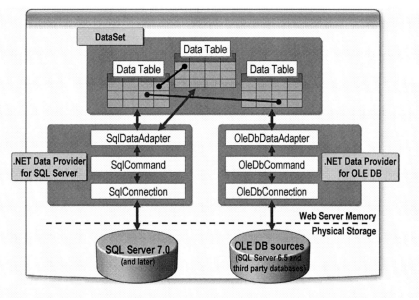

Introduction

The ADO.NET object model provides a structure that can be used to access data from various data sources. There are two main components that comprise the ADO.NET object model: the **DataSet** object and the .NET Framework data provider.

DataSet objects

The **DataSet** object represents a local copy of data from a data source. The **DataSet** object is useful for holding local data that Web Forms can then access.

A **DataSet** object stores disconnected information. For example, to fill a **DataSet** object, you could use a connection object to query a database, and then store those query results in the **DataSet**. The **DataSet** object would maintain the results of the query, but it would not maintain any information about the connection. This normally disconnected nature of the **DataSet** object is a key difference from the ADO **Recordset**.

DataSet objects can also be constructed in memory without a data source. However, to serve as an actual data-management tool, a **DataSet** object must be able to interact with one or more data sources.

DataTable objects

The **DataSet** object stores data in one or more **DataTables**. Each **DataTable** object may be populated with data that comes from a unique data source. You can also establish relationships between two **DataTables** objects by using a **DataRelation** object.

For example, a **DataSet** may contain data from a SQL Server 2000 database, an OLE DB source, and an XML file, all of which are available to the same data-bound control. The **DataSet** may also use a **DataView**, which is a customizable view of a **DataTable**.

Data providers

The .NET data provider provides the link between the data source and the **DataSet**. Examples of the objects that are provided by the .NET data providers are listed in the following table.

.NET data provider objects	Purpose
Connection	Provides connectivity to the data source.
Command	Provides access to database commands.
DataReader	Provides data streaming from a single data source.
DataAdapter	Links the **DataSet** and the data provider. The **DataAdapter** object also reconciles changes that are made to the data in the **DataSet** when updating the data source.

Using the objects

The .NET Framework includes the .NET Framework Data Provider for SQL Server (for SQL Server version 7.0 or later), and the .NET Framework Data Provider for OLE DB. You use the .NET Framework Data Provider for SQL Server objects, **SqlConnection**, **SqlCommand**, **SqlDataReader**, and **SqlDataAdapter**, to read and manipulate data in a SQL Server 7.0 or later database. You use .NET Framework Data Provider for OLE DB objects, **OleDbConnection**, **OleDbCommand**, **OleDbDataReader**, and **OleDbDataAdapter**, to read and manipulate data in all of the other types of databases.

The .NET Framework Data Provider for OLE DB is almost identical to the .NET Framework Data Provider for SQL Server that you will be using in this module. The advantage of the .NET Framework Data Provider SQL Server is that it is specifically designed to work with the advanced features in SQL Server 7.0 and later.

ADO.NET namespaces

There are three namespaces that you import into your ASP.NET Web Form if you are using ADO.NET. You will always use the **System.Data** namespace; and you will also use either the **System.Data.SqlClient** or the **System.Data.OleDb** namespace, depending on the data source.

When using ADO.NET, you must import the **System.Data** namespace. To import this namespace, you use the **Imports** or **using** keyword, as shown in the following code example:

Visual Basic .NET

```
Imports System.Data
```

C#

```
using System.Data;
```

If you are working with data in a SQL Server 2000 database, you must also import the **System.Data.SqlClient** namespace. If you are working with data from other database sources, you need to import the **System.Data.OleDb** namespace. The following code example shows how to import both the **System.Data.SqlClient** and **System.Data.OleDb** namespaces:

Visual Basic .NET

```
Imports System.Data.SqlClient
Imports System.Data.OleDb
```

C#

```
using System.Data.SqlClient;
using System.Data.OleDB;
```

Multimedia: Using ADO.NET to Access Data

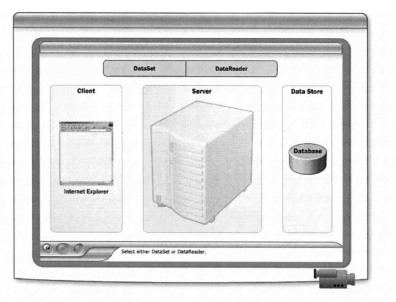

Introduction

In ADO.NET, the **DataSet** and **DataReader** classes are used for accessing data from a database. If you also intend to manipulate data in ASP.NET Web Forms, or return data to a database, you would use a **DataAdapter** object to fill a **DataSet** object. If you only intend to read the data into a data-bound control, you can use either a **DataAdapter** object, or a **Data Reader** object to fill the control.

Using a DataAdapter and a DataSet

DataSet objects are typically set up to use the following data access process:

1. When a user requests data, the **DataSetCommand** pulls data out of a data store and pushes it into a **DataTable**.

2. The page creates the **SqlConnection** and **SqlDataAdapter** objects, and populates a **DataSet** from the database by using the **SqlDataAdapter** object.

3. The data is transferred as XML data. Although the **DataSet** is transmitted as XML, ASP.NET and ADO.NET automatically transform the XML data into a **DataSet**, thereby creating a complete, yet simplified, programming model.

4. After the **DataTables** are transferred to the Web server, the link can be closed.

5. **DataSet** objects are designed to run in a disconnected environment; therefore, **Connection** and **DataAdapter** objects close as soon as the data transfer is complete.

6. A **DataView** is created and bound to a list-bound control that will be displayed.

   After the **DataSet** object is populated, the user can view and manipulate the data. While the data is being viewed and manipulated, there is no connection between the client and the Web server, nor is there a connection between the Web server and the database server. The design of the **DataSet** class makes this disconnected environment easy to implement. Because the **DataSet** object is stateless, it can be safely passed between the Web server and the client without using all of the server resources, such as database connections.

7. When the user is finished viewing and modifying the data, the client passes the modified **DataSet** object back to the ASP.NET page, which uses a **DataAdapter** object to reconcile the changes in the returned **DataSet** object with the original data that is in the database.

8. The data is then sent as XML data between the client and Web server, and then sent between the Web server and the database server.

Using a DataReader

DataReader objects are typically set up to use the following data access process:

1. When a user requests data, the **Command** object retrieves data into the **DataReader** object.

   DataReader objects typically contain only a single stored procedure data request or **SQLSelect** command.

2. The **DataReader** is a read-only, forward-only stream that is returned from the database.

3. You have the option of looping through the **DataReader** object data and displaying it programmatically, or you can bind a **DataReader** object to a list-bound control.

Comparing DataSets and DataReaders

DataSet	DataReader
Read/write access to data	Read-only
Includes multiple tables from different databases	Based on one SQL statement from one database
Disconnected	Connected
Bind to multiple controls	Bind to one control only
Forward and backward scanning of data	Forward-only
Slower access	Faster access
Supported by Visual Studio .NET tools	Manually coded

Introduction

DataSet objects allow you to store multiple **DataTables** of data that are retrieved from a data source. **DataSet** objects can also contain relationships between the data that is in the **DataTables**, and the **DataSet** objects can then apply these relationships when the data is retrieved or modified.

DataReader objects are lightweight objects that are used for reading data from a data source; **DataReader** objects provide forward-only, read-only access to the data that is in a database.

Choosing between DataSets and DataReaders

The choice between using **DataSet** or **DataReader** objects should be based on your intended use for the data. Generally, **DataReader** objects are used for reading data in one-time, read-only situations, such as when accessing a stored password, or filling in a list-bound control. **DataSet** objects are used for more complicated data operations, such as retrieving, displaying, and then updating a customer order entry.

Some of the issues to consider when selecting between **DataSet** and **DataReader** objects include:

- Access to data

  If you intend to both read from and write to your data source, you should use a **DataSet** object. **DataReader** objects are read-only connections and should be used when the data will be used in a read-only situation.

- Access to multiple databases

  If you intend to combine tables from one or more databases, you should use a **DataSet** object. **DataReader** objects are based on a single SQL statement from a single database.

- Binding to controls

  If you intend to bind the data to more than one control, you must use a **DataSet** object. **DataReader** objects can only be bound to a single control.

- Connection mode

  If you intend to access data in a disconnected mode, you should use a **DataSet** object. You can pull data from a **DataSet** object, even when the **DataSet** object is disconnected from the data source. **DataSet** objects only need a connection when filling from or updating to a data source. **DataReader** objects can only supply data when running in a connected mode.

- Data scanning

  If you intend to scan both backwards and forwards through the data, you must use a **DataSet** object. **DataReader** objects can only scan forwards as the data is streamed from the database.

- Access speed

  If you need high-speed access to your data source, use a **DataReader** object. **DataSet** objects are slower than **DataReader** objects when it comes to accessing data from a database because **DataSet** objects store the data in an object on the Web server. There is also more overhead in creating the **DataSet** object because of its ability to read and write data and scan forwards and backwards. **DataReader** objects are faster due to the lightweight nature of the object. There is very little overhead to using the **DataReader** object because it is forward-only and read-only.

- Tool support

  If you intend to use the visual tools in Visual Studio .NET to create the data connection, use a **DataSet** object. With **DataSet** objects, you have the choice of writing your own code or using the visual tools. With **DataReader** objects, you must write all the code yourself.

Practice: The ADO.NET Architecture

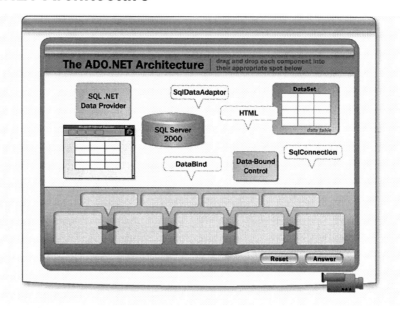

Introduction

In this practice, you will create a flowchart for using a **DataSet** object to access data from a database and to then display it in a browser.

▶ **To run this practice**

1. Open the file
   install_folder\Practices\Mod04\DataQuestions\2640A_DataQuestions.htm
   in Microsoft Internet Explorer.

2. Drag components into the appropriate outline on the bottom of the screen.

3. Click on the **Answer** button to see the correct solution.

   Any errors will be outlined in red.

4. Click on the **Reset** button to start over.

Lesson: Reading Data Using DataReaders

- **What Is a DataReader?**
- **Demonstration: Creating a DataReader Object**
- **Reading Data from a DataReader**
- **Practice: Organizing DataReader Code**

Introduction

For short and simple operations, such as displaying a single set of data directly to the user or accessing a single password with each data request, you do not need to create and maintain a **DataSet** object. Instead, you can use a simple **DataReader** object to select the required data and bind it to a control, or feed it to a function.

In this lesson, you will learn how to read data from a data source by using the **DataReader** class.

Lesson objectives

After completing this lesson, you will be able to:

- Explain how the **DataReader** class works.

- Create a **DataReader** object.

- Read data from a **DataReader** object.

What Is a DataReader?

- **Forward-only, read-only data access**
- **Connected to a data source**
- **Manage the connection yourself**
- **Manage the data yourself, or bind it to a list-bound control**
- **Advantages of DataReaders over DataSets**
  - Faster access to data
  - Uses fewer server resources

Introduction

When a large amount of data is being retrieved from a data source, holding memory open can become a problem. For example, reading 10,000 rows out of a database causes a **DataTable** object to allocate and maintain memory for those 10,000 rows for the lifetime of the table. If 1,000 users do this against the same computer at the same time, memory usage becomes critical.

To address the memory usage issues that **DataSet** objects can create, the **DataReader** class is designed to produce a read-only, forward-only data stream that is returned from the database. With a **DataReader** object, only one record at a time is ever in server memory and memory usage is never an issue. Using a **DataReader** class is similar to the ADO model in that you can use a server cursor in the **Recordset** to do the exact same thing.

Forward-only, read-only

The **DataReader** class provides a forward-only, read-only result set. Because many ASP.NET Web application data requests only require a read-only, forward-only data, the **DataReader** class is an ideal data access solution.

Connected to data source

ADO.NET includes two types of **DataReader** objects: the **SqlDataReader** object for SQL Server version 7.0 or later databases, and the **OleDbDataReader** object for the .NET Framework Data Provider for OLE DB.

You use the **OleDbCommand** or **SqlCommand** objects, and the **ExecuteReader** method, to transfer data into a **DataReader** object.

Manage the connection yourself

Unlike a **DataAdapter** object that opens and closes connections automatically, you need to manage the **DataReader** object connection yourself. The **DataReader** class is similar to the **DataAdapter** class in that you create a **Command** object from a SQL statement and a connection. However, with the **DataReader Command** object, you must explicitly open and close the **Connection** object.

Manage the data yourself

With **DataReader** objects, you have the option of looping through the data and displaying it programmatically, or binding the **DataReader** object directly to a data-bound control. With either option, you must write the code yourself.

Advantages of DataReaders over DataSets

The advantages of the **DataReader** class over the **DataSet** class are based on the lightweight nature of the **DataReader** model, including:

- Faster access to data

  DataReader objects are faster than **DataSet** objects, due to the lightweight nature of the **DataReader** class. There is more overhead in creating the **DataSet** object because **DataSet** objects have the ability to read and write data and scan forward and backward. There is very little overhead to a **DataReader** object because it is forward-only and read-only. This relative lack of overhead means that accessing data with a **DataReader** object is faster than accessing data with a **DataSet** object.

- Uses fewer server resources

  Large **DataSet** objects can quickly consume server memory, thereby causing server performance problems. Because the **DataReader** object is not an in-memory representation of the data, using a **DataReader** object has little effect on the availability of server memory.

Demonstration: Creating a DataReader Object

Try...
- Create the database connection object
- Create a Command object
- Open the database connection
- Call the ExecuteReader method
- Use the DataReader object

Finally...
- Close the DataReader object
- Close the Connection object

Introduction

In this demonstration, you will see how to create and use a **DataReader** object that calls the **Employee Sales by Country** stored procedure in the Northwind database.

The completed code for this demonstration is in the default.aspx page in the *install_folder*\Democode\Mod04*language*\DataReader\Solution folder. You can perform the following steps, or optionally open the solution code, set a breakpoint in the **Page_Load** event handler, and step through the code to explain it.

Open the Demonstration Project

1. In Visual Studio .NET, from the **File** menu, click **Open Solution**.

2. In the Open Solution window, click the **My Projects** shortcut.

3. Open the **Democode**, **Mod04**, *language*, and **DataReader** folders.

4. Select **DataReader.sln**, and then click **Open**.

Create the database connection object

In the following steps you will create a **connection** object to the Northwind database.

5. Open the code-behind file for default.aspx.

6. In the Page_Load event handler, enter the following code to create a database connection to the Northwind database:

```
Visual Basic .NET

Dim cn As SqlConnection = Nothing
Dim dr As SqlDataReader = Nothing
Try
    ' Create the database connection
    cn = New SqlConnection("data source=(local)\MOC;" _
        & "integrated security=true; " _
        & "initial catalog=Northwind")
```

```
C#

SqlConnection cn=null;
SqlDataReader dr=null;
try
{
    // Create the database connection
    cn = new SqlConnection
    ("data source=(local)\\MOC; integrated security=true; "+
    "initial catalog=Northwind");
```

Create a command object

7. Enter the following code to create a **Command** object that calls the **Employee Sales by Country** stored procedure:

```
Visual Basic .NET

' Create a command object
Dim cmdSelect As New SqlCommand()
cmdSelect.CommandText = "Employee Sales by Country"
cmdSelect.Connection = cn
cmdSelect.CommandType = CommandType.StoredProcedure

Dim p1 As New SqlParameter("@Beginning_Date", _
    SqlDbType.DateTime)
p1.Direction = ParameterDirection.Input
p1.Value = "1/1/96"
Dim p2 As New SqlParameter("@Ending_Date", _
    SqlDbType.DateTime)
p2.Direction = ParameterDirection.Input
p2.Value = "12/31/96"
cmdSelect.Parameters.Add(p1)
cmdSelect.Parameters.Add(p2)
```

```
C#

// Create a command object
SqlCommand cmdSelect = new SqlCommand();
cmdSelect.CommandText = "Employee Sales by Country";
cmdSelect.Connection = cn;
cmdSelect.CommandType = CommandType.StoredProcedure;

SqlParameter p1 = new
    SqlParameter("@Beginning_Date",SqlDbType.DateTime);
p1.Direction = ParameterDirection.Input;
p1.Value = "1/1/96";
SqlParameter p2 = new
    SqlParameter("@Ending_Date",SqlDbType.DateTime);
p2.Direction = ParameterDirection.Input;
p2.Value = "12/31/96";
cmdSelect.Parameters.Add(p1);
cmdSelect.Parameters.Add(p2);
```

Open the database connection

8. Enter the following code to open the connection to the Northwind database:

```
Visual Basic .NET

' Open the connection
cn.Open()
```

```
C#

// Open the connection
cn.Open();
```

Call the ExecuteReader method

9. Enter the following code to call the stored procedure and retrieve a **DataReader** object:

Visual Basic .NET

```
' Call the ExecuteReader method
dr = cmdSelect.ExecuteReader()
```

C#

```
// Call the ExecuteReader method
dr = cmdSelect.ExecuteReader();
```

Use the DataReader object

10. Enter the following code to display the order numbers from the **DataReader** object in the **ListBox** control:

Visual Basic .NET

```
' Use the DataReader object
While dr.Read()
    ListBox1.Items.Add(dr("OrderID").ToString())
End While
```

C#

```
    // Use the DataReader object
    while (dr.Read())
    {
        ListBox1.Items.Add(dr["OrderID"].ToString());
    }
} // end the "try" block
```

11. Enter the following code to create an exception handler:

Visual Basic .NET

```
Catch exc As Exception
    ' Handle error
    lblError.Text = exc.Message
```

C#

```
catch(Exception exc)
{
    // Handle error
    lblError.Text = exc.Message;
}
```

Close the DataReader and Connection objects

12. Enter the following code to close the **DataReader** and **Connection** objects:

```Visual Basic .NET
Finally
    'Close the DataReader object
    If Not (dr Is Nothing) Then
        dr.Close()
    End If
    ' Close the Connection object
    If Not (cn Is Nothing) Then
        cn.Close()
    End If
End Try
```

```C#
finally
{
    // Close the DataReader object
    if (dr!=null) dr.Close();

    // 7. Close the Connection object
    if (cn!= null) cn.Close();
}
```

13. Build and browse the default.aspx Web page.

The **ListBox** control should display all of the Order numbers that were retrieved from the stored procedure.

Reading Data from a DataReader

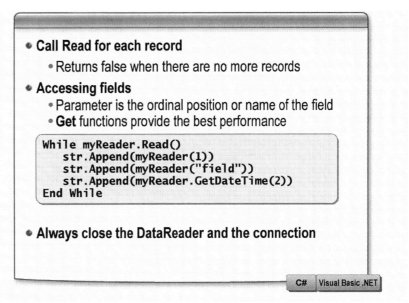

* **Call Read for each record**
    * Returns false when there are no more records
* **Accessing fields**
    * Parameter is the ordinal position or name of the field
    * **Get** functions provide the best performance

```
While myReader.Read()
    str.Append(myReader(1))
    str.Append(myReader("field"))
    str.Append(myReader.GetDateTime(2))
End While
```

* **Always close the DataReader and the connection**

C#   Visual Basic .NET

Introduction

Because **DataReaders** are forward-only, you need to add code that reads the result, handles the data stream, and that then either sorts the data or looks for a specific item.

Call Read for each record

After you have called the **ExecuteReader** method of the **Command** object, you can access a record in the **DataReader** object by calling the **Read** method. The default positioning in the **DataReader** object is before the first record; therefore, you must call the **Read** method before accessing any data. When there are no more records available, the **Read** method returns **false**.

The following code example shows how to read records from the authors table in the **pubs** database. The code loops through all of the records that are in the **DataReader** object **dr,** and then displays the **au_fname** field in the **Label** control **lblName:**

Visual Basic .NET

```
Try
  Dim s As New System.Text.StringBuilder()
  While dr.Read()
      s.Append(dr("au_fname"))
  End While
  lblName.Text = s.ToString()
...
```

C#

```
try
{
  System.Text.StringBuilder s;
  s = new System.Text.StringBuilder();
  while (dr.Read())
  {
      s.Append(dr["au_name"]);
  }
  lblName.Text = s.ToString();
...
```

Accessing fields

To access the data from the fields that are in the current record, you can access a field by ordinal position, by name, or by calling an appropriate **Get** method, such as **GetDateTime**, **GetDouble**, **GetInt32**, or **GetString**.

Tip Using an ordinal position is faster than using a string because the **DataReader** does not need to do a string compare.

The following code example reads the first name and last name fields, both string values, from the first record of the **DataReader** object **dr**, by using the **GetString()** method:

Visual Basic .NET

```
'Position 1 is the last name
'Position 2 is the first name
dr.Read()
lblName.Text = dr.GetString(1) + ", " + _
    dr.GetString(2)
```

C#

```
//Position 1 is the last name
//Position 2 is the first name
dr.Read();
lblName.Text = dr.GetString(1) + ", " +
    dr.GetString(2);
```

You can also reference, by name, the fields of data that are in the current record of the **DataReader** object. You can then call an appropriate conversion function. The following code example shows how to reference a field by name:

Visual Basic .NET

```
strName = CStr(dr("au_fname"))
```

C#

```
strName = dr["au_fname"].ToString();
```

Practice: Organizing DataReader Code

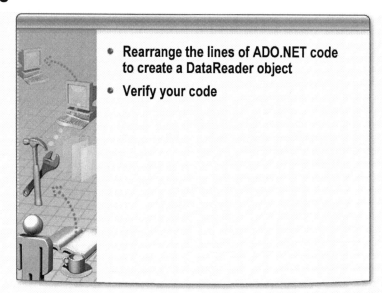

Introduction

In this practice, you will rearrange lines of ADO.NET code into the correct order to create a **DataReader** object.

▶ **To run the practice**

1. Using Internet Explorer, browse to
   http://localhost/upg/mod04-dataquestions/DataReaderCode.aspx.

2. Organize the lines of ADO.NET code into the correct order to create a **DataReader** object.

   Select a line of code and then click on the up or down arrows to move the code.

3. Verify your code organization by clicking on the **Check Answers** button.

Note   There are several correct answers to this practice. This practice focuses on the concepts creating a **DataReader** object and as a result does not include **Try...Catch...Finally...** blocks for error handling.

Lesson: Programmatically Accessing Data Using DataSets

- **The Connection Object**
- **The Command Object**
- **Calling Stored Procedures**
- **The DataAdapter Object**
- **Filling a DataSet**
- **Accessing DataTables**
- **Using a DataView**
- **Handling Errors**
- **Practice: Organizing DataSet Code**

Introduction

The **DataSet** object consists of a collection of records that you can use to locally store and manipulate data. Using a **DataSet** object allows a data-driven Web Form to continue to run while it is disconnected from data sources.

Creating a **DataSet** object from a database requires the use of a **Connection** object to connect to the database, a **Command** object to run the query, and a **DataAdapter** object to transfer the results to the **DataSet** object. In this lesson, you will learn how to programmatically use each of these objects to create and work with **DataSet** objects.

Lesson objectives

After completing this lesson, you will be able to:

- Programmatically create a **Connection** object.
- Programmatically create a **Command** object.
- Programmatically call a stored procedure.
- Explain how the components of a **DataAdapter** object interact.
- Programmatically fill a **DataSet** object.
- Programmatically access **DataTable** objects and individual data fields.
- Programmatically create a **DataView** object to present a subset of the data that is in a **DataTable** object.
- Handle the typical errors that are encountered while accessing data with ADO.NET.

The Connection Object

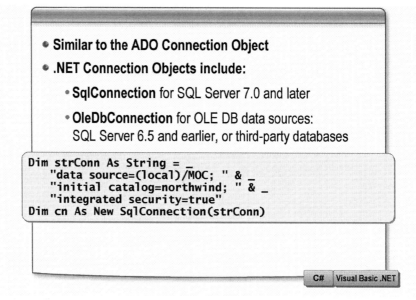

- Similar to the ADO Connection Object
- .NET Connection Objects include:
  - SqlConnection for SQL Server 7.0 and later
  - OleDbConnection for OLE DB data sources:
    SQL Server 6.5 and earlier, or third-party databases

```
Dim strConn As String = _
    "data source=(local)/MOC; " & _
    "initial catalog=northwind; " & _
    "integrated security=true"
Dim cn As New SqlConnection(strConn)
```

C#   Visual Basic .NET

Introduction

To transfer data between a database and your Web application, you must first have a connection to the database. To create a **Connection** object to access a database, you need to identify the name of the database server, the name of the database, and the required logon information.

Depending on the type of database that you are accessing, you can use either a **SqlConnection** or **OleDbConnection** object. You would use a **SqlConnection** object to connect to SQL Server 7.0 and later databases, while using **OleDbConnection** objects to connect to all of the other databases.

Creating a connection string

You create a **SqlConnection** object by passing in a connection string that provides the parameters that are needed to create a connection to the database.

The following example code creates a **SQLConnection** object to the Northwind SQL Server database:

Visual Basic .NET

```
Dim strConn As String = _
    "data source=(local)/MOC; " & _
    "initial catalog=northwind; " & _
    "integrated security=true"
Dim cn As New SqlConnection(strConn)
```

C#

```
string strConn =
    "data source=(local)//MOC; " +
    "initial catalog=northwind; " +
    "integrated security=true";
SqlConnection cn = new SqlConnection(strConn);
```

Connection object parameters

The following table describes some of the commonly used parameters of a **Connection** object:

Parameter	Description
Connection Timeout	The length of time, in seconds, to wait for a connection to the server before terminating the attempt and generating an exception. The default length of time is **15** seconds.
Data Source	The name of the SQL Server server to be used when a connection is open, or the file name to be used when connecting to a Microsoft Access database.
Initial Catalog	The name of the database.
Integrated Security	Determines whether or not the connection is to be a secure connection. **True**, **False**, and **SSPI** are the possible values. **SSPI** is the equivalent of **True**.
Password	The logon password for the SQL Server database.
Persist Security Info	Determines whether security information will be sent as part of the connection. When set to **False**, security-sensitive information, such as the password, is not returned as part of the connection, if the connection is open or has ever been in an open state. Setting this property to **True** can be a security risk. The default setting is **False**.
Provider	Used to set or return the name of the provider for the connection; this parameter is used only for **OleDbConnection** objects.
User ID	The SQL Server logon account name.

Authentication

There are two primary authentication methods that can be used for connecting a Web application to a SQL Server database: Microsoft Windows®-only authentication and mixed-mode authentication. The preferred method is Windows-only authentication, which is used when you set the integrated security parameter of the connection string to **True**.

When you use Windows-only authentication, you do not need to store user credentials, such as the user name and password, in your ASP.NET Web application. Therefore, you avoid transmitting the user credentials as part of the connection string. Instead, with Windows-only authentication, SQL Server verifies the network credentials of the ASP.NET Web application with a Windows domain controller.

The default identity for an ASP.NET Web application is the ASPNET Windows user account. The database administrator must grant permissions to this account to connect to and use the appropriate resources in the SQL Server database. You can change the ASP.NET Web application identity in the Web.config file.

Note   For more information about ASP.NET authentication, see Module 6, "Authenticating Users," in Course 2640, *Upgrading Web Development Skills from ASP to Microsoft ASP.NET*.

The Command Object

- Similar to the ADO Command Object
- .NET Command Objects include:
  - **SqlCommand** for SQL Server 7.0 and later
  - **OleDbCommand** for OLE DB data sources: SQL Server 6.5 and earlier, or third-party databases

```
Dim cmdAuthors As New SqlCommand( _
    "select count(DISTINCT city) from authors", cn)
Dim result As Integer = _
    Convert.ToInt32(cmdAuthors.ExecuteScalar())
```

| C# | Visual Basic .NET |

Introduction

The **Command** object is used to run SQL queries and stored procedures on a SQL Server database. You use the **Command** object to specify what command to run, and how to handle the results.

Creating a Command object

To run an SQL query or a stored procedure, you must first create a **Command** object and then specify the command text to run. The following code example shows how to create a **Command** object and initialize the **CommandText** and **Connection** properties:

Visual Basic .NET

```
'Use constructor
Dim cmdAuthors As New SqlCommand _
  ("select au_lname,au_fname from authors", cn)
...
'Or use properties
Dim cmdAuthors As SqlCommand
cmdAuthors.CommandText = _
  "select au_lname,au_fname from authors"
cmdAuthors.Connection = cn
```

C#

```
//Use constructor
SqlCommand cmdAuthors = new SqlCommand
  ("select au_lname,au_fname from authors", cn);
...
//Or use properties
SqlCommand cmdAuthors;
cmdAuthors.CommandText =
  "select au_lname,au_fname from authors";
cmdAuthors.Connection = cn;
```

Running a Command

To run a command, you call one of the three following methods: **ExecuteNonQuery**, **ExecuteReader**, or **ExecuteScalar**. You can use the **ExecuteNonQuery** method to perform catalog operations (for example, querying the structure of a database or creating database objects, such as tables), or to change the data that is in a database, without using a **DataSet**, by executing **UPDATE**, **INSERT**, or **DELETE** statements.

You can use the **ExecuteReader** method to run a command that returns records, such as a **SELECT** statement. The **ExecuteReader** method's return value is a **DataReader** object that can be used to read and process the returned records.

You can use the **ExecuteScalar** method to retrieve a single value (for example, an aggregate value) from a database. This method requires less code than using the **ExecuteReader** method.

The following code example shows how to use the **ExecuteScalar** method to obtain the number of different cities in which authors reside:

```vb
Visual Basic .NET

Dim cn As New SqlConnection( _
  "data source=(local)\MOC; integrated security=true; " + _
  "initial catalog=pubs")
cn.Open()

Dim cmdAuthors As New SqlCommand( _
  "select count(DISTINCT city) from authors", cn)

Dim result As Integer = _
  Convert.ToInt32(cmdAuthors.ExecuteScalar())
```

```csharp
C#

SqlConnection cn = new SqlConnection
  ("data source=(local)\\MOC; integrated security=true; " +
  "initial catalog=pubs");
cn.Open();

SqlCommand cmdAuthors = new SqlCommand
  ("select count(DISTINCT city) from authors", cn);

int result = (int) cmdAuthors.ExecuteScalar();
```

Calling Stored Procedures

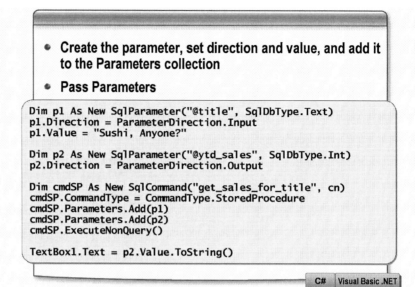

- **Create the parameter, set direction and value, and add it to the Parameters collection**
- **Pass Parameters**

```
Dim p1 As New SqlParameter("@title", SqlDbType.Text)
p1.Direction = ParameterDirection.Input
p1.Value = "Sushi, Anyone?"

Dim p2 As New SqlParameter("@ytd_sales", SqlDbType.Int)
p2.Direction = ParameterDirection.Output

Dim cmdSP As New SqlCommand("get_sales_for_title", cn)
cmdSP.CommandType = CommandType.StoredProcedure
cmdSP.Parameters.Add(p1)
cmdSP.Parameters.Add(p2)
cmdSP.ExecuteNonQuery()

TextBox1.Text = p2.Value.ToString()
```

C#   Visual Basic .NET

Introduction

A best practice for accessing databases from your Web application is to call a stored procedure that will access the database for you. Using stored procedures has several advantages over direct database access, including efficiency, security, and the protection of the database.

Types of stored procedures

The first step in using a stored procedure is to identify the type and name of the stored procedure that will be used. The method that you call to execute the stored procedure will vary depending on the type of stored procedure that you are calling:

- Return records stored procedures

  When you call a stored procedure that returns a set of records, you need to store that set of records either in a **DataSet**, or directly into a list-bound control by using a **DataReader**. If you want to use a **DataSet**, you need to use a **DataAdapter** and the **Fill** method. If you want to use a **DataReader**, you need to use a **Command** object and the **ExecuteReader** method, and then bind the returned record into a list-bound control.

- Return value stored procedures

  When you call a stored procedure that returns a value, call the **ExecuteScalar** method of the **Command** object, and then save the result in a variable of the appropriate data type.

- Perform action stored procedures

  When you call a stored procedure that performs some action on the database, but does not return a set of records or a value, use the **ExecuteNonQuery** method of the **Command** object.

To call a stored procedure

To call a stored procedure, you must change the **CommandType** property of the **Command** object to **CommandType.StoredProcedure**, and then specify the name of the stored procedure in the **CommandText** property. If the stored procedure requires parameters, you must create **Parameter** objects and add them to the **Parameters** collection of the **Command** object.

Parameters

When you use parameters with a SQL Server stored procedure, the names of the parameters that are added to the **Parameters** collection of the **Command** object must match the names of the parameters that are in the stored procedure; however, the order of the parameters is adaptable.

Note When using parameters in an OLE DB database, the order of the parameters in the **Parameters** collection must match the order of the parameters that are defined in the stored procedure.

The following table describes the types of parameters that are supported by many stored procedures.

Parameter	Function
Input	Used by your Web application to send specific data values to a stored procedure.
Output	Used by a stored procedure to send specific values back to the calling Web application.
InputOutput	Used by a stored procedure to both retrieve information that was sent by your Web application and to send specific values back to the Web application.
ReturnValue	Used by a stored procedure to send a return value back to the calling Web application.

After you have identified the parameters that a stored procedure supports, you need to add the parameters that you will use to the **Parameters** collection of the **Command** object.

Creating a parameter

To create a parameter, you need to first create a new **SqlParameter** object with the name and data type of the parameter, as specified by the stored procedure. Next, set the **Direction** property of the new parameter to indicate how the parameter is used by the stored procedure. If the stored procedure returns a return value, create a parameter named **returnValue**. If the parameter is an input parameter, set the **Value** property to specify the data that should be sent to the SQL Server database.

For example, the **get_sales_for_title** stored procedure takes one input parameter, named **@title** of type **Text**, and one output parameter, named **@ytd_sales** of type **Int**, as shown in the following code example:

```
CREATE PROCEDURE get_sales_for_title
@title varchar(80),   -- This is the input parameter.
@ytd_sales int OUTPUT -- This is the output parameter.
AS

-- Get the sales for the specified title and
-- assign it to the output parameter.
SELECT @ytd_sales = ytd_sales
FROM titles
WHERE title = @title

RETURN
```

To call the **get_sales_for_title** stored procedure, create an input parameter named **@title** and set its value to a valid book title such as "Sushi, Anyone?". Then create an output parameter named **@ytd_sales**. The following code example shows how to create the **@title** and **@ytd_sales** parameters:

Visual Basic .NET

```
Dim p1 As New SqlParameter("@title", SqlDbType.Text)
p1.Direction = ParameterDirection.Input
p1.Value = "Sushi, Anyone?"
Dim p2 As New SqlParameter("@ytd_sales", SqlDbType.Int)
p2.Direction = ParameterDirection.Output
```

C#

```
SqlParameter p1 =
  new SqlParameter("@title",SqlDbType.Text);
p1.Direction = ParameterDirection.Input;
p1.Value = "Sushi, Anyone?";
SqlParameter p2 =
  new SqlParameter("@ytd_sales",SqlDbType.Int);
p2.Direction = ParameterDirection.Output;
```

Configuring the Command object

After you have created the **Parameter** objects, use the **Add** method of the **Parameters** collection of the **Command** object. If a stored procedure has more than one parameter, it does not matter in what order you add the parameters because you create them by name. You must also set the **CommandType** property to **CommandType.StoredProcedure**. The following code example shows how to create a **Command** object to call a stored procedure, and how to add the parameters to the **Parameters** collection:

Visual Basic .NET

```
Dim cmdSP As New SqlCommand("get_sales_for_title", cn)
cmdSP.CommandType = CommandType.StoredProcedure
cmdSP.Parameters.Add(p1)
cmdSP.Parameters.Add(p2)
```

C#

```
SqlCommand cmdSP = new SqlCommand("get_sales_for_title", cn);
cmdSP.CommandType = CommandType.StoredProcedure;
cmdSP.Parameters.Add(p1);
cmdSP.Parameters.Add(p2);
```

Running a stored procedure with parameters

After you have added the parameters to the **Command** object, you call the appropriate method to run the command. The following code example shows how to call the **ExecuteNonQuery** method, and how to obtain the output parameter value for **@ytd_sales**:

```vb
Visual Basic .NET

cmdSP.ExecuteNonQuery()
TextBox1.Text = p2.Value.ToString()
```

```csharp
C#

cmdSP.ExecuteNonQuery();
TextBox1.Text = p2.Value.ToString();
```

The DataAdapter Object

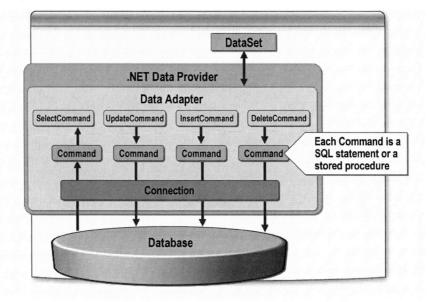

Introduction

A **DataAdapter** is used to retrieve data from a data source and to populate tables within a **DataSet**. The **DataAdapter** also saves changes, which are made to the **DataSet**, back to the data source. The **DataAdapter** uses the **Connection** object of the .NET data provider to connect to a data source. The **DataAdapter** then uses **Command** objects to select, update, insert, or delete data in the data source.

The **DataAdapter** class represents a set of database commands and a database connection that you use to fill a **DataSet** object and to update the data source. Each **DataAdapter** object exchanges data between a single **DataTable** object in a **DataSet** object and a single result set from a SQL statement or stored procedure.

ADO.NET provides two primary **DataAdapter** classes:

- **OleDbDataAdapter** class

    The **OleDbDataAdapter** class is suitable for use with any data source that is exposed by a.NET Framework Data Provider for OLE DB.

- **SqlDataAdapter** class

    The **SqlDataAdapter** class is optimized to work specifically with SQL Server version 7.0 or later. The **SqlDataAdapter** object is faster than the **OleDbDataAdapter** object because **SqlDataAdapter** works directly with SQL Server and it does not go through a .NET Framework Data Provider for OLE DB.

Note   DataAdapter classes for other types of data sources can be integrated with Visual Studio .NET.

Using Command objects

The **DataAdapter** object interacts with the data source through **Command** objects. The **DataAdapter** object has four command-type properties, which are used to select, insert, update, and delete data, as shown in the following table.

Property	Description
SelectCommand	Gets or sets an SQL statement or stored procedure that is then used to select records in the data source.
UpdateCommand	Gets or sets an SQL statement or stored procedure that is then used to update records in the data source.
InsertCommand	Gets or sets an SQL statement or stored procedure that is then used to insert new records into the data source.
DeleteCommand	Gets or sets an SQL statement or stored procedure that is then used for deleting records from the data source.

Each **Command** object will also have a reference to a **Connection** object. The **DataAdapter** manages this connection for you. If the connection is already open, the **DataAdapter** leaves the connection open after running a command. If the connection is closed, the **DataAdapter** will open the connection, run the command, and then close the connection.

Filling a DataSet

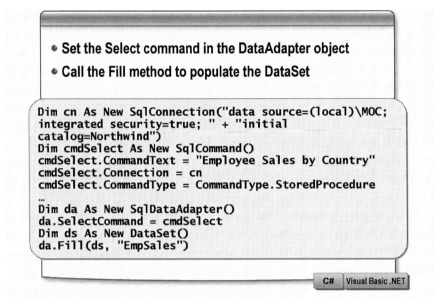

- Set the Select command in the DataAdapter object
- Call the Fill method to populate the DataSet

```
Dim cn As New SqlConnection("data source=(local)\MOC;
integrated security=true; " + "initial
catalog=Northwind")
Dim cmdSelect As New SqlCommand()
cmdSelect.CommandText = "Employee Sales by Country"
cmdSelect.Connection = cn
cmdSelect.CommandType = CommandType.StoredProcedure
...
Dim da As New SqlDataAdapter()
da.SelectCommand = cmdSelect
Dim ds As New DataSet()
da.Fill(ds, "EmpSales")
```

C#   Visual Basic .NET

Introduction

To fill a **DataSet** with the results of a query, you must create the necessary **Command** and **Connection** objects to run the query, along with creating a **DataSet** to hold the results of the query. Then, you create a **DataAdapter** object to use the **Command** object as a retrieval command. Finally, you call the **DataAdapter's Fill** method to run the query and fill the **DataSet** with the results.

The following code example shows how to create a **DataSet** from the
Northwind database stored procedure **Employee Sales by Country**:

```vb
Visual Basic .NET

Dim cn As New SqlConnection("data source=(local)\MOC;
integrated security=true; " + "initial catalog=Northwind")

Dim cmdSelect As New SqlCommand()
cmdSelect.CommandText = "Employee Sales by Country"
cmdSelect.Connection = cn
cmdSelect.CommandType = CommandType.StoredProcedure

Dim p1 As New SqlParameter("@Beginning_Date", _
  SqlDbType.DateTime)
p1.Direction = ParameterDirection.Input
p1.Value = "1/1/96"
Dim p2 As New SqlParameter("@Ending_Date", _
  SqlDbType.DateTime)
p2.Direction = ParameterDirection.Input
p2.Value = "12/31/96"
cmdSelect.Parameters.Add(p1)
cmdSelect.Parameters.Add(p2)

Dim da As New SqlDataAdapter()
da.SelectCommand = cmdSelect
Dim ds As New DataSet()
da.Fill(ds, "EmpSales")
```

```csharp
C#

SqlConnection cn = new SqlConnection
  ("data source=(local)\\MOC; integrated security=true; " +
  "initial catalog=Northwind");

SqlCommand cmdSelect = new SqlCommand();
cmdSelect.CommandText = "Employee Sales by Country";
cmdSelect.Connection = cn;
cmdSelect.CommandType = CommandType.StoredProcedure;

SqlParameter p1 = new SqlParameter("@Beginning_Date",
  SqlDbType.DateTime);
p1.Direction = ParameterDirection.Input;
p1.Value = "1/1/96";
SqlParameter p2 = new SqlParameter("@Ending_Date",
  SqlDbType.DateTime);
p2.Direction = ParameterDirection.Input;
p2.Value = "12/31/96";
cmdSelect.Parameters.Add(p1);
cmdSelect.Parameters.Add(p2);

SqlDataAdapter da = new SqlDataAdapter();
da.SelectCommand = cmdSelect;
DataSet ds = new DataSet();
da.Fill(ds,"EmpSales");
```

Accessing DataTables

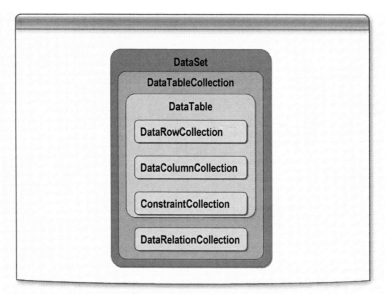

Introduction

The **DataSet** object can contain one or more tables. Each table is represented by a **DataTable** object and it can be accessed through the **DataTableCollection** object. There are also collection classes for rows, columns, constraints, and relations.

The DataTableCollection

After you have placed data in a **DataSet** object, you can programmatically access that data. You can use the **Tables** property to access the **DataTableCollection** object and work with specific tables. The **DataTableCollection** supports the acquiring of a **DataTable** object by name or by ordinal position. The following code example shows how to retrieve the **DataTable** object for the **Top Ten** table:

```
Visual Basic .NET

'Specify table name
Dim dt As DataTable = ds.Tables("EmpSales")
'or specify ordinal
Dim dt As DataTable = ds.Tables(0)
```

```
C#

//Specify table name
DataTable dt = ds.Tables["EmpSales"];
//or specify ordinal
DataTable dt = ds.Tables[0];
```

Rows and columns

Row and columns in the **DataSet** are represented by the **DataRowCollection** and **DataColumnCollection** classes, respectively. The **DataRowCollection** object is accessed through the **Rows** property, and the **DataColumnCollection** object is access through the **Columns** property.

Each column in a **DataTable** is represented by a **DataColumn** object. The **DataColumn** object provides the properties and methods that are necessary to access column metadata. The following code example shows how to obtain the column names for the EmpSales **DataTable**:

Visual Basic .NET

```
Dim c As DataColumn
For Each c In  ds.Tables("EmpSales").Columns
    ListBox1.Items.Add(c.ColumnName)
Next c
```

C#

```
foreach (DataColumn c in ds.Tables["EmpSales"].Columns)
{
  ListBox1.Items.Add(c.ColumnName);
}
```

Each row in a **DataTable** is represented by a **DataRow** object. The **DataRow** object provides the properties and methods that are necessary to access row metadata and row values. The following code example shows how to add the OrderID, FirstName, and LastName fields from a row in the EmpSales **DataTable** to a list-box control:

Visual Basic .NET

```
Dim r As DataRow
For Each r In  ds.Tables("EmpSales").Rows
  ListBox2.Items.Add((r("OrderID").ToString() _
  + r("FirstName") + " " + r("LastName")))
Next r
```

C#

```
foreach (DataRow r in ds.Tables["EmpSales"].Rows)
{
  ListBox2.Items.Add(r["OrderID"].ToString()
  + r["FirstName"] + " " + r["LastName"]);
}
```

Accessing individual fields

Both the **DataRowCollection** and **DataColumnCollection** objects have a **Count** property that enables you to determine the number of rows or columns that are in a **DataTable** object, as shown in the following code example:

Visual Basic .NET

```
rowCount = ds.Tables("EmpSales").Rows.Count
colCount = ds.Tables("EmpSales").Columns.Count
```

C#

```
rowCount = ds.Tables["EmpSales"].Rows.Count;
colCount = ds.Tables["EmpSales"].Columns.Count;
```

Counting the rows and columns of the **DataTable** object allows you to access the individual fields in the **DataTable** object. You can either access fields by ordinal (0-based) position or by name. Using ordinals gives your code better performance because you will avoid string-comparison searches. In the following code, X is the index of the row of data that you want to access:

Visual Basic .NET

```
myObject = ds.Tables(0).Rows(x)(1)
myObject = ds.Tables(0).Rows(x)("fieldname")
```

C#

```
myObject = ds.Tables["EmpSales"].Rows[x][1];
myObject = ds.Tables["EmpSales"].Rows[x]["fieldname"];
```

Using a DataView

- A DataView can be customized to present a subset of data from a DataTable
- The DefaultView property returns the default DataView of the table

```
Dim dv As New DataView(ds.Tables("EmpSales"))
dv.RowFilter = "SaleAmount > 1000"
dv.Sort = "OrderID"
Dim r As DataRowView
For Each r In  dv
    ListBox3.Items.Add(r("orderid").ToString() _
    + r("LastName") + " " + r("FirstName"))
Next r
```

| C# | Visual Basic .NET |

Introduction

ADO.NET provides a **DataView** class, which offers a flexible interface when working with **DataSet** objects. A **DataView** object allows you to filter and sort rows in a **DataTable** object. By using a **DataView** object, you can provide multiple views of the data without requerying the data source. The **DataView** object can be useful for displaying different views of the data on a Web Form, or for code that requires a different view of the data to work correctly.

DefaultView

Each **DataTable** object in a **DataSet** object has a **DefaultView** property, which returns the default view for the table. The following code example shows how you can access the default **DataView** object dv, of a **DataTable** object named **Authors**:

Visual Basic .NET

```
Dim dv As DataView = ds.Tables("EmpSales").DefaultView
```

C#

```
DataView dv = ds.Tables["EmpSales"].DefaultView;
```

Customized DataView

You can also create a custom **DataView** object that is based on a subset of the data that is in a **DataTable** object. For example, you can set the **DataView RowFilter** property by using a filter expression. The filter expression must evaluate to **True** or **False**. You can also set the **DataView** object **Sort** property by using a sort expression. The sort expression can include the names of the **DataColumn** objects or a calculation.

The following code example shows how to create a **DataView** with a filter that retrieves only sales over $1,000, sorted by OrderID:

```
Visual Basic .NET

Dim dv As New DataView(ds.Tables("EmpSales"))
dv.RowFilter = "SaleAmount > 1000"
dv.Sort = "OrderID"
Dim r As DataRowView
For Each r In  dv
  ListBox3.Items.Add(r("orderid").ToString() _
   + r("LastName") + " " + r("FirstName"))
Next r
```

```
C#

DataView dv = new DataView(ds.Tables["EmpSales"]);
dv.RowFilter = "SaleAmount > 1000";
dv.Sort = "OrderID";
foreach(DataRowView r in dv)
{
  ListBox3.Items.Add(r["orderid"].ToString()
   + r["LastName"] + " " + r["FirstName"]);
}
```

Handling Errors

- **SqlException class describes the exception that occurs**
- **SqlException contains a collection of SqlError objects**

Properties	Description
Class	Gets the severity level of the error
LineNumber	Gets the line number within the Transact-SQL command batch or the stored procedure that contains the error
Message	Gets the text describing the error
Number	Gets a number that identifies the type of error

Introduction

The **SqlException** class contains the exception that is thrown when SQL Server returns a warning or error. The **SqlException** class is created whenever the .NET Framework Data Provider for OLE DB encounters a situation that it cannot handle. The **SqlException** class always contains at least one instance of a **SqlError** object. You can use the severity level of the **SqlException** class to assist you in determining the content of a message that is displayed by an exception.

SQL Server errors

SQL Server errors share common properties and are identified by a number and a severity level:

- The **SqlError** class and common properties.

  Each **SqlError** object has the common properties that are shown in the following table.

Property	Description
Class	Gets the severity level of the error that was returned from the SQL Server.
LineNumber	Gets the line number within the Transact-SQL command batch or the stored procedure that contains the error.
Message	Gets the text describing the error.
Number	Gets a number that identifies the type of error.

  Note For a complete list of **SqlError** class properties, see the Visual Studio .NET documentation.

- SQL Server error numbers.

  The **Number** property allows you to determine the specific error that occurred. For example, the following table lists some common SQL Server error numbers and their descriptions.

Number	Description
17	Invalid server name.
4060	Invalid database name.
18456	Invalid user name or password.

- SQL Server severity levels.

  The following table describes SQL Server error severity levels, which are accessed through the **Class** property of the **SqlError** class.

Severity	Description	Action
11-16	Generated by user.	Can be corrected by the user.
17-19	Software or hardware errors.	You can continue working, but you might not be able to execute a particular statement. **SqlConnection** remains open.
20-25	Software or hardware errors.	The server closes **SqlConnection**. The user can reopen the connection.

Capturing Errors

The following code example shows how to capture the error information by using the **SqlException** and **SqlError** classes:

```
Visual Basic .NET

Try
...
Catch exc As SqlException
  Dim s As New System.Text.StringBuilder()
  Dim myErrors As SqlErrorCollection = exc.Errors
  s.AppendFormat("Class: {0}", exc.Class)
  s.AppendFormat("Error #{0}: {1} on line {2}.", _
      exc.Number, exc.Message, exc.LineNumber)
  s.AppendFormat("Error reported by {0} while" _
      + " connected to {1}", exc.Source, exc.Server)
  s.Append("Neither record was written to database.")
  s.Append("Errors collection contains:")

  Dim errItem As SqlError
  For Each errItem In  myErrors
      s.AppendFormat("Class: {0}", errItem.Class)
      s.AppendFormat("Error #{0}: {1} on line {2}.", _
          errItem.Number, errItem.Message, errItem.LineNumber)
      s.AppendFormat("Error reported by {0} while" _
          + " connected to {1}", errItem.Source, _
          errItem.Server)
  Next errItem
  lblError.Text = s.ToString()
End Try
```

```
C#

try
{...}
catch (SqlException exc)
{
  System.Text.StringBuilder s = new
      System.Text.StringBuilder();
  SqlErrorCollection myErrors = exc.Errors;
  s.AppendFormat("Class: {0}", exc.Class);
  s.AppendFormat("Error #{0}: {1} on line {2}.",
      exc.Number, exc.Message, exc.LineNumber);
  s.AppendFormat("Error reported by {0} while"
      + " connected to {1}", exc.Source, exc.Server);
  s.Append("Neither record was written to database.");
  s.Append("Errors collection contains:");

  foreach (SqlError errItem in myErrors)
  {
      s.AppendFormat("Class: {0}", errItem.Class);
      s.AppendFormat("Error #{0}: {1} on line {2}.",
          errItem.Number, errItem.Message,
          errItem.LineNumber);
      s.AppendFormat("Error reported by {0} while"
          + " connected to {1}", errItem.Source,
          errItem.Server);
  }
  lblError.Text = s.ToString();
}
```

Practice: Organizing DataSet Code

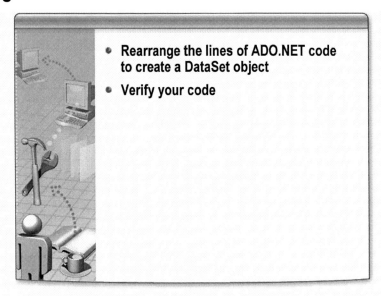

Introduction

In this practice, you will rearrange lines of ADO.NET code into the correct order to create a **DataSet** object.

▶ **To run the practice**

1. Using Internet Explorer, browse to
    http://localhost/upg/mod04-dataquestions/DataSetCode.aspx.

2. Organize the lines of ADO.NET code into the correct order to create a
    DataSet object.

    Select a line of code and then click on the up or down arrows to move the
    code.

3. Verify your code organization by clicking on the **Check Answers** button.

Note   There are several correct answers to this practice. This practice focuses
on the concepts creating a **DataSet** object and as a result does not include
Try...Catch...Finally... blocks for error handling.

Lesson: Visually Generating DataSets

- Advantages of Visually Generating a DataSet
- Visually Generating a DataSet
- What Are Typed DataSets?
- Instructor-led Practice: Visually Generating a DataSet

Introduction

Creating a **DataSet** from a database requires the use of a **Connection** object to connect to the database, a **Command** object to run the query, and a **DataAdapter** object to transfer the results to the **DataSet** object. These objects can be coded by hand, or generated visually by using the Data tools available in Visual Studio .NET. In this lesson, you will learn how to visually generate and work with **DataSets**.

Lesson objectives

After completing this lesson, you will be able to:

- Explain the advantages of visually generating **DataSet** objects.
- Visually create a **DataSet** object from a data source table.
- Visually create a **DataSet** object from a data source stored procedure.
- Explain the advantages of typed **DataSets**.

Advantages of Visually Generating a DataSet

- Efficient development
- Creates a typed DataSet
- Can generate a stand-alone DataSet

Introduction	Generating **DataSets** with the tools that are available in Visual Studio .NET has several advantages over creating DataSets programmatically.
Efficient development	A fully functioning **DataSet** and the supporting **DataAdapter**, **Command**, and **Connection** objects can require dozens of lines of code. With the tools that are available in Visual Studio .NET, the same **DataSet** and supporting objects can be generated in a dozen steps.
Creates a typed DataSet	When you build a **DataSet** object by using the tools that are in Visual Studio .NET, the default is a typed **DataSet**. In a typed **DataSet**, column names become properties of the **DataSet** object. Looking for a property is faster than parsing a string and then looking up that string to find the column.
Generating a stand-alone DataSet	With the tools in Visual Studio .NET, you can build a **DataSet** object that is not connected to any other data source, thereby allowing you to design and run your ASP.NET Web application with the support of a local relational database.

To generate a stand-alone **DataSet**:

1. From the **Data** section of the Visual Studio .NET **Toolbox**, drag a **DataSet** onto the editor.

2. Select **Typed dataset** to create a typed **DataSet** with a built-in schema that is based on an existing **DataSet** object in the project.

   or,

   Select **Untyped dataset** to create a **DataSet** without a schema.

Note For more information on creating stand-alone typed **DataSets**, see the Visual Studio .NET documentation.

Visually Generating a DataSet

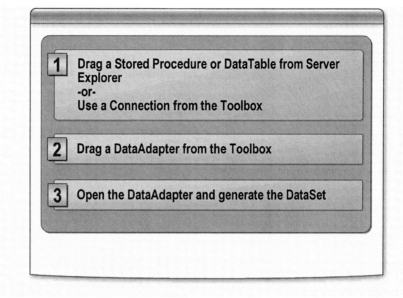

1 Drag a Stored Procedure or DataTable from Server Explorer
   -or-
   Use a Connection from the Toolbox

2 Drag a DataAdapter from the Toolbox

3 Open the DataAdapter and generate the DataSet

Introduction

With Visual Studio .NET, you can visually create **DataSets** from stored procedures or directly from the tables in your data source.

Generating a DataSet from a stored procedure

You can establish a connection to a data source stored procedure from within the Visual Studio .NET IDE. Server Explorer, which is part of the Visual Studio .NET IDE, allows you to browse for servers that are running SQL Server and other databases. By using Server Explorer, you simplify the process of establishing a connection to a data source, thereby getting the opportunity to verify the connection during design time.

To create a **DataSet** object from a stored procedure:

1. Drag the stored procedure from Server Explorer onto the editor.

2. Drag a **DataSet** and **DataAdapter** from the Toolbox.

3. Link the **DataSet** to the **Command**.

Generating a DataSet from a DataTable

There are a number of procedures for visually generating a **DataSet** object in Visual Studio .NET. Select the appropriate procedure based on the type of data source that you are working with.

From a SQL Server 7.0 Table

The server list in Server Explorer only displays the servers that are running SQL Server 7.0 or later. If you need to connect to a different type of database, you use the **Data Links Properties** dialog box.

To connect to a SQL Server 7.0 table:

1. In Server Explorer, expand the list of servers, expand the database that you want to use, and then expand the **Stored Procedures** or **Tables** list.

   Server Explorer displays the list of stored procedures and tables that are in the selected database.

2. Within the list of stored procedures or tables, click the specific stored procedure or table to which you want to connect, and drag it to the open project.

   Visual Studio .NET automatically configures a connection and a **DataAdapter** to connect to that table.

   A **SqlConnection** and **SqlDataAdapter** objects or an **OleDbConnection** and **OleDbDataAdapter** objects are added to the project, and the objects are then displayed at the bottom of the Web Form.

Using the DataLinks dialog box

You can also use the **Data Connections** option, located at the top of the Server Explorer list, to connect to SQL Server databases or OLE DB data sources.

To connect to a data source by using the **Data Links** dialog box:

1. In Server Explorer, right-click **Data Connections**, and then click **Add Connection**.

   In the resulting **Data Link Properties** dialog box, select the data type to which you will connect.

2. After selecting the data type, click **Next** or select the **Connection** tab and provide the necessary information to connect to the data source.

3. After you have created a connection from the **Data Link Properties** dialog box, you can click on the connection and drag it to the project, just as you would drag a connection from the SQL Servers list in Server Explorer.

   An **OleDbConnection** object is added to the project and displayed in the designer at the bottom of the Web Form. Depending on the type of item that you drag from Server Explorer, an **OleDbDataAdapter** object or **OleDbCommand** object may be created as well. For example, dragging a table always creates an **OleDbDataAdapter** object.

   Note If you add a data connection to a SQL Server 7.0 or later database, Visual Studio .NET will still create **SqlConnection**, **SqlCommand**, and **SqlDataAdapter** objects instead of their OLE DB counterparts.

Using the Toolbox

You can also visually generate a data provider data source from the Toolbox section of the Visual Studio .NET IDE.

To create **Connection** and **DataAdapter** objects by using items from the Toolbox:

1. From the **Data** section of the Visual Studio .NET Toolbox, drag a **Connection** to the editor.

2. Drag a **DataAdapter** to the editor.

3. Set properties to link the data source, **Connection** object, and **DataAdapter** object.

Generating a DataSet

After you have created a **Connection** object and **DataAdapter** object, you create the **DataSet** object that will store the values that are returned from the database.

To generate a **DataSet** from a **DataAdapter**:

1. On the ASP.NET page where you have created the **Connection** and **DataAdapter** objects, right-click the **DataAdapter** object and click **Generate Dataset**.

2. In the **Generate Dataset** dialog box, enter a name for the new **DataSet**, select **Add this dataset to the designer**, and then click **OK**.

   The **Generate Dataset** dialog then creates a strongly typed **DataSet** in an .xsd file. This .xsd file allows you to reference, by name, the tables and fields that are in the **Dataset**.

What Are Typed DataSets?

A DataSet with defined schema information

* Type mismatch errors are caught when code is compiled
* Allows IntelliSense
* Access tables and columns by name instead of using collection-based methods

```
'Using typed properties and methods
Dim r1 As BooksDataSet.TitlesRow = _
    dsBooks.Titles.NewTitlesRow()
r1.Title = "First book"
dsBooks.Titles.AddTitlesRow(r1)

'Using untyped properties and methods
Dim r2 As DataRow = _
    dsBooks.Tables("Titles").NewRow()
r2("Title") = "Second book"
dsBooks.Tables("Titles").Rows.Add(r2)
```

C#   Visual Basic .NET

Introduction

In addition to late-bound access to values through weakly typed variables, the **DataSet** object provides access to data through a strongly typed metaphor. Tables and columns that are part of the **DataSet** can be accessed by using user-friendly names and strongly typed variables.

Definition

A *typed DataSet* is an instance of an existing **DataSet** class for which schema information has been defined.

Type mismatch is caught at compilation

A typed **DataSet** provides strongly typed methods, events, and properties, which means that you can access tables and columns by name, instead of using collection-based methods. This access by name greatly improves the readability of the code.

Allows IntelliSense

Having a typed **DataSet** also allows the Microsoft IntelliSense® feature in the Visual Studio .NET code editor to complete lines of code automatically as you type them.

Access by name

Additionally, the typed **DataSet** provides access to values by name at compile time. With a strongly typed **DataSet**, type mismatch errors are found when the code is compiled, rather than being found at run time.

The following code example shows how to add a new row to a Titles table, which features a Title column and a Price column. The first row is added by using typed **DataSet** properties and methods. The second row is added by using untyped properties and methods:

Visual Basic .NET

```
'Using typed properties and methods
Dim r1 As BooksDataSet.TitlesRow = _
  dsBooks.Titles.NewTitlesRow()
r1.Title = "First book"
r1.Price = 29.99
dsBooks.Titles.AddTitlesRow(r1)

'Using untyped properties and methods
Dim r2 As DataRow = _
  dsBooks.Tables("Titles").NewRow()
r2("Title") = "Second book"
r2("Price") = 39.99
dsBooks.Tables("Titles").Rows.Add(r2)
```

C#

```
//Using typed properties and methods
BooksDataSet.TitlesRow r1 = dsBooks.Titles.NewTitlesRow();
r1.Title = "First book";
r1.Price = 29.99;
dsBooks.Titles.AddTitlesRow(r1);

//Using untyped properties and methods
DataRow r2 = dsBooks.Tables["Titles"].NewRow();
r2["Title"] = "Second book";
r2["Price"] = 39.99;
dsBooks.Tables["Titles"].Rows.Add(r2);
```

Instructor-led Practice: Visually Generating a DataSet

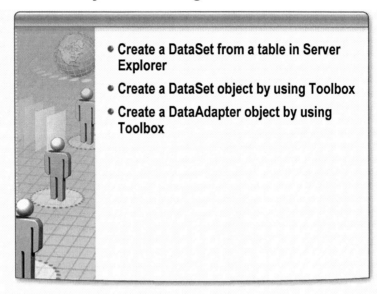

- Create a DataSet from a table in Server Explorer
- Create a DataSet object by using Toolbox
- Create a DataAdapter object by using Toolbox

Introduction

In this practice, you will use Sever Explorer to create and bind a **DataGrid** control to a **DataSet** object. You will also use the Toolbox **Data** tab to visually generate and design a **DataSet** object. Finally, you will use the Toolbox **Data** tab to visually generate and design a **DataAdapter** to use a stored procedure.

The completed code for this practice is in the *install_folder*\Practices\Mod04\ *language*\DataTools\Solution folder.

Open the Practice Solution

1. In Visual Studio .NET, from the **File** menu, click **Open Solution**.

2. In the Open Solution window, click the **My Projects** shortcut.

3. Open the **Practices**, **Mod04**, *language*, and **DataTools** folders.

4. Select **DataTools.sln**, and then click **Open**.

Create a DataSet object from a table in Server Explorer

In the following steps you will create a **DataSet** object from the **Northwind** database **Orders** table that is listed in **Sever Explorer**:

5. Open the Orders.aspx page.

6. Open Server Explorer and expand the **Servers**, *machinename*, **SQL Servers**, *machinename***MOC**, **Northwind**, and **Tables** folders.

7. Drag the Orders table from Server Explorer onto the Orders.aspx page.

Visual Studio .NET will create a **sqlConnection1** object, and **sqlDataAdapter1** object.

8. Select the **sqlDataAdapter1** object.

9. Right-click the **sqlDataAdapter1** object, and select **Generate Dataset**.

10. In the **Generate Dataset** dialog box, select **New**, and enter **OrdersDataSet** as the new **DataSet** name.

11. Click **OK**.

    Visual Studio .NET will create an **OrdersDataSet1** object and add an OrdersDataSet.xsd file to the project.

12. Select the **OrdersDataSet1** object.

13. In the Properties window, change the **Name** property to **dsOrders**.

14. Right-click the **DataGrid** control, and select **Property Builder**.

15. In the **General** properties pane, set the **DataSource** property to **dsOrders**.

16. Click **OK**.

17. In the **Page_Load** event handler, add the following code:

    ```
    Visual Basic .NET

    SqlDataAdapter1.Fill(dsOrders)
    grdOrders.DataBind()
    ```

    ```
    C#

    sqlDataAdapter1.Fill(dsOrders);
    grdOrders.DataBind();
    ```

18. Right-click the **Orders.aspx** page in Solution Explorer, and select **Set As Start Page**.

19. Build and browse the Orders.aspx page.

    The **DataGrid** control should display all of the records from the Orders table.

Create a DataSet object by using the Toolbox

In the following steps you will build a **DataSet** object that does not connect to a database by using the **Data** tools in the **Toolbox**:

20. Open the Books.aspx page.

21. Select the **Data** tab in the Toolbox window.

22. Drag a **DataSet** onto the Books.aspx page.

23. In the **Add Dataset** dialog box, select **Untyped dataset**, and then click **OK**.

    Visual Studio .NET creates a **DataSet1** object.

24. Select the **DataSet1** object.

25. In the Properties window, set the **Name** property to **dsBooks**.

26. In the Properties window, select the **Tables** property, and then click the **...** button.

27. In the **Tables Collection Editor** dialog box, click **Add**.

28. Set the **TableName** property to **Books**.

29. Set the **Name** property to **Books**.

30. Select the **Columns** property, and then click the **...** button.

31. In the **Columns Collection Editor** dialog box, perform the following steps:

    a. Click the **Add** button.

    b. Set the **ColumnName** property to **Title**.

    c. Set the **Name** property to **Title**.

    d. Click the **Add** button.

    e. Set the **ColumnName** property to **Price**.

    f. Set the **Name** property to **Price**.

32. Click **Close** to close the **Columns Collection Editor** dialog box.

33. Click **Close** to close the **Tables Collection Editor** dialog box.

34. Right-click the **DataGrid** control, and select **Property Builder**.

35. On the **General** tab, set the **DataSource** property to **dsBooks**, and then click **OK**.

36. In the **Page_Load** event handler, add the following code:

```
Visual Basic .NET

Dim r As DataRow = dsBooks.Tables("Books").NewRow()
r(0) = "The Psychology of Computer Cooking"
r(1) = "19.99"
dsBooks.Tables("Books").Rows.Add(r)
r = dsBooks.Tables("Books").NewRow()
r(0) = "The Gourmet Microwave"
r(1) = "21.59"
dsBooks.Tables("Books").Rows.Add(r)
grdBooks.DataBind()
```

```
C#

DataRow r = dsBooks.Tables["Books"].NewRow();
r[0] = "The Psychology of Computer Cooking";
r[1] = "19.99";
dsBooks.Tables["Books"].Rows.Add(r);
r = dsBooks.Tables["Books"].NewRow();
r[0] = "The Gourmet Microwave";
r[1] = "21.59";
dsBooks.Tables["Books"].Rows.Add(r);
grdBooks.DataBind();
```

37. Right-click the **Books.aspx** page in Solution Explorer, and select **Set As Start Page**.

38. Build and browse the Books.aspx page.

    The **DataGrid** control should display two rows of book data.

Create a DataAdapter object by using the Toolbox

In the following steps you will build a **DataAdapter** by using the **Data** tools in the **Toolbox**, and bind the **DataAdapter** to a **DataGrid** control:

39. Open the OrdersDetails.aspx page.

40. Select the **Data** tab in the Toolbox window.

41. Drag a **SqlDataAdapter** onto the OrderDetails.aspx page.

    Visual Studio .NET opens the Data Adapter Configuration Wizard.

42. In the **Data Adapter Configuration Wizard**, perform the following steps:

    a. Click **Next**.

    b. On the **Choose Your Data Connection** screen, click **New Connection**.

    c. In the **Data Link Properties** dialog box, enter **(local)\MOC** for the server name.

    d. Click Use Windows NT Integrated Security.

    e. Select the Northwind database.

    f. Click **OK** to close the **Data Link Properties** dialog box.

    g. Click **Next**.

    h. On the Choose a Query Type screen, select Use existing stored procedures, and then click Next.

    i. On the Bind Commands to Existing Stored Procedures screen, set the Select drop-down list to CustOrdersDetail, and then click Next.

    j. On the View Wizard Results screen, click Finish.

       Visual Studio .NET creates a **SqlDataAdapter1** object, and a **SqlConnection1** object.

43. Right-click the **SqlDataAdapter1** object and select **Generate Dataset**.

44. In the **Generate Dataset** dialog box, select **New**, and enter **OrdersDetailsDataSet** as the new **DataSet** name.

45. Click **OK**.

    Visual Studio .NET creates an **OrdersDetailsDataSet1** object and adds an OrdersDetailsDataSet.xsd file to the project.

46. Select the **OrdersDetailsDataSet1** object.

47. In the Properties window, change the **Name** property to **dsOrdersDetails**.

48. Right-click the **DataGrid** control, and select **Property Builder**.

49. In the **General** properties pane, set the **DataSource** property to **dsOrdersDetails**.

50. Click **OK**.

51. In the **Page_Load** event handler, add the following code:

```
Visual Basic .NET

SqlSelectCommand1.Parameters("@OrderID").Value = 10249
SqlDataAdapter1.Fill(dsOrdersDetails)
grdOrdersDetails.DataBind()
```

```
C#

sqlSelectCommand1.Parameters["@OrderID"].Value = 10249;
sqlDataAdapter1.Fill(dsOrdersDetails);
grdOrdersDetails.DataBind();
```

52. Right-click the **OrdersDetails.aspx** page in Solution Explorer, and select
Set As Start Page.

53. Build and browse the OrdersDetails.aspx page.

The **DataGrid** control should display two product records for order 10249.

Lesson: Data-Bound Controls

- **Using Data-Bound Controls**
- **Instructor-led Practice: Binding a DataGrid Control to a DataSet**
- **Binding a Data-Bound Control to a DataReader**
- **Demonstration: Customizing the DataGrid Control**

Introduction

In this lesson, you will learn how to display the data from an ADO.NET connection on an ASP.NET Web Form. You will specifically learn about data-bound controls, which are the controls that can be populated automatically with data from a data source.

Lesson objectives

After completing this lesson, you will be able to:

- Explain what data-bound controls are and how they are used.
- Bind a **DataGrid** control to a **DataSet** object.
- Bind a data-bound control to a **DataReader** object.
- Customize the appearance of a **DataGrid** control.

Using Data-Bound Controls

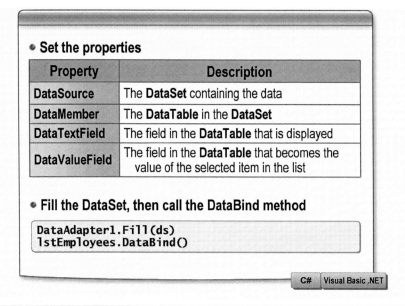

* **Set the properties**

Property	Description
DataSource	The **DataSet** containing the data
DataMember	The **DataTable** in the **DataSet**
DataTextField	The field in the **DataTable** that is displayed
DataValueField	The field in the **DataTable** that becomes the value of the selected item in the list

* **Fill the DataSet, then call the DataBind method**

```
DataAdapter1.Fill(ds)
lstEmployees.DataBind()
```

C#   Visual Basic .NET

Introduction

ASP.NET includes a set of data-bound controls, such as the **DataGrid**, **DataList**, and **DataRepeater** controls, which make displaying data from a data source simple and flexible. Developers only need to bind these controls to a data source to display the selected data.

Types of data-bound controls

There are two types of data-bound controls: multirecord controls and single-value controls. Multirecord controls can display multiple records at the same time. The **ListBox** control and the **DataGrid** control are examples of multirecord controls.

Single-value controls can only display one value at a time. The **TextBox** control is an example of a single-value control. Typically, single-value controls are used inside of multirecord controls to allow tasks such as editing field values.

The following table lists the multirecord controls.

Control	Description
CheckBoxList	A multiple-selection check box group that can be dynamically generated by using data binding.
DataGrid	A control that displays the fields of a data source as columns in a table.
DataList	A control that displays a template-defined, data-bound list.
DropDownList	A single selection, drop-down list control.
ListBox	A list control that allows single or multiple item selection.
RadioButtonList	A single-selection radio button group that can be dynamically generated through data binding.
Repeater	A data-bound list that uses a template. The **Repeater** control has no built-in layout or styles, so you must explicitly declare all Hypertext Markup Language (HTML) layout, formatting, and style tags within the control's templates.

Setting data-bound control properties

Data-bound controls in ASP.NET have specific data binding properties. The following table describes the properties that you must set to bind a data-bound control to a data source.

Property	Description
DataSource	Specifies the data source containing the data. A data source can be a **DataSet**, **DataReader**, **DataTable**, or **DataView** object.
DataMember	Specifies the **DataTable** in the **DataSet**.
DataTextField	Specifies the field in the **DataTable** that will be displayed in the list.
DataValueField	Specifies the field in the **DataTable** that becomes the value of the selected item in the list.

The **DataTextField** and the **DataValueField** properties are used by the **ListBox**, **DropDownList**, **CheckBoxList**, and **RadioButtonList** controls because these controls can only display one field from a row of the **DataSet**.

Binding controls

To bind a control such as the **DataGrid** control, you first need to set the **DataSource** property of the control to a **DataSet**, **DataReader**, **DataTable**, or **DataView** object, and then call the **DataBind** method.

Note The **DataGrid** and other Web server controls can support binding to other types of collection classes, such as the **ArrayList** class. Data-bound controls are not limited to just working with databases.

If you set the **DataSource** property of the **DataGrid** control directly to a **DataSet** object, the **DataTable** object with the index of 0 is used by default. To specify a different **DataTable** object, set the **DataMember** property of the **DataGrid** control to the name of the preferred **DataTable** object.

The following code example shows how to bind the **Authors** table, of the **ds DataSet** object, to a **DataGrid** control named **dg**:

```
Visual Basic .NET

dg.DataSource = ds
dg.DataMember = "Authors"
dg.DataBind()
```

```
C#

dg.DataSource = ds;
dg.DataMember = "Authors";
dg.DataBind();
```

The following code example shows how you can also use the **Tables** collection of the **DataSet** object **ds** to assign the **DataTable** object **Authors** directly to the **DataSource** property of the **DataGrid** control that is named **dg**:

Visual Basic .NET

```
dg.DataSource = ds.Tables("Authors")
dg.DataBind()
```

C#

```
dg.DataSource = ds.Tables["Authors"];
dg.DataBind();
```

Example of using a custom view

If you want to display a different view of the data in the **DataGrid** control, you will need to create a new **DataView** object from the **DataSet** object, and then bind that **DataView** object to the **DataGrid** control.

The following code example shows how to bind a **DataView** object **dv**, filtered for the state of California, to a **DataGrid** control **dg**:

Visual Basic .NET

```
Dim dv As New DataView(ds.Tables("Authors"))
dv.RowFilter = "state = 'CA'"
dg.DataSource = dv
dg.DataBind()
```

C#

```
DataView dv = new DataView(ds.Tables["Authors"]);
dv.RowFilter = "state = 'CA'";
dg.DataSource = dv;
dg.Databind();
```

Instructor-led Practice: Binding a DataGrid Control to a DataSet

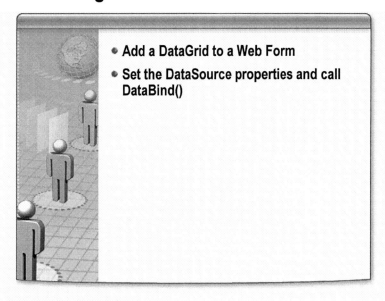

* Add a DataGrid to a Web Form
* Set the DataSource properties and call DataBind()

Introduction

In this practice, you will see how to bind a **DataGrid** control to an existing **DataSet** object.

The completed code for this practice is in the EmployeeSales.aspx page in the *install_folder*\Practices\Mod04\language\BoundGrid\Solution folder.

Open the Practice Solution

1. In Visual Studio .NET, from the **File** menu, click **Open Solution**.

2. In the Open Solution window, click the **My Projects** shortcut.

3. Open the **Practices**, **Mod04**, *language*, and **BoundGrid** folders.

4. Select **BoundGrid.sln**, and then click **Open**.

Bind a DataSet to a DataGrid control

In the following steps you will create a **DataGrid** control named **grdEmployeeSales**.

5. Open the EmployeeSales.aspx page.

6. Using the Toolbox, put a **Button** control and a **DataGrid** control on the EmployeeSales.aspx page.

7. Set the **DataGrid** control's ID property to **grdEmployeeSales**.

8. Set the **Button** control's **Text** property to **Bind**.

9. Set the **Button** control's ID property to **cmdBind**.

10. Create a **Click** event handler for the **Button** control.

Set the DataSource properties and call DataBind()

In the following steps you will bind the **grdEmployeeSales DataGrid** control to an existing **DataSet** object.

11. In the **Click** event handler, enter the following code:

```
Visual Basic .NET

Dim ds As DataSet = _
    GetEmployeeSales(DateTime.Parse("1/1/96"), _
    DateTime.Parse("12/31/96"))

grdEmployeeSales.DataSource = ds
grdEmployeeSales.DataBind()
```

```
C#

DataSet ds = GetEmployeeSales(
    DateTime.Parse("1/1/96"),
    DateTime.Parse("12/31/96"));

grdEmployeeSales.DataSource = ds;
grdEmployeeSales.DataBind();
```

Note The **GetEmployeeSales** method builds a **DataSet** by calling the **Employee Sales by Country** stored procedure in the Northwind database.

12. Build and browse the EmployeeSales.aspx page.

13. Click the **Bind** button.

The **DataGrid** control will display six bound columns of data that have been returned from the **Employee Sales by Country** stored procedure.

Binding a Data-Bound Control to a DataReader

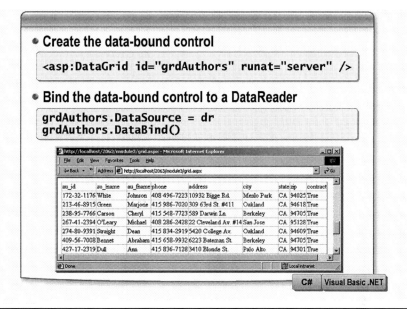

Introduction

In addition to looping through **DataReader** object data and displaying it programmatically, you can bind a **DataReader** object to a data-bound control.

Binding to a DataReader

To bind a **DataReader** object to a data-bound control, you set the **DataSource** property of the data-bound control to the **DataReader** object. The following example code creates a **DataReader** object **dr**, binds it to a **DataGrid** control **grdAuthors**, and then closes the **DataReader** and **Connection** objects:

```
Visual Basic .NET

Dim conn As New SqlConnection _
  ("data source=(local)\MOC; integrated security=true; " + _
  "initial catalog=pubs")
Dim cmdAuthors As New SqlCommand( _
  "select au_lname,au_fname from Authors", conn)
Dim dr As SqlDataReader = Nothing
Try
    conn.Open()

    'bind the datareader to a DataGrid
    dr = cmdAuthors.ExecuteReader()
    grdAuthors.DataSource = dr
    grdAuthors.DataBind()
Catch
Finally
    'close the datareader and the connection
    dr.Close()
    conn.Close()
End Try
```

C#

```csharp
SqlConnection conn = new SqlConnection
  ("data source=(local)\\MOC; integrated security=true; " +
  "initial catalog=pubs");
SqlCommand cmdAuthors = new SqlCommand
  ("select au_lname,au_fname from Authors", conn);
SqlDataReader dr = null;
try
{
  conn.Open();

  //bind the datareader to a DataGrid
  dr = cmdAuthors.ExecuteReader();
  grdAuthors.DataSource = dr;
  grdAuthors.DataBind();
}
catch{}
finally
{
  //close the datareader and the connection
  dr.Close();
  conn.Close();
}
```

Demonstration: Customizing the DataGrid Control

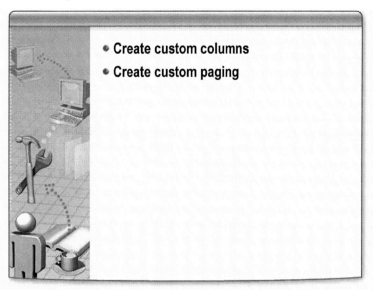

- Create custom columns
- Create custom paging

Introduction

In this demonstration, you will see how to customize the presentation of a **DataGrid** control.

The completed code for this demonstration is in the EmployeeSales.aspx page in the *install_folder*\Democode\Mod04*language*\CustomGrid\Solution folder.

Open the demonstration project

1. In Visual Studio .NET, from the **File** menu, click **Open Solution**.

2. In the Open Solution window, click the **My Projects** shortcut.

3. Open the **Practices**, **Mod04**, *language*, and **CustomGrid** folders.

4. Select **CustomGrid.sln**, and then click **Open**.

Create custom columns

In the following steps you will create custom column headers and a **Select** column in the **DataGrid** control on the EmployeeSales.aspx Web Form.

5. Open EmployeeSales.aspx.

6. Select the **DataGrid** control and then click the **Property Builder** hyperlink in the Properties window.

7. In the **Properties** dialog box, on the **Columns** tab, clear the **Create columns automatically at run time** check box.

8. Add a bound column to the **Selected columns** list:

   a. Set the **Header text** value to **Order ID**.

   b. Set the **Data Field** value to **OrderID**.

9. Add a second bound column to the **Selected columns** list:

   a. Set the **Header text** value to **Sale Amount**.

   b. Set the **Data Field** value to **SaleAmount**.

10. Add a third bound column to the **Selected columns** list:

    a. Set the **Header text** value to **Last Name**.

    b. Set the **Data Field** value to **LastName**.

11. Add a fourth bound column to the **Selected columns** list:

    a. Set the **Header text** value to **First Name**.

    b. Set the **Data Field** value to **FirstName**.

12. Expand the **Button Column** list, and add a **Select** column to the select columns list.

13. Set the **Header text** value to **Command**.

14. Click **OK**.

15. Create an event handler for the **grdEmployeeSales SelectedIndexChanged** event.

    In Visual Basic .NET, use the **Class Name** and **Method Name** drop-down boxes to create the event.

    In C#, use the **Events** (lightning-bolt) button, in the Properties window, to create the event.

16. In the **grdEmployeeSales_SelectedIndexChanged** event handler, add the following code to copy the selected text into the **lblName** label:

Visual Basic .NET

```
If grdEmployeeSales.SelectedIndex <> -1 Then
   lblName.Text = grdEmployeeSales.Items( _
      grdEmployeeSales.SelectedIndex).Cells(0).Text
End If
```

C#

```
if (grdEmployeeSales.SelectedIndex != -1)
   lblName.Text =
      grdEmployeeSales.Items
      [grdEmployeeSales.SelectedIndex].Cells[0].Text;
```

17. Save your changes.

18. Build the project (because you added code).

19. View the EmployeeSales.aspx page in a browser and test the page.

Create custom paging

In the following steps you will create custom paging with 15 rows on each page.

20. In Visual Studio .NET, open EmployeeSales.aspx.

21. Select the **DataGrid** control and then click the **Property Builder** hyperlink in the Properties window.

22. In the **Properties** dialog box, on the **Paging** tab, perform the following steps:

    a. Select the **Allow paging** check box.

    b. Set the **Page size** field to **15**.

    c. Set the **Numeric buttons** to **5**.

    d. Click **OK**.

23. In the code-behind file for the EmployeeSales.aspx page, create a **PageIndexChanged** event handler for the **DataGrid** control.

    In Visual Basic .NET, use the **Class Name** and **Method Name** drop-down boxes to create the event.

    In C#, use the **Events** button in the Properties window to create the event.

24. Add the following code to the **grdEmployeeSales_PageIndexChanged** event handler to implement paging:

Visual Basic .NET

```
grdEmployeeSales.CurrentPageIndex = e.NewPageIndex
Dim ds As DataSet = _
   GetEmployeeSales(DateTime.Parse("1/1/96"), _
   DateTime.Parse("12/31/96"))

grdEmployeeSales.DataSource = ds
grdEmployeeSales.DataBind()
grdEmployeeSales_SelectedIndexChanged(Nothing, Nothing)
```

C#

```
grdEmployeeSales.CurrentPageIndex = e.NewPageIndex;
DataSet ds = GetEmployeeSales(
   DateTime.Parse("1/1/96"),
   DateTime.Parse("12/31/96"));

grdEmployeeSales.DataSource = ds;
grdEmployeeSales.DataBind();
grdEmployeeSales_SelectedIndexChanged(null, null);
```

25. Save your changes.

26. Build the project (because you added code).

27. View the EmployeeSales.aspx page in a browser.

28. Click the page numbers to move through the **DataSet**.

Lesson: Best Practices for Secure and Reliable Data Access

- Use stored procedures
- Use Windows-only authentication or hash the users password
- Use Try...Catch...Finally error handling
- Only send validated strings to the database

Introduction

Anytime you work with a database, you must ensure that the database is protected from unauthorized access. There are several best practices to follow to ensure that your Web application accesses a database in a secure and reliable manner.

Stored procedures

The preferred method of accessing databases from your Web application is to call a stored procedure that will access the database for you. Some of the advantages of using stored procedures include:

- Modular programming

  Stored procedures are classic examples of modular programming. You create the procedure once, test it once, store it on the database server, and then call it any number of times from multiple Web applications. Any updates or changes to the database are hidden from all of the accessing Web applications by the stored procedure.

- Distribution of work

  Stored procedures can be created independently by a developer who specializes in database programming, whereas the Web applications that will use the stored procedure can be created in parallel by other developers. This distribution of work allows each developer to focus on their own specialty, and meet their own development deadlines.

- Increased database security

  Using stored procedures provides increased security for a database by limiting direct access. Only the tested and proven stored procedures that are developed by the database programmer are allowed to access the database directly. Because other Web applications and developers do not directly access the database, there is a minimum risk of accidental damage to the structure or to the content of the database.

  Using **SQL** or **Transact-SQL** statements directly in ASP.NET code is also a security risk because the statements can give a hacker information about the database and its structure. In addition to this risk, with direct access to a database, you also have the security issue of trying to determine what kind of permissions you should give to the Webuser account on the individual tables.

- Faster execution

  If a procedure requires a large amount of **Transact-SQL** code, or if a procedure is performed repetitively, using stored procedures can be faster than direct database access by using **Transact-SQL** statements. Direct access through **Transact-SQL** statements requires that the statements be sent from the client each time that they run. The statements are then compiled and optimized every time that they are executed by the database server.

  Stored procedures are parsed and optimized when they are created, and an in-memory version of the procedure can be used after the procedure is executed for the first time. The pre-parsing and optimization of stored procedures can greatly reduce processing time at the SQL Server when compared to direct access through **Transact-SQL** statements.

- Reduce network loads

  An operation that requires hundreds of lines of **Transact-SQL** code can sometimes be performed through a single statement that calls a stored procedure. Sending one call over the network, rather than hundreds of lines of code, reduces network loads.

- Provides flexibility

  Because database access is through the stored procedure, the database developer can change the structure of the database without breaking the Web applications that use it. This protection allows for continual improvement of the database without putting the rest of the system at risk.

Windows-only authentication

Windows-only authentication is the preferred authentication method to use when connecting a Web application to a SQL Server database. When you use Windows-only authentication, the SQL Server database does not need the user name and password. Only a confirmation that the user has been authenticated by a trusted source is required to process the database request.

Warning Using mixed-mode authentication to access a SQL Server database from a Web application is a security risk and it is not recommended.

Hash passwords

If your stored procedures require passwords, or if you decide to use mixed-mode authentication, all passwords should be hashed before being transmitted. Hashing protects the password from interception.

Note   For more information authentication in ASP.NET Web applications, see Module 6, "Authenticating Users," in Course 2640, *Upgrading Web Development Skills from ASP to Microsoft ASP.NET.*

Use Try...Catch...Finally error handling

When using connections with either **DataAdapter** or **DataReader** objects, you need to always use a **Try...Catch...Finally** statement to ensure that if anything in the process fails, the connection will be closed. Otherwise, the connection may be left open indefinitely.

A typical **Try... Catch... Finally** block would look similar to the following code example:

Visual Basic .NET

```
Dim conn As New SqlConnection("connect_string")
Try
  conn.Open()
  'Data related operations
Catch
  'Error handling code
Finally
  'Always close connections
  conn.Close()
```

C#

```
SqlConnection conn = new SqlConnection("connect_string");
try
{
  conn.Open();
  //Data related operations
}
catch
{
  //Error handling code
}
finally
{
  //Always close connections
  conn.Close();
}
```

Only send validated strings to the database

Any strings, especially those coming directly from the user, such as the content of a text box, should be validated before being stored or used by the Web application. Sending a string from a user to a database without validating the content allows hackers to insert code directly into the database with potentially harmful results.

Lab 4: ADO.NET

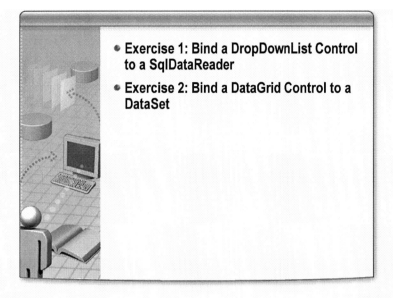

* Exercise 1: Bind a DropDownList Control to a SqlDataReader
* Exercise 2: Bind a DataGrid Control to a DataSet

Objectives

After completing this lab, you will be able to:

- Bind a **DataReader** object to a data-bound control.

- Create a typed **DataSet** from a **DataAdapter** object.

- Call stored procedures to retrieve and update data.

- Bind a **DataGrid** control to a **DataSet**.

- Configure paging and column display in a **DataGrid**

Note This lab focuses on the concepts in this module and as a result may not comply with Microsoft security recommendations.

Prerequisites

Before working on this lab, you must have:

- Knowledge of how to write **Try**...**Catch**...**Finally** exception-handling code.

- Knowledge of how to use Server Explorer to create connections and browse databases.

- Knowledge of how to bind **DataReaders** and **DataSets** to data-bound controls.

Scenario

In this lab, you will work with the Products.aspx Web Form, which displays a **DropDownList** control and a **DataGrid** control. The purpose of the Web Form is to allow a user to select a supplier in the **DropDownList** control, and then to view the products from that supplier in the **DataGrid** control.

You will write the code that is needed to bind the **DropDownList** control to supplier names, and you will then write the code that is needed to bind the **DataGrid** control to products, based on the selected supplier. You will also write the code that is needed to allow the user to edit product information on the **DataGrid** control.

Solution

The solution project for this lab is located in the *install_folder*\Labfiles\Lab04\ *language*\Solution folder, where *language* is CS or VB. You can also view the solution Web Form at http://localhost/upg/lab04-*language*-solution/ Products.aspx.

Estimated time to complete this lab: 60 minutes

Exercise 1
Bind a DropDownList Control to a SqlDataReader

In this exercise, you will modify the Northwind Traders product editing Web Form to display a list of suppliers in a drop-down combo box. You will create a **Connection** object and a **Command** object. You will then run a command to retrieve the names of all of the suppliers and bind the returned **SqlDataReader** to a data-bound, **DropDownList** control.

▶ Open the Lab04 Solution

1. In Visual Studio .NET, from the **File** menu, click **Open Solution**.

2. In the Open Solution window, click the **My Projects** shortcut.

3. Open the **Labfiles**, **Lab04**, *language*, and **Starter** folders.

4. Select **Lab04.sln**, and then click **Open**.

▶ Create a DataReader

1. Open the Products.aspx page in Design view.

   The controls in the following table have already been provided on the Products.aspx page.

Control	Description
lstNames	A **DropDownList** control that you will modify to display the names of all of the suppliers.
grdProducts	A **DataGrid** control that you will modify to display the products for a select supplier. You will also modify this control to allow editing of the data.
lblError	A **Label** control that you will use to display any errors that occur at runtime.

2. Drag a **SqlConnection** object from the Toolbox to the Products.aspx page.

3. Rename the **SqlConnection** object.

   In the solution for this lab, the object is named **cnNorthwind1**.

4. Set the **ConnectionString** property to a connection string that connects to the local Northwind Traders database.

   The SQL Server instance is named **(local)\MOC**.

   The solution for this lab uses the following connection string:

```
data source=(local)\MOC;initial
catalog=Northwind;integrated security=SSPI;persist security
info=True;packet size=4096
```

5. Open the code-behind file for the Products.aspx page, and perform the following steps inside the **Page_Load** event handler:

   a. Set the **lblError.Text** property to an empty string, thereby ensuring that any error messages are cleared when the page loads.

   b. Create an **If** block to determine if the **IsPostBack** property is false.

      The code for the remaining steps will appear inside this **If** block, and should only run if **IsPostBack** is false.

   c. Define a variable of type **SqlDataReader** and set it to **Nothing** (Visual Basic .NET) or **null** (C#).

      In the solution for this lab, the variable is named **dr**.

   d. Define a variable of type **SqlCommand** and create a new instance of **SqlCommand**.

      In the solution for this lab, the variable is named **cmGetSuppliers**.

   e. Configure the **SqlCommand** variable to call the **GetSupplierNames** stored procedure, and to use the **SqlConnection** object you created in Step 3.

   f. Open the connection on the **SqlConnection** object that you created in Step 3.

   g. Call the **SqlCommand** variable's **ExecuteReader** method to execute the command and return a **SqlDataReader** object. Assign the return result to the **SqlDataReader** variable.

   h. Set the **DataSource** property of **lstNames** to the **SqlDataReader** variable.

   i. Set the **lstNames** property values according to the information in the following table.

Property	Value
DataTextField	CompanyName
DataValueField	SupplierID

   j. Call the **lstNames** control's **DataBind** method.

   k. Close the **SqlDataReader** variable.

      Closing the variable will make the connection available for other objects.

   l. After the call to the **Close** method, add the following code to create an **[All]** entry in the list:

   Visual Basic .NET

   ```
   lstNames.Items.Insert(0, New ListItem("[All]", "0"))
   lstNames.SelectedIndex = 0
   ```

   C#

   ```
   lstNames.Items.Insert(0,new ListItem("[All]","0"));
   lstNames.SelectedIndex = 0;
   ```

Your code should look similar to the following:

Visual Basic .NET

```vbnet
lblError.Text = ""
If Not Me.IsPostBack Then
    Dim dr As SqlDataReader = Nothing
    Dim cmGetSuppliers As SqlCommand = Nothing
    cmGetSuppliers = New SqlCommand( _
        "GetSupplierNames", cnNorthwind1)
    cmGetSuppliers.CommandType = CommandType.StoredProcedure
    cnNorthwind1.Open()
    dr = cmGetSuppliers.ExecuteReader()
    lstNames.DataSource = dr
    lstNames.DataTextField = "CompanyName"
    lstNames.DataValueField = "SupplierID"
    lstNames.DataBind()
    dr.Close()
    lstNames.Items.Insert(0, New ListItem("[All]", "0"))
    lstNames.SelectedIndex = 0
End If
```

C#

```csharp
lblError.Text = "";
if (!this.IsPostBack)
{
    SqlDataReader dr = null;
    SqlCommand cmGetSuppliers = null;
    cmGetSuppliers = new SqlCommand
        ("GetSupplierNames",cnNorthwind1);
    cmGetSuppliers.CommandType =
        CommandType.StoredProcedure;
    cnNorthwind1.Open();
    dr = cmGetSuppliers.ExecuteReader();
    lstNames.DataSource = dr;
    lstNames.DataTextField = "CompanyName";
    lstNames.DataValueField = "SupplierID";
    lstNames.DataBind();
    dr.Close();
    lstNames.Items.Insert(0,new ListItem("[All]","0"));
    lstNames.SelectedIndex = 0;
}
```

▶ **Enable structured error handling**

1. Perform the following steps to place the **Page_Load** event handler code inside a **Try...Catch...Finally** block:

   a. Surround all of the code inside the **If** block by a **Try** block.

   b. Move the variable declaration for the **SqlDataReader** above the **Try** block.

      Moving the variable declaration will change the scope of the variable to make it accessible in the **Finally** block.

   c. Write a **Catch** block to catch a generic **Exception** type, and assign the error message to the **lblError Label** control's **Text** property.

   d. Write a **Finally** block to close the **SqlDataReader** and **SqlConnection** objects.

   Your code should look similar to the following:

```
Visual Basic .NET

lblError.Text = ""
If Not Me.IsPostBack Then
   Dim dr As SqlDataReader = Nothing
   Try
       Dim cmGetSuppliers As SqlCommand = Nothing
       cmGetSuppliers = New SqlCommand( _
           "GetSupplierNames", cnNorthwind1)
       cmGetSuppliers.CommandType = _
           CommandType.StoredProcedure
       cnNorthwind1.Open()
       dr = cmGetSuppliers.ExecuteReader()
       lstNames.DataSource = dr
       lstNames.DataTextField = "CompanyName"
       lstNames.DataValueField = "SupplierID"
       lstNames.DataBind()
       dr.Close()
       lstNames.Items.Insert(0, New ListItem("[All]", "0"))
       lstNames.SelectedIndex = 0
   Catch exc As Exception
       lblError.Text = exc.Message
   Finally
       If Not IsNothing(dr) Then dr.Close()
       If Not IsNothing(cnNorthwind1) _
           Then cnNorthwind1.Close()
   End Try
End If
```

C#

```
lblError.Text = "";
if (!this.IsPostBack)
{
    SqlDataReader dr = null;
    try
    {
        SqlCommand cmGetSuppliers = null;
        cmGetSuppliers = new SqlCommand
            ("GetSupplierNames",cnNorthwind1);
        cmGetSuppliers.CommandType =
            CommandType.StoredProcedure;
        cnNorthwind1.Open();
        dr = cmGetSuppliers.ExecuteReader();
        lstNames.DataSource = dr;
        lstNames.DataTextField = "CompanyName";
        lstNames.DataValueField = "SupplierID";
        lstNames.DataBind();
        dr.Close();
        lstNames.Items.Insert(0,new ListItem("[All]","0"));
        lstNames.SelectedIndex = 0;
    }
    catch (Exception exc)
    {
        lblError.Text = exc.Message;
    }
    finally
    {
        if (dr != null) dr.Close();
        if (cnNorthwind1 != null) cnNorthwind1.Close();
    }
}
```

2. Build and browse the Products.aspx page.

    The **DropDownList** control should display **[All]**. You should be able to use the list to select any company name.

Exercise 2
Bind a DataGrid Control to a DataSet

In this exercise, you will modify the Northwind Traders product editing Web Form to display a list of products whenever an item is selected in the **DropDownList** control. You will create a **SqlDataAdapter** control to call stored procedures to select and update products for a specific supplier. You will then customize the **DataGrid** control to allow the user to edit and update of the products.

▶ **Create a typed DataSet**

1. Open the Products.aspx page.

2. Drag a **SqlDataAdapter** control from the Toolbox onto the Products.aspx page.

3. In the Data Adapter Configuration Wizard, set the **Select** command to call the **GetProducts** stored procedure, and to set the **Update** command to call the **UpdateProduct** stored procedure.

4. Rename the **SqlDataAdapter** object.

   In the solution for this lab, the **SqlDataAdapter** is named **daProducts**.

5. Use the **SqlDataAdapter** object to create a typed **DataSet** named **ProductsDataSet**.

6. Rename the **ProductsDataSet1** typed **DataSet**.

   In the solution for this lab, the type **DataSet** is named **dsProducts**.

▶ **Configure the DataGrid control**

1. Use the Properties window to select an AutoFormat type for the **grdProducts** control.

   In the solution for this lab, the AutoFormat is set to **Professional 1**.

2. Use the Property Builder to connect **grdProducts** to the typed **DataSet**.

3. Use the Property Builder to add an **Edit, Update, Cancel** column.

   You must also manually add the **ProductID**, **ProductName**, **SupplierID**, **CategoryID**, **QuantityPerUnit**, **UnitPrice**, **UnitsInStock**, **UnitsOnOrder**, **ReorderLevel**, and **Discontinued** columns.

4. Set the **ProductID**, **ProductName**, **SupplierID**, and **CategoryID** columns to be read-only.

5. Configure the paging on **grdProducts** to allow 10 rows per page.

6. Clear the **DataSource** property and click **OK**.

   You will set this property programmatically later.

▶ **Bind the DataGrid Control**

1. Create a private method, named **BindDataGrid**, with the following function signature:

```
Visual Basic .NET
Private Sub BindDataGrid()

End Sub
```

```
C#
```

```
private void BindDataGrid()
{
}
```

2. In the **BindDataGrid** method, use the **SqlDataAdapter** object to fill the typed **DataSet**.

3. Check the **Value** property of the currently selected **lstNames** control item:

   a. If the value is 0, then **[All]** is selected, and you must bind **DataGrid** control **grdProducts** to the entire **DataSet** object **dsProducts**.

   b. If the value is not 0, then a specific company is selected and you must filter and bind the products for that company. Create a **DataView** from **dsProducts**, and filter the records so that only the records with a **SupplierID** equal to the selected **lstNames** value are selected. Then, bind the **DataView** to **grdProducts**.

4. Place all of the **BindDataGrid** method code inside a **Try...Catch...Finally** block.

   The **Catch** block should assign the error message to the **lblError.Text** property, and the **Finally** block should be empty.

   Your completed **BindDataGrid** method should look similar to the following:

```
Visual Basic .NET

Try
    daProducts.Fill(dsProducts)
    Dim ItemValue As String = _
        lstNames.Items(lstNames.SelectedIndex).Value
    If ItemValue = "0" Then
        grdProducts.DataSource = dsProducts
        grdProducts.DataBind()
    Else
        Dim dv As New DataView(dsProducts.GetProducts)
        dv.RowFilter = "SupplierID=" + ItemValue
        grdProducts.DataSource = dv
        grdProducts.DataBind()
    End If
Catch exc As Exception
    lblError.Text = exc.Message
End Try
```

```csharp
C#

try
{
    string ItemValue =
        lstNames.Items[lstNames.SelectedIndex].Value;
    daProducts.Fill(dsProducts);
    if (ItemValue == "0")
    {
        grdProducts.DataSource = dsProducts;
        grdProducts.DataBind();
    }
    else
    {
        DataView dv = new DataView(dsProducts.GetProducts);
        dv.RowFilter = "SupplierID=" + ItemValue;
        grdProducts.DataSource = dv;
        grdProducts.DataBind();
    }
}
catch (Exception exc)
{
    lblError.Text = exc.Message;
}
```

5. Modify the **Page_Load** event handler so that the last call in the **Try** block is to the **BindDataGrid** method, which will cause the **grdProducts** control to display all of the suppliers when the page loads.

    Note You must ensure the data reader, **dr**, is closed before calling **BindDataGrid**.

6. Build and browse the Products.aspx page.

    The **grdProducts DataGrid** control should display all of the products in the Northwind Traders database.

    Note You will not be able to update any of the data until you complete the next steps, which create event handlers.

▶ Create the SelectedIndexChanged event handler

1. Add an event handler for the **lstNames SelectedIndexChanged** event.

    In Visual Basic .NET, use the **Class Name** and **Method Name** drop-down boxes to create the event.

    In C#, use the **Event** button, in the Properties window, to create the event.

2. In the **lstNames_SelectedIndexChanged** event handler, set the **CurrentPageIndex** property of **grdProducts** to 0.

    Anytime the list is changed, the **DataGrid** control must be returned to the first displayable page.

3. Call the **BindDataGrid** method.

   BindDataGrid will update the **DataGrid** control when the user selects different company names in the list.

4. Place all of the **lstNames_SelectedIndexChanged** event handler code inside a **Try...Catch** block.

   The **Catch** block should assign the error message to the **lblError.Text** property.

   Your completed **lstNames_SelectedIndexChanged** event handler should look similar to the following code:

   Visual Basic .NET

```vb
Try
   grdProducts.CurrentPageIndex = 0
   BindDataGrid()
Catch exc As Exception
   lblError.Text = exc.Message
End Try
```

   C#

```csharp
try
{
   grdProducts.CurrentPageIndex = 0;
   BindDataGrid();
}
catch (Exception exc)
{
   lblError.Text = exc.Message;
}
```

▶ **Create the EditCommand event handler**

1. Add an event handler for the **grdProducts_EditCommand** event.

2. In the **grdProducts_EditCommand** event handler, set the **EditItemIndex** property to the currently selected index, thereby engaging editing on that row, and then call **BindDataGrid**.

3. Place all of the **grdProducts_EditCommand** event handler code inside a **Try…Catch** block.

   The **Catch** block should assign the error message to the **lblError.Text** property.

   Your completed **grdProducts_EditCommand** event handler should look similar to the following code:

```
Visual Basic .NET

Try
    grdProducts.EditItemIndex = e.Item.ItemIndex
    BindDataGrid()
Catch exc As Exception
    lblError.Text = exc.Message
End Try
```

```
C#

try
{
    grdProducts.EditItemIndex = e.Item.ItemIndex;
    BindDataGrid();
}
catch (Exception exc)
{
    lblError.Text = exc.Message;
}
```

▶ **Create the UpdateCommand event handler**

1. Add an event handler for the **grdProducts_UpdateCommand** event.

2. In the **grdProducts_UpdateCommand** event handler, you may perform the following steps, or paste the code in from the *install_folder*\Labfiles\Lab04*language*\Starter\Update-*language*.txt:

   a. Use the **SqlDataAdapter** object to fill the typed **DataSet**.

   b. Create a variable of type **ProductsDataSet.GetProductsRow**.

      In the solution for this lab, this variable is named **r**.

   c. Call the typed **DataSet's GetProducts.FindByProductID** method to retrieve the row that is being updated.

      Pass **e.Item.Cells(1).Text**, converted to an **Int32**, as the argument to **FindByProductID**.

   d. Create a variable of type **TextBox**.

      In the solution for this lab, this variable is named **tb**.

   e. Call the **BeginEdit** method on the **GetProductsRow** variable.

f. Set the **TextBox** variable equal to the **e.Item.Cells(10).Controls(0)** property.

g. Set the **GetProductsRow** variable's **Discontinued** property to the value in the **TextBox**.

You will need to convert the **Text** property of the **TextBox** variable to a **Boolean** value.

h. Set the **TextBox** variable equal to the **e.Item.Cells(5).Controls(0)** property.

i. Set the **GetProductsRow** variable's **QuantityPerUnit** property to the value in the **TextBox**.

j. Set the **TextBox** variable equal to the **e.Item.Cells(9).Controls(0)** property.

k. Set the **GetProductsRow** variable's **ReorderLevel** property to the value in the **TextBox**.

You will need to convert the **Text** property of the **TextBox** variable to an **Integer** value.

l. Set the **TextBox** variable equal to the **e.Item.Cells(6).Controls(0)** property.

m. Set the **GetProductsRow** variable's **UnitPrice** property to the value in the **TextBox**.

You will need to convert the **Text** property of the **TextBox** variable to a **Decimal** value.

n. Set the **TextBox** variable equal to the **e.Item.Cells(7).Controls(0)** property.

o. Set the **GetProductsRow** variable's **UnitsInStock** property to the value in the **TextBox**.

You will need to convert the **Text** property of the **TextBox** variable to a **Integer** value.

p. Set the **TextBox** variable equal to the **e.Item.Cells(8).Controls(0)** property.

q. Set the **GetProductsRow** variable's **UnitsOnOrder** property to the value in the **TextBox**.

You will need to convert the **Text** property of the **TextBox** variable to a **Integer** value.

r. Call the **EndEdit** method on the **GetProductsRow** variable.

s. Call the **Update** method on the **SqlDataAdapter** object.

t. Set the **EditItemIndex** property of the **grdProducts** control to **-1**, which will turn off the editing mode.

u. Call the **BindDataGrid** method to rebind the **grdProducts** control.

3. Place all of the **grdProducts_UpdateCommand** event handler code inside a **Try...Catch...Finally** block.

The **Catch** block should assign the error message to the **lblError.Text** property, and the **Finally** block should be empty.

Your completed **grdProducts_EditCommand** event handler should look similar to the following code:

```vb
Visual Basic .NET

Try
    daProducts.Fill(dsProducts)
    Dim r As ProductsDataSet.GetProductsRow = _
        dsProducts.GetProducts.FindByProductID( _
        Convert.ToInt32(e.Item.Cells(1).Text))


    Dim tb As TextBox
    r.BeginEdit()
    tb = CType(e.Item.Cells(10).Controls(0), TextBox)
    r.Discontinued = Convert.ToBoolean(tb.Text)
    tb = CType(e.Item.Cells(5).Controls(0), TextBox)
    r.QuantityPerUnit = tb.Text
    tb = CType(e.Item.Cells(9).Controls(0), TextBox)
    r.ReorderLevel = Convert.ToInt16(tb.Text)
    tb = CType(e.Item.Cells(6).Controls(0), TextBox)
    r.UnitPrice = Convert.ToDecimal(tb.Text)
    tb = CType(e.Item.Cells(7).Controls(0), TextBox)
    r.UnitsInStock = Convert.ToInt16(tb.Text)
    tb = CType(e.Item.Cells(8).Controls(0), TextBox)
    r.UnitsOnOrder = Convert.ToInt16(tb.Text)
    r.EndEdit()
    daProducts.Update(dsProducts)
    grdProducts.EditItemIndex = -1
    BindDataGrid()
Catch exc As Exception
    lblError.Text = exc.Message
End Try
```

```csharp
C#

try
{
    daProducts.Fill(dsProducts);
    ProductsDataSet.GetProductsRow r =
        dsProducts.GetProducts.FindByProductID(
        Convert.ToInt32(e.Item.Cells[1].Text));
    TextBox tb;
    r.BeginEdit();
    tb = (TextBox) e.Item.Cells[10].Controls[0];
    r.Discontinued = Convert.ToBoolean(tb.Text);
    tb = (TextBox) e.Item.Cells[5].Controls[0];
    r.QuantityPerUnit = tb.Text;
    tb = (TextBox) e.Item.Cells[9].Controls[0];
    r.ReorderLevel = Convert.ToInt16(tb.Text);
    tb = (TextBox) e.Item.Cells[6].Controls[0];
    r.UnitPrice = Convert.ToDecimal(tb.Text);
    tb = (TextBox) e.Item.Cells[7].Controls[0];
    r.UnitsInStock = Convert.ToInt16(tb.Text);
    tb = (TextBox) e.Item.Cells[8].Controls[0];
    r.UnitsOnOrder = Convert.ToInt16(tb.Text);
    r.EndEdit();
    daProducts.Update(dsProducts);
    grdProducts.EditItemIndex = -1;
    BindDataGrid();
}
catch (Exception exc)
{
    lblError.Text = exc.Message;
}
```

▶ **Create the CancelCommand event handler**

1. Add an event handler for the **grdProducts_CancelCommand** event.

2. In the **grdProducts_CancelCommand** event handler, set the **EditItemIndex** property to -1 to cancel editing, and call the **BindDataGrid** method.

3. Place all of the **grdProducts_CancelCommand** event handler code inside a **Try...Catch** block.

   The **Catch** block should assign the error message to the **lblError.Text** property.

   Your completed **grdProducts_CancelCommand** event handler should look similar to the following code:

```vbnet
Visual Basic .NET

Try
    grdProducts.EditItemIndex = -1
    BindDataGrid()
Catch exc As Exception
    lblError.Text = exc.Message
End Try
```

```
C#

try
{
    grdProducts.EditItemIndex = -1;
    BindDataGrid();
}
catch (Exception exc)
{
    lblError.Text = exc.Message;
}
```

▶ **Create the PageIndexChanged event handler**

1. Add an event handler for the **grdProducts_PageIndexChanged** event.

2. In the **grdProducts_PageIndexChanged** event handler, set the
   CurrentPageIndex property of **grdProducts** to the value of
   e.NewPageIndex, and then call the **BindDataGrid** method.

3. Place all of the **grdProducts_PageIndexChanged** event handler code
   inside a **Try...Catch** block.

   The **Catch** block should assign the error message to the **lblError.Text**
   property.

   Your completed **grdProducts_PageIndexChanged** event handler should
   look similar to the following code:

```
Visual Basic .NET

Try
    grdProducts.CurrentPageIndex = e.NewPageIndex
    BindDataGrid()
Catch exc As Exception
    lblError.Text = exc.Message
End Try
```

```
C#

try
{
    grdProducts.CurrentPageIndex = e.NewPageIndex;
    BindDataGrid();
}
catch (Exception exc)
{
    lblError.Text = exc.Message;
}
```

4. Build and browse the Products.aspx page.

   You should be able to edit and update any of the products that are displayed
   on the **DataGrid** control.

msdn training

Module 5: Managing State in a Microsoft ASP.NET Web Application

Contents

Overview

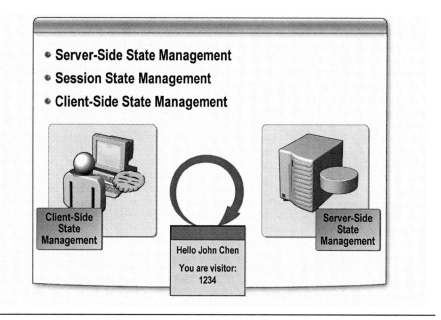

Introduction

State management is the process by which you maintain the same information throughout multiple requests for the same or different Web pages. State is user- or application-specific data that must persist across multiple Web requests. This user- or application-specific data can include data, such as the user's name, that persists for only a single session, along with data, such as the number of visitors, that persists across an entire Web application.

Hypertext Transfer Protocol (HTTP) is a stateless protocol; therefore, Web applications must provide their own state management.

Microsoft® ASP.NET provides a number of options for state management that can be used to save information between requests, thereby maintaining the continuity of user information (state) throughout a user's visit to a Web site.

In this module, you will learn about server-side state management and client-side state management. You will also learn how to manage state in an ASP.NET Web application.

Note The code examples in this module are provided in both Microsoft Visual Basic® .NET and C#.

Objectives

After completing this module, you will be able to:

- Manage application state by using the server-side state management options that are available to ASP.NET Web applications.

- Manage session state by using the server-side state management options that are available to ASP.NET Web applications.

- Manage session state by using the client-side state management options that are available to ASP.NET Web applications.

Lesson: Server-Side State Management

* Application and Session State Management
* Technologies for Server-Side State Management
* The Global.asax File
* Using Application Variables
* Practice: Using Application State

Introduction

In ASP.NET, you can maintain two different kinds of server-side state: application state and session state. In this lesson, you will learn the differences between session and application state. You will also learn how to initialize and use static variables for managing application state and how to manage application state by using the Global.asax file.

Although application state can be displayed to users, it is generally used to manage the Web application. Application state is typically used by administrators for tracking statistics, server locations, and registration information. A Web site user will rarely see application state values unless they log on as an administrator.

Lesson objectives

After completing this lesson, you will be able to:

* Explain the differences between session and application state.

* Explain the technologies that are available for server-side state management

* Store application state in the Global.asax file.

* Initialize, set, and read application variables.

Application and Session State Management

* **Application state is accessible from all of the sessions in the Web application**
* **Session state is limited to a single browser session**

Introduction

Server-side state management involves two types of state management:

- Application state

  In application state, information is available to all of the users of a Web application. The storing, updating, and displaying of the number of visitors to a Web application is an example of application state maintenance.

- Session state

  In session state, information is available only to the user of a specific session of a Web application. Providing a user with customization options, such as selecting and displaying a preferred color scheme across several Web pages, is an example of session state maintenance.

Application state

In application state, information is available to all of the sessions in Web application.

The advantages of using application state are:

- Ease of implementation.

  Application state is easy to use, and it should be familiar to Active Server Pages (ASP) Web application developers. Also, application state is consistent with the other Microsoft .NET Framework classes.

- Global scope.

  Because application state is accessible to all of the Web pages in an application, storing information in application state consists of keeping only a single copy of specific information (as opposed to keeping multiple copies of information in session state or in individual pages).

The disadvantages of using application state are:

- Global scope.

  The global scope of application state can also be a disadvantage. Variables that are stored in application state are global only to the particular process in which the application is running, and each application process can have different values. You cannot, therefore, rely on application state to store unique values or to update global counters in Web garden and Web farm configurations.

- Durability.

  Because the global data that is stored in application state is volatile, the data will be lost if the Web server process containing it is destroyed, most likely from a Web server failure, upgrade or shutdown.

- Resource requirements.

  Application state requires server memory, which can affect the performance of the Web server, as well as the scalability of the application.

Session state

Session state is similar to application state, except that it is limited to the current browser session. If different users are using a Web application, each user will have an individual session state. In addition, if the same user leaves the Web application and then returns later, that user will also have a different session state than the one he or she had previously.

The advantages of using session state are:

- Ease of implementation.

  Session state is easy to use, and it should be familiar to ASP developers. Session state is consistent with the other .NET Framework classes.

- Session-specific events.

  Session management events can be raised and then used by your application.

- Durability.

  Data that is placed in session-state variables can endure Internet Information Services (IIS) restarts and worker-process restarts without losing session data because the data is stored in another process space.

- Platform scalability.

  Session state can be used in both multicomputer and multiprocess configurations, thereby optimizing scalability scenarios.

- Cookieless support.

  Session state works with browsers that do not support HTTP cookies; however, session state is most commonly used with cookies to provide user identification facilities to a Web application.

The disadvantage of using session state is its performance. Session state variables stay in memory until they are either removed or replaced; therefore, the variables can degrade server performance. Session state variables containing blocks of information, such as large **DataSet** objects, can adversely affect Web server performance as the Web server load increases.

Technologies for Server-Side State Management

- **State server**
  - Stores session state in memory or in a database
- **The Cache object**
  - Volatile storage of data at the application level
- **The Global.asax file**
  - Handles application events that can be used to initialize variables
- **Custom database**
  - Could store any type of state data

Introduction

ASP.NET Web applications offer a number of options that are available for storing state on the server side.

State server

You can use a state server to store session information on the server side. A state server is the best option for Web farms and for when the information store is large. The state server can run in memory or on a Microsoft SQL Server™ server.

The advantages of using state server on a database to maintain state are:

- *Security*. Access to databases is typically very secure, requiring rigorous authentication and authorization.

- *Capacity*. You can store as much information as you want in a database.

- *Persistence*. Database information can be stored as long as you want, and it is not subject to the availability of the Web server.

- *Robustness and data integrity*. Databases include various facilities that can be used for maintaining data, including triggers and referential integrity, transactions, and so on. By keeping information regarding transactions in a database (rather than in session state, for example), you can recover from errors more readily.

- *Accessibility*. The data that is stored in your database is accessible to a wide variety of information-processing tools.

- *Wide support*. There are a large range of database tools and configurations are available for the creation of custom state servers.

The disadvantages of using state server on a database to maintain state are:

- *Complexity*. Using a database to support state management implies more complex hardware and software configurations.

- *Performance*. Poor construction of the relational data model can lead to scaling problems. Also, leveraging too many queries to the database can adversely affect server performance.

The Cache object

One feature in ASP.NET is the **Cache** object, which can be used for caching data at the application level. The **Cache** object supports versatile state management options, such as event-driven updates to the cache, as well as expiration dates for cached items. However, objects in the cache are volatile and may be removed based on conditions, such as high levels of memory load. The **Cache** object is suitable for storing read-only or noncritical data that is used to increase performance of the Web application.

Note   For more information about the **Cache** object, see Appendix B, "Improving Microsoft ASP.NET Web Application Performance Using Caching," in Course 2640, *Upgrading Web Development Skills from ASP to Microsoft ASP.NET*.

The Global.asax file

The Global.asax file, also known as the ASP.NET application file, is a declarative file that is used to handle events while your Web application is running. The Global.asax file is similar to the Global.asa file in an ASP page. The Global.asax file can coexist with the Global.asa file, thereby allowing you to combine both ASP and ASP.NET Web applications on a Web server.

Custom database

A custom state management database is an option for server-side state management, and it is available in ASP and in ASP.NET. A custom state management database can also be used to maintain a user's preferred state across sessions by matching settings with persistent cookies on the user's computer.

The Global.asax File

- **Similar to the global.asa file in ASP**
- **Only one Global.asax file per Web application**
- **Used to handle application and session events**
  - Events that are fired when a page is requested
  - Events that are fired when the requested page is sent
  - Conditional application events

Introduction

The Global.asax file, also known as the ASP.NET application file, is a declarative file that is used to handle events while your Web application runs. The Global.asax file is similar to the Global.asa file that is in ASP. The Global.asax file can coexist with the Global.asa file, thereby allowing you to combine ASP and ASP.NET Web applications.

Some of the characteristics of the Global.asax file are:

- Every ASP.NET Web application supports one Global.asax file per Web application.

- The Global.asax file is stored in the virtual root folder of the Web application.

- The Global.asax file can handle application and session (start and end) events that can be used to initialize application and sessions variables.

- The Global.asax file is optional. If you do not define the file, the ASP.NET page framework assumes that you have not defined any application or session event handlers.

Categories of events

The Global.asax file supports three categories of events:

- Events that are fired when a page is requested.

- Events that are fired when the requested page is sent.

- Conditional application events.

Using Application Variables

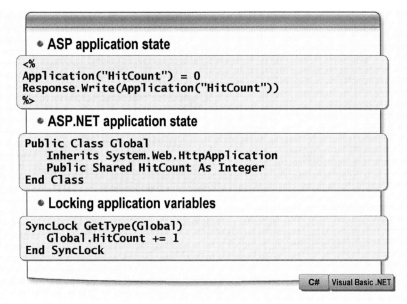

Introduction

Application state is data that has application scope. Application scope refers to the data that is accessible from any Web Form and any session in the Web application, beginning when the Web application starts, until the Web application shuts down.

ASP application state

In ASP, application state is managed by using the **Application** object. The **Application** object supports the storing of variant data types, and COM object references. Application events can be written in the Global.asa file to initialize application variables, or to perform actions upon shutdown. The following code example shows the syntax for creating and reading an **Application** object variable:

```
<%
Application("HitCount") = 0
Response.Write(Application("HitCount"))
%>
```

ASP.NET application state compatibility

ASP.NET supports an **Application** property for programming model backward compatibility with ASP pages. The **Application** property uses syntax that is similar to the ASP **Application** object, but this property stores and manages Microsoft .NET types. These two application state objects, the **Application** property and the **Application** object, are incompatible; therefore, state that is saved in an ASP Web application can not be used in ASP.NET Web applications.

Note For more information on migrating application state, see Module 9, "Migrating ASP Web Applications to Microsoft ASP.NET," in Course 2640, *Upgrading Web Development Skills from ASP to Microsoft ASP.NET*.

Storing application state in ASP.NET

You can store application state in ASP.NET by creating shared (Visual Basic .NET), or static (C#) members in your **HttpApplication** derived class. By default, when you create a new Web project by using Microsoft Visual Studio® .NET, a class named **Global** is created in the Global.asax file. The **Global** class inherits from **HttpApplication**, and it is available to all .aspx pages. Using global variables for state management is faster than using the **Application** property because your code has direct access to global variables, whereas the **Application** property must perform lookups and conversions.

The following code example shows the code-behind file for initializing a global variable named **HitCount** to zero:

```vbnet
Visual Basic .NET

Public Class Global
  Inherits System.Web.HttpApplication

  'Declare any application state variables
  'as public static members here
  Public Shared HitCount As Integer

  Sub Application_Start(ByVal sender As Object, _
        ByVal e As EventArgs)
    HitCount = 0
  End Sub
...
End Class
```

```csharp
C#

public class Global : System.Web.HttpApplication
{
  //Declare any application state variables
  //as public static members here
  public static int HitCount = 0;

  protected void Application_Start(Object sender, EventArgs e)
  {
    HitCount = 0;
  }
...
}
```

To update a global variable, you must lock the variable to prevent concurrent access from multiple Web Forms. You can use the **SyncLock** statement in Visual Basic .NET, or the **lock** keyword in C#, to prevent concurrent access when updating a global variable. The easiest lock to implement is on the type of the **Global** class, although this locks the entire class. You can also lock individual variables if they are reference types derived from the **Object** class.

The following code example shows how to update the **HitCount** global variable from an .aspx page:

```
Visual Basic .NET

Public Class MyForm
  Inherits System.Web.UI.Page
...
  Private Sub Page_Load(ByVal sender As System.Object, _
          ByVal e As System.EventArgs) Handles MyBase.Load
      'The following block locks the Global class
      'and prevents concurrent access to HitCount
      SyncLock GetType(Global)
          Global.HitCount += 1
      End SyncLock
  End Sub
...
End Class
```

```
C#

public class MyForm : System.Web.UI.Page
{
...
  private void Page_Load(object sender, System.EventArgs e)
  {
      //The following block locks the Global class
      //and prevents concurrent access to HitCount
      lock(typeof(Global))
      {
          Global.HitCount++;
      }
  }
...
}
```

Practice: Using Application State

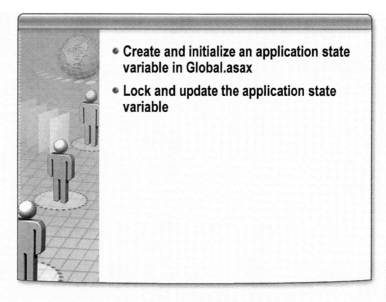

- Create and initialize an application state variable in Global.asax
- Lock and update the application state variable

Introduction

In this practice, you will learn how to use application state in ASP.NET. You will modify a Web Form to display the total number of visitors. The number of visitors will be stored as a variable on the **Global** class in the Global.asax file. The number of visitors will be incremented each time the page is loaded by any browser.

The code for this practice is in the *install_folder*\Practices\Mod05*language* folder.

Open the practice project

1. In Visual Studio .NET, from the **File** menu, click **Open Solution**.
2. In the Open Solution window, click the **My Projects** shortcut.
3. Open the **Practices**, **Mod05**, and *language* folders.
4. Select **state.sln**, and then click **Open**.

Create and initialize an application variable

In the following steps you will create and initialize an application variable named **NumberofVisitors**.

5. Open the code-behind file for the Global.asax file.
6. In the **Global** class, create a shared (Visual Basic .NET), or static (C#) variable named **NumberofVisitors** of type integer, as shown in the following code example:

```
Visual Basic .NET

Public Shared NumberofVisitors As Integer
```

```
C#

public static int NumberofVisitors;
```

7. In the **Application_Start** event handler, initialize the **NumberofVisitors** variable to 0, as shown in the following code example:

```
Visual Basic .NET

Sub Application_Start(ByVal sender As Object, _
        ByVal e As EventArgs)
  Global.NumberofVisitors = 0
End Sub
```

```
C#

protected void Application_Start(Object sender,
        EventArgs e)
{
   Global.NumberofVisitors = 0;
}
```

Lock and update the application state variable

In the following steps you will add the necessary code to the **Page_load** event to lock and increment the **NumberofVisitors** variable.

8. Open the code-behind file for AppState.aspx.

9. In the **Page_Load** event handler, increment the **NumberofVisitors** variable by 1, as shown in the following code example:

```
Visual Basic .NET

SyncLock GetType(Global)
   Global.NumberofVisitors += 1
End SyncLock
```

```
C#

lock(typeof(Global))
{
   Global.NumberofVisitors++;
}
```

10. Assign the value of **NumberofVisitors** to **txtHits.Text**, as shown in the following code example:

```
Visual Basic .NET

txtHits.Text = Global.NumberofVisitors.ToString()
```

```
C#

txtHits.Text = Global.NumberofVisitors.ToString();
```

11. Build and browse the AppState.aspx Web page.

Each time you refresh the page, the number of visitors on the page should increase by one. If you start a second instance of a browser and view the same page, you should see the same number of visitors, plus one.

Lesson: Session State Management

- **Using Session Variables**
- **Initializing Session Variables**
- **Session Duration**
- **Scalable Storage of Session Variables**
- **Using SQL Server for Session Storage**
- **Using Cookieless Sessions**

Introduction

In ASP.NET, you can maintain two kinds of server-side state: application state and session state. In this lesson, you will learn how to manage session state, including using state servers and databases. You will also learn how to configure session-state attributes.

You use the **Session** property to store the information that is needed for a particular user session. Variables that are stored in the **Session** property will not be discarded when the user goes between the different pages in the Web application. Instead, these variables will persist for the entire user session.

Lesson objectives

After completing this lesson, you will be able to:

- Set and read session variables.

- Initialize session variables.

- Modify the timeout period session attribute.

- Describe the out of process methods that are used for scalable storage of session state.

- Explain how to set up scalable storage of session variables using SQL Server.

- Initialize an ASP.NET Web application to use cookieless sessions.

Using Session Variables

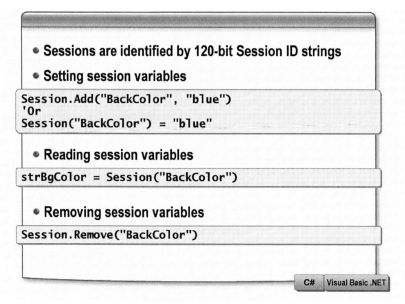

- **Sessions are identified by 120-bit Session ID strings**
- **Setting session variables**

```
Session.Add("BackColor", "blue")
'Or
Session("BackColor") = "blue"
```

- **Reading session variables**

```
strBgColor = Session("BackColor")
```

- **Removing session variables**

```
Session.Remove("BackColor")
```

C#   Visual Basic .NET

Introduction

ASP.NET provides the session variables that are needed to maintain session state. The ideal data to store in session state variables is short-lived, sensitive data that is specific to an individual user session.

Scalability

With ASP.NET, session state can be used in both multicomputer and multiprocess configurations, thereby optimizing the scalability scenarios of a Web application.

Identifying and tracking a session

Each active Web application session is identified and tracked by using a 120-bit **SessionID** string containing only the ASCII characters that are allowed in the Uniform Resource Locators (URLs). The **SessionID** strings are communicated across client-server requests, either by means of an HTTP cookie or a modified URL, with the **SessionID** string embedded, and commonly referred to as cookieless **SessionID**, depending on how you configure the Web application settings.

Server-side state management requires a cookie to store the **SessionID** on the client computer. Because the duration of a **SessionID** is very short, just the duration of a session, the mechanism that is used by ASP.NET to store session information, either in a SQL Server database or in a state server, is also used to allow the application to be scalable, but not for long-term storage. If you want to implement long-term storage of user session information, you must require that users register and enter their personal information, and then you need to implement your own storage solution by using a database that permanently stores the entered personal information of the registered users.

Adding session variables

To use session variables in ASP.NET, you simply use a string key and set a value. The following code example shows the changing of the background color by providing a key named **BackColor**, and a value **Blue**, both of which identify the item that you are storing:

Visual Basic .NET

```
'You can use the Add method
Session.Add("BackColor", "blue")
'Or you can use the indexer
Session("BackColor") = "blue"
```

C#

```
//You can use the Add method
Session.Add("BackColor", "blue");
//Or you can use the indexer
Session["BackColor"] = "blue";
```

Reading session variables

To read a session variable in an ASP.NET page, you read the value from the **Session** property by using the indexer, as shown in the following code example:

Visual Basic.NET

```
strBgColor = Session("BackColor")
```

C#

```
strBgColor = (string)Session["BackColor"];
```

Removing session variables

You can remove session variables by using the **Remove**, **RemoveAt**, and **RemoveAll** methods. The following code example shows how to remove the BackColor variable by using the **Remove** method:

Visual Basic .NET

```
Session.Remove("BackColor")
```

C#

```
Session.Remove("BackColor");
```

Initializing Session Variables

* **The Session object stores infromation for a particular user session**

* **Session_Start event**

```
Sub Session_Start(ByVal Sender As Object, _
     ByVal e As    EventArgs)
   Session("BackColor") = "beige"
   Session("ForeColor") = "black"
End Sub
```

* **Session_End event**

```
Sub Session_End(ByVal sender As Object, _
     ByVal e As EventArgs)
   Application("sCount") = _
      CInt(Application("sCount")) - 1
End Sub
```

| C# | Visual Basic .NET |

Introduction

You initialize session variables in the **Session_Start** event handler in the Global.asax file. You can also use the **Session_End** event to run code whenever a session ends.

Session_Start event

A **Session_Start** event exists in the Global.asax file. This event is called whenever a new session begins. You can write code to perform session variable initialization in the **Session_Start** event. The following code example illustrates how session variables are initialized to store the default preferred color scheme for a new session:

Visual Basic .NET

```
Sub Session_Start(ByVal Sender As Object, _
    ByVal e As EventArgs)
  Session("BackColor") = "beige"
  Session("ForeColor") = "black"
End Sub
```

C#

```
protected void Session_Start(Object sender, EventArgs e)
{
  Session["BackColor"] = "beige";
  Session["ForeColor"] = "black";
}
```

Session_End event

A **Session_End** event exists in the Global.asax file. This event is called whenever a session ends, either through a call to the **Abandon** method, or by timing out. You can write code in the **Session_End** event to perform specific actions when the session ends. The following code example shows how to update a session-count variable when a session ends:

Visual Basic .NET

```
Sub Session_End(ByVal Sender As Object, _
    ByVal e As EventArgs)
  Application("sCount") = CInt(Application("sCount"))-1
End Sub
```

C#

```
protected void Session_End(Object sender, EventArgs e)
{
  Application["sCount"] = ((int)Application["sCount"])-1;
}
```

Session Duration

* **Sessions have a set duration time after last access**
    * Default is 20 minutes
* **Session duration can be changed in Web.config**

```
<configuration>
    <system.web>
        <sessionState timeout="10" />
    </system.web>
</configuration>
```

Introduction

Because HTTP is a stateless protocol, ASP.NET has no means of detecting when a user leaves a Web site. Instead, ASP.NET tracks how much time has passed without the user requesting a page. If the amount of time exceeds a specified timeout value, ASP.NET assumes that the user has left the Web site, and it removes all of the items in session state that are associated with that user.

Default session duration

By default, a session times out when a user has not requested a page for more than 20 minutes. If the same user requests a page after 20 minutes, a new session is created for that user.

Note Setting a shorter session duration makes your Web site save resources on your Web server.

Modify session duration

You can modify the session duration in the Web.config file. Web.config files are standard, human-readable Extensible Markup Language (XML) files that you can open and modify with any text editor. For example, in the following Web.config file, the session duration is set to 10 minutes:

```
<configuration>
    <system.web>
        <sessionState timeout="10" />
    </system.web>
</configuration>
```

Abandoning a session

Just as in ASP, you can explicitly end a session by calling the **Abandon** method. For example, if your Web site allows users to log in and to log out, you can end the session when the user logs out of your Web site. Using the **Abandon** method is a useful way to conserve server resources. Calling the **Abandon** method will force the **Session_End** event to run. The following code example shows how to end a session by using the **Abandon** method:

```vbnet
Visual Basic .NET

Private Sub cmdLogOut_Click(ByVal sender As Object, _
    ByVal e As System.EventArgs)
  Session.Abandon()
End Sub
```

```csharp
C#

private void cmdLogOut_Click(object sender,
    System.EventArgs e)
{
  Session.Abandon();
}
```

Scalable Storage of Session Variables

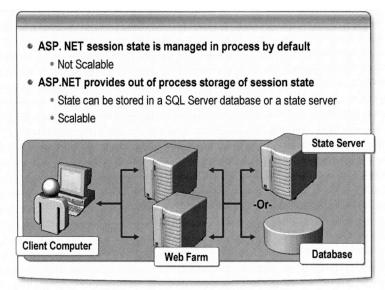

Introduction

By default, the session state is managed *in process*, which means that all of the information that is added to the session state is stored in the Web server that is running the ASP.NET Web application. However, storing session state in process has some significant disadvantages.

Disadvantage of storing session state in process

One of the major disadvantages of storing session state in process is that it limits the scalability of your Web site. You cannot configure multiple Web servers to handle requests by using in process session state storage.

Out-of-process session-state storage

ASP.NET provides two methods that can be used to store session state out of process, which are:

- Managing session state with a SQL Server database.

- Managing session state with a separate ASP.NET state server.

  Any Microsoft Windows®–based server could be an ASP.NET state server.

To store session state out of process, you must modify the Web.config file to set the **sessionstate** mode to the value **sqlserver** or **stateserver**, and then specify the location of the SQL Server or state server. The **sqlserver** option is similar to the **stateserver** option, except that, in the former, the information persists to a SQL Server database rather than being stored in the state server computer's memory.

Advantage of out-of-process session-state storage

The main advantage of separating the storage of session state from the Web application is that you can then use an external state server or a computer running SQL Server to store session state, thereby making the Web application scalable. To have scalable ASP.NET Web applications, session state is shared across multiple servers that are supporting the Web farm scenario. In a Web farm scenario, multiple servers are configured to handle user requests; therefore, users can be routed dynamically from one server to another without losing their session variables. Moreover, session variables can then be retrieved from any server of the Web farm because the session variables are stored in a separate computer that is running SQL Server or state server.

Using SQL Server for Session Storage

1 Configure the session state in Web.config

   • Mode is set to **sqlserver** or **stateserver**

```
<sessionState mode="SQLServer"
sqlConnectionString="data source=SQLServerName;
Integrated security=true" />
```

2 Configure the SQL server

```
c:\> OSQL -S SQLServerName -E <InstallSqlState.sql
```

   • InstallSqlState.sql creates several stored procedures and
temporary databases for storing the variables

Introduction

You can use SQL Server as a session store. To configure SQL Server to store session state, you must perform the following two steps:

1. Configure the **sessionState** element in the Web.config file of your Web application.
2. Configure SQL Server.

Configure the session state in Web.config

In the Web.config file, you must modify the configuration settings to set the **mode** attribute of the **sessionState** to **sqlserver** or **stateserver**. You must then modify the **sqlconnectionstring** attribute to identify the name of the computer that is running SQL Server or the state server.

For example, if you use the **sqlserver** mode with integrated security, you must set the session state in Web.config as shown in the following code example:

```
<sessionState mode="SQLServer"
  sqlConnectionString="data source=SQLServerName;
    Integrated security=true" />
```

Configure the
SQL Server

To configure the SQL Server, you must use the command line tool, OSQL.exe, which is provided by SQL Server.

InstallSqlState.sql installs the database that is called ASPState, which is then used to save the application and session variables.

To install the ASPState database by using integrated security, use the following code:

```
c:\> OSQL -S SQLServerName -E <InstallSqlState.sql
```

Important   The switches for the OSQL command are case-sensitive.

If you use a state server instead of SQL Server, you must start the ASP.NET Windows service instead of installing a database.

Using Cookieless Sessions

- **Each active session is identified and tracked using a SessionID included in the URL**

  `http://server/(h44a1e55c0breu552yrecob1)/page.aspx`

    - Cannot use absolute URLs with SessionIDs
    - Most browsers limit the URL size to 255 characters, which limits the use of cookieless SessionIDs

- **Session state is configured in the <SessionState> section of Web.config**

  `<sessionState cookieless="true" />`

Introduction

Each active browser session can be identified and tracked by using a **SessionID**. The **SessionID** is communicated across client-server requests by using an HTTP cookie or by the inclusion of the **SessionID** in the URL. By default, the **SessionID** is stored in cookies.

Users can, however, disable cookies through a setting in their browsers. If the cookie cannot be added to a user's browser, every request that is made by the user starts a new user session. Any session data that was associated with that user is lost when a new page is requested.

Cookieless sessions

The ASP.NET page framework includes an option to enable cookieless sessions. Cookieless sessions enable you to take advantage of session state even with browsers that have cookie support disabled.

When a user makes their first request to a Web site with cookieless sessions enabled, the URL that is used for the request is automatically modified to include the user's **SessionID**. For example, when a user makes a request for http://server/page.aspx, the request is automatically modified to:

`http://server/(h44a1e55c0breu552yrecob1)/page.aspx`

The part of the URL that appears in parentheses is the **SessionID** for the current user.

After the **SessionID** is embedded in the URL of the first page request, the **SessionID** then tracks the user throughout his or her visit to the Web site.

Limitation of cookieless sessions

There are certain limitations to using cookieless sessions, including:

- If you choose to use cookieless sessions, you cannot use absolute URLs when linking between pages. You must design your Web site in a way that every link uses a URL that is relative to the current page.

- Most browsers limit the URL size to 255 characters.

Setting up a cookieless session

You can set up cookieless sessions by modifying the **cookieless** attribute of the **sessionState** element in the Web.config file. By default, the **cookieless** attribute is set to **false**. Changing the **cookieless** attribute to **true** enables cookieless sessions, as shown in the following XML:

```
<sessionState cookieless="true" />
```

Lesson: Client-Side State Management

- **Client-Side State Management**
- **What Are Cookies?**
- **Using Cookies to Store Session Data**
- **Retrieving Information from a Cookie**
- **Using ViewState to Store Session Data**
- **Practice: Using the VewState Property**

Introduction

Cookies are a means by which the Web application can cause a client to return a packet of information to the Web server with each HTTP request. The returned information can then be used to maintain state with the client across multiple requests. Cookies are sent to the client as part of the HTTP header in a client request, and then returned in a server response.

In this lesson, you will learn how to use cookies to store session data, and then learn how to retrieve that data from a cookie. You will also learn about cookieless sessions and setting up cookieless sessions.

Lesson objectives

After completing this lesson, you will be able to:

- Explain the options that are available for client-side state management.
- Explain how cookies can be used to store session and user data.
- Use cookies to store session data.
- Retrieve information from a cookie.
- Use the **ViewState** property to store session data.

Client-Side State Management

- **Cookies**
  - Persistent cookies stored as a text file
- **Query strings**
  - Information appended to the end of a URL
- **Hidden fields**
  - Field retains values between multiple requests for the same page
- **The ViewState property**
  - Hidden control retains values between multiple requests for the same page

Introduction

In ASP.NET Web applications there are several technologies that can be used for client-side state management.

Cookies

A cookie is a text file that can be used to store the small amounts of information that are needed to maintain state on the client side.

The advantages of using cookies are:

- No server resources are required.

  A cookie is stored on the client and read by the server during requests from the client.

- Simplicity.

  A cookie is a lightweight, text-based structure with simple key-value pairs.

- Configurable expiration.

  A cookie can expire when the browser session ends, or it can exist indefinitely on the client computer, subject to the expiration rules on the client.

The disadvantages of using cookies are:

- Limited size.

  Most browsers place a 4096-byte limit on the size of a cookie, although the support for the 8192-byte cookie size is becoming common.

- User-configured refusal.

  Some users disable their browser or client devices ability to receive cookies, thereby limiting the functionality of a cookie.

- Security.

  Cookies are subject to tampering. Users can manipulate cookies on their computer, which can potentially represent a security compromise or cause the Web application that is dependent on the cookie to fail.

- Durability.

  The durability of the cookie on a client computer is based on the cookie expiration processes on the client, and on user intervention.

Note Cookies are often used for personalization, customizing content for a known user. In most of these customizing scenarios, identification is the issue rather than authentication, so it is enough to merely store the user name, account name, or a unique user ID (such as a globally unique identifier, or GUID) in a cookie and use it to access the user personalization infrastructure of a site.

Query strings

A query string is information that is appended to the end of a URL. This type of state management is typically used to maintain selection information between one page and the next. A typical example of a query string might look similar to the following:

```
http://www.contoso.com/listwidgets.aspx?category=basic&price=1
00
```

In the preceding URL path, the query string starts with the question mark (**?**) and includes two attribute-value pairs, category and price.

The advantages of using query strings to maintain session state are:

- No server resources are required.

  The query string is contained in the HTTP request for a specific URL.

- Broad support.

  Almost all browsers and client devices support the passing of values in a query string.

- Simple implementation.

  ASP.NET provides full support for query strings, including support for the different techniques of reading query strings by using the **HttpRequest.Params** property.

The disadvantages of using query strings to maintain session state are:

- Security.

  The information in the query string is directly visible to the user through the browser user interface (UI). The query values are exposed to the Internet through the URL; therefore, it is possible that security may be an issue.

- Limited capacity.

  Most browsers and client devices impose a 255-character limit on URL length.

Hidden fields

You can store page-specific information in a hidden field, which resides on the Web page, as a way of maintaining the state of your page. If you use hidden fields, it is best to store only small amounts of frequently changed data on the client. ASP.NET provides the **HtmlInputHidden** control, which offers hidden field functionality.

Note If you use hidden fields, you must submit your pages to the server by using the **HTTP POST** method rather than requesting the page by using the page URL (the **HTTP GET** method).

The advantages of using hidden fields to maintain state are:

- No server resources are required.

    The hidden field is stored and read from the page.

- Wide-ranging support.

    Almost all browsers and client devices support Web pages with hidden fields.

- Simple implementation.

    ASP.NET provides the **HtmlInputHidden** control, which offers hidden field functionality.

The disadvantages of using hidden fields to maintain state are:

- Security.

    The hidden field can be tampered with. The information in the hidden field can be seen if the page output source is viewed directly, thereby creating a potential security issue.

- Limited storage structure.

    The hidden field does not support rich structures. Hidden fields offer a single value field in which to place information. To store multiple values, you must implement delimited strings and add the needed code to parse those strings.

- Performance.

    Because hidden fields are stored in the page itself, storing large values can cause the page to slow down when users display it and when they post it.

The ViewState property

ASP.NET Web Forms provide the **ViewState** property as a built-in structure for automatically retaining values between multiple requests for the same Web page. The **ViewState** property is maintained as a hidden field in the Web page.

You can use **ViewState** hidden field to store your own page-specific values across round trips to the client. For example, if your application is maintaining user-specific information—that is, information that is used in the page but not necessarily part of any control—you can store it in view state.

The advantages of using the **ViewState** property to maintain state are:

- No server resources required.

  The view state is contained in a structure within the page code.

- Simple implementation.

  ASP.NET Web Forms provide the **ViewState** property as a built-in structure.

- Automatic retention of page and control state.

- Enhanced security features.

  The values in view state are hashed, compressed, and encoded for Unicode implementations, thereby representing a higher state of security than available by using hidden fields.

The disadvantages of using the **ViewState** property to maintain state are:

- Performance.

  Because the **ViewState** hidden field is stored in the page itself, storing large values can cause the page to slow when users display it and when they post it.

- Security.

  The view state is stored in a hidden field on the page. Although the **ViewState** property stores data in a hashed format, the data can be tampered with. The information in the hidden field can also be seen if the page output source is viewed directly, creating a potential security issue.

Note   This module only covers cookies in detail. For more information about **ViewState** and query strings, see the Visual Studio .NET documentation.

What Are Cookies?

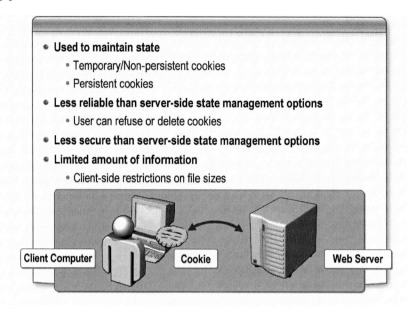

Introduction	Most Web applications use cookies for client-side state management.
Cookies	A cookie is a small amount of data that is stored either in a text file on the file system of the client computer, or in-memory in the client-browser session. A cookie contains page-specific information that the server sends to the client, as well as the page output.

You can use cookies to store information about a particular client, session, or application. The cookies are stored on the client computer, and when the browser requests a page, it sends the information in the cookie, as well as the requested information. The server is authorized to read the cookie and extract its value. Every cookie contains the information of the domain that issued the cookie. You can have several cookies issued for one domain.

Types of cookies

The two types of cookies are:

- Temporary

  Temporary cookies, also called session or non-persistent cookies, exist only in the memory of the browser. When the browser is shut down, any temporary cookies that were added to the browser are lost.

- Persistent

  Persistent cookies are similar to temporary cookies, except that persistent cookies have a finite expiration period. When a browser requests a page that creates a persistent cookie, the browser saves that cookie to the user's hard disk. You can create a persistent cookie that will remain for months, or even years, on the client computer. With Microsoft Internet Explorer, persistent cookies are stored in a file named username@domainname.txt, which is created on the client's hard disk.

Expiration

Cookies can expire when the browser session ends (temporary cookies), or they can exist indefinitely on the client computer, based on the expiration rules that are on the client (persistent cookies).

Users can also choose to delete cookies from their computer before the cookie expires. Therefore, there is no guarantee that a persistent cookie will remain on a user's computer for the period of time that is specified.

Security

Cookies are less secure than the available server-side state management options. Cookies are also subject to tampering. Users can manipulate cookies on their computers, which can potentially represent a security compromise or can cause the Web application that is dependent on the cookie to fail.

Limited information

There is also a limit on how much information you can store in a cookie because client computers have restrictions on file sizes. In addition to file size restrictions, each individual cookie can contain a limited amount of information, no more than 4 kilobytes (KB).

Example

For example, consider creating a cookie, named Username, which contains the name of a visitor to your Web site. To create this cookie, the Web server will send an HTTP header to the client, as shown in the following code example:

```
Set-Cookie: Username=John+Chen; path=/; domain=microsoft.com;
Expires=Tuesday, 01-Feb-05 00.00.01 GMT
```

The header in the preceding code example instructs the browser to add an entry to its cookie file. The browser adds the cookie, named Username, with the value John Chen.

The **domain** attribute in the preceding code example restricts where the cookie can be sent by the browser. In the preceding code example, the cookie can be sent only to the Microsoft.com Web site. The cookie will never be sent to any other Web site on the Internet.

After the Web server creates a cookie, the browser returns the cookie in every request that it makes to that specific Web site, Microsoft.com. The browser returns the cookie in a header that looks similar to the following:

```
Cookie: Username: John+Chen
```

The cookies that are stored in a text file format are the persistent cookies. By default, this file is stored in the \Documents and Settings*Username*\Cookies folder.

When persistent cookies are stored by using Internet Explorer, the format of the text file is:

```
Username@DomainName.txt
```

Using Cookies to Store Session Data

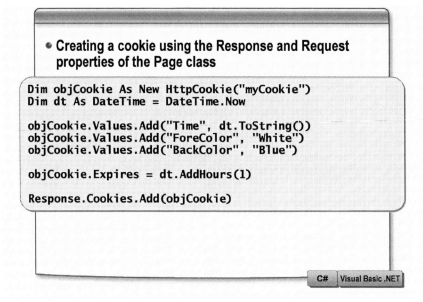

- Creating a cookie using the Response and Request properties of the Page class

```
Dim objCookie As New HttpCookie("myCookie")
Dim dt As DateTime = DateTime.Now

objCookie.Values.Add("Time", dt.ToString())
objCookie.Values.Add("ForeColor", "White")
objCookie.Values.Add("BackColor", "Blue")

objCookie.Expires = dt.AddHours(1)

Response.Cookies.Add(objCookie)
```

C#   Visual Basic .NET

Introduction

In ASP, you created and retrieved cookies by using the **Cookies** collection in the **Response** and **Request** objects. In ASP.NET, you can create and retrieve cookies by using the **Cookies** property of the **Response** and **Request** properties of the **Page** class. The **Cookies** property represents a collection of cookies and it returns an instance of the **HttpCookieCollection** class.

Creating a cookie in ASP

In ASP, you would use the following code to create a new cookie named **myCookie** with values for the keys **Date**, **ForeColor**, and **BackColor**:

```
Response.Cookies("myCookie")("Time") = Now
Response.Cookies("myCookie")("ForeColor") = "White"
Response.Cookies("myCookie")("BackColor") = "Blue"
```

Creating a cookie in ASP.NET

In ASP.NET, the following code creates a cookie named **myCookie**:

Visual Basic .NET

```
Dim objCookie As New HttpCookie("myCookie")
```

C#

```
HttpCookie objCookie = new HttpCookie("myCookie");
```

The following code adds key-value pairs, with values for the keys **Date**, **ForeColor**, and **BackColor**:

Visual Basic .NET

```
Dim dt As DateTime = DateTime.Now
objCookie.Values.Add("Time", dt.ToString())
objCookie.Values.Add("ForeColor", "White")
objCookie.Values.Add("BackColor", "Blue")
```

C#

```
DateTime dt = DateTime.Now;
objCookie.Values.Add("Time", dt.ToString());
objCookie.Values.Add("ForeColor", "White");
objCookie.Values.Add("BackColor", "Blue");
```

Making a cookie persistent

The following code sets the expiration time of the cookie to one hour:

Visual Basic .NET

```
objCookie.Expires = dt.AddHours(1)
```

C#

```
objCookie.Expires = dt.AddHours(1);
```

If you do not add the preceding code while creating a cookie, the cookie that is created is a temporary cookie. The temporary cookie is added to the memory of the browser, but it will not be recorded to a file. When the user shuts down the browser, the cookie is deleted from memory.

Adding the expiration time code turns a temporary cookie into a persistent cookie. The persistent cookie is saved to the hard disk. With a persistent cookie, if the user closes the browser and opens it again, the user can access the same Web page again until the persistent cookie expires. The expiration of the persistent cookie depends on the expiration time that was set in the code. In the preceding code, the persistent cookie will be deleted after one hour.

Note Persistent cookies are often used to store information about user names and user IDs so that the Web server can then identify the same users when they return to the Web site.

Adding a cookie to the cookie collection

The final step in creating a cookie is to add the new cookie to the cookie collection in the **Response** object. The following code adds the new cookie to the cookie collection of the **Response** object:

Visual Basic .NET

```
Response.Cookies.Add(objCookie)
```

C#

```
Response.Cookies.Add(objCookie);
```

Retrieving Information from a Cookie

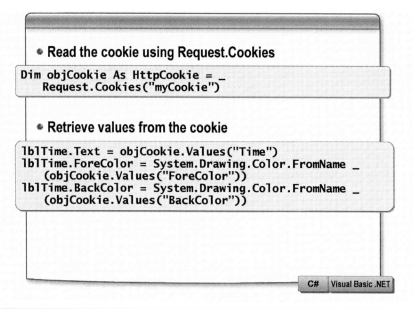

Introduction	Retrieving information from a cookie involves reading a cookie and retrieving the key-value pairs from the cookie.
Read a cookie	A cookie is returned to the server by the client in an HTTP **"Cookie:"** header. Multiple cookies, separated by semicolons, can appear in this header. To read an existing cookie, you access the cookies collection of the **Request** object, as shown in the following code:

Visual Basic

```
Dim objCookie As HttpCookie = Request.Cookies("myCookie")
```

C#

```
HttpCookie objCookie = Request.Cookies["myCookie"];
```

Retrieve values from the cookie	The following code displays the values that are retrieved from a cookie:

Visual Basic .NET

```
lblTime.Text = objCookie.Values("Time")
lblTime.ForeColor = System.Drawing.Color.FromName _
                            (objCookie.Values("ForeColor"))
lblTime.BackColor = System.Drawing.Color.FromName _
                            (objCookie.Values("BackColor"))
```

C#

```
lblTime.Text = objCookie.Values["Time"];
lblTime.ForeColor = System.Drawing.Color.FromName
                            (objCookie.Values["ForeColor"]);
lblTime.BackColor = System.Drawing.Color.FromName
                            (objCookie.Values["BackColor"]);
```

Using ViewState to Store Session Data

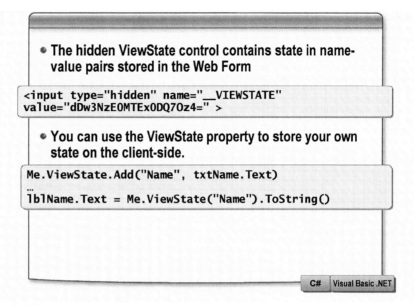

Introduction

ASP.NET uses a hidden control named __VIEWSTATE in the Web Form that records the state of the controls on the Web Form. You can also use the __VIEWSTATE hidden control to store your own data on the client-side.

Hidden fields in ASP

In ASP, you can create a hidden field and store the values in the hidden field across multiple Web requests. ASP.NET continues to support the creation of custom hidden fields, and offers a complete system for state management with the hidden __VIEWSTATE control.

The ViewState property

The **Page** class has a **ViewState** property that provides access to the **ViewState** properties that are saved in the Web Form. Using the **ViewState** property, you can add and retrieve data to the hidden __VIEWSTATE control.

The following code example shows how to store a user name, entered in a **TextBox** control, into a property named **Name**. Note that you should check for the existence of a property before creating a new one.

```
Visual Basic .NET

If Me.ViewState("Name") Is Nothing Then
  Me.ViewState.Add("Name", txtName.Text)
Else
  Me.ViewState("Name") = txtName.Text
End If
```

```
C#

if (this.ViewState["Name"] == null)
  this.ViewState.Add("Name",txtName.Text);
else
  this.ViewState["Name"] = txtName.Text;
```

The following code example shows how to retrieve a user name from the same **Name** property in the **ViewState** property and display it in a **Label** control. Note that you should check to make sure a property is present before retrieving it.

Visual Basic .NET

```
If Not (Me.ViewState("Name") Is Nothing) Then
  lblName.Text = Me.ViewState("Name").ToString()
End If
```

C#

```
if (this.ViewState["Name"] != null)
  lblName.Text = this.ViewState["Name"].ToString();
```

Practice: Using the ViewState Property

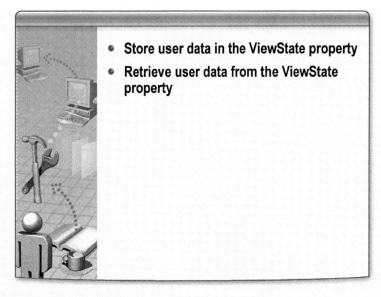

- Store user data in the ViewState property
- Retrieve user data from the ViewState property

Introduction

In this practice, you will learn how to use the **ViewState** property to store client-side state. You will modify a Web Form to store a user's name and their individual color preference.

The code for this practice is in the *install_folder*\Practices\Mod05*language* folder.

Open the practice project

1. In Microsoft Visual Studio® .NET, from the **File** menu, click **Open Solution**.

2. In the Open Solution window, click the **My Projects** shortcut.

3. Open the **Practices**, **Mod05**, and *language* folders.

4. Select **state.sln**, and then click **Open**.

Store data in the ViewState property

In the following steps you will store the user's name and color selection in the **ViewState** property.

5. Open the ViewState.aspx file in design view.

The top of this Web form will display the current user name and color choice. However, when the form first loads, the user name is blank, and there is no color choice. You will write code to make the top of the form display the user name and color from the ViewState property.

The bottom of the Web form allows the user to change the name and color by entering a new value, and clicking the appropriate button. You will write the code to make the buttons store the user's choices in the ViewState property.

6. Open the ViewState.aspx code-behind file.

7. Locate the **cmdChangeColor_Click** event handler. Before the call to the **UpdateForm** method, write code that retrieves the color selected in the **lstColor Listbox** control and stores it as a **Color** property in the **ViewState** property. Your code should look like the following:

Visual Basic .NET

```
If Me.ViewState("Color") Is Nothing Then
   Me.ViewState.Add("Color", lstColor.SelectedItem.Text)
Else
   Me.ViewState("Color") = lstColor.SelectedItem.Text
End If
```

C#

```
if (this.ViewState["Color"] == null)
   this.ViewState.Add("Color",lstColor.SelectedItem.Text);
else
   this.ViewState["Color"] = lstColor.SelectedItem.Text;
```

8. Locate the **cmdChangeName_Click** event handler. Before the call to the **UpdateForm** method, write code that stores the user name from the **txtName TextBox** control in a **Name** property in the **ViewState** property. Your code should look like the following:

Visual Basic .NET

```
If Me.ViewState("Name") Is Nothing Then
   Me.ViewState.Add("Name", txtName.Text)
Else
   Me.ViewState("Name") = txtName.Text
End If
```

C#

```
if (this.ViewState["Name"] == null)
   this.ViewState.Add("Name",txtName.Text);
else
   this.ViewState["Name"] = txtName.Text;
```

Retrieve data from the ViewState property.

In the following steps you will retrieve the user's name and color selection from the **ViewState** property.

9. Locate the **UpdateForm** method. Add code that retrieves the user name and color, assigns these values to the appropriate labels, and then changes the **ForeColor** property of the labels. When complete, your code should look like the following:

```
Visual Basic .NET

If Not (Me.ViewState("Name") Is Nothing) Then
    lblName.Text = Me.ViewState("Name").ToString()
End If
If Not (Me.ViewState("Color") Is Nothing) Then
    Dim color As String = Me.ViewState("Color").ToString()
    lblColor.Text = color
    lblName.ForeColor = _
        System.Drawing.Color.FromName(color)
    lblColor.ForeColor = _
        System.Drawing.Color.FromName(color)
End If
```

```
C#

if (this.ViewState["Name"] != null)
    lblName.Text = this.ViewState["Name"].ToString();
if (this.ViewState["Color"] != null)
{
    string color = this.ViewState["Color"].ToString();
    lblColor.Text = color;
    lblName.ForeColor =
        System.Drawing.Color.FromName(color);
    lblColor.ForeColor =
        System.Drawing.Color.FromName(color);
}
```

10. Build and browse the ViewState.aspx Web page.

11. Enter a user name and a color, and click the **Change Name**, and **Change Color** buttons.

    The top of the Web form should display the name and color you just selected.

12. Start a second browser and browse to the same URL for ViewState.aspx.

13. Enter a different user name and color, and click the **Change Name** and **Change Color** buttons.

    The top of the Web form should display the name and color you just selected. Note that the choices for this browser session are stored and tracked separately from the previous browser session.

Lab 5: Storing Application and Session Data

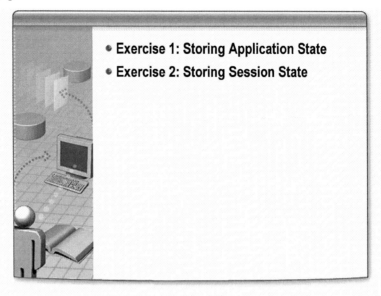

- ● Exercise 1: Storing Application State
- ● Exercise 2: Storing Session State

Objectives

After completing this lab, you will be able to:

- ■ Store application state by setting fields on the **Global** class.

- ■ Store session state by using the **Session** object.

Note This lab focuses on the concepts in this module and as a result may not comply with Microsoft security recommendations.

Prerequisites

Before working on this lab, you must have:

- ■ Knowledge of how to use Visual Studio .NET.

- ■ Knowledge of how to use Microsoft ADO.NET.

- ■ Knowledge of how to use data-bound controls.

Scenario

This lab is based on creating and managing a basic shopping basket for Web users who are accessing an online book store. The Web site has two ASP.NET Web Forms. The Books.aspx page displays a list of available books. On the Books.aspx page, the user can enter which book they want to purchase and a quantity. The user then clicks an **Add to Basket** button to add the book purchase to the shopping basket. The user can continue adding items to the basket as often as they want.

By clicking a **Show Basket** button, the user is shown the Basket.aspx page, which shows the current contents of the user's shopping basket.

Most of the functionality for retrieving the data from the SQL Server Pubs database, and then binding it to data-bound controls, is already implemented. You will focus on modifying the code that is needed to store the list of books in application state. You will also write the code that is needed to store the shopping basket information in session state.

Estimated time to complete this lab: 60 minutes

Exercise 1
Storing Application State

In this exercise, you will modify the Global.asax file to create a **DataSet** object that contains all of the book titles that are in the Pubs database. You will then store the **DataSet** object in application state for use by all browser sessions.

▶ **Open the Lab05 Solution**

1. In Visual Studio .NET, from the **File** menu, click **Open Solution**.
2. In the Open Solution window, click the **My Projects** shortcut.
3. Open the **Labfiles**, **Lab05**, *language*, and **Starter** folders.
4. Select **Lab05.sln**, and then click **Open**.

▶ **Modify Global.asax to store a DataSet in application state**

1. Open the Global.asax code-behind file.
2. Locate the first TODO comment at the top of the file.
3. Create a variable on the **Global** class of type **BooksDataSet** that is named **dsBooks**.

   This variable is an application state-accessible **DataSet**. Your code should look similar to the following code example:

   Visual Basic .NET

   ```
   'TODO: Add a shared BooksDataSet field
   Public Shared dsBooks As BooksDataSet = Nothing
   ```

   C#

   ```
   //TODO: Add a static BooksDataSet field
   public static BooksDataSet dsBooks=null;
   ```

4. In the **Application_Start** event handler, uncomment all of the code before the TODO comment that reads **Fill the DataSet**.

   Tip In Visual Studio .NET, you can quickly comment code by highlighting the lines of code and pressing **ctrl-k**, **ctrl-c**. You can use **ctrl-k**, **ctrl-u** to uncomment highlighted code.

5. After the TODO comment, create a new **BooksDataSet** DataSet object for **dsBooks**.

6. Call the **sqlDABooks.Fill** method to fill **dsBooks** with book data from the database.

Your completed code for Steps 5 and 6 should look similar to the following code example:

Visual Basic .NET

```
'TODO: Fill the DataSet
Global.dsBooks = New BooksDataSet()
sqlDABooks.Fill(Global.dsBooks, "Books")
```

C#

```
//TODO: Fill the DataSet
dsBooks = new BooksDataSet();
sqlDABooks.Fill(dsBooks,"Books");
```

▶ **Modify Books.aspx to bind the DataSet to the DataGrid control**

1. Open the Books.aspx code-behind file.

2. Locate the **BindBooksGrid** method.

3. In the **BindBooksGrid** method, bind the **grdBooks** DataGrid control to the **dsBooks** DataSet that you stored in application state.

Your code should look similar to the following code example:

Visual Basic .NET

```
'TODO: Bind the grdBooks DataGrid control
grdBooks.DataSource = Global.dsBooks
grdBooks.DataBind()
```

C#

```
//TODO: Bind the grdBooks DataGrid control
grdBooks.DataSource = Global.dsBooks;
grdBooks.DataBind();
```

4. Build and browse the Books.aspx page.

The **grdBooks** DataGrid control should display all of the book titles, with their corresponding prices, from the Pubs database.

Exercise 2
Storing Session State

In this exercise, you will create a shopping basket to keep track of the title and quantity information as the user adds book titles to his or her shopping basket. A **BasketDataSet** typed DataSet is provided for you that defines the records and fields of the shopping basket. You will add code to the Global.asax, Books.aspx, and Basket.aspx pages to store and retrieve the **DataSet** as the user adds, modifies, and deletes items in the shopping basket.

▶ **Modify Global.asax to create session state**

1. Open the code-behind file for Global.asax.

2. In the **Session_Start** event handler, locate the TODO comment, and create a new instance of the **BasketDataSet** class.

3. Store the **BasketDataSet** object in session state by using the identifier **Basket**, as shown in the following code example:

Visual Basic .NET

```
'TODO: Create shopping basket and store in session state

Dim dsBasket As New BasketDataSet()
Session("Basket") = dsBasket
```

C#

```
//TODO: Create shopping basket and store in session state

BasketDataSet dsBasket = new BasketDataSet();
Session["Basket"] = dsBasket;
```

▶ **Modify Books.aspx to use session state**

1. Open the Books.aspx code-behind file.

2. Locate the TODO comment in the **grdBooks_ItemCommand** event handler.

3. Uncomment all of the code before and after the TODO comment.

4. After the TODO comment, retrieve the **BasketDataSet** object from session state.

   Your code should look similar to the following code example:

   Visual Basic .NET

   ```
   'TODO: Retrieve the basket from session state
   Dim dsBasket As BasketDataSet = _
      CType(Session("Basket"), BasketDataSet)
   ```

   C#

   ```
   //TODO: Retrieve the basket from session state
   BasketDataSet dsBasket =
      (BasketDataSet) Session["Basket"];
   ```

▶ **Modify Basket.aspx to use session state**

1. Open the Basket.aspx code-behind file.

2. Locate the **BindBasketGrid** method.

3. In the **BindBasketGrid** method, retrieve the **BasketDataSet** object from session state.

4. Bind the **grdBasket** DataGrid control to the **BasketDataSet** object.

   Your completed code for Steps 3 and 4 should look similar to the following code example:

   Visual Basic .NET

   ```
   'TODO: Bind the grdBasket DataGrid control
   Dim dsBasket As BasketDataSet = _
      CType(Session("Basket"), BasketDataSet)
   grdBasket.DataSource = dsBasket
   grdBasket.DataBind()
   ```

   C#

   ```
   //TODO: Bind the grdBasket DataGrid control
   BasketDataSet dsBasket =
      (BasketDataSet) Session["Basket"];
   grdBasket.DataSource = dsBasket;
   grdBasket.DataBind();
   ```

5. In the **grdBasket_UpdateCommand** event handler, locate the TODO comment that reads **Retrieve basket from session state**.

6. Uncomment the code before and after the TODO comment.

7. After the TODO comment, retrieve the **BasketDataSet** object from session state.

   Your code should look similar to the following code example:

   Visual Basic .NET

   ```
   'TODO: Retrieve basket from session state
   Dim dsBasket As BasketDataSet = _
      CType(Session("Basket"), BasketDataSet)
   ```

   C#

   ```
   //TODO: Retrieve basket from session state
   BasketDataSet dsBasket =
      (BasketDataSet) Session["Basket"];
   ```

8. In the **grdBasket_DeleteCommand** event handler, locate the TODO comment that reads **Retrieve basket from session state**.

9. Uncomment all of the code after the TODO comment.

10. After the TODO comment, retrieve the **BasketDataSet** object from session state.

    Your code should look similar to the following code example:

    Visual Basic .NET

    ```
    'TODO: Retrieve basket from session state
    Dim dsBasket As BasketDataSet = _
       CType(Session("Basket"), BasketDataSet)
    ```

    C#

    ```
    //TODO: Retrieve basket from session state
    BasketDataSet dsBasket =
       (BasketDataSet) Session["Basket"];
    ```

11. Build and browse the Books.aspx page.

12. Add some items to the shopping basket and then view the shopping basket page.

    You should be able to edit and delete books that are in the shopping basket.

▶ **Use cookieless sessions**

1. Modify the Web.config file to use cookieless sessions.

2. Build and browse the Books.aspx page.

3. Add some items to the shopping basket, and verify that the URL contains the session identifier for the current session.

msdn training

Module 6:
Authenticating Users

Contents

Overview

- **ASP.NET Authentication Methods**
- **Implementing Windows Authentication in ASP.NET Web Applications**
- **Implementing Forms-Based Authentication in ASP.NET Web Applications**

Introduction

This module introduces the different types of authentication methods that are supported by Microsoft® ASP.NET and explains how to implement Microsoft Windows®–based and Forms-based authentication in an ASP.NET Web application.

Note The code samples in this module are provided in both Microsoft Visual Basic® .NET and C#.

Objectives

After completing this module, you will be able to:

- Describe the authentication methods that are supported by ASP.NET.

- Implement Windows-based authentication in an ASP.NET Web application.

- Implement Forms-based authentication in an ASP.NET Web application.

Lesson: ASP.NET Authentication Methods

* Comparing Authentication Methods in ASP and ASP.NET
* Multimedia: The ASP.NET Authentication Methods
* Selecting an ASP.NET Authentication Method
* Windows Authentication Methods
* Configuring Authentication, Authorization, and Impersonation in Web.config
* Practice: Selecting an ASP.NET Authentication Method

Introduction

This lesson introduces the authentication methods, supported by ASP.NET, which are used to authenticate ASP.NET Web applications.

Lesson objectives

After completing this lesson, you will be able to:

■ Compare the authentication methods that are supported by Active Server Pages (ASP) and ASP.NET.

■ Explain how ASP.NET authentication methods work.

■ Explain the Windows authentication methods.

■ Configure authentication, authorization, and impersonation in the Web.config file.

■ Select an ASP.NET authentication method to authenticate the user of an ASP.NET Web application.

Comparing Authentication Methods in ASP and ASP.NET

- **ASP authentication methods**

  - Windows-based authentication

  - Forms-based authentication

    After authentication, user identity is stored in the session state variable

    Requires users to have cookies enabled on their computers

- **ASP.NET authentication methods**

  - Windows-based authentication

  - Forms-based authentication

  - .NET Passport authentication

Introduction

In traditional ASP, there are two main choices for identifying, and therefore, authenticating, users. You can use the authentication methods that are included with Internet Information Services (IIS), which is Windows-based authentication, or you can use Forms-based authentication, which is where you would build a logon Web form, collect user information, and then store that information in Session-level variables (Session state).

In ASP.NET, Windows-based and Forms-based authentication are still the two primary methods that are used for authenticating users. However, with ASP.NET, Forms-based authentication has become much easier to implement and more powerful than it was when used with traditional ASP.

ASP Forms-based authentication

Forms-based authentication in ASP is based on a custom logon Web Form that you create. All unauthenticated users are directed to this logon Web page for authentication before they are allowed access to protected Web pages.

ASP Forms-based authentication relies on the maintenance of Session state to determine the identity of the user. After Forms-based authentication is implemented, the secured Web pages cannot be accessed by the user unless a specific Session variable is set by the ASP Web application. If this Session variable is not set, your ASP code redirects the user to a logon page.

To maintain Session state in ASP Web applications, the user must have cookies enabled on his or her browser. Therefore, Forms-based authentication will work only for those users who have cookies enabled on their computers.

ASP Forms-based authentication follows the following steps when authenticating users:

1. A client generates a request for a protected ASP Web page.

2. The IIS authentication mode is set to Anonymous access, so the request passes directly through IIS to ASP.

3. The protected Web page checks whether a valid Session variable is attached to the client's request.

   If there is no Session variable attached to the request:

   a. The protected Web page redirects the user to a logon Web page, where the user then enters the required credentials, usually a user name and a password.

   b. The application code that is in the logon Web page checks the user's credentials to confirm the user's identity, usually against the credentials that are stored in a database or in the Microsoft Active Directory® directory service. If the user is authenticated, the logon Web page creates a Session variable that contains the authentication information about the user.

   c. If authentication fails, the Web page request is returned with an Access Denied message.

   If a valid Session variable is attached to the request, the user has been authenticated to view the Web page and access is then granted to the requested, secure Web page.

ASP.NET Forms-based authentication

The following list outlines some of the benefits of using Forms-based authentication in ASP.NET. When using Forms-based authentication in ASP.NET:

- You do not need to add code to each secure Web page to prevent access to that Web page.

- All secure Web Forms are listed in the ASP.NET Web application's Web.config file.

- The Web.config file lists the name of the logon Web Form.

- ASP.NET automatically redirects unauthenticated users to the logon Web page and appends the name of the originally requested Web page in the Uniform Resource Locator (URL).

Multimedia: The ASP.NET Authentication Methods

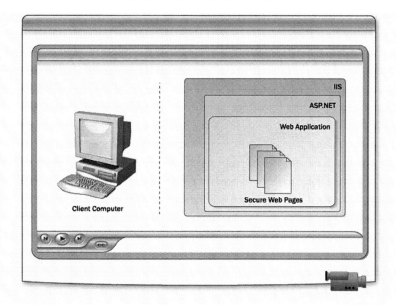

Introduction

ASP.NET implements authentication through three types of authentication methods. In this animation, you will see the following three types of authentication methods that you can use to secure ASP.NET Web applications:

- Windows-based authentication

- Forms-based authentication

- Microsoft .NET Passport authentication

Windows-based authentication

With Windows-based authentication, the ASP.NET Web application relies on the Windows operating system to authenticate the user. ASP.NET uses Windows-based authentication in conjunction with IIS authentication.

With Windows-based authentication, the user requests a secure Web page from the Web application, and the request then goes through IIS. If the user's credentials do not match those of an authorized user, IIS rejects the request. The user then has to enter his or her name and password on the logon Web page. The credentials are again verified by IIS. If the credentials match, IIS then directs the original Web page request to the Web application. The secure Web page is then returned to the user.

Forms-based authentication

In Forms-based authentication, nonauthenticated requests are redirected to a Web page by using Hypertext Transfer Protocol (HTTP) client-side redirection. The user provides credentials and submits them to the ASP.NET Web application. If the ASP.NET Web application validates the credentials on the Web page, the Web server issues an authentication cookie to the user. Subsequent requests from the user are issued with the authentication cookie in the request headers, and the user is then authenticated based on those request headers.

Microsoft .NET Passport authentication

.NET Passport authentication is a centralized authentication service, provided by Microsoft, which offers a single logon option, as well as a core profile services for member sites. Users that sign up to use .NET Passport single sign-in service (SSI) are authenticated to access Web sites by using a single .NET Passport account. .NET Passport is an XML Web service, and it is an integral part of the Microsoft .NET Framework.

Selecting an ASP.NET Authentication Method

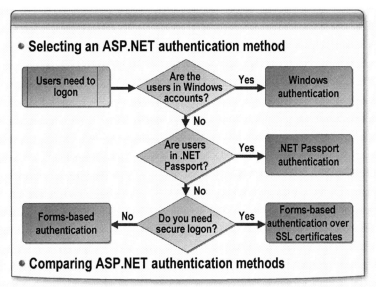

Introduction

The three authentication methods—Windows-based, Forms-based, and .NET Passport—that are supported by ASP.NET are each best suited for specific requirements. Based on the ASP.NET Web application requirements, you can then determine a suitable authentication method.

Selecting an ASP.NET authentication method

You can use the preceding flowchart to assist in selecting the most appropriate authentication method, based on the requirements of your individual ASP.NET Web application. The flowchart endpoints contain the appropriate authentication methods for specific requirements.

Comparing ASP.NET authentication methods

Each ASP.NET authentication method also has the following advantages and disadvantages:

Windows authentication

■ Advantages:

- Windows authentication uses the existing Windows infrastructure; therefore, it is most appropriate for situations in which you have a fixed number of users with existing Windows user accounts. If you are developing an intranet Web site for your organization, you can use Windows authentication. Your organization may already have Windows user accounts that are configured for each employee.

- You can use Windows authentication to control access to sensitive information. For example, you may want users in the Human Resources group to have access to directories that contain employee resumes and salary details. You can use Windows-based authentication to prevent employees in other Windows groups, such as the Developers group, from accessing these sensitive documents.

- Disadvantages:

  - Windows-based authentication requires a valid Windows user account for each user who accesses a restricted Web page.

  - Integrated Windows authentication does not work through a proxy server. Therefore, Windows-based authentication is not suitable for most Internet Web applications.

Forms-based authentication

- Advantages:

  - Forms-based authentication is an appropriate solution if you want to set up a custom user registration system for your Web application. The advantage of Forms-based authentication is that it works with most browsers and has broad support on the Internet.

- Disadvantages:

  - The primary disadvantage of Forms-based authentication is that it requires you to write the authentication logic yourself.

.NET Passport Authentication

- Advantages:

  - Users benefit from using .NET Passport authentication because they can use the same user name and password to sign in to many Internet Web sites. Therefore, users are less likely to forget their passwords. For example, both Microsoft Hotmail® and Microsoft MSN® use .NET Passport to authenticate users. You do not need to set up and maintain a database to store user registration information. Microsoft does all of that maintenance for you.

  - .NET Passport authentication provides you with templates to customize the appearance of the registration and sign-in pages of your Web application.

- Disadvantages:

  - There are two disadvantages with .NET Passport authentication. First, there is a subscription fee to use the single sign-in service. Second, .NET Passport authentication requires that each user have a valid .NET Passport account.

Windows Authentication Methods

Windows Authentication Method	Password transmission format	Usable across a proxy?	Minimum client requirements
Basic	Clear text	Yes	Most browsers
Digest	Hashed	Yes	Internet Explorer 5.5
Integrated Windows	Hashed with NTLM or Kerberos ticket	No	Internet Explorer 2.0 for NTLM; Windows 2000 and Internet Explorer 5.0 for Kerberos

Introduction

There are three types of Windows authentication that you can enable in IIS: Basic, Digest, and Integrated Windows authentication. Each authentication type has advantages and disadvantages.

About the Windows authentication methods

All three authentication methods use Windows user accounts to authenticate your Web application users. Only Digest authentication requires the presence of a Windows 2000 domain on your network and that all user accounts that are authenticated by Digest must be domain user accounts. The other Windows authentication methods, Basic and Integrated Windows, can use local or domain user accounts.

Configuring Authentication, Authorization, and Impersonation in Web.config

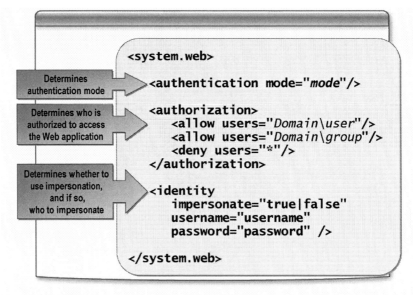

Introduction

The <system.web> section in the Web.config file specifies the root element for the ASP.NET configuration section. Within this configuration section, you can set the authentication, authorization, and impersonation options for your ASP.NET Web application.

<authentication> section

In Web.config, you set the authentication method for an ASP.NET Web application in the <authentication> subsection of the <system.web> section. The *mode* parameter is set to one of the authentication methods that are supported by ASP.NET: **Windows**, **Forms**, **Passport**, or **None**.

The following code example sets the authentication mode to **Windows**:

```
<system.web>
  <authentication mode="Windows" />
</system.web>
```

<authorization> section

In Web.config, you set the authorization parameters for an ASP.NET Web application in an <authorization> subsection of the <system.web> section.

Note Authorization settings apply to the entire Web application unless they are contained in a <location> section or child Web.config files. You will learn more about the <location> section in the topic "Securing a Single Web Page" in this lesson.

You can add multiple <allow> and <deny> sections to the <authorization> section to allow or deny access to users and roles. The meaning of a user or a role is dependent on the type of IIS authentication that your ASP.NET Web application is configured to use. For Basic and Integrated Windows authentication, users are computer or domain users, and roles are computer or domain groups.

You can specify specific users and roles in the <allow> and <deny> sections of the Web.config file. You can also use wildcard characters to control access to the categories of users, such as anonymous or unauthenticated users, as described in the following table.

Wildcard character	<allow> section	<deny> section
*	Permit access to anyone.	Deny access to anyone.
?	Permit access to anonymous users.	Deny access to unauthenticated users.

For example, the following code example denies access to all anonymous users:

```
<authorization>
  <deny users="?"/>
</authorization>
```

The following code example allows access to the users who are named Bob and Alice:

```
<authorization>
  <allow users="Domain\Bob, Domain\Alice"/>
  <deny users="*"/>
</authorization>
```

When you are allowing access to specific users or groups, it is important to remember to deny access to everyone else, as the preceding example illustrates.

Note It is not advisable to authorize users individually, because doing so may disclose sensitive information if the Web.config file is compromised.

You can enable role-based security by using the **roles** attribute. The following code example allows only users that are assigned to the Administrators role to access the ASP.NET Web application, whereas it denies access to all of the other users:

```
<authorization>
  <allow roles="Domain\Administrators"/>
  <deny users"*"/>
</authorization>
```

The ordering of the <allow> and <deny> elements in the <authorization> section is important. ASP.NET iterates through the subelements of the <authorization> section until it finds a rule that matches the current user. Therefore, the following configuration section will never permit access to anyone because the <deny> element appears first:

```
<authorization>
  <deny users"*"/>
  <allow roles="Domain\Administrators"/>
  <allow users="Domain\Bob, Domain\Alice"/>
</authorization>
```

Impersonation settings

A special Windows account named **ASPNET** is used if **impersonate** is set to **false**, which is the default value.

You use the <identity> element to enable impersonation. Impersonation allows the server to execute code under the security context of a request entity or as an anonymous user. In ASP.NET, impersonation is optional, and, by default, it is disabled.

The <identity> element must be under the <system.web> section in the Web.config or machine.config file. The following code example shows the syntax that is used with the <identity> element:

```
<identity impersonate="true|false"
    username="username"
    password="password" />
```

In the preceding code example, the **username** and **password** attributes specify the credentials to use if **impersonate** is set to **true**.

Practice: Selecting an ASP.NET Authentication Method

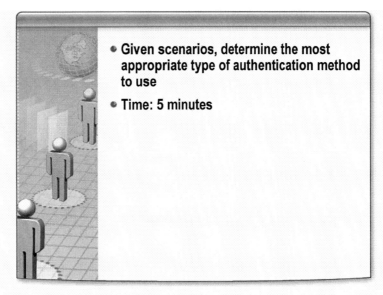

Introduction

Given the following scenarios, determine the most appropriate type of authentication method to use.

1. You want to secure a series of Web pages on a corporate intranet Web site. All of the users on the network have accounts in the Windows 2000 Active Directory.

   _____

2. You want to secure a series of Web pages that are available on the Internet. You want to control access to the Web pages by using accounts that are stored in a Microsoft SQL Server™ database.

   _____

3. You want to secure a series of Web pages that are available on the Internet. You do not have the capacity to store user information, but you want to be able to verify access to the Web pages.

   _____

Lesson: Implementing Windows Authentication in ASP.NET Web Applications

- **Enabling Windows Authentication in ASP.NET Web Applications**
- **Reading User Information**
- **Demonstration: Implementing Windows Authentication in ASP.NET Web Applications**

Introduction

In this lesson, you will learn how to implement Windows-based authentication for an ASP.NET Web application.

Lesson objectives

After completing this lesson, you will be able to:

- Describe how to enable Windows authentication for an ASP.NET Web application.

- Read the user information of an authenticated user by using Windows-based authentication.

- Implement Windows authentication for an ASP.NET Web application.

Enabling Windows Authentication in ASP.NET Web Applications

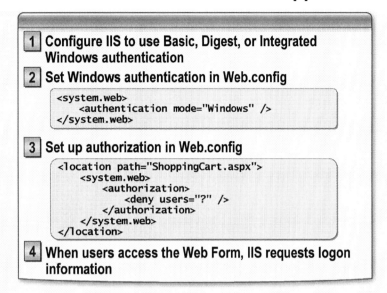

1 Configure IIS to use Basic, Digest, or Integrated Windows authentication

2 Set Windows authentication in Web.config

```
<system.web>
    <authentication mode="Windows" />
</system.web>
```

3 Set up authorization in Web.config

```
<location path="ShoppingCart.aspx">
    <system.web>
        <authorization>
            <deny users="?" />
        </authorization>
    </system.web>
</location>
```

4 When users access the Web Form, IIS requests logon information

---

Introduction

Authenticating users in ASP.NET Web applications by using Windows-based authentication is a four-step process:

1. Configure IIS.
2. Set up authentication in the Web.config file.
3. Set up authorization in the Web.config file.
4. IIS requests logon information from the user.

Configure IIS

The first step in securing ASP.NET Web applications by using Windows-based authentication involves configuring IIS by using one or more of its three authentication mechanisms:

- Basic authentication.
- Digest authentication.
- Integrated Windows authentication.

Typically, you enable either Basic authentication or Integrated Windows security. If you want your Web application to be compatible with Netscape browsers, you should use Basic authentication. If you are not using a firewall or proxy server, you can use Integrated Windows authentication.

Set up authentication

The second step in securing ASP.NET Web applications by using Windows-based authentication is to set ASP.NET security to Windows-based authentication in the Web.config file. The security settings in Web.config are included in the <authentication>, <authorization>, and <identity> sections of the Web.config file.

For an ASP.NET Web application, set the authentication method to "Windows" in the <authentication> subsection of the <system.web> section of the Web.config file, as shown in the following code example:

```
<system.web>
  <authentication mode="Windows" />
</system.web>
```

Set up authorization

The third step in securing ASP.NET Web applications by using Windows authentication is to add authorization settings to Web.config. The authorization settings arc in the <authorization>subsection of the <system.web> section.

The following code example denies all anonymous users access to all the files and subfolders that are within the SecureFiles virtual directory:

```
<location path="SecureFiles">
  <system.web>
      <authorization>
          <deny users="?" />
      </authorization>
    </system.web>
</location>
```

IIS requests logon information from users

The last step in the process of enabling Windows authentication consists of IIS requesting logon information from the user. IIS requests logon information when users try to access a Web Form from the ASP.NET Web application. The user must provide his or her user name and password. If the user's credentials are approved by IIS, the user obtains access to the requested, secure Web page.

Reading User Information

- After authentication, the Web server can read the user information from any Web page of the ASP.NET Web application

```
lblAuthUser.Text = User.Identity.Name
lblAuthType.Text =
        User.Identity.AuthenticationType
lblIsAuth.Text = User.Identity.IsAuthenticated
```

C# | Visual Basic .NET

Introduction

After the process of Windows-based authentication is complete, the Web server can read the user information from any Web page of the ASP.NET Web application. The Web server reads the user identity by using the **User.Identity.Name** property. The Web server can also identify the IIS authentication mechanism that is used to authenticate the user by using the **User.Identity.AuthenticationType** property. In addition, the Web server can also test if the user is authenticated by using **User.Identity.IsAuthenticated** property.

The following code example shows how to write the code that allows the Web server to read user information:

Visual Basic .NET

```
lblAuthUser.Text = User.Identity.Name
lblAuthType.Text = User.Identity.AuthenticationType
lblIsAuth.Text = User.Identity.IsAuthenticated
```

C#

```
lblAuthUser.Text = User.Identity.Name;
lblAuthType.Text = User.Identity.AuthenticationType;
lblIsAuth.Text = User.Identity.IsAuthenticated;
```

Note **User.Identity** is an object of the **WindowsIdentity** class.

Demonstration: Implementing Windows Authentication in ASP.NET Web Applications

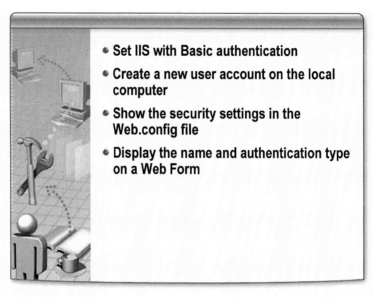

- **Set IIS with Basic authentication**
- **Create a new user account on the local computer**
- **Show the security settings in the Web.config file**
- **Display the name and authentication type on a Web Form**

Introduction

In this demonstration, you will see how to set up IIS to use Windows-based authentication by using Basic IIS authentication. You will then see how to create a new user account on the local computer, and how to set up authentication and authorization in the Web.config file. Then, you will see some demonstrations of accessing secure and nonsecure Web pages. Finally, you will be able to connect to a secure Web page on the Instructor computer.

The files for this demonstration are in the Auth solution file, which is in either the Mod06\VB\Auth or Mod06\CS\Auth folder.

▶ **To run the demonstration**

Set IIS with Basic authentication

In the following steps, you will configure IIS to use Basic authentication.

1. Right-click **My Computer**, and then click **Manage**.
2. Expand **Services and Applications**, expand **Internet Information Services**, and then click **Web Sites**.
3. Right-click **Default Web Site**, and then click **Properties**.
4. Click the **Directory Security** tab, and then click **Edit** to open the **Authentication Methods** dialog box.
5. Select the **Basic authentication (password is sent in clear text)** check box and click **Yes** in the **Internet Service Manager** dialog box.

Note Make sure that the **Anonymous access** check box is selected. Verify that the **Digest authentication for Windows domain servers** check box and the **Integrated Windows authentication** check box are cleared.

6. Type *machinename* in the **Default domain** field, because this demonstration will be done with a local account, not a domain account.

7. Click **OK** to close the **Authentication Methods** dialog box.

8. Click **OK** to close the **Default Web Site Properties** dialog box. In the **Inheritance Overrides** dialog box, click **OK**.

Create a new user account on the local computer

In the following steps, you will create a new local user account.

9. In the Computer Management console, under **System Tools**, expand **Local Users and Groups**, and then select **Users**.

10. Right-click the Users folder and then click **New User**.

Enter the following information in the **New User** dialog box.

Field Name	Value
User name	someone
Full name	someone
Description	someone demo account
Password	Secret1
Confirm password	Secret1

a. Clear the **User must change password at next logon** check box.

b. Select the **User cannot change password** check box.

c. Click **Create** and then click **Close**.

In the right-hand window of the **Computer Management** dialog box, you should see the user **someone**.

Show the security settings in the Web.config file

In the following step, you will show the Web.config file settings for the ASP.NET Web application.

11. Open the Auth solution and view the Web.config file in Microsoft Visual Studio® .NET.

There is an <authentication> section set up with Windows-based authentication.

There are two <location> sections that are needed to secure the following two Web pages: SecurePageDemo1.aspx and SecurePageDemo2.aspx. With the current IIS setting, if a user tries to access one of these Web pages, Basic authentication will be used. If a user tries to access any of the other Web pages, Anonymous authentication will be used.

Display the name and authentication type on a Web Form

In the following steps, you will demonstrate how the authentication changes that you have made affect access to the ASP.NET Web application.

12. Open the SecurePageDemo1.aspx code-behind file and explain the purpose of the properties **User.Identity.Name** and **User.Identity.AuthenticationType**.

Note   **User** is a property of the **Page** class.

---

13. Build the project.

14. Open a new browser and browse to:

Visual Basic .NET

```
http://localhost/upg/
    Mod06-VB-auth/NonSecurePageDemo.aspx
```

C#

```
http://localhost/upg/
    Mod06-CS-auth/NonSecurePageDemo.aspx
```

15. Browse to:

Visual Basic .NET

```
http://localhost/upg/Mod06-VB-auth/SecurePageDemo1.aspx
```

C#

```
http://localhost/upg/Mod06-CS-auth/SecurePageDemo1.aspx
```

16. Show that the **Connect to localhost** dialog box appears.

17. Click **Cancel** to show that you get a Server Error because access to the Web Form is denied.

18. Browse to:

Visual Basic .NET

```
http://localhost/upg/Mod06-VB-auth/SecurePageDemo2.aspx
```

C#

```
http://localhost/upg/Mod06-CS-auth/SecurePageDemo2.aspx
```

19. Show that the **Connect to localhost** dialog box also appears.

20. Type the credentials **User name** as **someone** and **Password** as **Secret1** and then click **OK**.

You should see the user name **someone** and authentication type **Basic** displayed on the SecurePageDemo2.aspx page.

You can now access any of the secured Web pages, so long as you do not close the browser. If you close the browser, you have to go through the authentication process again.

21. Browse to :

Visual Basic .NET

```
http://localhost/upg/Mod06-VB-auth/SecurePageDemo1.aspx
```

C#

```
http://localhost/upg/Mod06-CS-auth/SecurePageDemo1.aspx
```

22. Show that this time you are not asked to enter your credentials.

Lesson: Implementing Forms-Based Authentication in ASP.NET Web Applications

- Overview of Implementing Forms-Based Authentication
- Configuring the Web.config File for Forms-Based Authentication
- Creating a Logon Web Form
- Verifying User Credentials
- Hashing User Credentials
- Demonstration: Implementing Forms-Based Authentication

Introduction

In this lesson, you will learn how to implement Forms-based authentication in an ASP.NET Web application.

Lesson objectives

After completing this lesson, you will be able to:

- List the steps for implementing Forms-based authentication in ASP.NET Web applications.
- Configure Web.config for Forms-based authentication.
- Create a logon Web page.
- Verify user credentials
- Hash user credentials.
- Implement Forms-based authentication in an ASP.NET Web application.

Overview of Implementing Forms-Based Authentication

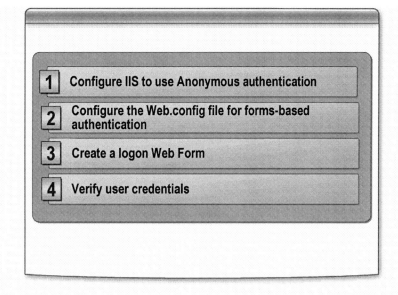

1   Configure IIS to use Anonymous authentication

2   Configure the Web.config file for forms-based authentication

3   Create a logon Web Form

4   Verify user credentials

Introduction

When a client first requests a Web page from a secure ASP.NET Web application that uses Forms-based authentication, the client is redirected to a logon Web page.

The logon Web page requires the user to enter his or her credentials, such as a user name and password. The logon Web page then verifies the user's credentials. After the user is authenticated, the logon Web page returns a cookie to the client and redirects the client to the Web page originally requested.

Implementing Forms-based authentication

Implementing Forms-based authentication involves the following steps:

1. Configuring IIS to use Anonymous authentication.

2. Configuring the Web.config file, which involves specifying the authentication mode for the ASP.NET Web application.

3. Creating a logon Web Form, which involves creating a Web Form that will collect the user's credentials.

4. Verifying the user's credentials, which involves authenticating the user and generating a cookie for the client.

   If the user is authenticated, the client is redirected to the originally requested Web page.

Important   Forms-based authentication protects only files that are handled by the aspnet_isapi application. The file types protected by the aspnet_isapi application include .aspx, asmx, ascx, and .config files. ASP files, which are handled by the asp application, are not protected by Forms-based authentication.

Configuring the Web.config File for Forms-Based Authentication

* **Web.config settings:**

```
<authentication mode = "Forms">
    <forms name="formsauth"
                loginURL="login.aspx"/>
</authentication>

<authorization>
    <deny users="?">
<authorization>
```

Introduction

To implement Forms-based authentication in ASP.NET Web applications involves:

1. Configuring the Web.config file.

2. Creating a logon Web Form.

3. Verifying user credentials.

Configuring the Web.config file

The first step in implementing Forms-based authentication is to configure the ASP.NET Web application's Web.config file. To set the ASP.NET Web application's authentication method to Forms-based, you must configure the following elements and attributes in the Web.config file:

■ Set the **mode** attribute of the **<authentication>** element to the value **Forms**.

■ Set the **name** attribute of the **<forms>** element to the suffix that will be used for the cookies.

■ Set the **loginURL** attribute of the **<forms>** element to the URL of the Web page to which unauthenticated requests are redirected.

■ Set the **users** attribute of the **<deny>** element to the value **?** to deny access to any users who are not authenticated by the ASP.NET Web application.

The following code example shows how to configure the Web.config file to set the authentication method to Forms-based for an ASP.NET Web application:

```
<authentication mode = "Forms">
  <forms name="formsauth" loginURL="login.aspx"/>
</authentication>

<authorization>
  <deny users="?">
<authorization>
```

Note The <authorization> section of the Web.config file is the same whether you use Windows-based or Forms-based authentication.

Creating a Logon Web Form

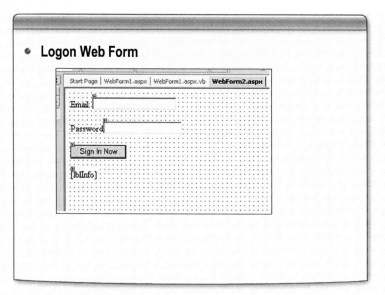

Introduction

To implement Forms-based authentication in ASP.NET Web applications involves:

1. Configuring the Web.config file.
2. Creating a logon Web Form.
3. Verifying user credentials.

The second step is to create a logon Web Form.

Creating a logon Web form

The second step in implementing Forms-based authentication is to create a logon Web Form. The logon Web Form usually consists of ASP.NET server controls that allow the users to provide their credentials and a button to which the users can use to send their user credentials to the Web server. Typically, a user's credentials include a user name and a password.

The following code is an example of what a logon Web Form looks like after it is created:

```
<form id="Login" method="post" runat="server">
  <P>Email:  <asp:TextBox id="txtEmail" runat="server">
    </asp:TextBox></P>
  <P>Password<asp:TextBox id="txtPassword" TextMode="password"
    runat="server">
    </asp:TextBox></P>
  <P><asp:Button id="cmdLogin" Text="Sign In Now"
    OnClick="cmdLogin_Click" runat="server">
    </asp:Button></P>
  <P><asp:Label id="lblInfo" runat="server">
    </asp:Label></P>
</form>
```

Verifying User Credentials

- **Authenticating the user and generating a cookie for the client**
- **Redirecting the client to the requested Web page**

```
Private Sub cmdLogin_Click( ByVal sender As System.Object, _
        ByVal e As System.EventArgs) Handles cmdLogin.Click

    Dim strCustomerId As String

    'Validate User Credentials
    strCustomerId = Login(txtEmail.Text, txtPassword.Text)

    If (strCustomerId <> "") Then
        FormsAuthentication.RedirectFromLoginPage _
            (strCustomerId, False)
    Else
        lblInfo.Text = "Invalid Credentials: Please try again"
    End If

End Sub
```

C#   Visual Basic .NET

Introduction

To implement Forms-based authentication in ASP.NET Web applications involves:

1. Configuring the Web.config file.
2. Creating a logon Web Form.
3. Verifying user credentials.

Verifying user credentials

The third step in implementing Forms-based authentication is to verify the user credentials. Verifying user credentials involves writing code for the following purposes:

- Authenticating the user's credentials.
- Generating a cookie if the user's credentials are valid.
- Redirecting the client to the originally requested Web page.

The code for authenticating the user's credentials resides in an event handler of the logon Web Form. Typically, the verification code would be contained in a button's **Click** event handler.

Redirect the request

If the user's credentials are valid, you may need to redirect the client to the originally requested Web page by calling the **System.Web.Security.FormsAuthentication.RedirectFromLoginPage** method.

The **RedirectFromLoginPage** method takes two parameters: **userName**, which specifies the name of the user for Forms-based authentication purposes, and **createPersistentCookie**. If the value of **createPersistentCookie** is **true**, a *persistent authentication cookie*, which is a cookie that is written to the client file system, is created on the user's computer. Otherwise, a temporary (nonpersistent) authentication cookie is created on the user's computer.

The following example code uses a custom function named **Login** to validate the user name and password, and then calls the **RedirectFromLoginPage** method, if the user name and password are valid:

```vbnet
Visual Basic .NET

Private Sub cmdLogin_Click( _
  ByVal sender As System.Object, _
  ByVal e As System.EventArgs) _
  Handles cmdLogin.Click

  Dim strCustomerId As String
  'Validate User Credentials
  strCustomerId = Login(txtEmail.Text, txtPassword.Text)

  If (strCustomerId <> "") Then
      FormsAuthentication.RedirectFromLoginPage _
          (strCustomerId, False)
  Else
      lblInfo.Text = "Invalid Credentials: Please try again"
  End If

End Sub
```

```csharp
C#

private void cmdLogin_Click(object sender, EventArgs e)
{
  string strCustomerId;
  //Validate User Credentials
  strCustomerId = Login(txtEmail.Text, txtPassword.Text);

  if (strCustomerId != "")
  {
      FormsAuthentication.RedirectFromLoginPage
          (strCustomerId, false);
  }
  else
  {
      lblInfo.Text = "Invalid Credentials: Please try again";
  }
}
```

Hashing User Credentials

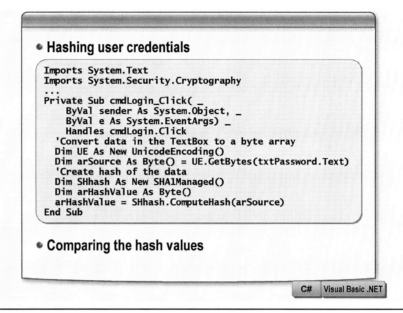

Introduction

When users provide personal information to a Web page, such as a password or credit card information, it is very important to maintain the security of this information. As a Web developer, you must use every precaution to prevent this information from being obtained and used by nonauthorized users.

In general, you should consider not saving the actual information that is provided by the user, but instead, you can save an encrypted version of the information. The .NET Framework provides a group of classes that you can use to hash, or encrypt, this type of information.

What is a hash?

A hash is a similar to a thumbprint. Your thumbprint uniquely identifies you, but by itself, it does not reveal anything about you. A hash is a unique and extremely compact numerical representation of a piece of data, and it is computationally improbable to find two distinct inputs that hash to the same value.

A hash is derived by applying a mathematical algorithm to arbitrary-length binary data that is going to be hashed. These mathematical algorithms are called *hash functions*. The result of applying the mathematical algorithm is a fixed-length hash, which is then associated with the original information.

Example of using a hash

By storing the hash of the information, rather than the information itself, you ensure information security. For example, if a Web application needs to verify that a user knows a password, you can compare the hash of the password that was entered by the user with the hash of the password that is stored by the Web application. In this scenario, the password is not stored by the Web application, only the hash is stored, thereby presenting less risk to the user because even if the system is compromised, the password itself cannot be retrieved, only the hash can be accessed.

How to verify user passwords by using hashing

The following steps describe the steps that an ASP.NET Web application, that is using Forms-based authentication, goes through to verify user passwords by using hashing:

1. The ASP.NET Web application retrieves the user name and password from the logon Web page that was submitted by the client.

2. The ASP.NET Web application hashes the user password that was obtained from the logon Web page.

3. The ASP.NET Web application queries a database to obtain the hash for the user name that was obtained from the logon Web page.

4. The ASP.NET Web application compares the hash that was obtained from the database with the resulting hash that was obtained from hashing the user password that was obtained from the logon Web page. If the hashes are the same, the user supplied the correct password.

5. If the user name and password match, the user will receive a cookie that will be used to identify them for subsequent requests. If the user name and password do not match the client is redirected to the logon Web page.

Important   Whenever you require a user to provide private information, you should use a Secure Sockets Layer (SSL) connection. For more information on SSL, see Module 8, "Protecting Communication Privacy and Data Integrity," in Course 2300, *Developing Secure Web Applications.*

Verifying user passwords by using .NET Framework Hash classes

To verify user passwords by using hashing, you must create a hash for the user password that was obtained from the logon Web page and then compare that hash to the hash that is stored in a database for that same user. The .NET Framework classes that you use to create a hash are in the **System.Security.Cryptography** namespace.

To create a hash for the user password that was obtained from the logon Web page, you call the **System.Security.Cryptography.**_classname_**.ComputeHash** method by passing in the user password as a byte array or **Stream**. The **ComputeHash** method returns a byte array that contains the hash of the user password. To compare the user password hash and the hash that was obtained from the database, thereby determining whether they are equal, you must loop through the byte arrays and compare each element.

The following code example shows how to hash a password that a user has entered in the txtPassword **TextBox** control:

```
Visual Basic .NET

Imports System.Text
Imports System.Security.Cryptography
...
Private Sub cmdLogin_Click( _
  ByVal sender As System.Object, _
  ByVal e As System.EventArgs) _
  Handles cmdLogin.Click

    'Convert data in the TextBox to a byte array
    Dim UE As New UnicodeEncoding()
    Dim arSource As Byte() = UE.GetBytes(txtPassword.Text)

    'Create hash of the data
    Dim SHhash As New SHA1Managed()
    Dim arHashValue As Byte()
    arHashValue = SHhash.ComputeHash(arSource)

End Sub
```

```
C#

using System.Text;
using System.Security.Cryptography;
...
private void cmdLogin_Click(object sender, EventArgs e)
{
    //Convert data in the TextBox to a byte array
    UnicodeEncoding UE = new UnicodeEncoding();
    byte[ ] arSource = UE.GetBytes(txtPassword.Text);

    //create hash of the data
    SHA1 SHhash = new SHA1Managed();
    byte[ ] arHashValue;
    arHashValue = SHhash.ComputeHash(arSource);
}
```

Comparing hash values   The following code example assumes that **arHash1** and **arHash2** contain two hashed values, and the code determines whether the hashed values are equal:

```
Visual Basic .NET

Dim i As Integer
Dim bSame As Boolean = True
For i = 0 To arHash1.Length - 1
  If arHash1(i) <> arHash2(i) Then
      bSame = False
      Exit For
  End If
Next
```

```
C#

int i;
bool bSame = true;
for (i = 0;i < arHash1.Length; i++)
 {
  if (arHash1(i) != arHash2(i))
  {
      bSame = false;
      break;
  }
}
```

Demonstration: Implementing Forms-Based Authentication

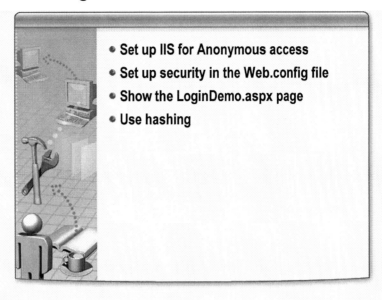

- • Set up IIS for Anonymous access
- • Set up security in the Web.config file
- • Show the LoginDemo.aspx page
- • Use hashing

Introduction

In this demonstration, you will see how to set up IIS to use Forms-based authentication with Anonymous authentication. You will then see how to set up authentication and authorization in the Web.config file. Then, you will see how the logon Web page works, along with some demonstrations of accessing secure and nonsecure Web pages. Finally, you will connect to a secure page on the Instructor computer.

The files for this demonstration are in the Auth solution file, which is in either the Mod06\VB\Auth or Mod06\CS\Auth folder.

▶ **To run the demonstration**

Set up IIS for Anonymous access

In the following steps, you will configure IIS to use only Anonymous authentication.

1. Right-click **My Computer** and then click **Manage**.
2. Navigate to **Services and Applications**, expand **Internet Information Services**, and then click **Web Sites**.
3. Right-click **Default Web Site** and click **Properties**.
4. Click the **Directory Security** tab and then click **Edit** to open the **Authentication Methods** dialog box.
5. Clear the **Basic authentication** (password is sent in clear text) check box.

Note Verify that the check boxes **Digest authentication for Windows domain servers** and **Integrated Windows authentication** are cleared and that the **Anonymous access** check box is selected.

---

6. Click **OK** to close the **Authentication Methods** dialog box, and then click **OK** again.
7. Click **OK** on the **Inheritance Overrides** dialog box.

Set up the security in the Web.config file

In the following steps, you will edit the Web.config file to use Forms-based authentication.

8. Open the Web.config file. Using the **<!--** and **-->** comments, comment the <system.web> section that contains the "Windows" authentication mode and uncomment the <system.web> section containing the authentication mode "Forms."

   Explain the new <authentication> section that redirects all of the nonauthenticated requests to the LoginDemo.aspx page.

   The same two pages (SecurePageDemo1.aspx and SecurePageDemo2.aspx) have been set up as secure pages.

9. Save the changes in the Web.config file.

Show the LoginDemo.aspx page

In the following steps, you will demonstrate how the changes affect access to the Web application.

10. Open the LoginDemo.aspx.vb or the LoginDemo.aspx.cs code-behind file and show the following:

    - The **cmdLogin_Click** event handler that validates the user name and password by calling the **Login** function, and that then calls **RedirectFromLoginPage**, if the credentials are valid.

    - The first parameter of **RedirectFromLoginPage** is the user identity that you want to save in the cookie.

      During the user Session, this user identity can then be read from any page by using **User.Identity.Name**.

    - The **RedirectFromLoginPage** creates a temporary (nonpersistent) authentication cookie (second parameter is set to **false**).

    - To use **RedirectFromLoginPage**, you have to import **System.Web.Security**.

    - The code of the **Login** function. Show how the **Login** function calls the **GetPassword** stored procedure to verify the entered credentials against those credentials that are stored in the database.

    - Open SQL Server Enterprise Manager, and then open the **Northwind** database on the *Servername***MOC** instance and show the record in the **Login** table.

    Important   When you see the **Northwind** database, notice that with Forms-based authentication, unlike with Windows-based authentication, it is up to you as the developer to design and manage a database of users.

    ---

11. Build the project.

12. Open a new browser and browse to:

Visual Basic .NET

```
http://localhost/upg/
    Mod06-VB-auth/NonSecurePageDemo.aspx
```

C#

```
http://localhost/upg/
    Mod06-CS-auth/NonSecurePageDemo.aspx
```

13. Browse to:

Visual Basic .NET

```
http://localhost/upg/Mod06-VB-auth/SecurePageDemo1.aspx
```

C#

```
http://localhost/upg/Mod06-CS-auth/SecurePageDemo1.aspx
```

14. Show that you are automatically redirected to the LoginDemo.aspx page.

15. Show that the new URL contains a parameter with the URL to the SecurePageDemo1.aspx page. This parameter is needed to redirect the user to the requested Web page, if the credentials are correct.

16. Log on using the username **someone** with an invalid password, such as **password**, and then click **Sign In Now**.

    The sign-in will fail because the password is invalid.

17. Log on using the username **someone** with a password of **Secret1**, and then click **Sign In Now** again.

    You will be redirected to the SecurePageDemo1.aspx page.

18. You should see the user name **1** (which is the identity that is stored in the cookie in LoginDemo.aspx) and the authentication type **Forms** displayed on the SecurePageDemo1.aspx page.

    You can now access any of the secured Web pages, so long as you do not close the browser. If you close the browser, you have to go through the authentication process again because the cookie is temporary (non-persistent).

19. Browse to:

Visual Basic .NET

```
http://localhost/upg/Mod06-VB-auth/SecurePageDemo2.aspx
```

C#

```
http://localhost/upg/Mod06-CS-auth/SecurePageDemo2.aspx
```

20. Show that this time you are not asked to enter your credentials.

Use Hashing

In the following steps, you will change the function that is used to process the user credentials so that the Web Form uses hashing.

21. In Visual Studio .NET, open the code-behind file for LoginDemo.aspx.

22. In the **cmdLogin_Click** event handler, comment out the first line of code, which calls the **Login** function.

23. Uncomment the line of code that calls the **LoginWithHashing** function.

24. Explain what each of the main sections of the **LoginWithHashing** function do.

25. Build and browse LoginDemo.aspx and log on using the username **someone** with a password of **Secret1**.

Lab 6: Authenticating Users

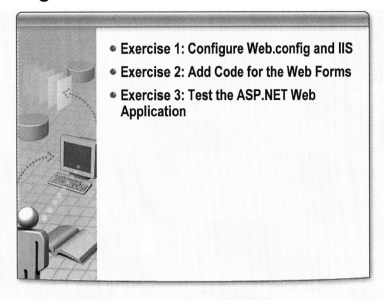

Objectives

After completing this lab, you will be able to:

- Secure Web Forms by using Forms-based authentication.

- Hash passwords and then store them in a SQL Server database.

- Retrieve hashed values from a SQL Server database.

Note This lab focuses on the concepts in this module and as a result may not comply with Microsoft security recommendations. For instance, this lab does not comply with the recommendation that secure information be transmitted by using SSL.

Prerequisites

Before working on this lab, you must have:

- Knowledge of how to use Visual Studio .NET.

- Knowledge of ASP.NET authentication methods.

- Knowledge of Microsoft ADO.NET.

Scenario

Your company wants to provide managers access to private employee information, but correspondingly, also want to ensure that non-managers cannot access this private employee information. The managers in your company use a variety of computer operating systems and browsers.

A Web Form has been created that displays the employee information in a **DataGrid** control. You must secure this page and provide a method for authenticating users, the managers, before they can access this page. The managers also want to have the ability to grant access to other users, with the intention being that only an authenticated manager would be able to add new users.

The user passwords are stored in a SQL Server database. It is important that passwords are hashed before storing them in the SQL Server database. However, you should keep user names unencrypted so that passwords can be reset by an administrator if needed.

You have been provided with the user interface (UI) portion of the Login and AddUser Web Forms. You have been asked to provide the code logic for these pages.

The files for this lab are in the *install_folder*/Labfiles/Lab06/*language*/Starter folder. The solution for this lab can be found in the *install_folder*/Labfiles/Lab06/*language*/Solution folder.

Estimated time to complete this lab: 60 minutes

Exercise 1
Configure Web.config and IIS

In this exercise, you will use the Web.config file to enable Forms-based authentication and secure two Web Forms. You will also configure IIS to allow the use of Forms-based authentication.

Scenario

You need to enable Forms-based authentication by using the Web.config file. You also want to add configuration information to the Web.config file that secures both the EmployeeInfo.aspx and the AddUser.aspx pages. If an unauthenticated user tries to access either of these pages, that user should be redirected to the Login.aspx page.

▶ **Open the Lab06 Solution**

1. In Visual Studio .NET, from the **File** menu, click **Open Solution**.

2. In the Open Solution window, in the shortcut list, click **My Projects**.

3. Expand the **Labfiles**, **Lab06**, *language*, and **Starter** folders.

4. Select **AuthLab.sln**, and then click **Open**.

▶ **Edit the Web.config file**

1. In Solution Explorer, double-click **Web.config** to open the file in the editor.

2. Add a **system.web** element that enables Forms-based authentication and directs all unauthenticated requests to Login.aspx.

   This **system.web** element contains one child element, which in turn contains one additional child element. What are the two child elements within the **system.web** section?

   _____

   _____

   _____

3. Add two **location** elements, one each for EmployeeInfo.aspx and AddUser.aspx, that will deny access to all unauthenticated users.

   What are the child elements that are within the **location** element?

   _____

   _____

   _____

4. Save the changes in the Web.config file.

   Your Web.config file should match the Web.config file in the solution project for this lab.

▶ **Configure IIS**

You need to configure the default Web site to allow anonymous access to the ASP.NET Web application and disable any other authentication methods.

1. On the **Start** menu, right-click **My Computer**, and then click **Manage**.

2. In the **Computer Management** console, expand **Services and Applications**, expand **Internet Information Services**, and then expand **Web Sites**.

3. Right-click **Default Web Site,** and then click **Properties**.

4. In the **Default Web Site Properties** dialog box, on the **Directory Security** tab, in the **Anonymous access and authentication control** section, click **Edit**.

5. In the **Authentication Methods** dialog box, verify that the **Anonymous access** check box is selected, and then clear all of the check boxes in the Authenticated access section.

   Your configuration should look like the following illustration.

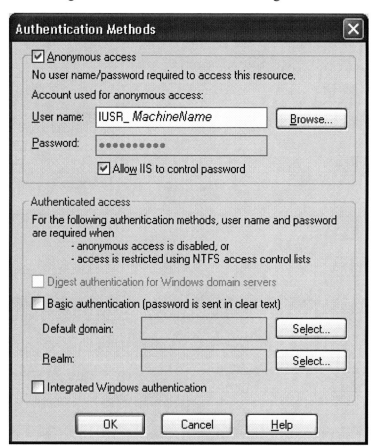

6. Click **OK** to close the **Authentication Methods** dialog box, and then click **OK** again to close the **Default Web Site Properties** dialog box.

Note If you see an **Inheritance Overrides** dialog box after making changes in the **Authentication Methods** dialog box, click **OK**.

Exercise 2
Add Code for the Web Forms

In this exercise, you will provide the code for two Web Forms: a Web Form that will be used to add new users to the database, and a logon Web Form.

In the following steps, you will add the logic that is needed to the code-behind file for Login.aspx. The **Click** event handler for the **cmdLogin** button has been added to the page. In the **Click** event handler, three functions are called. You need to add code to these three functions.

▶ **Code the Logon Web Form**

1. In Solution Explorer, right-click **Login.aspx** and choose **View Code**.

2. In the **HashPass** function, add code that hashes the password that is provided by the user.

   To complete this task, do the following steps:

   a. Create a **System.Security.Cryptography.SHA1Managed** object and a **System.Text.UnicodeEncoding** object.

   b. Create a byte array to store the results of the **UnicodeEncoding** object's **GetBytes** method. Pass the user-supplied password to the **GetBytes** method.

   c. Create a second byte array and store the results of the **SHA1Managed** object's **ComputeHash** method (to which you pass the first byte array).

   d. Return the second byte array, which contains the hashed password.

3. In the **GetStoredPass** function, add code that calls the **GetSavedPassword** stored procedure that is in the Northwind database, and retrieve the hashed password that correlates to the user name that was supplied in the username **TextBox** control.

   To complete this task, do the following steps:

   a. Create a **SqlConnection** object that uses the following connection string:

   ```
   Visual Basic .NET

   "data source=(local)\MOC; initial catalog=Northwind;
       integrated security=true"
   ```

   ```
   C#

   @"data source=(local)\MOC; initial catalog=Northwind;
       integrated security=true"
   ```

   b. Create a **SqlCommand** object that passes **GetSavedPassword** as the command text and uses the **SqlConnection** object.

   c. Set the **SqlCommand CommandType** property to **CommandType.StoredProcedure**.

   d. Add three parameters to the **SqlCommand** object. The **GetSavedPassword** stored procedure requires the following three parameters: an input parameter called **@Username**, an output parameter called **@Pword**, and a return value parameter named **@ReturnValue**.

Use the following table to create each of the three **SqlParamter** objects.

Parameter name	Parameter type and size	Parameter value
@Username	NChar (30) as Input	username TextBox.Text
@Pword	Binary (20) as Output	None
@ReturnValue	Int (4) as ReturnValue	None

e. Open the connection, run the **ExecuteNonQuery** method on the **SqlCommand** object, and then close the connection.

f. When the stored procedure matches a user name and password pair, it will return a value of **1**. If the **ReturnValue** parameter is **1**, store the **Password** parameter value as a byte array and then return the byte array. Otherwise, return **null** (**Nothing** in Visual Basic .NET).

4. View the code in the **ComparePassword** function that has been provided for you.

   This code steps through the byte array of the retrieved password and compares each value in that array to the array for the supplied password. If the passwords match, the function returns **true**; otherwise, the function returns **false**.

5. View the code in the **Click** event handler.

   The provided code completes the following steps:

   a. If the **ComparePasswords** function returns **true**, the code redirects the user to the originating page.

   b. If the user did not reach the Login page from an originating page, then the code redirects the user to the default.aspx Web Form.

▶ **Code the AddUser Web Form**

You will now add code to the AddUser.aspx Web Form. This Web Form allows authenticated users to add other uses to the SQL Server database. Similar to the Login Web Form, this new Web Form uses a stored procedure.

1. In Solution Explorer, right-click **AddUser.aspx** and choose **View Code**.

2. In the **Click** event handler for Button1, add code that performs the following steps:

   a. Hash the password that was entered in the password **TextBox** control.

      The code for this step is identical to the code that you used in the Login page for hashing the password.

   b. Create a **SqlConnection** object that uses the following connection string:

```
Visual Basic .NET

"data source=(local)\MOC; initial catalog=Northwind;
    integrated security=true"
```

```
C#

@"data source=(local)\MOC; initial catalog=Northwind;
    integrated security=true"
```

   c. Create a **SqlCommand** object that passes **AddUser** as the command text and uses the **SqlConnection** object.

   d. Set the **SqlCommand CommandType** property to **CommandType.StoredProcedure**.

   e. Add three parameters to the **SqlCommand** object.

      The **AddUser** stored procedure requires the following three parameters: an input parameter called **@Username**, an input parameter called **@Password**, and an output parameter named **@UserID**.

      Use the following table to create each of the three **SqlParamter** objects.

Parameter name	Parameter type and size	Parameter value
@Username	NChar (30) as Input	username TextBox.Text
@Password	Binary (20) as Input	hashed password
@UserID	Int (4) as Output	None

   f. Open the connection, run the **ExecuteNonQuery** method on the **SqlCommand** object, and then close the connection.

   g. If the stored procedure executes properly, display the UserID for the newly added user.

Exercise 3
Test the ASP.NET Web Application

In this exercise, you will test the security of your newly created ASP.NET Web application.

▶ **Build and browse**

1. In Solution Explorer, right-click **default.aspx** and then choose **Build and Browse**.

   The **Welcome Managers!** page displays.

2. Click the link to access the employee information.

   What happens? Why?

   _____

   _____

   If you were not redirected to the Login Web Form, check your Web.config file to ensure that the EmployeeInfo.aspx page is protected.

3. In the Login Web Form, type your name and any password, and then click the button.

   What happens?

   _____

   _____

4. In the Login Web Form, enter **someone** for a username and **Secret1** for a password, and then click the button.

   What happens? Why?

   _____

   _____

5. In Solution Explorer, right-click **default.aspx** and then choose **View in Browser**.

6. Click the **Add a new user** link.

   What happens? Why?

   _____

   _____

7. Type a user name and password, and then click **Submit**.

   A message appears on the screen that the user has been added to the SQL Server database.

8. In Solution Explorer, right-click the Login page, and then choose **View in Browser**.

9. Log on as the user that you just added.

msdn®training

Module 7: Creating and Consuming XML Web Services

Contents

Microsoft®

Overview

- **Introduction to XML Web Services**
- **Creating an XML Web Service**
- **Creating an XML Web Service Client**

Introduction

The Internet has helped facilitate better communication within and between organizations by providing fast access to information. However, for many organizations, browsing data-driven Web pages does not adequately satisfy their business needs. Programmable Web sites that directly link organizations, applications, and services would better meet these business needs. This direct linking of applications is the role of the XML Web service. By linking your Web sites and applications to XML Web services, you have the opportunity to expand the functionality that your Web site offers to users.

In this module, you will learn how to call an XML Web service directly by using a browser and by proxy from a Web Form. You will also learn how to create and publish XML Web services by using Microsoft® Visual Studio® .NET.

Note The code examples in this module are provided in both Microsoft Visual Basic® .NET and C#.

Objectives

After completing this module, you will be able to:

- Explain why XML Web services were developed and how they function.
- Use the template in Visual Studio .NET to create an XML Web service.
- Create a Web reference proxy for an XML Web service Web method, and call that Web method from a Web Form.

Lesson: Introduction to XML Web Services

- **What Is an XML Web Service?**
- **Why Use XML Web Services?**
- **.NET XML Web Service Architecture**
- **Multimedia: XML Web Service Execution Model**

Introduction

XML Web services provide a simple, flexible, standards-based model that can be used to connect applications over the Internet. XML Web services allow you to take advantage of the existing Internet infrastructure and protocols that are available to integrate applications. This standards-based model allows you to integrate applications that are developed on almost any platform, operating system, or programming language.

In this lesson, you will learn why XML Web services were developed, and how they function.

Lesson objectives

After completing this lesson, you will be able to:

- Explain what an XML Web Service is.
- Explain the major difficulties of integrating Web applications over the Internet and clarify how XML Web Services address most of these issues.
- Explain the architecture of XML Web Services.
- Explain the XML Web Service execution model.

What Is an XML Web Service?

Introduction

One of the challenges that you may encounter in creating feature-rich Web sites is application integration. When creating feature-rich Web sites, you often need to link a number of independent applications into a single, easy-to-use solution. An issue that may arise when linking independent applications is that the applications that you want to combine may be found on a variety of hardware platforms, running different operating systems, and may be written in a number of different programming languages.

There are three methods for linking multiple disparate applications:

1. The simplest method is to create and maintain custom interfaces from one application to another. The problem with this model is that the number of interfaces is a multiple of the number of applications that are being linked. Each additional application added to the system requires a new link to every other application in the system.

2. An alternative method for linking applications is to add a single middleware application to handle all links between the individual applications. The advantage of this model is that each application only needs one interface to the middleware. The problem with this model is one group needs to handle and maintain the middleware to manage the conversions and security of all of the links. Additionally, the interface between the applications and the middleware is often proprietary.

3. XML Web services provide a simple, flexible, standards-based model that can be used for linking applications over the Internet. The XML Web service interface and security are handled locally, while the connection protocol is based on World Wide Web Consortium (W3C) standards.

Example

As an example of how XML Web services can be used, the preceding slide shows an ASP.NET Web Form that incorporates data from three different XML Web services:

- The Weather XML Web service might be an academic site that is running on a very small Web server that is a front end for a computer system that predates the Internet.

- The Money Exchange XML Web service might be running on a Web server farm.

- The Airfare XML Web service might be written in COBOL and running on a very large mainframe.

All of these XML Web services are contacted over the Internet by using the same Internet protocols and XML Web service model.

Why Use XML Web Services?

- **XML Web services are programmable logic accessible by standard Web protocols**

Issues with distributed applications	XML Web service features
Lack of standards	W3C standard, language and platform independent
Different data types	Uses SOAP-formatted XML
Server/client failures	Uses Request / Response Model
Connection duration	Short lived
State management	Stateless architecture
Security	Allows passwords, SSL, and encryption

Introduction

One of the challenges that you may encounter in creating feature-rich Web applications is to integrate with other applications. When the support applications are located on a variety of platforms, each using a different operating system and language, application integration can become extremely difficult.

XML Web services are designed to simplify application integration by using the Internet and standard protocols that connect distributed applications in an efficient, secure, and reliable architecture model. The Microsoft .NET XML Web services combine many of the strengths of earlier distributed object models, while adding the flexibility of the .NET environment.

XML Web services are similar to components in that they represent black-box functionality that developers can use to add features to a Web Form, to Microsoft Windows® applications, or even to another XML Web service, without the developer having to worry about how the supporting service is implemented.

Issues with distributed applications

Some of the issues that arise with distributed applications, which XML Web services are designed to mitigate, include:

- Lack of standards

    Different operating systems support different standards. Connecting disparate operating systems often involves developing custom interfaces or middleware to translate between systems.

    XML Web services are based on a W3C standard that is still evolving. As a result of this evolving standard, the generic features of XML Web services are fixed; however, new features may be added to XML Web services in the future.

    Unlike current component technologies, XML Web services do not use protocols that are specific to certain object models. XML Web services communicate by using standard Web protocols and data formats. Any server that supports these Web standards can access or host XML Web services. Because each application must translate into only one standard protocol, multiple sets of middleware are not required.

    XML Web services are designed to interact directly with other applications over the Internet. As a result, XML Web services do not have user interfaces (UIs); instead, XML Web services provide standard-defined interfaces that are called *contracts*, which describe the services that the XML Web Service provides.

    A client of an XML Web service can be written in any programming language. As a result of this language flexibility, you do not need to learn a new language every time you want to use an XML Web service.

- Different data types

    Different operating systems support different data types. Sometimes, there is not total compatibility of data types across different operating systems. Therefore, you must consider how to handle data types that are not compatible across different operating systems.

    XML Web services communicate by using standard Web data formats. All requests and responses are transmitted in SOAP-formatted XML.

    By using the Web Service Description Language (WSDL) to build links to XML Web services, data types are automatically aligned between the client and server. This automatic data marshaling avoids the translation problems that are common to many of the current component technologies.

- Server/client failures

    Because components of distributed applications are often remote, there are more possible points for client or server failure. Failure of any one of these individual points can cause the entire distributed application to fail. Therefore, you must consider how to handle server failures and the loss of server response.

    XML Web services offer structured error handling through a **Try...Catch...Finally** model. Restructured error handling allows failures in a call to an XML Web service can be actively identified and handled in the **Catch...**block. When the error cannot be handled, the **Finally...** block is used to close the connection and release resources.

■ State management

If a server is storing state on behalf of a client, and the client or server fails, then you must consider how the other computer will be notified of the failure. You also must consider if it is necessary to reclaim the resources on the server that were in use by the client.

Each request/response from the XML Web service is a new object, with a new state. As a result, XML Web services do not become locked when there are failures at the server or client.

Unless the XML Web services uses some form of state management service to maintain state between requests, state is not maintained.

Note For more information about managing state, see Module 5, "Managing State in a Microsoft ASP.NET Web Application," in Course 2640, *Upgrading Web Development Skills from ASP to Microsoft ASP.NET.*

■ Security

In distributed applications, there are a number of opportunities for security threats. Not only must you consider authentication and authorization, but you also must consider how to secure the communication between a client and a server, and how to guard against man-in-the-middle attacks, denial-of-service attacks, replay attacks, and so on.

The default protocols that are used by XML Web services are not secure.

By default, XML Web services respond to any request that includes the correct attributes. You can require passwords before access to the XML Web service is allowed to increase security by limiting access.

The SOAP protocol, which is used by XML Web services by default, uses unencrypted XML. You can use Secure Sockets Layer (SSL) to encrypt the entire message, and to encrypt specific sections of the SOAP envelope, depending on your security needs.

.NET XML Web Service Architecture

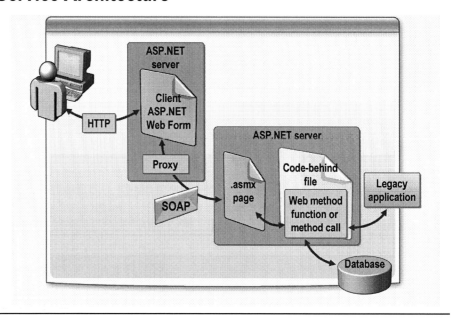

Introduction

XML Web services are designed to function as an interface between clients on the Internet and to either local Web method functions, calls to legacy applications or method calls to databases.

Note The focus of this module is on consuming a .NET XML Web service from ASP.NET Web Forms. The preceding illustration shows the .NET XML Web Service architecture. The underlying W3C version of this diagram would not necessarily show the client application type, server type, proxy, or code-behind file.

Client ASP.NET Web Form

The ASP.NET Web Form that calls an XML Web service is known as the client application. The client application does not call the XML Web service directly; instead, it uses a proxy to manage the interaction.

Proxy

A proxy is code that looks exactly like the object that it is meant to represent; however, the proxy does not contain any of the application logic. Instead, the proxy contains marshaling and transport logic. A proxy object resides on the client server, and it allows the client to access an XML Web service as if it were a local COM object.

SOAP Envelope

XML Web service requests and responses are encoded by using XML data that is structured into SOAP envelopes. The use of these standard Internet protocols allows any client application with access to the Internet to call any XML Web service.

The following is the SOAP request for the **GetForecast** Web method of the XML Web service **Weather**:

```xml
<?xml version="1.0" encoding="utf-8"?>
<soap:Envelope xmlns:xsi="http://www.w3.org/2001/XMLSchema-
instance" xmlns:xsd="http://www.w3.org/2001/XMLSchema"
xmlns:soap="http://schemas.xmlsoap.org/soap/envelope/">
  <soap:Body>
    <GetForecast xmlns="http://localhost/upg/mod07-cs-
Weather">
      <cityName>Seattle</cityName>
    </GetForecast>
  </soap:Body>
</soap:Envelope>
```

ASP.NET server

Any server can support XML Web services and any servers that can support ASP.NET Web Forms can also support .NET XML Web services.

.asmx File

Visual Studio .NET uses the same code-behind architecture with XML Web services that it uses with Web Forms. Because XML Web services do not use UI-related items, such as response objects and Web controls, the .asmx file is limited to high-level information, including a **language** attribute, a **class** attribute, and a **codeBehind** attribute.

Code-behind file

The .asmx.vb or .asmx.cs code-behind file contains the WebMethods for the XML Web service. These WebMethods can be stand-alone functions, or they can be a method that calls to a local database or to an earlier existing application.

Multimedia: XML Web Service Execution Model

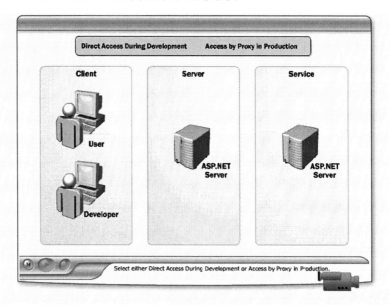

Introduction	In this animation, you will see how XML Web services interact with browsers and other Web Forms.
XML Web service model	Before an XML Web service can be accessed over the Internet, the XML Web service developer must have created a minimum XML Web service, including:

1. Created the .asmx file that includes the namespace, classes, properties, and Web methods of the XML Web service.

2. Declared at least one function or method call as a **WebMethod**, which can then be accessed over the Internet.

Access from a browser

Direct access to an XML Web service is typically only done by developers and it involves sending the Uniform Resource Locator (URL) request in Hypertext Transfer Protocol (HTTP) by using a browser. The XML Web service responds with a list of the Web methods and properties in XML. The user then has the opportunity to send a request directly to the XML Web service and to receive the results in XML.

This direct access process is not recommended for normal runtime use; however, it does allow developers to test the XML Web service's functionality.

To directly access an XML Web service from a browser:

1. The client browser issues an HTTP-GET request directly to the XML Web service.

   You can also directly access the XML Web service by using HTTP-PUT; however, you will not receive a service description.

2. The XML Web service sends the service description to the client.

   When you call an XML Web service from a browser, you are redirected to the Hypertext Markup Language (HTML) description page, which lists the methods that are included in the XML Web service.

3. Call a method of the XML Web service from the browser.

   When you call a method of an XML Web service from the browser, the protocol that is used is HTTP, and the data is returned as XML.

Access from a Web Form

ASP.NET Web Forms typically call the WebMethods of an XML Web service at runtime by using a call to a proxy on the local Web Server, which in turn calls the XML Web service.

Before the Web Form can call the XML Web service, the developer must create a WebReference to the XML Web service. The WebReference creates the XML Web service proxy source code that is contained in a .vb or .cs file.

To call an XML Web service from a Web Form during runtime:

1. The client browser issues an HTTP-GET request to the Web Form server.

2. The server parses and compiles the page.

   The page then compiles a proxy object into the Web application assembly in the /bin folder.

3. The code on the Web Form invokes the proxy to call the XML Web service.

   The proxy creates an instance of the WebReference that then calls the WebMethods of the XML Web service.

4. The Web Form uses the data that is returned by the XML Web service and a response is then sent to the client.

Lesson: Creating an XML Web Service

- **The .asmx File**
- **The .asmx Code-Behind File**
- **Demonstration: How to Create an XML Web Service**
- **Demonstration: How to Test an XML Web Service**

Introduction

In this lesson, you will learn how to use Visual Studio .NET to create an XML Web service. You will also learn how to create a Web method, and how to modify the **description** attributes to expose information about the Web method over the Internet.

Lesson objectives

After completing this lesson, you will be able to:

- Explain the elements of the .asmx file.
- Explain the elements of the .asmx.vb or asmx.cx code-behind file.
- Create an XML Web service in Visual Studio .NET.
- Test an XML Web service by using direct access from a browser.

The .asmx File

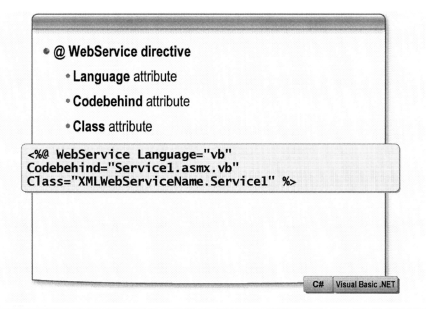

Introduction

When you create an XML Web service with Visual Studio .NET, two primary files are created that comprise the XML Web service: the *Name*.asmx file and the *Name*.asmx.vb or *Name*.asmx.cs code-behind file. The .asmx file identifies the Web page as an XML Web service, and the code-behind file contains the XML Web service logic.

.asmx file

Because there is no UI in an XML Web service, the .asmx file only contains the file type information and a directive to the code-behind file.

The code in an .asmx file is as follows:

Visual Basic .NET

```
<%@ WebService Language="vb"
Codebehind="Service1.asmx.vb"
Class="XMLWebServiceName.Service1" %>
```

C#

```
<%@ WebService Language="c#"
Codebehind="Service1.asmx.cs"
Class="XMLWebServiceName.Service1" %>
```

@ WebService directive

.asmx files have a **@ WebService** directive that specifies information about where the Web service code is located, the language in which it is written, and which class implements the Web service.

The attributes of the **@ WebService** directive are:

- **Language**

    The **Language** attribute defines the language in which the script on the Web file is written. Some of the values for this attribute are: **vb**, **c#**, and **JScript**.

- **Codebehind**

    The **Codebehind** attribute identifies the name and the location of the .asmx.vb or .asmx.cs code-behind file that contains the logic of the XML Web service.

- **Class**

    The **Class** attribute identifies the base class that supports this instance of an XML Web service.

    In a .asmx file, you must define a class that encapsulates the functionality of the XML Web service. This defined class should be public, and should inherit from the XML Web service base class.

    The XML Web service base class is **System.Web.Services.WebService**. By default, Visual Studio .NET creates the following class for a new XML Web service:

Visual Basic .NET

```
Public Class Service1
Inherits System.Web.Services.WebService
```

C#

```
public class Service1 : System.Web.Services.WebService
```

The .asmx Code-Behind File

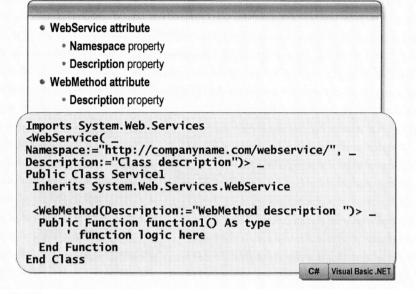

- WebService attribute
  - Namespace property
  - Description property
- WebMethod attribute
  - Description property

```
Imports System.Web.Services
<WebService( _
Namespace:="http://companyname.com/webservice/", _
Description:="Class description")> _
Public Class Service1
  Inherits System.Web.Services.WebService

  <WebMethod(Description:="WebMethod description ")> _
    Public Function function1() As type
        ' function logic here
    End Function
End Class
```

C#   Visual Basic .NET

Introduction

The code-behind file, *Name*.asmx.vb or *Name*.asmx.cs, is the file that carries the XML Web service logic. This logic can consist of a local function or a method call to another application.

Visual Studio .NET uses the same code-behind architecture with XML Web services that it uses with Web Forms. However, both XML Web services and Web Forms can be implemented by using a single file.

The following code example shows a sample XML Web service code-behind file that was created in Visual Studio .NET:

```
Visual Basic .NET

Imports System.Web.Services

<WebService(Namespace := _
  "http://organizationname.com/webservice/", Description := _
  "This XML Web Service provides math services.")> _
  Public Class Service1
      Inherits System.Web.Services.WebService

      Public Sub New()
          'CODEGEN: This call is required by the
          'ASP.NET Web Services Designer
          InitializeComponent()
      End Sub 'New

          <WebMethod(Description := _
          "This WebMethod returns a random number")> _
          Public Function RandomNumber(minValue As Integer, _
          maxValue as Integer) As Integer

          Dim r As New _
              Random(System.DateTime.Now.Millisecond)
          Return r.Next(minValue, maxValue)

      End Function 'RandomNumber

End Class 'Service1
```

```csharp
C#

using System;
using System.Collections;
using System.ComponentModel;
using System.Data;
using System.Diagnostics;
using System.Web;
using System.Web.Services;

[WebService(Namespace=
  "http://organizationname.com/webservice/",
  Description="This XML Web Service provides math services.")]

public class Service1 : System.Web.Services.WebService
{
  public Service1()
  {
      //CODEGEN: This call is required by the ASP.NET Web
Services Designer
      InitializeComponent();
  }

  [WebMethod(Description=
      "This WebMethod returns a random number")]
  public int RandomNumber(int minValue,int maxValue)
  {
      Random r = new Random(System.DateTime.Now.Millisecond);
      return r.Next(minValue,maxValue);
  }
}
```

WebService attribute

The **WebService** attribute allows you to provide additional metadata that can be used to describe your Web service.

The **WebService** attribute has the properties that are shown in the following table.

Property	Description
Description	A descriptive message for the XML Web service.
Name	The name for the XML Web service. The default value is the name of the class that is implementing the XML Web service.
Namespace	Gets or sets the default XML namespace to use for the XML Web service.

To help developers of clients for your XML Web service, you should always use the **Namespace** and **Description** properties as follows:

- **Namespace** property

  Each XML Web service requires a unique namespace, which makes it possible for client applications to differentiate among XML Web services that might use the same method name. The default namespace for XML Web services that are created in Visual Studio .NET is http://tempuri.org/. You should change the **Namespace** property to a unique name to identify your Web service, such as http://*organizationname.com/webservice*. Although the namespace resembles a typical URL, you should not assume that it is viewable in a Web browser; the namespace is merely a unique identifier.

  Note   You may want to provide a Web page at the namespace location that contains information about the XML Web services that you are providing.

- **Description** property

  The **Description** property lets the developer provide a text message that is displayed to prospective consumers of the XML Web service. This message is displayed when description documents, such as the Service Description and the Service help page, for the XML Web service are generated.

WebMethod attribute

Each method that will be exposed from the XML Web service must be contain a **WebMethod** attribute. This attribute is required to create a Web-callable method. If a method does not have the **WebMethod** attribute, the method will not be exposed by the XML Web service and it will only be available to local calls.

Visual Studio .NET creates a default **"Hello World"** Web method, which can be activated by removing the comment tags on the XML Web service page. You can edit the default Web method, or use the default Web method as a test case and add your own Web methods to the XML Web service.

An XML Web service may have more than one **WebMethod** attribute, and each **WebMethod** attribute may have one or more of the properties that are shown in the following table.

Property	Description
BufferResponse	Gets or sets whether the response for this request is buffered.
CacheDuration	Gets or sets the number of seconds the response should be held in the cache.
Description	A descriptive message describing the XML Web service method.
EnableSession	Indicates whether session state is enabled for an XML Web service method.
MessageName	The name that is used for the XML Web service method in the data that is passed to and returned from an XML Web service method.
TransactionOption	Indicates the transaction support of an XML Web service method.

Note For more information on the **WebMethod** properties, see the Visual Studio .NET Help.

Demonstration: How to Create an XML Web Service

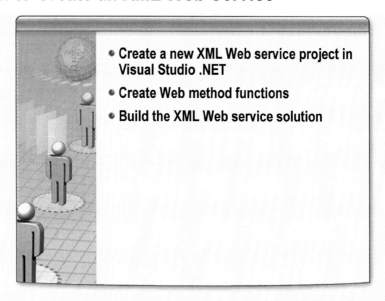

- Create a new XML Web service project in Visual Studio .NET
- Create Web method functions
- Build the XML Web service solution

Introduction

In this demonstration, you will see how to create a simple XML Web service with a **WebMethod** attribute that returns a weather forecast when you enter a city name.

Create a new XML Web service project in Visual Studio .NET

Visual Studio .NET provides templates and a default XML Web service method to help you get started in creating XML Web services.

1. Open Visual Studio .NET, and create a new **ASP.NET Web Service** project named http://localhost/upg/mod07-cs-Weather, or http://localhost/upg/mod07-vb-Weather.

    Visual Studio .NET will automatically create a number of new files and folders including those that are shown in the following table.

Files and Folders	Contents
install_folder\ mod07-*language*-Weather\Service1.sln	The solution file listing all of the files that are included in the solution.
\Inetpub\wwwroot\upg\ mod07-*language*-Weather\ Service1.asmx	The XML Web service.
\Inetpub\wwwroot\upg\ mod07-cs-Weather\Service1.asmx.vb or \Inetpub\wwwroot\upg\ mod07-vb-Weather\Service1.asmx.cs	The code-behind file containing the Web methods.
Inetpub\wwwroot\upg\ mod07-cs-Weather\ mod07-cs-Weather.csproj or Inetpub\wwwroot\upg\ mod07-vb-Weather\ mod07-vb-Weather.vbproj	The project file.

2. Open the default .asmx file, Service1.asmx, in Code view by right-clicking the file in Solution Explorer and clicking **View Code**.

   Note that the default name of the class is **Service1**, and that Visual Studio .NET has automatically opened the code-behind file, Sevice1.asmx.vb or Sevice1.asmx.cs.

3. Change or add the namespace.

   Every XML Web service needs a unique namespace for the client application to distinguish it from the other services that are on the Internet.

   By default, Visual Studio .NET XML Web services in Visual Basic .NET use http://tempuri.org/. Although http://tempura.org/ is useful for development purposes, it is not suitable for published XML Web Services.

   In Visual Studio .NET, namespaces are handled differently for Visual Basic .NET or C#:

   - Visual Basic .NET

     If you are using Visual Basic .NET, change the default URL that Visual Studio .NET provides. Modify the **Namespace** property above the **Service1** class to appear as in the following code example:

     ```
     <WebService( _
     Namespace:="http://localhost/upg/mod07-vb-Weather"> _
     Public Class Service1
     ```

   - C#

     If you are using C#, Visual Studio .NET does not generate a default namespace. Therefore, you must add a **WebService** attribute and then add the **Namespace** property to that attribute. Add the **WebService** attribute and **Namespace** property above the **Service1** class, as in the following code example:

     ```
     [WebService(
     Namespace="http://localhost/upg/mod07-cs-Weather")]
     public class Service1 : System.Web.Services.WebService
     ```

4. Add a description for the Web Service **Class**.

   Your code should look like the following:

   Visual Basic .NET

   ```
   <WebService( _
   Namespace:="http://localhost/upg/mod07-vb-Weather", _
   Description:="Provides weather services.")> _
   Public Class Service1
   ```

   C#

   ```
   [WebService(
   Namespace="http://localhost/upg/mod07-cs-Weather",
   Description="Provides weather services.")]
   public class Service1 : System.Web.Services.WebService
   ```

5. Save all of the files.

Create Web method functions

Almost any kind of function can be written as a Web method, from a simple local calculation to a complex database query.

Visual Studio .NET creates a default "HelloWorld" function on the XML Web service page. This function can be activated by removing the comment tags.

6. Uncomment the Visual Studio .NET generated "HelloWorld" Web method.

   Having this default Web method allows you to ensure that the XML Web service is functioning correctly, regardless of the status of our own Web method.

7. Add a Web method named **GetForecast** that accepts a string city name, and returns a string forecast. For the city of Seattle, return the value **Rain**. For all other cities, return the value **Forecast unavailable**.

   Your code should look similar to the following code example:

   ```
   Visual Basic .NET

   <WebMethod()> _
   Public Function GetForecast( _
         ByVal cityName As String) As String

      Select Case cityName
          Case "Seattle"
              Return "Rain"
          Case Else
              Return "Forecast unavailable"
      End Select
   End Function
   ```

   ```
   C#

   [WebMethod()]
   public string GetForecast(string cityName)
   {
      switch(cityName)
      {
          case "Seattle" :
              return "Rain";
          default:
          return "Forecast unavailable";
      }
   }
   ```

8. Add a description to the **WebMethod** directive. Your code should look like the following:

```
Visual Basic .NET

<WebMethod(Description:="Returns a weather forecast for the
given city.")> _
```

```
C#

[WebMethod(Description="Returns a weather forecast for the
given city.")]
```

9. Save the file.

Build the XML Web service solution

After your functions are written, you need to build the XML Web service solution before you can test the logic. As with Web Forms, ASP.NET compiles the XML Web service into Microsoft intermediate language (MSIL) for later execution.

10. Build the XML Web service

Building the solution updates the following files:

- \Inetpub\wwwroot\upg\mod07-*language*-Weather\bin\ mod07-*language*-Weather.dll

- \Inetpub\wwwroot\upg\mod07-*language*-Weather\bin\ mod07-*language*-Weather.pdb

Demonstration: How to Test an XML Web Service

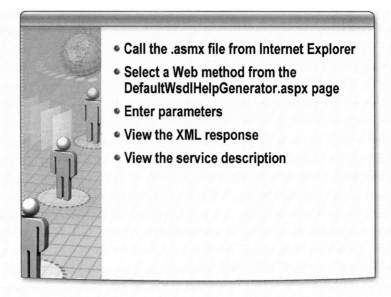

* Call the .asmx file from Internet Explorer
* Select a Web method from the DefaultWsdlHelpGenerator.aspx page
* Enter parameters
* View the XML response
* View the service description

Introduction

In this demonstration, you will see how to access the XML Web service that was created in the previous demonstration by using HTTP-GET. You will then see how to test the two available Web methods in the XML Web service.

To test an XML Web service, you can call the service directly from a browser by using HTTP-GET. This process, called *direct access*, is typically used by developers at design time to identify and test XML Web services. Direct access allows you to view the methods, properties, and output of an XML Web service in a developer-friendly environment.

You can also use the HTTP-POST protocol to access an XML Web service. Although you will not access the default page, DefaultWsdlHelpGenerator.aspx, the final response from the XML Web service will be identical to an HTTP-GET request.

Call the .asmx file from Internet Explorer

After you have identified an XML Web service to call, use the *Name*.asmx URL to navigate to the HTML description page, DefaultWsdlHelpGenerator.aspx. This page provides information about what the XML Web service does, the available Web methods that it contains, and the Web method parameters and responses that the Web methods contain. You can also use the HTML description page to test the functionality of the XML Web service.

1. Browse to the XML Web service in Microsoft Internet Explorer by viewing

   Visual Basic .NET

   ```
   http://localhost/upg/mod07-vb-Weather/Service1.asmx
   ```

   C#

   ```
   http://localhost/upg/mod07-cs-Weather/Service1.asmx
   ```

   In Visual Studio .NET, you can also view local XML Web services by right-clicking the .asmx file in Solution Explorer and then clicking **Build and Browse**. You can also view the XML Web service from Visual Studio .NET with a remote browser by right-clicking the .asmx file in Solution Explorer and then clicking **Browse with…**.

Select a Web method from the DefaultWsdlHelp Generator.aspx page

When you access the HTML description page for an XML Web service, the browser displays all of the available XML Web service Web methods.

2. Click GetForecast.

Enter parameters

To call a Web method with parameters, fill in the automatically generated form and then click **Invoke**. The Web Form passes the name of the method, the required parameters, and the values of those parameters to the URL of the XML Web service.

3. In the **cityName** field, type **Seattle**

4. Click **Invoke**.

View the XML response

XML Web services always return data in XML format.

5. Show the XML response.

View the service description

The WSDL contract or service description contains an XML description of the XML Web service and its contents.

6. Click the **Service Description** link at the top of the initial description page and show the Web service description.

Lesson: Creating an XML Web Service Client

* Using Proxies to Call XML Web Services
* Demonstration: How to Use a Proxy to Call an XML Web Service
* Handling XML Web Service Exceptions
* How to Find an XML Web Service

Introduction

To call an XML Web service programmatically from a Web Form, you need to create a proxy to manage the call. In this lesson, you will learn how to create a Web reference proxy for an XML Web service method, and then how to call the Web method from the client Web Form.

Lesson objectives

After completing this lesson, you will be able to:

- Create a proxy to call an XML Web service.
- Incorporate content from an XML Web service into your Web application.
- Handle exceptions from an XML Web service.
- Find an XML Web service by using a Universal Description, Discovery, and Integration Universal Description, Discovery, and Integration (UDDI) Web site.

Using Proxies to Call XML Web Services

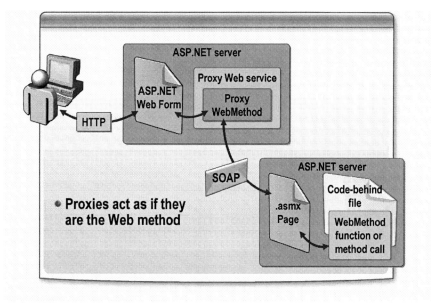

Introduction

To call an XML Web service from a Web application, you need to create a Web reference to the XML Web service in the Web Application project. The Web reference in turn creates the proxy object that is used to communicate with the XML Web service by using SOAP.

What is a proxy?

A proxy is code that looks exactly like the class that it is meant to represent, but it does not contain any of the application logic. Instead, the proxy class contains marshaling and transport logic. A proxy object allows a client to access an XML Web service as if it were a local COM object. The proxy must be on the same computer as Web application.

Visual Studio .NET automatically creates a proxy, named reference.vb or reference.cs, when you add a Web reference to an XML Web service. When you create the Web reference, Visual Studio .NET creates the reference file, which is the proxy code.

Created from the .asmx.wsdl file

Visual Studio .NET automatically creates a proxy when you select **Add Web Reference** from the **Project** menu and enter the XML Web service URL. The .asmx.wsdl file on the XML Web service server is used to identify the Web methods and parameters that are available in the XML Web service.

Changing the URL

When Visual Studio .NET creates a proxy, it sets the Web reference URL to a static location. You can change this URL at design time or runtime by using the **Url** property of the proxy. The following code example shows how to create a proxy and set the **Url** property:

Visual Basic .NET

```
Dim myProxy As New localhost.Service1()
myProxy.Url = "http://newUrl"
```

C#

```
localhost.Service1 myProxy = new localhost.Service1();
myProxy.Url = "http://newUrl";
```

Interact with SOAP

Proxies and XML Web services interact by using SOAP, which is an XML protocol that is used for exchanging structured and typed information.

Note To see a preview of the SOAP messages from an XML Web service, access the XML Web service URL directly from a browser by using HTTP-GET and review the code that is displayed by the HTML description page.

Access process

The process that a Web Form follows when accessing an XML Web service by using a proxy is:

1. The user sends a URL request to a Web Form that, in turn, requires the Web Form to call an XML Web service.

2. The Web Form instantiates the proxy, which then calls the XML Web service by using SOAP.

   The following is the SOAP request for the **GetForecast** Web method:

```
<?xml version="1.0" encoding="utf-8"?>
<soap:Envelope xmlns:xsi="http://www.w3.org/2001/XMLSchema-
instance" xmlns:xsd="http://www.w3.org/2001/XMLSchema"
xmlns:soap="http://schemas.xmlsoap.org/soap/envelope/">
  <soap:Body>
      <GetForecast xmlns="http://localhost/upg/mod07-cs-
Weather">
          <cityName>Seattle</cityName>
      </GetForecast>
  </soap:Body>
</soap:Envelope>
```

3. The XML Web service sends a response to the proxy by using SOAP.

The following is the SOAP response from the **GetForecast** XML Web method:

```
<?xml version="1.0" encoding="utf-8"?>
<soap:Envelope xmlns:xsi="http://www.w3.org/2001/XMLSchema-
instance" xmlns:xsd="http://www.w3.org/2001/XMLSchema"
xmlns:soap="http://schemas.xmlsoap.org/soap/envelope/">
  <soap:Body>
     <GetForecastResponse
xmlns="http://localhost/upg/mod07-cs-Weather">
        <GetForecastResult>Rain</GetForecastResult>
     </GetForecastResponse>
  </soap:Body>
</soap:Envelope>
```

4. The Web Form consumes the response from the XML Web service.

5. The updated Web Form is returned to the user.

Manage interactions and support asynchronous calls

When you create a proxy by using Visual Studio .NET, a number of methods and properties that support programmatic access to the XML Web service are available. The members that are available to a proxy include:

■ Members built into the proxy

The infrastructure for making asynchronous calls from a Web Form to an XML Web service is built into the proxy class, created automatically by Visual Studio .NET, when you add a Web reference. A **Begin***WebMethodName* method and an **End***WebMethodName* method are automatically created in the proxy for every Web method of the XML Web service:

- **Begin***WebMethodName*

  The **Begin** method is used to start asynchronous communication with the XML Web service method, *WebMethodName*.

- **End***WebMethodName*

  The **End** method is used to finish asynchronous communication with the XML Web service method, *WebMethodName*, and retrieve the completed reply from the XML Web service method.

For example, creating a Web reference to the **Weather** XML Web service creates a proxy with two additional methods: **BeginGetForecast** and **EndGetForecast**.

Note For more information on asynchronously calling an XML Web service, see "Communicating with XML Web Services Asynchronously" in the Visual Studio .NET documentation.

■ Members Inherited from **SoapHttpClientProtocol**

A proxy inherits a number of methods and properties from the **System.Web.Services.Protocols.SoapHttpClientProtocol** class. These methods and properties can be used to manage interactions with the XML Web service. Some of the proxy properties include:

- **Timeout**

    The **Timeout** property indicates the amount of time, in milliseconds, an XML Web service client waits for a synchronous XML Web service request to complete.

- **Url**

    The **Url** property gets or sets the base URL of the XML Web service that the client requests.

Note   For more information on **SoapHttpClientProtocol** members, see "SoapHttpClientProtocol Members" in the Visual Studio .NET documentation.

Demonstration: How to Use a Proxy to Call an XML Web Service

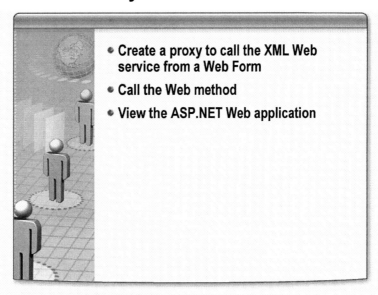

* Create a proxy to call the XML Web service from a Web Form
* Call the Web method
* View the ASP.NET Web application

Introduction

In this demonstration, you will see how to create a proxy in a Web Form to allow access to the **Weather** XML Web service that was created in a previous demonstration.

Open the demonstration project

1. In Visual Studio .NET, from the **File** menu, click **Open Solution**.

2. In the Open Solution window, in the **Look in** list, click **My Projects**.

3. Expand the **Democode, Mod07**, *language*, and **Client** folders.

4. Select **Client.sln**, and then click **Open**.

Create a proxy to call the XML Web service from a Web Form

5. On the **Project** menu, click **Add Web Reference**.

   Notice that Visual Studio .NET offers direct links to UDDI to help find production XML Web services and test XML Web services for use during development.

6. In the **Address** field of the **Add Web Reference** dialog box, type the URL of the XML Web service that you are accessing, and press ENTER:

   Visual Basic .NET

   ```
   http://localhost/upg/mod07-vb-Weather/Service1.asmx
   ```

   C#

   ```
   http://localhost/upg/mod07-cs-Weather/Service1.asmx
   ```

   Notice that Visual Studio .NET now displays the DefaultWsdlHelpGenerator.aspx page that lists all of the available Web methods. This list allows you to access these Web methods by using HTTP-GET and to review the input and output parameters.

7. Click **Add Reference**.

Visual Studio .NET creates a Web reference to the XML Web service, with the name of the server that is hosting the XML Web service.

As you created a Web reference to http://localhost/upg/ mod07-*language*-Weather/Service1.asmx, Visual Studio .NET will name the Web reference **localhost**.

Call the Web method

8. Open the Weather.aspx file in Design view.

9. Double-click the **Get Forecast** button to create a **Click** event handler.

10. In the **cmdGetForecast_Click** event handler, add the following code to create an instance of the proxy, and to call the **GetForecast** Web method.

Visual Basic .NET

```
Dim weatherProxy As New localhost.Service1()
lblForecast.Text = weatherProxy.GetForecast(txtCity.Text)
```

C#

```
localhost.Service1 weatherProxy = new localhost.Service1();
lblForecast.Text = weatherProxy.GetForecast(txtCity.Text);
```

View the ASP.NET Web application

11. Right-click the **Weather.aspx** file in Solution Explorer and click **Build and Browse**.

12. Enter **Seattle** and click the **Get Forecast** button.

The forecast of **Rain** should be displayed.

Handling XML Web Service Exceptions

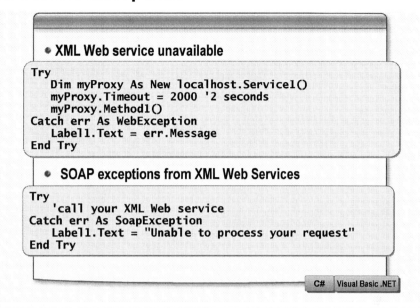

Introduction

There are two major sources of error that you can encounter when you use an XML Web service: inability to access the XML Web service, and errors that are internal to the XML Web service. Your Web Form needs to be able to identify and handle both types of errors.

XML Web service unavailable

To test the availability of an XML Web service from an ASP.NET Web Form, you need to set a timeout for the XML Web service proxy inside of a **Try…Catch…Finally** block and then handle the timeout exception:

- Set the **Timeout** parameter in the proxy

  Set the **Timeout** property of the XML Web service proxy to a value in milliseconds, as shown in the following code:

  ```
  ProxyName.Timeout = value in millisec
  ```

- Handle any timeout exceptions

  The following code calls the XML Web service, catches any timeout exception, and then displays an error message in Label1:

  Visual Basic .NET

  ```
  Try
      Dim myProxy As New localhost.Service1()
      myProxy.Timeout = 2000 '2 seconds
      'call the XML Web service
      myProxy.Method1()
  Catch err As WebException
      Label1.Text = err.Message
  End Try
  ```

```C#
try
{
    localhost.Service1 myProxy = new localhost.Service1();
    myProxy.Timeout = 2000; //2 seconds
    //call the XML Web service
    myProxy.Method1();
}
catch (WebException err)
{
    Label1.Text = err.Message;
}
```

SOAP Exceptions from XML Web services

XML Web service internal errors result in error messages from the XML Web service in the form of SOAP exceptions. If an XML Web service is unable to process a request, it may return an error message by using an instance of the **System.Web.Services** class **SoapException** object. To handle these exceptions, you need to use a **Try...Catch...Finally** statement.

The following code catches **SoapException** objects and displays an error message in Label1:

```Visual Basic .NET
Try
  'call your XML Web service
Catch err As SoapException
  Label1.Text = "Unable to process your request"
End Try
```

```C#
try
{
  //call your XML Web service
}
catch (SoapException err)
{
  Label1.Text = "Unable to process your request";
}
```

How to Find an XML Web Service

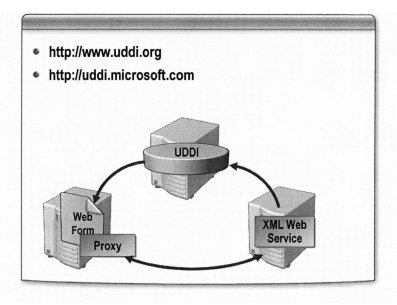

Introduction

You can find existing XML Web services to consume from your Web application by using one or more of a series of discovery services. These discovery services are evolving and changing rapidly as the development and use of XML Web services gains acceptance in the Internet community.

Finding an XML Web service

The process for finding and binding to an XML Web service is as follows:

1. The XML Web service developer publishes a description and location for their XML Web service to a UDDI Web site.

2. The Web application developer queries the UDDI Web site to find a listing of available XML Web services that meet your requirements.

3. Build a proxy object from the WSDL document.

    A proxy class is code that looks exactly like the class that it is meant to represent; however, the proxy class does not contain any of the application logic. Instead, the proxy class contains marshaling and transport logic. A proxy object allows the client Web application to access an XML Web service as if it were a local object.

4. Use the proxy object to bind the XML Web service.

UDDI specification

The UDDI specification defines a standard method for publishing and discovering information about XML Web services and the organizations that supply them.

Organizations individually register information about the XML Web services that they expose. After the information has been registered, it becomes freely available to anyone who needs to discover which XML Web services are exposed by a particular organization.

Note For more information on UDDI, see the UDDI Web site at http://www.uddi.org or the Microsoft UDDI Project Web site at http://uddi.microsoft.com

Lab 7: Creating and Consuming XML Web Services

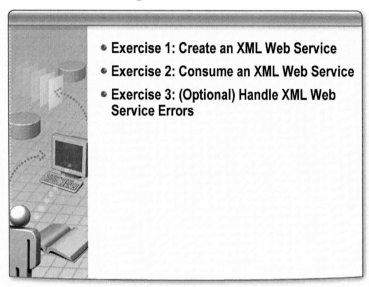

- • Exercise 1: Create an XML Web Service
- • Exercise 2: Consume an XML Web Service
- • Exercise 3: (Optional) Handle XML Web Service Errors

Objectives

After completing this lab, you will be able to:

- Create an XML Web service.
- Test an XML Web service by using a browser.
- Consume an XML Web service programmatically by using a proxy.
- (Optional) Handle XML Web service errors by using a **Try...Catch...Finally** block.

Note This lab focuses on the concepts in this module and as a result may not comply with Microsoft security recommendations.

Prerequisites

Before working on this lab, you must have:

- Knowledge of how to add a Web reference to a Web Form.
- Knowledge of how to create an XML Web service.
- Knowledge of how to call an existing XML Web service.
- Knowledge of how to create event handlers for server controls.
- Knowledge of ASP.NET structured error handling.

For more information

For detailed steps on how to complete the tasks in this lab, refer to the demonstrations in Module 7, "Creating and Consuming XML Web Services," in Course 2640, *Upgrading Web Development Skills from ASP to Microsoft ASP.NET*.

Scenario

In this lab, you will create an XML Web service that enables you to calculate payments for a loan when given a specific interest rate, number of payments, present value, future value, and payment type. You will also create a client Web page that provides a UI for a user to interact with the Web service. When the user presses a **Calculate** button, the XML Web service is called to perform the actual work. The result is then displayed back to the user.

Solution

The solution project for this lab is located in the *install_folder*\Labfiles\Lab07\ *language*\Solution folder, where *language* is CS or VB. You can also view the solution Web Form at http://localhost/upg/lab07-*language*-solution/ LoanCalculator/default.aspx.

Estimated time to complete this lab: 45 minutes

Exercise 1
Create an XML Web Service

In this exercise, you will create an XML Web Service that will calculate payment information for loans. You will create one Web method named **Pmt** that calculates the necessary payment per time period, given a specific interest rate, number of payments, present value, future value, and payment type.

▶ **Open the Lab07 Solution**

1. In Visual Studio .NET, from the **File** menu, click **Open Solution**.

2. In the Open Solution window, click the **My Projects** shortcut.

3. Expand the **Labfiles**, **Lab07**, *language*, and **Starter** folders.

4. Select **Lab07.sln**, and then click **Open**.

   This solution file contains a Web application project named **LoanCalculator** and an XML Web Service project named **FinancialServices**. The **FinancialServices** project has not been modified from its default creation state.

▶ **Create the XML Web Service**

The starter file for this lab contains the actual code to calculate interest rates. In the following steps you will rename the starter XML Web service files, add descriptions, and access the interest rate code.

1. In the **FinancialServices** project, rename the Service1.asmx file to LoanService.asmx.

2. Open the LoanService.asmx file.

3. Change the class name from **Service1** to **LoanService**. If you are using C#, you will also need to change the name of the constructor to **LoanService**.

4. In the **WebService** attribute, set the **Namespace** to **http://localhost/upg/FinancialServices/LoanService**. Set the **Description** to **This Web service performs loan related financial calculations**.

   Note   If you are using C#, you will have to add the **WebService** attribute.

5. Use the following code to create an enumeration of payment types just under the **LoanService** class declaration:

```
Visual Basic .NET

Public Class LoanService
    Inherits System.Web.Services.WebService

    Public Enum PaymentType
        BeginningOfPeriod
        EndOfPeriod
    End Enum
```

```
C#

public class LoanService : System.Web.Services.WebService
{
    public enum PaymentType

        BeginningOfPeriod,
        EndOfPeriod
```

6. Open the pmt.txt file located at
   Install_folder>\Labs\Lab07\language\Starter.

   This file contains the source code for the **Pmt** function.

7. Copy and paste the code into the LoanService.asmx file.

8. Add a **WebMethod** attribute to the **Pmt** function.

9. Set the WebMethod **Description** property for the **Pmt** method to
   Calculates the payment for a loan based on constant payments and a constant interest rate.

10. Build the project and fix any build errors that occur.

▶ **Test the XML Web Service**

In the following steps you will test your new XML Web service by directly accessing the XML Web service from a browser.

1. Use Internet Explorer to browse to http://localhost/upg/lab07-*language*/ FinancialServices/LoanService.asmx.

2. Test the **Pmt** Web method to ensure that it is operating correctly.

   You can use the values that are shown in the following table as a test.

Field	Value
rate	0.00833
numPeriods	60
presentValue	50000
futureValue	0
paymentStart	0

   The result should look like the XML shown in the following illustration.

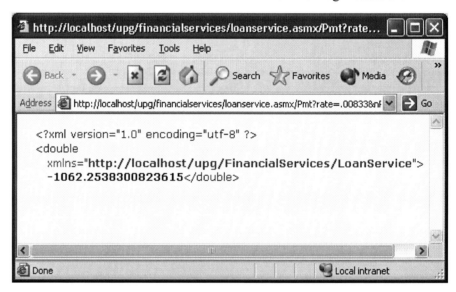

Exercise 2
Consume an XML Web Service

In this exercise, you will create a Web Form with controls to let users input loan information. When the user presses the **Calculate** button, the Web Form uses a proxy to call the **LoanService** XML Web Service that you created in Exercise 1. You will display the result from the **LoanService** XML Web Service in a **Textbox** control.

▶ **Create and call the proxy**

In the following steps you will create a Web reference to the XML Web service that you created in Exercise 1.

1. In the LoanCalculator Web application project, open the default.aspx page and note the names of the **Textbox** controls on the Web page.

2. Add a Web reference to the **LoanService** XML Web service that you created in Exercise 1.

Note   The code for Steps 3 and 4 is available in comments in the starter code. You can uncomment the code if you prefer not to type the code for these steps.

---

3. Locate the **cmdCalculate_Click** event handler, and create an instance of the **LoanService** proxy:

```
Visual Basic .NET

'Create instance of LoanService proxy
Dim proxy As New localhost.LoanService()
```

```
C#

//Create instance of LoanService proxy
localhost.LoanService proxy =
    new localhost.LoanService();
```

4. Call the **Pmt** method, passing the appropriate **Textbox** values as parameters.

5. Assign the return result to the **txtResult** textbox:

```
Visual Basic .NET

'Convert payment text type to PaymentType enumeration
Dim pt As localhost.PaymentType
pt = pt.Parse(pt.GetType(), txtPaymentType.Text)
'Call Pmt method on proxy
Dim result As Double = _
   proxy.Pmt(Convert.ToDouble(txtRate.Text), _
   Convert.ToDouble(txtNPER.Text), _
   Convert.ToDouble(txtPV.Text), _
   Convert.ToDouble(txtFV.Text), _
   pt)
'Convert result to text
txtResult.Text = result.ToString()
```

```
C#

//Convert payment text type to PaymentType enumeration
localhost.PaymentType pt;
pt = (localhost.PaymentType)
   localhost.PaymentType.Parse(
   typeof(localhost.PaymentType),
   txtPaymentType.Text);
//Call Pmt method on proxy
double result =proxy.Pmt(
   Convert.ToDouble(txtRate.Text),
   Convert.ToDouble(txtNPER.Text),
   Convert.ToDouble(txtPV.Text),
   Convert.ToDouble(txtFV.Text),
   pt);
//Convert result to text
txtResult.Text = result.ToString();
```

6. Build the project and fix any build errors that occur.

▶ **Test the XML Web Service Call**

In the following steps you will test your new **LoanCalculator** Web Form.

1. Use Internet Explorer to browse to the Web Form.

2. Test the Web Form to ensure that the call to the XML Web service is working properly.

    You can use the values from Exercise 1 as a test.

Exercise 3 (Optional)
Handle XML Web Service Errors

In this exercise, you will modify the LoanService.asmx file to throw an ArgumentException error if the loan calculation results in a NaN (not a number) result. You will also modify the LoanCalculator default Web Form to handle the generated SOAP exception by displaying the error message on the Web page.

▶ **Throw an exception**

In the following steps you will add code to the XML Web service to throw an exception when the value of the result is not a number.

1. In the **FinancialServices** project, open the LoanService.asmx file in Code view, and locate the **Pmt** WebMethod.

2. Just before the last line of code where the result is returned, add code to check the value of the result.

   If it is NaN (not a number), throw an ArgumentException error with the message **One or more arguments does not fall within the valid range**. You can use the double class's **IsNaN** method to determine if the result is NaN.

   Your code should look like the following:

```
Visual Basic .NET

If Double.IsNaN(result) Then
    Throw New ArgumentException("One or more arguments " & _
        "does not fall within the valid range.")
End If
```

```
C#

if (double.IsNaN(result))
    throw new ArgumentException("One or more arguments " +
        "does not fall within the valid range.");
```

3. Build the project and ensure that it compiles with no errors.

▶ **Handle an exception**

In the following steps you will add code to the **Catch...** block in the Web Form that handles the exception from the XML Web service.

1. In the LoanCalculator project, open the default.aspx file in Code view, and locate the **Calculate** button's click event.

2. Place all of code in this event handler inside a **Try** block.

3. Write a catch handler for the **Try...Catch...Finally** block that catches an error of type SoapException and displays the **SoapException.Message** property in the **lblError** label's **Text** property.

4. Build the project and fix any build errors that occur.

▶ **Test the error handling**

In the following steps you will test your error handling by entering invalid values into the Web Form.

1. Use Internet Explorer to browse to the Web Form.

2. Test the Web Form to ensure that the call to the XML Web service is working properly.

   You can use the values from Exercise 1 as a test.

3. Test the Web Form to ensure that the error handing is working properly.

   You can use the following values to cause a **SoapException** and test your code.

Field	Value
rate	0.00833
numPeriods	600000
presentValue	50000
futureValue	0
paymentStart	0

msdn® training

Module 8: Calling COM Components

Contents

Overview

- **ASP.NET and COM Interoperability**
- **Calling COM Objects from ASP.NET Web Forms**

Introduction

In this module, you will learn how to connect Microsoft® ASP.NET applications to existing COM objects.

Note The code examples in this module are provided in both Microsoft Visual Basic® .NET and C#.

Module objectives

After completing this module, you will be able to:

- Explain how ASP.NET and COM objects interact.
- Access a COM object from an ASP.NET Web application.

Lesson: ASP.NET and COM Interoperability

- Introduction to COM Interoperability
- ASP and ASP.NET COM Interoperability Differences
- Multimedia: The Runtime Callable Wrapper
- Overview of the Runtime Callable Wrapper

Introduction

ASP.NET Web applications can work with a number of types of applications including COM components and COM+ services. This lesson explains how ASP.NET Web applications and COM objects interact.

Lesson objectives

After completing this lesson, you will be able to:

- Explain the differences between Microsoft .NET and COM objects.

- Explain the differences between how Active Server Pages (ASP) and ASP.NET access COM objects.

- Explain how ASP.NET Web applications can access existing COM objects by using a runtime callable wrapper (RCW).

- Explain what an RCW is.

Introduction to COM Interoperability

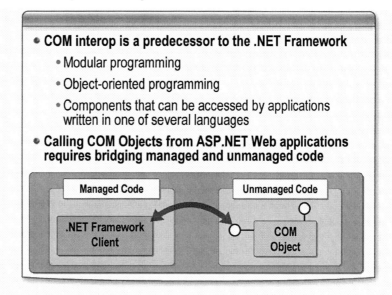

Introduction	When creating new ASP.NET Web applications or upgrading your Web site from ASP to ASP.NET, you do not need to replace your existing COM components with .NET objects. You can use your tested and functioning COM objects, and then gradually migrate individual COM components to .NET on an as-needed basis.

COM interop is a .NET predecessor

COM interop is the precursor to the Microsoft .NET Framework. COM objects are a method for reusing code that includes:

- Modular programming.

  Each COM component is a stand-alone set of functions that can be called by other functions. A single application may include a number of COM components that are shared with other applications. The same modularity is true for .NET objects.

- Object-oriented programming.

  COM components follow a simplified object model. However, COM objects are not the same as .NET objects.

- Components that can be accessed by applications that are written in one of several programming languages.

  COM components can be access by applications that are written in Visual Basic .NET and C++. .NET objects can likewise be accessed by applications that are written in any .NET-based programming language.

Bridging managed and unmanaged code

ASP.NET Web applications run as managed code in the .NET Framework. COM objects run in unmanaged code. Because of this code difference, .NET applications cannot directly access COM objects, and COM objects cannot directly access .NET objects.

ASP and ASP.NET COM Interoperability Differences

- **ASP and ASP.NET COM interoperability differences include:**

	ASP	ASP.NET
Lifetime Management	Set to **Nothing**	Garbage collection
Binding	Late binding	Early binding
Interface Access	IDispatch only	All Interfaces

Introduction

ASP and ASP.NET differ in how they interact with COM objects in several important ways.

Lifetime management

ASP handles the COM object lifetime by using exit subroutines or by setting an object reference to **Nothing** (Visual Basic Scripting Edition). Setting an object reference to **Nothing** causes the COM object to be released from memory.

In ASP.NET, the common language runtime manages the lifetime of objects in its environment and uses garbage collection to remove unreferenced objects. Therefore, setting an object reference to **Nothing** (Visual Basic .NET) or **null** (C#) does not actually remove the COM object from memory until garbage collection occurs.

Binding

ASP uses late binding to create and call COM object methods. Using late binding means that type information for a COM object is not determined until the COM object is created. This lack of type information can lead to runtime errors. For example, if you call a COM object method with the wrong number of parameters, you will not receive an error until you make the method call at runtime.

ASP.NET Web Forms use early binding by using types, from the COM object's type library, at compile time. With ASP.NET, you will know if a method call has the wrong number or types of parameters at compile time, rather than at runtime. In addition, Microsoft Visual Studio® .NET uses the type library information to provide Microsoft IntelliSense® ToolTips as you use COM types.

Interface access

ASP is limited to only the **IDispatch** interface and automation types when working with COM objects.

ASP.NET Web Forms can access all of the interfaces and types that are provided by COM objects, including custom interfaces. This compete interface access allows you to incorporate more functionality from the COM object than was possible with ASP.

Multimedia: The Runtime Callable Wrapper

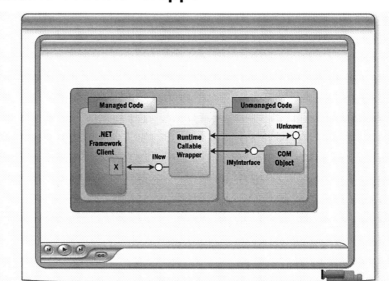

Introduction

Although COM objects have always been available to ASP, the difficulty with accessing COM objects was that you needed to create and manage your own connection between ASP code and the COM object.

ASP.NET uses .NET COM interop to create, use, and release COM objects. Because all COM objects are unmanaged code, .NET COM interop uses RCWs to make COM objects available to managed code. The purpose of the RCW is to marshal calls between a .NET Framework client and a COM object.

Animation

In this animation, you will see how a .NET client calls a COM object by using an RCW as an adapter between the .NET managed code and an unmanaged COM object.

Programming with managed code in .NET does not require you to abandon your existing code, such as COM objects. However, objects in managed code cannot directly access objects in unmanaged code. To call a COM object, the .NET runtime uses an RCW.

Creating a COM object

You create a COM Object in Visual Studio .NET, just as you would create any other managed objects, by using the **New** keyword. The .NET Framework first creates an RCW as an adapter between the .NET client and the COM object. The RCW then creates an instance of the COM object.

When you import a COM object into your project, an assembly is created that then collects all of the information that is needed to call the COM object by creating type descriptions of the COM object.

At runtime, the RCW exposes .NET interfaces that represent the COM object. These .NET interfaces support the methods, properties, and events from the COM object's interfaces. The RCW translates data formats between the .NET data types and those data types that are used by the COM object.

For an example of how the RCW translates data formats between the .NET data types and those data types that are used by the COM object, consider a COM component that receives a city name and then returns a weather report for that city:

1. The .NET client calls the method with the .NET **String** data type.

2. The RCW will translate this **String** into a **BSTR** data type, which is the COM representation of a string.

3. When the method call returns with a COM data type, the RCW translates the output parameters and the return values from the COM object into .NET types.

Releasing a COM object

Unlike ASP, setting COM objects to **Nothing** (Visual Basic .NET) or **null** (C#) does not cause the COM object to shut down in ASP.NET. The **Nothing** setting only removes the reference to the RCW. The RCW and COM object remain in memory until the runtime performs garbage collection.

Overview of the Runtime Callable Wrapper

- **Used by managed clients to call methods on a COM object**
- **Marshals method calls**
  - Converts .NET data types to and from COM data types
- **Implements COM interfaces**
  - Exposes **IDispatch** methods, properties, and events, as well as custom interfaces
  - Exposes **IErrorInfo** error data
  - Consumes **IUnknown** to identify COM objects

Introduction

The RCW is a proxy that exposes a COM object to a .NET client, such as an ASP.NET Web Form. The RCW appears to be an ordinary .NET object in your ASP.NET Web Form, but its primary function is to marshal calls between your ASP.NET code and the COM object. The RCW hides the differences between the managed .NET and unmanaged COM programming models.

The .NET runtime also creates a COM callable wrapper to reverse the process, thereby enabling a COM client to call a method on a .NET object.

Note This lesson does not cover how to expose .NET objects to COM because this is rarely done in ASP.NET. For more information on calling .NET objects from a COM client, see "COM callable wrapper" in the .NET Framework software development kit (SDK) documentation.

Calling a COM object method

To call a COM object method, the runtime uses a RCW. RCWs contain all of the information that is needed to call the COM object. The RCW maintains a cache of interface pointers on the COM object that it wraps, and the RCW then releases its reference on the COM object when the RCW is garbage collected.

Marshaling method calls

The primary function of the RCW is to marshal method calls between managed and unmanaged code. The RCW provides marshaling for method arguments and method return values whenever the client and server have different representations of the data that is passed between them. For example, when a .NET Framework client passes a **String** type as part of an argument to a managed object, the wrapper converts the **String** type to a **BSTR** type. Should the COM object return a **BSTR** type to its managed caller, the caller receives a **String** type. The RCW enables both the client and the server to send and receive the data types that are familiar to each of them. Some other types require no conversion. For instance, a standard wrapper will always pass a 4-byte integer between managed and unmanaged code without converting the type.

Implements COM interfaces

The RCW implements the same interfaces that the COM object implements, and the RCW then exposes the methods, properties, and events from the object's interfaces to .NET. The RCW also consumes the COM object interfaces that are listed in the following table.

Interface	Description
IConnectionPoint and **IConnectionPointContainer**	The RCW converts the objects that expose the connection-point event style to delegate-based events.
IDispatch	This interface is used for late binding to COM objects through Reflection.
IErrorInfo	If the COM object that is being wrapped implements the **IErrorInfo** interface, the exceptions that are generated by the RCW contain the information that is provided by the interface.
IProvideClassInfo	If the COM object that is being wrapped implements the **IProvideClassInfo** interface, the wrapper extracts the type information from this interface to provide better type identity.
IUnknown	Used by the RCW to identify the COM object, provide type coercion, and control lifetime management.
	Each interface is based on the fundamental COM interface, **IUnknown**. The methods of **IUnknown** allow navigation to the other interfaces that are exposed by the COM object.

Lesson: Calling COM Objects from ASP.NET Web Forms

- How to Call a COM Object
- Threading Models
- .NET COM Interop Error Handling
- Demonstration: .NET COM Interop

Introduction

This lesson explains how to access COM objects from an ASP.NET Web application.

Lesson objectives

After completing this lesson, you will be able to:

- Create and call methods on a COM object from an ASP.NET Web application.

- Adjust the threading model in an ASP.NET Web application to support access to a COM object.

- Manage errors from a COM object.

How to Call a COM Object

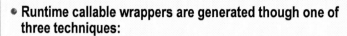

- **Runtime callable wrappers are generated though one of three techniques:**
  - Adding a reference to a COM component in a Visual Studio .NET project
  - Using the Type Library Importer
  - Creating a custom wrapper

```
Imports System.Runtime.InteropServices
...
Dim TObj As New Converter.CTemperatureClass()
Dim ITemperatureRef As Converter.ITemperature = TObj
txtCelsius.Text =
ITemperatureRef.GetCelsius(0).ToString()
Marshal.ReleaseComObject(TObj)
```

| C# | Visual Basic .NET |

Introduction

In ASP, you created a COM object by passing the programmatic identifier (PROGID) of the COM object to the **CreateObject** method. In ASP.NET, you create a COM object by using the **New** keyword, just as you would create a .NET object.

Generating runtime callable wrappers

RCWs are generated as .NET classes in an assembly. RCWs are generated in one of three ways:

- Adding a reference to a COM component in a Visual Studio .NET project

  Visual Studio .NET automatically converts the COM types that are in a type library to metadata in an assembly and references the RCW assembly that is in your project.

- Using the Type Library Importer

  The Type Library Importer provides command-line switches that can be used to adjust metadata in the assembly file, imports types from an existing type library, and generates an assembly and a namespace containing the RCW.

  The same is true for DCOM components. ASP.NET just needs a type library in order to generate the RCW.

- By creating custom wrappers

  If you need detailed control, or require high levels of performance optimization, you can create type definitions and create your own wrapper; however, this requires advanced programming skills.

Adding a reference in Visual Studio .NET

Visual Studio .NET generates an assembly that contains metadata when you add a reference to a specific type library. This reference automatically converts the COM types that are in a type library into metadata in an assembly.

To add a reference to a type library in Visual Studio .NET:

1. Install the COM DLL or EXE file manually on your computer and use Regsrv32.exe to add a component to the registry (unless a Microsoft Windows® installation program performs the installation for you).

2. In Visual Studio .NET, on the **Project** menu, click **Add Reference**.

3. Click the **COM** tab.

4. In the **Component Name** list, double-click the **type library**, and then click **OK**.

Employ the Type Library Importer

The Type Library Importer (Tlbimp.exe) is a command-line tool that converts the classes and interfaces that are contained in a COM type library into metadata. This command-line tool creates an assembly and namespace for the type information automatically. You must reference the assembly from your project to access the RCW. The Type Library Importer provides command-line switches to adjust metadata in the resulting assembly file, to import types from an existing type library, and to generate an assembly and a namespace.

While the Type Library Importer converts an entire type library to metadata at once, it cannot generate type information for a subset of the types that are defined in a type library.

To generate an assembly from a type library:

1. To produce the Loanlib.dll assembly in the **Loanlib** namespace, type the following command:

```
tlbimp Loanlib.tlb
```

2. Add the **/out:** switch to produce an assembly with an altered name, such as Loanlib_RCW.dll.

   Altering the RCW assembly name can help distinguish it from the original COM dynamic-link library (DLL). The following example uses the **/out:** switch of the Type Library Importer to alter the generated assembly's name:

```
tlbimp Loanlib.dll /out: Loanlib_RCW.dll
```

Creating custom wrappers

The advantage of creating a custom wrapper is that you can attain higher communication performance. As you understand the functions of the COM object, you can optimize the wrapper and avoid some of the restraints that are imposed by managed code.

Writing a custom wrapper is an advanced technique that you will seldom perform. However, if you need to create custom wrappers, there are two methods to accomplish this task:

- If you have access to Microsoft Interface Definition Language (MIDL) source, you can modify the MIDL source by applying type library file attributes and import the type library.

- You can apply interop-specific attributes to the imported types and generate a new assembly.

Note For additional information on generating a custom wrapper, see "Customizing Standard Wrappers" in the .NET Framework SDK documentation.

Creating the COM Object

To create a COM object, you create an instance of the RCW class. The following code example shows how to create the RCW for a temperature converter COM object:

Visual Basic .NET

```
Dim TObj as New Converter.CTemperatureClass()
```

C#

```
Converter.CTemperature TObj = new
  Converter.CTemperatureClass();
```

Using different interfaces

When you create a COM object, you can call the methods on the default interface. However, if the COM object supports other interfaces, you can use those interfaces through casting. You cast COM object interfaces just as you would .NET object interfaces. The following code example shows how to cast the temperature converter COM object to the **ITemperature** interface to call temperature-specific methods:

Visual Basic .NET

```
Dim TObj As New Converter.CTemperatureClass()
Dim ITemperatureRef As Converter.ITemperature = TObj
txtCelsius.Text = ITemperatureRef.GetCelsius(0).ToString()
```

C#

```
Converter.CTemperature TObj = new
  Converter.CTemperatureClass();
Converter.ITemperature ITemperatureRef =
  (Converter.ITemperature) TObj;
txtCelsius.Text = ITemperatureRef.GetCelsius(0).ToString();
```

Releasing the COM object

In ASP, you could set an object reference to **Nothing** to release the COM object. In ASP.NET, you can still set object references to **Nothing** (Visual Basic .NET) or to **null** (C#), but these settings do not actually release the COM object. Instead, these settings only remove the reference to the RCW. The COM object and any of the resources that it references are held in memory until garbage collection occurs. To increase scalability in your ASP.NET Web applications, you need to release COM objects as soon as possible.

To explicitly release a COM object, call the **Marshal.ReleaseComObject** method. This method will force the RCW to call the **Release** method on the COM object. Provided that there are no other references to the COM object, it will immediately remove itself from memory. You must import the **System.Runtime.InteropServices** namespace to use the Marshal class methods. The following code example shows how to release the temperature COM object:

Visual Basic .NET

```
Imports System.Runtime.InteropServices
...
Marshal.ReleaseComObject(TObj)
```

C#

```
using System.Runtime.InteropServices;
...
Marshal.ReleaseComObject(TObj);
```

Threading Models

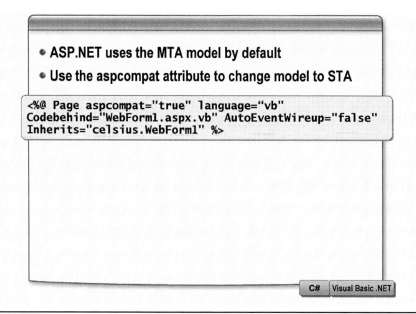

Introduction

ASP uses single-threaded apartments (STAs) that contain only one thread, whereas ASP.NET, by default, uses multithreaded apartments (MTAs).

For interoperability, the common language runtime creates and initializes an apartment when calling a COM object. A managed thread can create and enter an STA or an MTA. When a COM object's apartment model and a thread-generated apartment are compatible, COM permits the calling thread to make calls directly to the COM object. If the apartment types are incompatible, COM marshals all of the calls between the client and the COM object to ensure proper synchronization semantics.

aspcompat attribute

For the best performance, you want the client to use the same apartment model as the COM object. By default, ASP.NET uses the MTA. If you are using STA COM objects in your Web Form, you can use the **aspcompat** attribute to configure the Web Form to use an STA. The following code example shows how to set the **aspcompat** attribute in your page directive:

Visual Basic .NET

```
<%@ Page aspcompat="true" language="vb"
Codebehind="WebForm1.aspx.cs" AutoEventWireup="false"
Inherits="celsius.WebForm1" %>
```

C#

```
<%@ Page aspcompat="true" language="c#"
Codebehind="WebForm1.aspx.cs" AutoEventWireup="false"
Inherits="celsius.WebForm1" %>
```

.NET COM Interop Error Handling

- **ASP.NET uses structured exception handling for COM errors**
- **COMException class contains error information**

```
Imports System.Runtime.InteropServices
...
Try
    txtFahrenheit2.Text = _
        TObj.GetFahrenheit(- 300).ToString()

Catch exc As COMException
    txtError.Text = exc.Message
    txtHResult.Text = exc.ErrorCode.ToString()

Finally
    Marshal.ReleaseComObject(TObj)
End Try
```

C#   Visual Basic .NET

Introduction

ASP does not provide structured exception handling; therefore, you must check for any COM errors after each method call. The following code example shows how to handle COM errors in ASP. This example causes a temperature conversion error because the Celsius parameter value of -300 is below absolute zero:

```
<% On Error Resume Next
Set TObj = CreateObject("Converter.Temperature")
F = TObj.GetFahrenheit(0)
If Err.Number <> 0 Then
  Response.Write Err.Description
Else
  Response.Write F
End If
F = TObj.GetFahrenheit(-300)
If Err.Number <> 0 Then
  Response.Write Err.Description
Else
  Response.Write F
End If
%>
```

In ASP.NET, you can trap errors by using structured error handling, and if the COM object that is being wrapped implements the **IErrorInfo** interface, the exceptions that are generated by the RCW will contain the information that is provided by the interface.

A best practice is to always use a **Try...Catch...Finally** statement to ensure that if anything in the call or COM object fails, the error will be identified and the COM object will be released in the **Finally** statement. Otherwise, the COM object and any resources that it is holding will remain in memory until garbage collection occurs.

COMException class

The **COMException** class represents an error that was returned from a COM object. You can use the **COMException** class to retrieve information about the error, such as the HRESULT. If the COM object supports the **IErrorInfo** interface, this additional information is also available through the **COMException** class properties.

Note For more information on the **IErrorInfo** interface, see the online documentation.

Some of the methods of **COMException** class include those shown in the following table.

Method	Description
ErrorCode	HRESULT returned from the call.
HelpLink	If **IErrorInfo->HelpContext** is non-zero, the string is formed by concatenating **IErrorInfo->GetHelpFile** and "#" and **IErrorInfo->GetHelpContext**. Otherwise, the string is returned from **IErrorInfo->GetHelpFile**
InnerException	Always **Nothing** (Visual Basic .NET), or **null** (C#).
Message	String returned from **IErrorInfo->GetDescription**.
Source	String returned from **IErrorInfo->GetSource**.
StackTrace	The stack trace.
TargetSite	The name of the method that returned the failing HRESULT.

The following code example shows how to use structured exception handling and the **COMException** class to handle a COM error:

```
Visual Basic .NET

Imports System.Runtime.InteropServices
...
Dim TObj As New Converter.CTemperatureClass()
Try
  txtFahrenheit1.Text = TObj.GetFahrenheit(0).ToString()
  txtFahrenheit2.Text = TObj.GetFahrenheit(- 300).ToString()

Catch exc As COMException
  txtError.Text = exc.Message
  txtHResult.Text = exc.ErrorCode.ToString()

Finally
  Marshal.ReleaseComObject(TObj)

End Try
```

```
C#

using System.Runtime.InteropServices;
...
Converter.CTemperature TObj = new
  Converter.CTemperatureClass();
try
{
  txtFahrenheit1.Text = TObj.GetFahrenheit(0).ToString();
  txtFahrenheit2.Text = TObj.GetFahrenheit(-300).ToString();
}
catch (COMException exc)
{
  txtError.Text = exc.Message;
  txtHResult.Text = exc.ErrorCode.ToString();
}
finally
{
  Marshal.ReleaseComObject(TObj);
}
```

Demonstration: .NET COM Interop

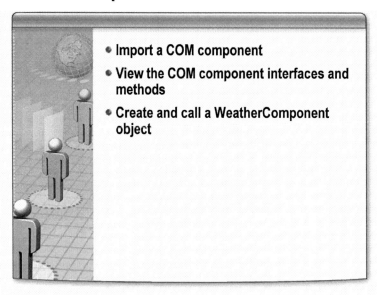

* Import a COM component
* View the COM component interfaces and methods
* Create and call a WeatherComponent object

Introduction

In this demonstration, you will see how to use .NET COM interop to create, call, and release a COM object.

The completed code for this demonstration is in the default.aspx page in the *install_folder*\Democode\Mod08*language*\Interop\Solution folder. You can perform the following steps, or optionally, open the solution code, set a breakpoint in the **cmdGetForecast_Click** event handler, and step through the code to explain it.

Open the Demonstration Project

1. In Visual Studio .NET, from the **File** menu, click **Open Solution**.

2. In the Open Solution window, in the **Look in** list, click **My Projects**.

3. Expand the **Democode, Mod08**, *language*, and **Interop** folders.

4. Select **Interop.sln**, and then click **Open**.

5. Open the default.aspx file in Design view, and explain the controls that are used to obtain a city name from the user, and to return a forecast when the user clicks the **Get Forecast** button.

Import the COM component

In the following steps you will import the COM component by adding a reference to it in Visual Studio .NET.

6. From the **Project** menu, select **Add Reference**.

7. In the **Add Reference** dialog box, perform the following steps:

   a. Select the **COM** tab.

   b. Select the **WeatherComponent 1.0 Type Library** and click **Select**. The components are listed in alphabetical order.

   c. Click **OK**.

   If you expand the **References** list in Solution Explorer, you can see that an entry exists for **WeatherComponent**.

View the COM component interfaces and methods

In the following steps, you will use the Object Browser to examine the **WeatherComponent** methods and types in .NET.

8. From the **View** menu, select **Other Windows, Object Browser**.

9. Expand **interop.weathercomponent**, and **WeatherComponent**.

10. Select the **IWeather** interface, and then in the right pane, select the **GetForecast** method.

11. Explain how the method types are shown at the bottom of the Object Browser. The types for the **GetForecast** method parameter and return value are **String**.

Create and call a WeatherComponent object

In the following steps you will create an instance of the proxy for the **WeatherComponent** COM class. You will use the proxy to create a **WeatherComponent** COM object and call the object to retrieve a forecast for the given city.

12. Open the code-behind file for default.aspx.

13. Add an **Imports** statement (Visual Basic .NET) or **using** statement (C#) for the **System.Runtime.InteropServices** namespace.

    This namespace allows you to reference the **Marshal** class in a later step.

14. Locate the **cmdGetForecast_Click** event handler.

15. Add the following code to the **cmdGetForecast_Click** event handler:

```
Visual Basic .NET

Dim weatherObject As _
    WeatherComponent.CWeatherClass = Nothing
Try
    weatherObject = New WeatherComponent.CWeatherClass()
    lblForecast.Text = _
        weatherObject.GetForecast(txtCity.Text)
Finally
    Marshal.ReleaseComObject(weatherObject)
End Try
```

```
C#

WeatherComponent.CWeatherClass weatherObject = null;
try
{
    weatherObject = new WeatherComponent.CWeatherClass();
    lblForecast.Text =
        weatherObject.GetForecast(txtCity.Text);
}
finally
{
    Marshal.ReleaseComObject(weatherObject);
}
```

16. Build and browse the default.aspx file. Enter **Seattle** for the city name and click the **Get Forecast** button. The result should be **Rain**. Any other city name should return **Forecast unavailable**.

Lab 8: Calling COM Components

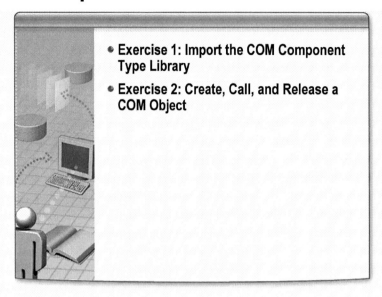

Objectives

After completing this lab, you will be able to:

- Import a COM component type library into your Visual Studio .NET project.
- Create and call a COM object by using an RCW.
- Explicitly release a COM object.

Prerequisites

Before working on this lab, you must have:

- Knowledge of how to import COM type libraries into Visual Studio .NET.
- Knowledge of how to create and call COM objects.

Solution

The solution project for this lab is located in the *install_folder*\Labfiles\Lab08*language*\Solution folder, where *language* is CS or VB. You can also view the solution Web Form at http://localhost/upg/lab08-*language*-solution/default.aspx.

Estimated time to complete this lab: 30 minutes

Exercise 1
Import the COM Component Type Library

In this exercise, you will import the type library for the Converter.dll COM component. This component contains a COM object that converts temperatures between Celsius and Fahrenheit. After importing the type library, you will use the Object Viewer to discover which interfaces and methods are available in the Converter.dll COM component.

▶ **Open the Lab08 Solution**

1. In Visual Studio .NET, from the **File** menu, click **Open Solution**.

2. In the Open Solution window, click the **My Projects** shortcut.

3. Expand the **Labfiles, Lab08,** *language*, and **Starter** folders.

4. Select **Lab08.sln**, and then click **Open**.

▶ **Import the type library**

1. From the **Project** menu, click **Add Reference**.

2. In the **Add Reference** dialog box, select the **COM** pane.

3. Locate and then click the **Converter 1.0 Type Library**, and then click the **Select** button.

4. Click **OK**.

▶ **Add the aspcompat attribute**

1. Open the default.aspx page in the designer.

2. Add the **aspcompat="true"** attribute to the **Page** directive.

▶ **View the COM object**

1. From the **View** menu, click **Other Windows, Object Browser**.

2. Expand the **interop.converter** object and locate the **ITemperature** interface.

3. Select the **ITemperature** interface and examine the methods and parameters that are declared in the interface.

Exercise 2
Create, Call, and Release a COM Object

In this exercise, you will implement **To Celsius** and **To Fahrenheit** buttons on the ASP.NET Web Form. You will create an instance of the **Converter** COM object, and call the **GetCelsius** and **GetFahrenheit** methods to perform temperature conversions. You will also add error-handling code to handle any COM exceptions that are raised by the **Converter** COM object.

▶ **Create and call the COM object**

1. Open the code-behind file for the default.aspx page and locate the **cmdToCelsius_Click** event handler.

2. In the **cmdToCelsius_Click** event handler, create a **Try...Catch...Finally** block.

3. In the **Try** block, create an instance of the **Converter** COM object.

4. Call the **GetCelsius** method, passing the **txtFahrenheit.Text** property as the parameter.

5. Assign the return value to the **txtCelsius.Text** property.

   Your code should look similar to the following code example:

   Visual Basic .NET

   ```
   Dim TObj As Converter.CTemperatureClass = Nothing
   Try
      TObj = New Converter.CTemperatureClass()
      txtCelsius.Text = TObj.GetCelsius( _
         Convert.ToDouble(txtFahrenheit.Text)).ToString()
   ```

   C#

   ```
   Converter.CTemperature TObj = null;
   try
   {
      TObj = new Converter.CTemperatureClass();
      txtCelsius.Text = TObj.GetCelsius(
         Convert.ToDouble(txtFahrenheit.Text)).ToString();
   }
   ```

▶ **Create an exception handler**

1. In the **Catch...** block, catch an exception of type **COMException**.

2. Obtain the **HRESULT** and the error message, and then assign them to the **lblError.Text** property.

   Your code should look similar to the following code example:

   Visual Basic .NET

   ```
   Catch exc As COMException
      Dim strError As New StringBuilder()
      strError.AppendFormat("HRESULT: {0:X}; ", exc.ErrorCode)
      strError.AppendFormat("Message: {0}", exc.Message)
      lblError.Text = strError.ToString()
   ```

   C#

   ```
   catch (COMException exc)
   {
      StringBuilder strError = new StringBuilder();
      strError.AppendFormat("HRESULT: {0:X}; ",exc.ErrorCode);
      strError.AppendFormat("Message: {0}",exc.Message);
      lblError.Text = strError.ToString();
   }
   ```

3. Add a second **Catch...** block to handle all other errors.

4. Assign the error message to the **lblError.Text** property.

   Your code should look similar to the following code example:

   Visual Basic .NET

   ```
   Catch
      lblError.Text = "Please enter a valid number."
   ```

   C#

   ```
   catch
   {
      lblError.Text = "Please enter a valid number.";
   }
   ```

▶ **Release the COM Object**

1. Add an **Imports** statement (Visual Basic .NET) or **using** statement (C#), for the **System.Runtime.InteropServices** namespace, to the top of the default.aspx code-behind file.

2. Return to the **cmdToCelsius_Click** event handler. In the **Finally...** block, explicitly release the COM object.

   Your code should look similar to the following code example:

   Visual Basic .NET

   ```
   Finally
      Marshal.ReleaseComObject(TObj)
   End Try
   ```

   C#

   ```
   finally
   {
      Marshal.ReleaseComObject(TObj);
   }
   ```

3. Repeat all of the steps in this exercise until this point to implement the **cmdToFahrenheit_Click** event handler.

4. Build and browse the Web Form.

5. Enter Fahrenheit or Celsius values and convert them.

   You should receive an error for any value below absolute zero (~ -273 Celsius or ~ -460 Fahrenheit). You can use the following table for test values.

Celsius	Fahrenheit
0	32
100	212
50	122
-40	-40
-300(causes error)	-500(causes error)

Course Evaluation

Your evaluation of this course will help Microsoft understand the quality of your learning experience.

At a convenient time before the end of the course, please complete a course evaluation, which is available at http://www.CourseSurvey.com.

msdn training

Module 9: Migrating ASP Web Applications to Microsoft ASP.NET

Contents

Overview

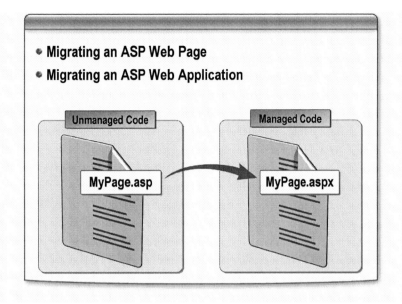

Introduction

Migrating Active Server Pages (ASP) Web pages and applications to Microsoft® ASP.NET requires more than just changing the Web page extension from .asp to .aspx. Migrating to ASP.NET also requires the changing of the programming model from unmanaged to managed code, as well as altering the Web page language from Microsoft Visual Basic® 6.0 or Microsoft Visual C++® to Visual Basic .NET or C#.

Note The code examples in this module are provided in both Visual Basic .NET and C#.

Objectives

After completing this module, you will be able to:

■ Plan and implement the migration of individual ASP Web pages to ASP.NET.

■ Plan and implement the migration of complete ASP Web applications to ASP.NET.

Lesson: Migrating an ASP Web Page

* Guidelines for Selecting a Migration Strategy
* Migrating Web Pages
* Migrating Code
* Migrating Configuration and Security

Introduction

In this lesson, you will examine the various strategies that can be used for migrating ASP Web pages to ASP.NET. You will also learn about the major issues that you must consider and resolve when planning to migrate an ASP Web page.

After completing this lesson, you will be able to plan for and implement the migration of an ASP Web page to ASP.NET.

Lesson objectives

After completing this lesson, you will be able to:

- Select a strategy for migrating from ASP to ASP.NET.

- Explain the major issues to be addressed when migrating an ASP Web page to ASP.NET.

- Explain the major issues to be addressed when migrating ASP code to ASP.NET.

- Explain the major issues to be addressed when migrating the configuration and security design of an ASP Web page to ASP.NET.

Guidelines for Selecting a Migration Strategy

Ordered by effort:

1. **Do not migrate any ASP Web pages at this time**
   - Design new ASP pages to be easily converted in the future

2. **Migrate one portion of the Web application at a time**
   - Consider functional boundaries such as COM interop, state management, and data access when deciding which Web pages to port

3. **Re-create entire Web pages**
   - When code and control changes will outweigh the remaining code

4. **Migrate the entire Web application**
   - For small or modular Web applications

Introduction

Both ASP and ASP.NET Web applications can run side-by-side on a Web server without one Web application adversely affecting the other. This independence is primarily due to the fact that separate file extensions (.asp and .aspx) and separate configuration models (metabase/registry and Extensible Markup Language (XML)-based configuration files) are used in the two technologies. Also, the two technologies use completely separate runtime processes.

Deciding on a migration strategy requires you to develop a return on investment (ROI) analysis that is based on the condition of your existing Web site, the value of the benefits from migrating to ASP.NET, and the cost of the migration. By using this analysis, you can develop a priority list for the changes that you would like to implement and a migration plan that supports these priorities.

Do not migrate any Web pages at this time

You may find that you cannot justify migrating any of your Web site to ASP.NET in the near future. There may be insufficient resources to accomplish the migration, or the Web site may be entering a peak time of important activity, during which introducing change would bring too much risk. In this scenario, it makes sense to continue maintaining your Web site in ASP.

If you decide to leave a Web site running on ASP, you can make the most of routine page updates or additions, thereby making the Web site easier to migrate to ASP.NET in the future. Some of the design guidelines to follow for creating ASP Web pages that can easily be migrated to ASP.NET include:

- Use a single programming language on a Web page.

- Declare functions inside **<script>** blocks, not inside **<%...%>** blocks.

- Use **Response.Write** instead of render functions that include code mixed with Hypertext Markup Language (HTML).

- Avoid nested include files.

- Use parentheses on all methods.

- Declare properties, and avoid using default properties.
- Organize utility functions into single files.
- Organize global variables into single files.
- Explicitly free resources by calling **Close** methods.

Migrate one portion of the Web application at a time

It is practical to have one section of a Web application running ASP and another section of that same Web application running ASP.NET. For example, if you must move a large, rapidly changing Web site to ASP.NET, the best strategy may be to migrate one Web page or section at a time. This strategy could involve creating some or all of the following plans:

- Create all new Web pages in ASP.NET.
- Combine page updates with page migration.
- Establish a priority list of the pages to migrate, as time permits.

Consider migrating User Interfaces (UIs) early in the Web application migration process. The Web controls, **InputValidation**, **SmartNavigation**, and **ViewState** controls, that are available in ASP.NET allow you to create efficient and user-friendly UI pages.

Also consider line-of-business (LOB) boundaries when you migrate a Web site to ASP.NET. For example, you may decide to migrate an independent payroll system before a heavily integrated expense system.

Within a line of business, there may be further boundaries, such as COM interop, state management, and Microsoft ActiveX® Data Objects (ADO) data access that you can use to identify related groups of pages when deciding what pieces of the Web site to migrate.

A possible priority listing for migrating pages in an ASP Web application might be:

1. UI pages that feature complex controls.
2. Pages with state management.
3. Pages with ADO data access.

Re-create entire Web pages

Re-creating entire ASP pages as ASP.NET Web Forms may be the best migration strategy when the code and control changes exceed 50 percent of the code that is on the Web page. For example, a Web page that collects user data would be a good candidate for re-creation if most of the controls are changing from design-time controls to Web server controls with validation.

Migrate the entire Web application

The last migration strategy is to migrate the entire Web application. The advantage of migrating the entire Web application is that you do not need to maintain parts of the Web application in ASP after the migration is complete.

Migrating Web Pages

- **Maintain ASP compatibility**
  - Keep track of ASP to ASP.NET links
  - Use parallel state management
- **Add an @ Page directive**
  - **Language** attribute must be in the @ **Page** directive
- **Structural changes**
  - All functions variables must be declared inside a **<script>** block
  - Only one server-side language per page
  - Render Functions are no longer supported, use **Response.Write**

Introduction

In ASP, you could write code wherever you wanted. You could write code inline with HTML markup, as a part of the **<% %>** render blocks, or you could write code in subroutines within render blocks. Also, you could write code in **<script>** declaration blocks, either as arbitrary code or as subroutines. The code in render blocks within ASP was executed in a linear fashion, but arbitrary code in a **<script>** block was not. This difference in execution often resulted in confusion because the ASP Web application code was sometimes executed out of sequence with developers' expectations.

ASP.NET solves the out-of-sequence execution problem by imposing limitations on what types of code may be written. As a result of these limitations, there are a number of issues that a developer must consider when migrating ASP pages to ASP.NET.

Maintain ASP compatibility

Unless you migrate an entire ASP Web application to ASP.NET, the individual pages that you port to ASP.NET must still work with the ASP pages that have not been ported. There are a few critical issues to consider when maintaining ASP and ASP.NET compatibility:

- Identifying all .asp and .aspx links and keeping them up to date.

- Continuing the use of include files, but only use one per page.

- Creating parallel state management in ASP and ASP.NET.

  Remember that ASP session or application variables are not shared with ASP.NET.

Page Directives

In ASP, you must place all of the directives on the first line of a page, within the same block. For example:

Visual Basic Scripting Edition

```
<% LANGUAGE="VBSCRIPT" %>
```

In ASP.NET, you will be required to place the **Language** directive with a **Page** directive, as shown in the following code example:

Visual Basic .NET

```
<%@ Page Language="vb"%>
```

C#

```
<%@ Page Language="c#"%>
```

You can have as many lines of directives as you need, and the directives can be located anywhere in your .aspx file. However, a best practice is to place all of the directives at the beginning of the file.

Structural Changes

Structural changes are those that affect the layout and coding style of the page. You need to be aware of several structure changes from ASP to ASP.NET, thereby ensuring that your code will work in ASP.NET:

- All functions variables must be declared inside a <script> block.

  In ASP, you can declare subroutines and variables in **<%...%>** render blocks, as shown in the following code example:

  Visual Basic Scripting Edition

  ```
  <%
     Dim X
     Dim str
     Sub MySub()
        Response.Write "This is a string."
     End Sub
  %>
  ```

  In ASP.NET, declaring subroutines and functions in render blocks is not allowed. Variables are allowed in render blocks, but they are accessible only within the render block.

In ASP.NET, a best practice is to declare all subroutines, functions, and variables within **<script runat=server>** blocks, as shown in the following code example:

```
Visual Basic .NET

<script language="vb" runat="server">
   Dim str As String
   Dim x, y As Integer

   Function Add(I As Integer, J As Integer) As Integer
      Return (I + J)
   End Function
</script>
```

```
C#

<script language="c#" runat="server">
int Add(int I, int J)
{
   return (I + J);
}
</script>
```

- Only one server-side language per page.

  In ASP, you essentially have two choices for your programming language: Visual Basic Scripting Edition or Microsoft JScript®. You can mix and match blocks of script in either language on the same page.

  In ASP.NET, you can code in any common language runtime-compliant language. The languages that are currently provided by Microsoft include: C#, Visual Basic .NET, and JScript. Visual Basic Scripting Edition does not exist in Microsoft .NET, as it has been subsumed by Visual Basic .NET.

  In ASP.NET, each page may be in a different language; however, you cannot mix languages on the same page as you can in ASP.

- Render Functions are no longer supported.

  A Render Function is a subroutine that contains sections of HTML that are embedded throughout its body, as shown in the following code example:

```
Visual Basic Scripting Edition

<%Sub RenderMe()%>
<H3> This is HTML text being rendered. </H3>
<%End Sub%>
```

Render Functions are difficult to read and maintain, and they are no longer allowed in ASP.NET. The simplest way to replace a Render Function in ASP.NET is to replace HTML outputs with calls to **Response.Write**, as shown in the following code example:

```
Visual Basic .NET

<script language="vb" runat="server">
  Sub RenderMe()
      Response.Write( _
          "<H3> This is HTML text being rendered. </H3>")
  End Sub
</script>
```

```
C#

<script language="c#" runat="server">
void RenderMe()
{
  Response.Write(
      "<H3> This is HTML text being rendered. </H3>");
}
</script>
```

Depending on the complexity and amount of the rendering code, consider using custom Web controls instead of **Response.Write**. Custom Web controls allow you to set your **HTML** attributes programmatically and separate your code from the text on the Web page.

Migrating Code

* **Design-time controls are no longer supported**
  * Replace with Web controls
* **Function changes**
  * **ByVal** is now the default
* **Method changes**
  * Parentheses are now required
  * Default properties are no longer supported
  * The **Request** object has changed
* **Variable changes**
  * **Option Explicit** is now the default
  * **Let** and **Set** are no longer supported
  * **Variant** data type is no longer supported
  * **Date**, **Integer**, and **Long** data types have changed

Introduction

The major code changes between ASP and ASP.NET are that design-time controls are no longer available, and that Microsoft .NET-based languages require your code writing to be more explicit. For example, in Visual Basic Scripting Edition, you could omit elements, such as parentheses and default properties, from your code. In Visual Basic .NET and C#, you must include these elements.

Note The following changes from ASP to ASP.NET code are a subset that you are likely to encounter when migrating an ASP page to ASP.NET. Consult the Visual Basic .NET and C# documentation for a complete list of all of the language changes that have been implemented.

Design-time controls

In ASP, Microsoft Visual InterDev® supported the use of design-time controls, such as the **Grid** control, which created server-side script that generated an HTML table. These design-time controls do not function in ASP.NET, and therefore, they must be replaced with Web controls. For example, you can replace the **Grid** design-time control with the **DataGrid** Web control.

You must also delete the Visual InterDev 6.0 Scripting Object Model tags from the beginning and end of the ASP page. These tags will cause errors when running under ASP.NET, or when a page is opened in Microsoft Visual Studio® .NET.

Function changes

The major change to functions in ASP.NET is that the default setting for passing arguments is by value, or **ByVal**. By default, in Visual Basic, parameter arguments were passed by reference or **ByRef**. To pass arguments by reference in Visual Basic .NET, you must explicitly use the **ByRef** keyword in front of your parameters, as shown in the following code example:

Visual Basic .NET

```
Sub MyByRefSub (ByRef Value As Integer)
    Value = 53
End Sub
```

C#

```
void MyByRefSub (ref int Value)
{
    Value = 53;
}
```

Warning Most ASP code works correctly when arguments are passed by value. However, you will need to test code carefully to ensure that passing by value does not introduce subtle errors.

Method changes

The major changes to methods in ASP.NET involve being more explicit when writing a method, including:

- Parentheses are now required.

  In ASP, you can freely call methods on objects without using parentheses, as shown in the following code example:

Visual Basic Scripting Edition

```
Sub WriteText()
    Response.Write "Text here"
End Sub
WriteText
```

In ASP.NET, you must use parentheses with all of your method calls, even for methods that do not take any parameters, as shown in the following code example:

Visual Basic .NET

```
Sub WriteText()
    Response.Write("Text here")
End Sub
Call WriteText()
```

C#

```
void WriteText()
{
    Response.Write("Text here");
}
WriteText();
```

- Default properties are not supported.

  The concept of default properties no longer exists in Visual Basic .NET. If you have ASP code that relies on a default property that was provided by one of your objects, you will now need to change that code to reference the property explicitly, as shown in the following code example:

  Visual Basic Scripting Edition

  ```
  'Implicit retrieval of Column Value property
  Set Conn = Server.CreateObject("ADODB.Connection")
  Conn.Open("TestDB")
  Set RS = Conn.Execute("Select * from Products")
  Response.Write RS("Name")
  ```

  Visual Basic .NET

  ```
  'Explicit retrieval of Column Value property
  Conn = Server.CreateObject("ADODB.Connection")
  Conn.Open("TestDB")
  RS = Conn.Execute("Select * from Products")
  Response.Write (RS("Name").Value)
  ```

  C#

  ```
  //Explicit retrieval of Column Value property
  Conn = (ADODB.Connection)
      Server.CreateObject("ADODB.Connection");
  Conn.Open("TestDB");
  RS = Conn.Execute("Select * from Products");
  Response.Write (RS["Name"].Value);
  ```

- The **Request** object has changed.

  The core application programming interfaces (APIs) of ASP consist of a few intrinsic objects (**Request, Response, Server,** and so on) and their associated methods. With the exception of a few simple changes, these APIs continue to function correctly in ASP.NET.

  If the item that you are accessing contains exactly one value for the specified key, you do not need to modify your code. However, if there are multiple values for a given key, you need to use a different method to return the collection of values.

Also, be aware that collections in Visual Basic .NET are zero-based, whereas the collections in Visual Basic Scripting Edition are one-based. For example, in ASP, the individual query string values that are from a request to http://localhost/myweb/valuetest.asp?values=10&values=20 would be accessed as shown in the following code example:

Visual Basic Scripting Edition

```
<%
    'This will output "10"
    Response.Write Request.QueryString("values")(1)

    'This will output "20"
    Response.Write Request.QueryString("values")(2)
%>
```

In ASP.NET, the **QueryString** property is a **NameValueCollection** object from which you need to retrieve the **Values** collection before you can retrieve the actual item that you want. Be aware that the first item in the collection is retrieved by using an index of zero rather than one, as shown in the following code example:

Visual Basic .NET

```
<%
    'This will output "10"
    Response.Write( _
        Request.QueryString.GetValues("values")(0))

    'This will output "20"
    Response.Write( _
        Request.QueryString.GetValues("values")(1))
%>
```

C#

```
<%
    //This will output "10"
    Response.Write(
        Request.QueryString.GetValues("values")[0]);

    //This will output "20"
    Response.Write(
        Request.QueryString.GetValues("values")[1]);
%>
```

The following code will respond identically when run on ASP or ASP.NET:

Visual Basic Script or .NET

```
<%
   'This will output "10,20"
   Response.Write (Request.QueryString("values"))
%>
```

C#

```
<%
   //This will output "10,20"
   Response.Write (Request.QueryString["values"]);
%>
```

Variable changes

The following variable changes are those that you are most likely to encounter when migrating a page to ASP.NET:

- **Option Explicit** is now the default.

  In ASP, the **Option Explicit** keywords were available but were not enforced. In Visual Basic .NET, **Option Explicit** is now the default; therefore, all variables need to be declared.

- **LET** and **SET** are no longer supported.

  You can no longer use the **LET** or **SET** statements. Objects should be assigned to one another directly, as shown in the following code example:

```
MyObj1 = MyObj2
```

- The **Variant** data type is no longer supported.

  The **Variant** data type is not supported in Visual Basic .NET. All ASP variables will change from **Variant** types to **Object** types. Most variables that are used in your Web application can and should be changed to a corresponding primitive type. If your variable is an object type in Visual Basic, you will need to declare it explicitly as an **Object** type in ASP.NET.

- The **Date** type has changed.

  In Visual Basic Scripting Edition, the **Variant** type stored dates in a double format by using four bytes. In Visual Basic .NET, the **Date** type uses the common language runtime **DateTime** type, which has an eight-byte integer representation.

  You may encounter some unexpected problems when you are performing certain operations with **Date** type variables because the underlying type has been changed. Be sure to declare such variables as the **Date** or **DateTime** type, which will enforce correct date and time calculations, and will also enforce correct marshaling when passing these data types to COM objects.

  Using **Date()** to get the current date is not supported in ASP.NET; instead, you need to use **DateTime.Now**.

■ The **Integer** type and **Long** type have changed.

Numeric variables in ASP were represented as two-byte **Integers** in the **Variant** data type. In Visual Basic .NET, **Integer** types are now four bytes and **Long** types are now eight bytes.

In ASP.NET, you should declare any numeric variables as type **Short**. The **Short** type is a two-byte value that most accurately represents the old ASP numeric types. The **Short** type will also marshal correctly to COM objects.

Migrating Configuration and Security

* **Application configuration changes to the XML file Web.config**

* **Input control validation and a ValidationSummary control are now available**

* **Structured exception handling is supported with Try...Catch...Finally blocks**

* **Security is set in the Web.config file**

    * Authentication

    * Authorization

    * Identity

Introduction

ASP.NET moves all of the configuration and security settings for the Web application to the XML file, Web.config. This shift allows you to control the configuration and security settings from a single, secure, and developer-accessible file.

Application configuration changes

In ASP, all Web application configuration information is stored in the system registry and the Internet Information Services (IIS) Metabase. This architecture makes it difficult to view or modify configuration settings because the correct administration tools are often unavailable.

In ASP.NET, each Web application has its own Web.config file that resides in the main application directory. This Web.config file is used to control the custom configuration, behavior, and security of your Web application.

Input control validation

Migrating to ASP.NET provides you with an opportunity to review your code protection strategy and strengthen the robustness of your Web application. ASP.NET provides validation controls that can increase the protection of your code from user input errors. At a minimum, all strings from the user should be validated to protect your Web application from malicious code.

The integrated design of the ASP.NET validation controls and the ValidationSummary control also allow you to expand the usability of your Web page by integrating all of the error messages at a single location.

Structured exception handling

Although **On Error Resume Next** and **On Error Goto** are still allowed in Visual Basic .NET, neither of these methods is the best error-handling technique available in ASP.NET.

Visual Basic .NET has structured exception handling, using the **Try**, **Catch**, and **Finally** keywords. If possible, you should use this technique for error handling because it allows for a more powerful and consistent mechanism for resolving application errors.

The syntax of a **Try...Catch...Finally** statement is shown in the following code example:

```
Visual Basic .NET

Dim i As Integer
Try
  ' Start methods
  i = 5 / Convert.ToInt16(ValueBox.Text)
  ResultBox.Text = i.ToString()

Catch theError As Exception
  ' Collect and handle errors
  ErrorBox.Text = theError.Message

Finally
  ' Close connections and release resources
  ValueBox.Text = ""
End Try
```

```
C#

int i;
try
{
  // Start methods
  i = 5 / Convert.ToInt16(ValueBox.Text);
  ResultBox.Text = i.ToString();
}
catch (Exception theError)
{
  // Collect and handle errors
  ErrorBox.Text = theError.Message;
}
finally
{
  // Close connections and release resources
  ValueBox.Text = "";
}
```

Notice that you declare variables outside the **Try** block, so that even if the **Try** block fails, the **Finally** block can still close and release resources.

Security-related changes

ASP.NET security is primarily controlled by the settings in the security sections of your Web.config file. ASP.NET works together with IIS to provide a complete security model for your Web application, including:

- Authentication

  For authentication, ASP.NET supports the different authentication options that are shown in the following table.

Option	Description
Microsoft Windows®	Uses Windows authentication.
Forms	Uses cookie-based, custom logon forms.
Microsoft .NET Passport single sign-in (SSI)	Uses external Microsoft .NET Passport.
None	No authentication is performed.

  The preceding authentication options are the same options that are available to you in ASP, with the exception of the new .NET Passport SSI authentication option. The following configuration section enables Windows-based authentication for a Web application:

```
<configuration>
   <system.web>
      <authentication mode="Windows"/>
   </system.web>
</configuration>
```

- Authorization

  After your users have been authenticated, you can then turn your focus to authorizing the resources that you would like them to have access to. The following configuration section enables access for the group **clients**, while all other users are denied access:

```
<authorization>
   <allow users="clients"/>
   <deny users="*"/>
</authorization>
```

- Identity

  In ASP, you configured the identity of the ASP process by using the IIS tool. You could configure ASP to run as a specific account, or to impersonate the calling user's credentials.

  By default, ASP.NET runs as the ASPNET account, which is created when you install ASP.NET on a computer. By using the identity element, you can specify a different account to run under, or you can indicate that ASP.NET should impersonate. If you choose impersonation, ASP.NET will use the identity that was established by the IIS tool. For example, if IIS is using anonymous access to run as the account IUSER_*machinename*, ASP.NET will run as the account IUSER_*machinename*. The following code example shows how to use the identity element in the Web.config file to enable impersonation:

```
<identity>
   <impersonation enable = "true"/>
</identity>
```

Lesson: Migrating an ASP Web Application

- **Migrating ADO**
- **Migrating State Management**
- **Migrating COM Interop**
- **Porting an ASP Web Application to ASP.NET**

Introduction

In this lesson, you will examine the various major issues that you need to consider when planning to migrate ASP Web applications that use ADO, state management, and COM interop to ASP.NET. You will also learn the procedure for converting an ASP Web application to ASP.NET.

Lesson objectives

After completing this lesson, you will be able to:

- Explain how to manage data access when migrating an ASP Web application to ASP.NET.

- Explain how to migrate state management when migrating an ASP Web application to ASP.NET.

- Explain how to migrate COM interop when migrating an ASP Web application to ASP.NET.

- Follow a logical plan of action for porting an ASP application to ASP.NET.

Migrating ADO

ASP.NET offers several options for migrating data-driven ASP Web applications

Ordered by effort:

1. **Continue using ADO Recordsets**

2. **Use ADO Recordsets to fill ADO.NET DataSets and DataTables**

3. **Convert data access to ADO.NET objects**

   * DataSets

   * Data-bound controls

Introduction

Microsoft ADO.NET is not an extension of ADO; instead, ADO.NET is a new model for data access that builds on ADO, but is designed for a new disconnected paradigm. As a result of this change, when you update an ASP Web application to ASP.NET, you must either continue using ADO COM objects or redevelop your ADO data access in ADO.NET.

Continue using ADO

You can choose to continue using ADO objects in ASP.NET, which should yield basically equal performance. However, Visual Basic .NET does not support some of the features of Visual Basic Scripting Edition that are used with ADO, such as optional parameters. As a result of this language change to Visual Basic .NET, the continued use of ADO may require code review and revision.

Using Recordsets to fill DataSets and DataTables

You can combine ADO and ADO.NET by using the **Fill** method of the ASP.NET **OleDbDataAdaper** class to load the results sets from ADO **Recordsets**. This combination allows you to combine your existing data access objects with the **DataSet** object and data-bound controls that are available in ADO.NET. Any result sets that are created by commands or the contents from an existing ADO **Recordset** can be used to fill an ADO.NET **DataSet** object. The **DataAdapter** object copies each result set that is found in the **Recordset** into a **DataTable** object in the **DataSet** object.

The **Fill** link between ADO and ADO.NET is a one-way binding that you can use to copy data from the **Recordset** to the **DataSet** object. Updates to the **DataSet** object must be performed in ADO.NET. The following code example shows how to retrieve a **Recordset** by using ADO, and then load that object into a **DataSet** object by using an ADO.NET **OleDbDataAdaper** object:

Visual Basic .NET

```
'retrieve Recordset object
Dim adoRS As ADODB.Recordset
Try
  adoRS.Open(strCommand, strConn, _
      CursorTypeEnum.adOpenForwardOnly, _
      LockTypeEnum.adLockReadOnly, 1)

  'Fill a DataSet object from the Recordset object
  Dim oda As New OleDbDataAdapter()
  Dim ds As New DataSet()
  oda.Fill(ds, adoRS, "MyTable")
Finally
  adoRS.Close()
End Try
```

C#

```
//retrieve Recordset object
Recordset adoRS = new ADODB.Recordset();
try
{
  adoRS.Open(strCommand, strConn,
    CursorTypeEnum.adOpenForwardOnly,
    LockTypeEnum.adLockReadOnly, 1);

  //Fill a DataSet object from the Recordset object
  OleDbDataAdapter oda = new OleDbDataAdapter();
  DataSet ds = new DataSet();
  oda.Fill(ds, adoRS, "MyTable");
}
finally
{
  adoRS.Close();
}
```

Convert to ADO.NET

Converting all data handling from ADO to ADO.NET will increase data access performance and provide you with a variety of data handling and displaying tools. The primary data access objects in ADO.NET are the **DataSet** object for storing and manipulating data locally, and data-bound controls that provide flexible data presentation to the user.

Migrating State Management

- **Continue using Session and Application objects for ASP pages**
- **Use ASP.NET state management options for ASP.NET pages**

Option	Description
Inproc	Stored locally on server, similar to ASP
StateServer	Stored in a state service process locally, or remotely
SqlServer	Stored in a SQL Server database
Off	Session state is disabled

Introduction

The **Session** and **Application** objects are still available in ASP.NET; therefore, migrating ASP pages that use these objects is relatively easy. However, you cannot share the state that is stored in these objects between ASP and ASP.NET Web applications.

Sharing state between ASP and ASP.NET

Although your Web application can contain both ASP and ASP.NET pages, you cannot share state variables that are stored in the intrinsic **Session** or **Application** objects. You either need to duplicate this state information in both Web applications or create a custom solution, until your Web application is fully migrated to ASP.NET. An example of a custom solution would be storing state in a database, sharing information between the ASP and ASP.NET Web applications.

State management Options

In ASP.NET, you have additional options for your state storage model. These options finally allow you to go beyond a single Web server, supporting state management across a Web farm.

You configure your state management options in the **<sessionState>** section of the Web.config file. The following table lists the values for the **mode** attribute that specify where you will want to store your state information.

Value	Description
Inproc	Stored locally on the local server, similar to ASP.
StateServer	Stored in a state service; process locally or remotely.
SqlServer	Stored in a Microsoft SQL Server™ database.
Off	Session state is disabled.

Storing COM components

If you rely on storing references to your COM components in the **Session** or **Application** object, you cannot use the new state storage mechanisms (**StateServer** or **SqlServer**) within your Web application. You will need to use **Inproc**. This limitation is due in part to an object's need to be self-serializable. The managed components of .NET can be self-serialized relatively easily and they can therefore use the new state storage models.

Performance

In most situations, **Inproc** will continue to be the highest performing state management option, followed by **StateServer** and then **SqlServer**. You should perform you own tests with your Web application to ensure that the option you have selected will meet your performance goals.

Migrating COM Interop

- **Use aspcompat="true" to force STA**
- **Add references to COM components**

COM Component yype/method	ASP.NET setting/procedures
Custom STA	Use **ASPCOMPAT** and early binding
Custom MTA	Do not use **ASPCOMPAT**, do use early binding
Intrinsic Objects accessed through ObjectContext	Use **ASPCOMPAT** and early binding
OnStartPage, OnEndPage	Use **ASPCOMPAT** and Server.CreateObject(Type)

Introduction

The runtime callable wrapper (RCW) is used to interoperate with COM objects in ASP.NET. The RCW offers equivalent performance to ASP, with better performance in some situations because the RCW uses early binding. You can build custom wrappers in Visual C++ for even better performance, or simply convert COM objects to .NET objects for maximum performance.

COM-related changes

There are several issues that you need to be aware of when porting an ASP page that calls COM objects to ASP.NET, including:

- Threading model changes.

  ASP uses the single-threaded apartment (STA) model. The ASP.NET threading model is the multithreaded apartment (MTA) model. Anytime you mix these two models (such as a multithreaded ASP.NET page calling a single-threaded COM object), you lose performance ability because the COM threading rules require marshaling the method calls.

■ **aspcompat** compatibility attribute.

You can use STA COM components without having to change any code by including the **aspcompat** compatibility attribute on the ASP.NET page. Using this attribute will force your page to execute in STA mode, thereby ensuring that your component will continue to function optimally, as shown in the following code example:

Visual Basic .NET

```
<% @ Page aspcompat="true" Language="VB" %>
```

C#

```
<% @ Page aspcompat="true" Language="c#" %>
```

Setting the **aspcompat** attribute to **True** will also allow your page to call COM+ 1.0 objects that require access to the unmanaged ASP built-in objects. The COM+ 1.0 objects are accessible through the **ObjectContext** object.

■ Early binding versus late binding.

In ASP, all calls to COM objects occur through the **IDispatch** interface. This is known as late binding because calls to the actual objects are handled indirectly through the **IDispatch** interface at run time. In ASP.NET, you can continue to invoke your components in this manner, as shown in the following code example:

Visual Basic .NET

```
Dim Obj As Object
Obj = Server.CreateObject("ProgID")
Obj.MyMethodCall()
```

Note   C# does not support late binding by using the **Server.CreateObject** method. Therefore, when converting to C#, you must import the type library of the COM object and use early binding, as shown in the next example.

While the preceding code works, it is not the preferred technique for accessing your objects. Early binding allows you to interact with your components in a type-safe manner. With ASP.NET, you can take advantage of early binding and create your objects directly, as shown in the following code example:

Visual Basic .NET

```
Dim Obj As New MyObject
Obj.MyMethodCall()

'Or you can use Server.CreateObject
'with early binding

Dim Obj As MyObject
Obj = Server.CreateObject(MyObject)
Obj.MyMethodCall()
```

```
C#

MyObject Obj = new MyObject();
Obj.MyMethodCall();

//Or you can use Server.CreateObject
//with early binding

MyObject Obj = MyObject();
Obj = Server.CreateObject(MyObject);
Obj.MyMethodCall();
```

- **OnStartPage** and **OnEndPage** methods.

  One coding technique that needs some additional consideration when migrating an ASP Web page to ASP.NET is the use of the legacy **OnStartPage** and **OnEndPage** methods. If you rely on these methods to access ASP intrinsic objects, you will need to use the **ASPCOMPAT** directive and the **Server.CreateObject** to create your component in an early-bound approach, as shown in the following code example:

```
Visual Basic .NET

Dim Obj As MyObject
Obj = Server.CreateObject(MyObject)
Obj.MyMethodCall()
```

```
C#

MyObject Obj;
Obj = Server.CreateObject(MyObject);
Obj.MyMethodCall();
```

  Notice that instead of using ProgID, you can use the actual type in an early-bound manner. For this code to work, you will need to add a reference to your COM component in your Visual Studio .NET project so that the early-bound wrapper class is created for you. Creating the early bound wrapper class should be the only situation where you must continue to use **Server.CreateObject**.

COM summary

The following table is a summary of what you need to do to continue to use your COM components as efficiently as possible when migrating to ASP.NET.

COM component type/method	ASP.NET setting/procedures
Custom STA (Visual Basic Components or other components marked as "Apartment")	Use **ASPCOMPAT**, and use early binding.
Custom MTA (ATL or custom COM components marked as "Both" or "Free")	Do not use **ASPCOMPAT**; only use early binding.
Intrinsic Objects (accessed through **ObjectContext**)	Use **ASPCOMPAT**, and use early binding.
OnStartPage, **OnEndPage**	Use **ASPCOMPAT**, and use **Server.CreateObject(Type)**.

The preceding settings and procedures apply whether your components are deployed in COM or COM+.

Performance changes

Some overhead is added when you use .NET COM interop, as you will have an extra layer introduced because of the proxy object. In most situations, however, this overhead will not result in a performance reduction because the amount of actual CPU instructions for the interoperation to occur is still substantially less than that which is required in ASP by indirect **IDispatch** calls. You will gain more performance than you will lose.

For maximum performance, you can use newly created .NET managed objects. Review the COM objects that you use to identify which objects would result in the greatest performance improvements. You can then plan your COM object migration strategy accordingly.

Porting an ASP Web Application to ASP.NET

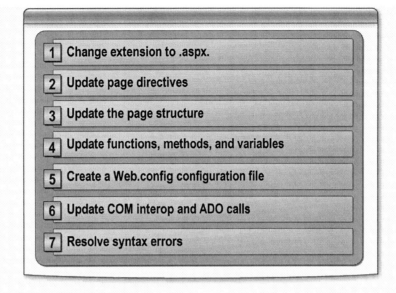

1 | Change extension to .aspx.

2 | Update page directives

3 | Update the page structure

4 | Update functions, methods, and variables

5 | Create a Web.config configuration file

6 | Update COM interop and ADO calls

7 | Resolve syntax errors

Introduction

The process of porting a Web application from ASP to ASP.NET is conceptually simple, but may be fairly labor-intensive, depending on the quality with which the original pages were written.

To port an ASP page to ASP.NET

The following steps are likely to be required when porting an ASP page to ASP.NET:

1. Change the file extension to .aspx.

   This changes the HTTP Handler from ASP to ASP.NET.

2. Update the **Page** directives.

   ASP.NET requires a single language that is declared in the @ **Page** directive.

3. Update the page structure.

   ASP.NET Web pages cannot use Render Functions.

4. Update functions, methods, and variables.

   ASP.NET code requires explicit coding; you must use parentheses, and declare properties and variables.

5. Create a Web.config file with the application configuration options.

   The Web.config file contains both Web page and Web application settings.

6. Update COM interop and ADO.

   Use the existing components or replace with .NET objects.

7. Resolve Syntax Errors.

Note For a detailed checklist of the steps that are required to be completed to port an ASP page to ASP.NET, see Appendix C, "Job Aid: Migrating ASP Web applications to Microsoft ASP.NET," in Course 2640, *Upgrading Web Development Skills from ASP to Microsoft ASP.NET.*

Lab 9: Migrating to ASP.NET

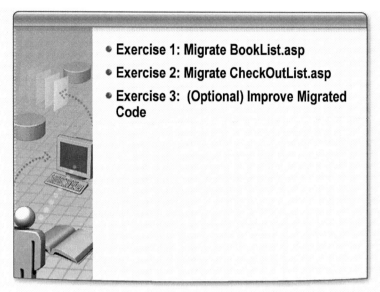

- Exercise 1: Migrate BookList.asp
- Exercise 2: Migrate CheckOutList.asp
- Exercise 3: (Optional) Improve Migrated Code

Objectives

After completing this lab, you will be able to:

- Make structural and functional changes to an ASP page to upgrade it to an ASP.NET Web Form.

- Make language changes to an ASP page to upgrade it to an ASP.NET Web Form.

- Improve performance in a migrated ASP page by converting data access to ADO.NET, and by modifying how state is managed.

- Improve readability and maintenance in a migrated ASP page by moving all of the functionality into a code-behind file.

Note This lab focuses on the concepts in this module and as a result may not comply with Microsoft security recommendations.

Prerequisites

Before working on this lab, you must have:

- Knowledge of how to use state management in ASP.NET.

- Knowledge of how to retrieve and update data by using ADO and ADO.NET.

- Knowledge of how to bind controls to data.

- Knowledge of how to repair problems in ASP pages, so that the pages run correctly in ASP.NET.

Scenario

For this lab, you will be using a simple library Web application that allows a user to check out books. The method by which the library Web application uses design-time controls and HTML to check out a book is not intended to be a real-world example. However, the process of migrating the Web application is a real-world scenario, and you will encounter numerous realistic problems as you migrate the Web application to ASP.NET.

The library Web application consists of two ASP pages. BookList.asp is the first page, and it displays a list of books, from the Pubs database, in a drop-down list control. The BookList.asp page also displays a list of library members by last name in a drop-down list control. The library member names are fictitious users of the library system, and are obtained from the Employees table in the Northwind database.

The user selects both a book title, and a library member name, and clicks a **Check Out Book** button. The **Check Out Book** button redirects the user to the CheckOutList.asp page.

The CheckOutList.asp page receives the title ID of the book, as well as the library ID of the user who is checking out the book. The CheckOutList.asp page stores this information, as well as the last name of the user, in a **Recordset** in application state. The CheckOutList.asp page then displays all of the records from the **Recordset** in an HTML table, which allows the user to see all of the books that are checked out. There is a link on the CheckOutList.asp page to return to the BookList.asp page.

Solution

The solution project for this lab is located in the *install_folder*\Labfiles\Lab09\ *language*\Solution folder, where *language* is CS or VB. You can also view the solution Web Form at http://localhost/upg/lab09-*language*-solution/ BookList.aspx.

Estimated time to complete this lab: 45 minutes

Exercise 1
Migrate BookList.asp

In this exercise, you will migrate the BookList.asp page. You will use **DropDownList** Web Form controls to replace the HTML **drop-down list** controls. You will also move all of the code out of the HTML portion of the Web form into a code-behind file. Finally, you will fix all of the language script so that it runs correctly as either Visual Basic .NET or C# code.

▶ Browse the existing simple library Web application

In the following steps you will review the ASP Web application that you will be migrating to ASP.NET.

1. Using Microsoft Internet Explorer, browse to http://localhost/upg/ lab09-SimpleLibrary/BookList.asp.

2. Select a book from the first drop-down list control.

3. Select a library member from the second drop-down list control.

4. Click the **Check Out Book** button to submit this information.

   You will be redirected to the CheckOutList.asp page. The CheckOutList.asp page should display the **Library ID**, **Title ID**, and **LastName** values that you just selected.

5. Click on the **Return to Book List** link to return to the BookList.asp page.

   You may repeat these steps to check out additional books and to observe how the Web application functions.

▶ Open the Lab09 Solution

1. In Visual Studio .NET, from the **File** menu, click **Open Solution**.

2. In the Open Solution window, click the **My Projects** shortcut.

3. Expand the **Labfiles**, **Lab09**, *language*, and **Starter** folders.

4. Select **Lab09.sln**, and then click **Open**.

▶ Copy and update the global.asa source code

In the following steps you will transfer the **Application_OnStart** subroutine from the global.asa file to the Global.asax file.

1. Open the *install_folder*\Labfiles\Lab09\SimpleLibrary\global.asa file in Visual Studio .NET.

2. Open the Global.asax.vb or Global.asax.cs file in Visual Studio .NET.

3. Copy the code that is inside the **Application_OnStart** subroutine from the global.asa page to the **Application_Start** event handler that is in the Global.asax code-behind file.

4. Locate the code that creates the connection strings for the Pubs and Northwind databases and delete the **Description** and **Driver** portions of the connection strings.

   These sections are not valid for ADO.NET connections.

5. Remove the code at the bottom of the **Application_Start** event handler that creates a **RecordSet** object.

   The code is after the comment, "'--Create RecordSet to store checked out items."

6. At the bottom of the **Application_Start** event handler, copy and paste the code from the DataSet-vb.txt or DataSet-cs.txt file that is located in the *install_folder*\Labfiles\Lab09*language*\Starter folder.

   Your completed code for the **Application_Start** event handler should look similar to the following code example:

Visual Basic .NET

```
'--Project Data Connection
Application("cnNorthwind_ConnectionString") = _
    "SERVER=(local)\MOC;APP=Microsoft Development " _
    + "Environment;DATABASE=Northwind;" _
    + "Trusted_Connection=Yes;"
Application("cnNorthwind_ConnectionTimeout") = 15
Application("cnNorthwind_CommandTimeout") = 30
Application("cnNorthwind_CursorLocation") = 3
Application("cnNorthwind_RuntimeUserName") = ""
Application("cnNorthwind_RuntimePassword") = ""
'--Project Data Connection
Application("cnPubs_ConnectionString") = _
    "SERVER=(local)\MOC;APP=Microsoft Development " _
    + "Environment;DATABASE=pubs;Trusted_Connection=Yes;"
Application("cnPubs_ConnectionTimeout") = 15
Application("cnPubs_CommandTimeout") = 30
Application("cnPubs_CursorLocation") = 3
Application("cnPubs_RuntimeUserName") = ""
Application("cnPubs_RuntimePassword") = ""

'Create DataSet with Title, Lastname,
'and LibraryID columns
Dim dsCheckOutList As New DataSet()
Dim Books As New System.Data.DataTable()
Dim TitleID As New System.Data.DataColumn()
Dim LastName As New System.Data.DataColumn()
Dim LibraryID As New System.Data.DataColumn()
dsCheckOutList.DataSetName = "NewDataSet"
dsCheckOutList.Tables.AddRange( _
    New System.Data.DataTable() {Books})
Books.Columns.AddRange( _
    New System.Data.DataColumn() _
    {TitleID, LibraryID, LastName})
Books.TableName = "Books"
TitleID.ColumnName = "TitleID"
LibraryID.ColumnName = "LibraryID"
LastName.ColumnName = "LastName"
Dim pk(1) As System.Data.DataColumn
pk(0) = TitleID
dsCheckOutList.Tables(0).PrimaryKey = pk
Application("CheckOutList") = dsCheckOutList
```

```csharp
C#

//--Project Data Connection
Application["cnNorthwind_ConnectionString"] =
   @"SERVER=(local)\MOC;APP=Microsoft Development "
   + "Environment;DATABASE=Northwind;"
   + "Trusted_Connection=Yes;";
Application["cnNorthwind_ConnectionTimeout"] = 15;
Application["cnNorthwind_CommandTimeout"] = 30;
Application["cnNorthwind_CursorLocation"] = 3;
Application["cnNorthwind_RuntimeUserName"] = "";
Application["cnNorthwind_RuntimePassword"] = "";
//--Project Data Connection
Application["cnPubs_ConnectionString"] =
   @"SERVER=(local)\MOC;APP=Microsoft Development "
   + "Environment;DATABASE=pubs;Trusted_Connection=Yes;";
Application["cnPubs_ConnectionTimeout"] = 15;
Application["cnPubs_CommandTimeout"] = 30;
Application["cnPubs_CursorLocation"] = 3;
Application["cnPubs_RuntimeUserName"] = "";
Application["cnPubs_RuntimePassword"] = "";

//Create DataSet with Title, Lastname, and
//LibraryID columns
System.Data.DataSet dsCheckOutList =
   new System.Data.DataSet();
System.Data.DataTable Books =
   new System.Data.DataTable();
System.Data.DataColumn TitleID =
   new System.Data.DataColumn();
System.Data.DataColumn LastName =
   new System.Data.DataColumn();
System.Data.DataColumn LibraryID =
   new System.Data.DataColumn();
dsCheckOutList.DataSetName = "NewDataSet";
dsCheckOutList.Tables.AddRange(
   new System.Data.DataTable[] {Books});
Books.Columns.AddRange(
   new System.Data.DataColumn[]
   {TitleID, LibraryID, LastName});
Books.TableName = "Books";
TitleID.ColumnName = "TitleID";
LibraryID.ColumnName = "LibraryID";
LastName.ColumnName = "LastName";
System.Data.DataColumn [] pk =
   new System.Data.DataColumn[1];
pk[0] = TitleID;
dsCheckOutList.Tables[0].PrimaryKey = pk;
Application["CheckOutList"] = dsCheckOutList;
```

7. Save changes.

► **Create the BookList.aspx user interface**

In the following steps you will create a new user interface that takes advantage of the controls available in ASP.NET.

1. Open the BookList.asp file in Visual Studio .NET.

    This file is located in *install_folder*\Labfiles\Lab09\SimpleLibrary. Keep this file open for the remainder of this exercise for reference.

2. Create a new Web Form named BookList.aspx.

3. In Design view for the BookList.aspx Web Form, change the **pageLayout** property to **FlowLayout**.

4. Type the text **Select the book to check out:**

    Alternatively, you can copy this text from the BookList.asp page.

5. Insert a **DropDownList** Web Form control named **lstTitles**.

6. Set the **lstTitles** control's **AutoPostBack** property to **True**.

7. On the next line, type the text **Select the library member checking out this book:**

    Alternatively, you can copy this text from the BookList.asp page.

8. Insert a **DropDownList** Web Form control named **lstNames**.

9. Set the **lstNames** control's **AutoPostBack** property to **True**.

10. On the next line, insert a **Button** Web Form control named **cmdCheckOutBook**.

11. Set the **Text** property for **cmdCheckOutBook** to **Check Out Book**.

► **Binding the DropDownList controls to data**

In the following steps you will bind controls on the UI to a **DataSet** object.

1. Open the code-behind file for BookList.aspx.

2. At the top of the code-behind file, import (Visual Basic .NET) or use (C#) the **System.Data.SqlClient** namespace.

3. Examine the BookList.asp file in HTML view.

    There are two large scripts that create a connection to the database and fill the HTML drop-down list controls with data. These scripts essentially data-bind the HTML drop-down list controls. Therefore, you must data bind the two **DropDownList** Web Form controls that you just created.

4. Perform the following steps in the **Page_Load** event handler in the BookList.aspx code-behind file:

   a. Use an **If** statement to check if this is a Web Form postback. The remaining steps should only be completed if this is not a Web Form postback.

   b. Create two new **SqlConnection** objects, but do not initialize any properties yet.

      In the solution for this lab, the variables are named **cnNwnd** and **cnPubs**.

   c. Create a new **SqlCommand** object, but do not initialize any properties yet.

      In the solution for this lab, the variable is named **cmdTmp**.

   d. Create a new **DataSet** object.

      In the solution for this lab, the variable is named **dsTmp**.

   e. Create a new **SqlDataAdapter** object.

      In the solution for this lab, the variable is named **daTmp**.

   f. Declare a **DataView** variable.

      In the solution for this lab, the variable is named **dvTmp**.

      Your code for the preceding steps should look similar to the following code example:

```
Visual Basic .NET

If Not IsPostBack Then
    'Initialize variables
    Dim cnNwnd As New SqlConnection()
    Dim cnPubs As New SqlConnection()
    Dim cmdTmp As New SqlCommand()
    Dim dsTmp As New DataSet()
    Dim daTmp As New SqlDataAdapter()
    Dim dvTmp As DataView
```

```
C#

if (!IsPostBack)
{
    //Initialize variables
    SqlConnection cnNwnd = new SqlConnection();
    SqlConnection cnPubs = new SqlConnection();
    SqlCommand cmdTmp = new SqlCommand();
    DataSet dsTmp = new DataSet();
    SqlDataAdapter daTmp = new SqlDataAdapter();
    DataView dvTmp;
```

   g. Initialize the connection strings for the **SqlConnection** objects by using the connection strings that are stored in application state.

      Initialize one connection string to use the **pubs** database, and the other connection string to use the **Northwind** database.

   h. Configure the **SqlCommand** object to use the **SqlConnection** object for the pubs database.

i. Set the **CommandTimeout** property of the **SqlCommand** object to 10.

j. Set the **CommandType** property of the **SqlCommand** object to **CommandType.StoredProcedure**.

k. Set the **SelectCommand** property of the **SqlDataAdapter** object to the **SqlCommand** object.

Your code for the preceding steps should look similar to the following code example:

Visual Basic .NET

```
'Configure Connection, Command, and DataAdapater
cnPubs.ConnectionString = _
    Application("cnPubs_ConnectionString")
cnNwnd.ConnectionString = _
    Application("cnNorthwind_ConnectionString")
cmdTmp.Connection = cnPubs
cmdTmp.CommandType = CommandType.StoredProcedure
cmdTmp.CommandTimeout = 10
daTmp.SelectCommand = cmdTmp
```

C#

```
//Configure Connection, Command, and DataAdapater
cnPubs.ConnectionString =
    Application["cnPubs_ConnectionString"].ToString();
cnNwnd.ConnectionString =
    Application["cnNorthwind_ConnectionString"]
        .ToString();
cmdTmp.Connection = cnPubs;
cmdTmp.CommandType = CommandType.StoredProcedure;
cmdTmp.CommandTimeout = 10;
daTmp.SelectCommand = cmdTmp;
```

l. Run the **GetTitles** stored procedure and fill a table named **Titles** in the **DataSet** object with the results, as shown in the following code example:

Visual Basic .NET

```
'Fill DataSet with Titles
cmdTmp.CommandText = "GetTitles"
daTmp.Fill(dsTmp, "Titles")
```

C#

```
//Fill DataSet with Titles
cmdTmp.CommandText = "GetTitles";
daTmp.Fill(dsTmp, "Titles");
```

m. Run the **GetNames** stored procedure and fill a table named **Names** in the **DataSet** object with the results, as shown in the following code example:

Visual Basic .NET

```
'Fill DataSet with Names
cmdTmp.Connection = cnNwnd
cmdTmp.CommandText = "GetNames"
daTmp.Fill(dsTmp, "Names")
```

C#

```
//Fill DataSet with Names
cmdTmp.Connection = cnNwnd;
cmdTmp.CommandText = "GetNames";
daTmp.Fill(dsTmp, "Names");
```

n. Create a **DataView** that sorts the Titles table by Title, and bind the resulting **DataView** to the **lstTitles DropDownList** Web Form control.

o. Set the **DataValueField** property to **title_id** to track the corresponding Title ID when a title is selected.

Your code for the preceding steps should look similar to the following code example:

Visual Basic .NET

```
'Sort and bind Titles table to lstTitles
dvTmp = New DataView(dsTmp.Tables("Titles"))
dvTmp.Sort = "Title"
lstTitles.DataSource = dvTmp
lstTitles.DataTextField = "title"
lstTitles.DataValueField = "title_id"
lstTitles.DataBind()
```

C#

```
//Sort and bind Titles table to lstTitles
dvTmp = new DataView(dsTmp.Tables["Titles"]);
dvTmp.Sort = "Title";
lstTitles.DataSource = dvTmp;
lstTitles.DataTextField = "title";
lstTitles.DataValueField = "title_id";
lstTitles.DataBind();
```

p. Create a **DataView** that sorts the Names table by LastName, and bind the resulting **DataView** to the **LstNames DropDownList** Web Form control.

q. Set the **DataValueField** to **LibraryID** to track the corresponding Library ID when a name is selected.

Your code for the preceding steps should look similar to the following code example:

```
Visual Basic .NET

'Sort and bind Names table to lstNames
dvTmp = New DataView(dsTmp.Tables("Names"))
dvTmp.Sort = "LastName"
lstNames.DataSource = dvTmp
lstNames.DataTextField = "LastName"
lstNames.DataValueField = "LibraryID"
lstNames.DataBind()
```

```
C#

//Sort and bind Names table to lstNames
dvTmp = new DataView(dsTmp.Tables["Names"]);
dvTmp.Sort = "LastName";
lstNames.DataSource = dvTmp;
lstNames.DataTextField = "LastName";
lstNames.DataValueField = "LibraryID";
lstNames.DataBind();
```

5. Build and browse the BookList.aspx Web Form.

Ensure that the two data-bound **DropDownList** controls display the titles and names correctly.

▶ **Add functionality for the Check Out Book button**

In the following steps you will enable the user to determine if the selected book is already checked out, and if the book is available, add the selected book to the checked-out list in application state. You will write code to add the selected book to the checked-out list in Application state. In the ASP Web application, this task was performed by the CheckOutList.asp page. Because you can handle this task on the same Web form, you will move the functionality into the **cmdCheckOutBook_Click** event handler.

1. Create a **Click** event handler for the **cmdCheckOutBook** button.

2. Retrieve the CheckOutList **DataSet** from Application state, as shown in the following code example:

```
Visual Basic .NET

Dim dsCheckOutList As DataSet
dsCheckOutList = Application("CheckOutList")
```

```
C#

DataSet dsCheckOutList;
dsCheckOutList = (DataSet)Application["CheckOutList"];
```

3. Determine if the selected book is already checked out by using the **Find** method to locate the row containing the selected book, as shown in the following code example:

Visual Basic .NET

```
Dim r As DataRow
r = dsCheckOutList.Tables(0).Rows.Find( _
    lstTitles.SelectedItem.Value)
```

C#

```
DataRow r;
r = dsCheckOutList.Tables[0].Rows.Find(
    lstTitles.SelectedItem.Value);
```

4. If the found row is **Nothing** (Visual Basic .NET) or **null** (C#), then the book has not been checked out. Lock the **Application** object to begin an update, as shown in the following code example:

Visual Basic .NET

```
If (r Is Nothing) Then
    Application.Lock()
```

C#

```
if (null == r)
{
    Application.Lock();
```

5. Create a new row in the **CheckOutList DataSet**.

6. Set the **LibraryID** field to **lstNames.SelectedItem.Value**.

7. Set the **LastName** field to **lstNames.SelectedItem.Text**.

8. Set the **TitleID** field to **lstTitles.SelectedItem.Value**.

9. Add the new row to the **CheckOutList DataSet**.

10. Unlock the **Application** object.

Your code for the preceding steps should look similar to the following code example:

Visual Basic .NET

```
r = dsCheckOutList.Tables(0).NewRow()
r("LibraryID") = lstNames.SelectedItem.Value
r("LastName") = lstNames.SelectedItem.Text
r("TitleID") = lstTitles.SelectedItem.Value
dsCheckOutList.Tables(0).Rows.Add(r)
Application.UnLock()
```

C#

```
r = dsCheckOutList.Tables[0].NewRow();
r["LibraryID"] = lstNames.SelectedItem.Value;
r["LastName"] = lstNames.SelectedItem.Text;
r["TitleID"] = lstTitles.SelectedItem.Value;
dsCheckOutList.Tables[0].Rows.Add(r);
Application.UnLock();
```

11. Complete the **If** statement by adding code to track whether or not the check out process was successful.

This tracking is done by using Session state. After unlocking the **Application** object, set **Session("CheckOutStatus")** to **True**. If the initial call to the **Find** method returned a valid row, set **Session("CheckOutStatus")** to **False**.

Your code for the preceding step should look similar to the following code example:

Visual Basic .NET

```
If (r Is Nothing) Then
...
   Session("CheckOutStatus") = True
Else
   Session("CheckOutStatus") = False
End If
```

C#

```
if (null == r)
{
...
   Session["CheckOutStatus"] = true;
}
else
{
   Session["CheckOutStatus"] = false;
}
```

12. After the **End If** statement, redirect the user to the CheckOutList.aspx Web Form, as shown in the following code example:

```
Visual Basic .NET

Response.Redirect("CheckOutList.aspx")
```

```
C#

Response.Redirect("CheckOutList.aspx");
```

13. Build BookList.aspx and ensure that it builds without any errors.

Exercise 2
Migrate CheckOutList.asp

In this exercise, you will migrate the CheckOutList.asp page. You will make numerous structural and language changes to ensure that the page runs correctly as an ASP.NET Web Form.

▶ Create the CheckOutList.aspx user interface

In the following steps you will create a new UI that takes advantage of the controls that are available in ASP.NET.

1. Open the CheckOutList.asp page in Visual Studio .NET.

   This file is located in *install_folder*\Labfiles\Lab09\SimpleLibrary. Keep this file open for the remainder of this exercise for reference.

2. Create a new Web Form named CheckOutList.aspx.

3. In Design view, change the **pageLayout** property to **FlowLayout**.

4. Insert a **Label** Web Form control named **lblCheckOutStatus**.

5. Clear the **Text** property of **lblCheckOutStatus**.

6. Type the text **Current list of who has checked out books:**

   Alternatively, you may copy this text from the CheckOutList.asp page.

7. On the next line, create a table with three column headers titled **Library ID**, **Title ID**, and **Last Name**, respectively.

8. Underneath the table, insert a **Repeater** Web Form control named **rptCheckOutList**.

9. Underneath the **Repeater** control, insert an HTML **Horizontal Rule** control.

10. Underneath the **Horizontal Rule** control, type the text **Return to Book List**

11. Highlight the text that you just typed, and from the **Insert** menu, select **Hyperlink**.

12. In the **Hyperlink** dialog box, type **BookList.aspx** in the **URL** field.

13. Click **OK**.

14. Switch to HTML view, and move the **Repeater** control so that it is after the </TR> element, but before the </TABLE> element.

   This will make the **Repeater** control display its data in the table.

   The **Repeater** control is all of the elements between the <asp:Repeater ...> element and the </asp:Repeater> element.

▶ Create the Page_Load event handler

In the following steps you will create a **Page_Load** event handler that informs the user if their book checkout was successful.

1. Open the code-behind file for the CheckOutList.aspx Web Form.

2. Perform the following steps in the **Page_Load** event handler:

   a. Retrieve the **Boolean** value from **Session("CheckOutStatus")**.

   b. If the **Boolean** value is **True**, set the **lblCheckOutStatus.Text** property to **Check out succeeded!**

   c. If the **Boolean** value is **False**, set the **lblCheckOutStatus.Text** property to **Check out failed because book already checked out!**

   d. Retrieve the CheckOutList **DataSet** from Application state and bind it to the **rptCheckOutList** Repeater control.

   Your completed **Page_Load** event handler should look similar to the following code example:

```
Visual Basic .NET

Dim s As Boolean = _
    CType(Session("CheckOutStatus"), Boolean)
If s Then
    lblCheckOutStatus.Text = "Check out succeeded!"
Else
    lblCheckOutStatus.Text = _
    "Check out failed because book already checked out!"
End If
Dim dsCheckOutList As DataSet = _
        Application("CheckOutList")
rptCheckOutList.DataSource = dsCheckOutList
rptCheckOutList.DataBind()
```

```
C#

bool s = (bool)Session["CheckOutStatus"];
if (s)
    lblCheckOutStatus.Text = "Check out succeeded!";
else
    lblCheckOutStatus.Text =
"Check out failed because book already checked out!";
DataSet dsCheckOutList =
    (DataSet)Application["CheckOutList"];
rptCheckOutList.DataSource = dsCheckOutList;
rptCheckOutList.DataBind();
```

▶ Configure the Repeater Web Form control

In the following steps you will configure the **Repeater** Web Form control to display the books that are checked out by the user.

1. View the HTML source for CheckOutList.aspx in the Design view.

2. Locate the **rptCheckOutList** Repeater control asp element, and insert the following code inside the asp element tags:

```
<ItemTemplate>
<tr>
   <td>
<%# DataBinder.Eval(Container, "DataItem.libraryid")%>
   </td>
   <td>
<%# DataBinder.Eval(Container, "DataItem.titleid")%>
   </td>
<td>
<%# DataBinder.Eval(Container, "DataItem.lastname")%>
   </td>
</tr>
</ItemTemplate>
```

3. Build and browse the BookList.aspx Web Form.

4. Select a book and user, and then click the **Check Out Book** button.

   On the CheckOutList.aspx Web Form, verify that the information that you just selected is displayed.

   Repair any remaining errors.

Exercise 3 (Optional)
Improve Migrated Code

In this exercise, you will update the library Web application to use state management more efficiently.

Scenario

This is a more advanced exercise to be completed only if you have time. The steps are not exact, but there are pointers to locations where you must update the code. You can refer to the solution code in *install_folder*\Labfiles\Lab09*language*\Solution\TimePermits if you have difficulties.

▶ **Improve state management**

In the following steps you will improve state management by shifting Application object references to shared (static) fields.

1. Open Global.asax in Visual Studio .NET.

2. Change all **Application** object references to use a shared (Visual Basic .NET) or static (C#) field.

   A recommendation is to use the following fields:

   ```
   Visual Basic .NET
   'Application state dataset
   Public Shared dsCheckOutList As DataSet
   Public Shared Northwind_ConnectionString As String
   Public Shared Pubs_ConnectionString As String
   ```

   ```
   C#

   //Application state dataset
   public static System.Data.DataSet dsCheckOutList;
   public static string Northwind_ConnectionString;
   public static string Pubs_ConnectionString;
   ```

3. Update any code in the .aspx files to use these fields instead of the **Application** object.

4. Build and browse the Web application.

msdn training

Module 10: Deploying Microsoft ASP.NET Web Applications

Contents

Overview

- **ASP.NET Web Application Deployment Methods**
- **Maintaining a Deployed ASP.NET Web Application**

Introduction

Microsoft® ASP.NET eliminates many of the deployment issues that occur in Active Server Pages (ASP) Web applications, thereby making it possible to deploy an ASP.NET Web application simply by copying all of the necessary files to the Internet Information Services (IIS) application directory, which is where the Web application will be deployed.

Previously, when deploying ASP Web applications, it was a simple procedure to deploy or replace static content and ASP files. However, other portions of the ASP Web application, such as the components and application-specific configuration settings, required greater effort to deploy, and therefore often necessitated a shutdown of the ASP Web application to replace the components and application-specific configuration settings.

Note The code samples in this module are provided in both Microsoft Visual Basic® .NET and C#.

Objectives

After completing this module, you will be able to:

- Deploy an ASP.NET Web application.
- Maintain a deployed ASP.NET Web application.

Lesson: ASP.NET Web Application Deployment Methods

- Files Needed to Deploy ASP.NET Web Applications
- Deploying ASP.NET Web Applications Manually
- Deploying ASP.NET Web Applications Using Windows Installer Files
- Demonstration: Creating a Web Setup Project

Introduction

ASP.NET Web applications can be deployed manually or by using Microsoft Visual Studio® .NET. Deploying ASP.NET Web applications manually requires that you copy the ASP.NET Web application files to the target Web server. You can deploy ASP.NET Web applications by using the Visual Studio .NET **Copy Project** command or the Visual Studio .NET Web Setup project. The Web Setup project creates the Microsoft Windows® Installer files (.msi files).

Lesson objectives

After completing this lesson, you will be able to:

- Determine the files that are needed to deploy ASP.NET Web applications.
- Deploy ASP.NET Web applications manually.
- Deploy ASP.NET Web applications by using Windows Installer files.

Files Needed to Deploy ASP.NET Web Applications

ASP.NET Web Application Files	Needed	Remove
.vbproj, .csproj		X
.vbproj.webinfo, .csproj.webinfo		X
.resx		X
.dll	X	
.aspx	X	
\bin directory and content	X	
.aspx.vb, .aspx.cs		X
Global.asax	X	
.exe	X	
.ascx	X	
.xml	X	
Web.config	X	

Introduction

Before you can deploy ASP.NET Web applications, you need to select the files that are necessary for deploying ASP.NET Web applications. You need to select the necessary files from the directory that contains the ASP.NET Web application. By not copying unnecessary files, you increase the security of your production environment by limiting the exposure of uncompiled code.

Files not needed to deploy ASP.NET Web applications

The files that are not needed in the production directory on the target Web server include:

- Visual Studio .NET solution files (.vbproj, .vbproj.webinfo, .csproj).

  The solution files are only required by Visual Studio .NET to develop the ASP.NET Web application and are not required to run the Web application in production.

- Resource (.resx) files.

  The resource files are compiled into the dynamic-link library (DLL) file and therefore do not need to be copied to the target Web server.

- Code-behind files (.vb, .cs).

  The code-behind files are compiled into the DLL file and therefore do not need to be copied to the target Web server.

Note You must copy the code-behind files if you are using dynamic compilation in your ASP.NET Web application. Dynamic compilation is enabled by using the **src** attribute in the @ **Page** directive.

Files needed to deploy ASP.NET Web applications

The files that are needed to deploy the ASP.NET Web applications include:

- The \bin directory and the DLL files that are within it.

  The \bin directory and the DLL files are the compiled resource files and the code-behind files.

- All Web Form, user control, and XML Web service files (.aspx, .ascx, .asmx).

  The Web Form, user control, and XML Web service files are the user and Web application interface files.

- Configuration files, including Web.config and Global.asax.

  If you have changed the configuration settings in the machine.config file on the development computer, you must make the same changes in the machine.config file on the production server.

- Any additional support files, such as Extensible Markup Language (XML) files, which are in the directory.

Deploying ASP.NET Web Applications Manually

- **When to deploy ASP.NET Web applications manually:**
  - You are deploying files to the same Web server
  - You are testing the ASP.NET Web application before final deployment
  - Your ASP.NET Web application is relatively simple
- **ASP.NET Web applications can be deployed manually using**
  - The **xcopy** command, Windows Explorer, or FTP
  - The Visual Studio .NET **Copy Project** command
- **IIS settings are not copied to target Web server**   —

Introduction

You can deploy an ASP.NET Web application manually by copying a collection of files to the target Web server.

The advantages of deploying your ASP.NET Web application files manually by copying include:

- Ease of deployment. The files and other resources can simply be copied to the target Web server.

- Ease of update. You can update the files on the Web server by simply copying the updated files to the Web server.

There are two disadvantages to manually deploying the ASP.NET Web applications:

- You must determine which files are needed to deploy the ASP.NET Web application and which files are not needed to deploy the ASP.NET Web application.

- You must manually configure IIS to deploy ASP.NET Web applications.

When to deploy ASP.NET Web applications manually

You can manually deploy an ASP.NET Web application if:

- You deploy the ASP.NET Web application files to the same Web server.

- You test the ASP.NET Web application before final deployment.

- Your ASP.NET Web application is relatively simple

Deploying ASP.NET Web applications manually

You can copy ASP.NET Web application files and resources to the target Web server by manually copying the files, or by using the Visual Studio .NET **Copy Project** command:

- To deploy an ASP.NET Web application by copying files.

  You can copy the files directly to the target Web server by using Windows Explorer, File Transfer Protocol (FTP) operations, or the command prompt's XCOPY command.

- To deploy an ASP.NET Web application by using the Visual Studio .NET **Copy Project** command:

  a. Open your ASP.NET Web application in Visual Studio .NET.

  b. On the **Project** menu, choose **Copy Project**.

  c. Select the destination project folder.

  d. Select the Web access method.

  e. Select the files to be copied.

Deployment and IIS Settings

If you choose to deploy your ASP.NET Web application by copying files manually, you will need to configure IIS to use the destination folder as a Web application. You can configure IIS manually by using the IIS console or by writing IIS scripts.

If you use the Visual Studio .NET **Copy Project** command to deploy an ASP.NET Web application, a new virtual directory is created for you during the copy process. However, any custom IIS settings that you have for the source Web application are not applied to the production copy of your ASP.NET Web application. The new virtual directory inherits all of the default settings from the Web application. You need to apply the appropriate IIS settings separately, either by developing and running IIS scripts or by manually applying the IIS settings that your Web application requires.

Deploying ASP.NET Web Applications Using Windows Installer Files

* **Windows Installer files makes it easy to deploy ASP.NET Web applications that contain features such as:**
    * Shared components
    * Legacy COM components
    * IIS settings
    * Web Application resources, such as message queues, Event logs, and performance counters
* **Visual Studio .NET Web Setup project creates Windows Installer files for ASP.NET Web applications**

Introduction

When deploying ASP.NET Web applications, especially larger and more complex ASP.NET Web applications, Visual Studio .NET allows you to create a Web Setup project. A Web Setup project creates a single Windows Installer file (.msi file) for the ASP.NET Web application. Although you can distribute your ASP.NET Web application by copying the necessary files to the required location, it is easier to deploy complex ASP.NET Web applications with Windows Installer files. The Windows Installer files can be distributed to the target Web server and installed similar to any other Windows Installer files.

When to use Windows Installer Files to deploy ASP.NET Web applications

When an ASP.NET Web application includes complex features, use the Windows Installer files to deploy that ASP.NET Web application, thereby ensuring that all of the necessary files and settings are installed properly on the target Web server.

There are many installation issues that are associated with complex ASP.NET Web applications. Complex ASP.NET Web applications include features such as:

- Shared components, such as global assemblies.

- Legacy Component Object Model (COM) components.

- Custom IIS settings, including security settings.

> **Note** While you can configure virtual directory access settings, you cannot configure IIS authentication settings. To configure IIS authentication settings, you must use a script file.

- Application resources, such as message queues, event logs, and performance counters.

A Web Setup project

A Web Setup project creates a Windows Installer file that can be deployed to a Web server so that users can later download and run the file from a Web site.

The following are the main steps to deploying a Web application by using the Web Setup project:

1. Create a new solution file and add new projects.

   Create a blank Visual Studio .NET solution and add the Web Setup project, and your ASP.NET Web application project, to that solution. Alternately, you can add a Web Setup project to an existing ASP.NET Web application Visual Studio .NET solution.

2. Configure the Web Setup project.

   Configure the Web Setup project. Configuring the Web Setup project involves specifying ASP.NET Web application properties, such as the virtual directory name, script access, indexing, and logging. Configuring the Web Setup project also involves selecting the ASP.NET Web application files that need to be deployed to the Web server.

3. Build the Web Setup project.

   Create the Windows Installer file. To create the Windows Installer file, on the **Build** menu, choose **Build** *ProjectName*.

Note   You cannot use a Web Setup project to automatically install the Microsoft .NET Framework on the target Web server. To install the Microoosft.NET Framework you must create a setup program. For more information, see the Microsoft MSDN® article, "Deploying .NET Applications: Lifecycle Guide," which is available at the following Uniform Resource Locator (URL): http://msdn.microsoft.com/library/default.asp?url=/library/en-us/dnbda/html/DALGDeploy.asp

---

Demonstration: Creating a Web Setup Project

- Create a new Solution file and add projects
- Configure the Web Setup project
- Build the Web Setup project
- Copy and test the ASP.NET Web application deployment
- Show the deployed files
- Remove the ASP.NET Web application

Introduction

In this demonstration, you will see the steps that are involved in creating a simple Web Setup project that is used to deploy an ASP.NET Web application.

▶ **To run this demonstration**

Note These steps are to be completed only by the instructor. Later in the demonstration, students will perform the steps on their computers.

Create a new Solution file and add projects

1. In Visual Studio .NET, create a new blank solution, **WebSetupDemo**, in the *install_folder*\Democode\Mod10 folder.

2. Add the XML project to this solution. The complete path is:

   install_folder\Democode\Mod10\XMLProject\XML.csproj

Note The Web Setup project creation is not language based. Although you are using a C#-based project for this demonstration, a Visual Basic .NET-based project works the same way.

3. Add a new Web Setup project named **SetupDemo** to the solution.

Configure the Web Setup project

4. In the File System window, select **Web Application Folder**.

5. In the Properties window, show the properties that you can set for the Web application, including the virtual directory name, script access, indexing, and logging properties.

6. In the left pane of the File System window, right-click the **Web Application Folder**, point to **Add**, and then click **Project Output**.

7. Explain each of the six outputs that can be added to the Web application folder.

   Refer to the following table for details on the six items.

Outputs	Purpose
Documentation Files	The files that are used for intellidoc documentation.
Primary output	The .dll or .exe file that is created when the Web application is compiled.
Localized resources	The satellite assemblies created if the Web project has been localized.
Debug Symbols	The debugging files (.pdb files) for this project.
Content Files	All content files (such as .aspx, .asmx, and .config files) for the project.
Source Files	The .cs or .vb files for the project.

8. Show the students that the Web application that you are deploying includes many of the XML and Extensible Stylesheet Language Transformation (XSLT) files that are needed for the Web application to run properly.

9. Select **Primary output** and **Content Files**, and then click **OK**.

10. In Solution Explorer, right-click **SetupDemo** and point to **View**.

11. With the **View** menu displayed, briefly explain what each of the following six views are used for.

View	Purpose
File System	Allows you to add the files and folders that are to be installed on the target Web server during installation.
Registry	Allows you to add custom settings to the registry during installation.
File Types	Allows you to specify file associations on the target Web server.
User Interface	Allows you to add the dialog boxes that display during installation.
Custom Actions	Allows you to add scripts and executable files that are run by the installation process. For example, you can run scripts to create a Microsoft SQL Server™ database or to configure IIS security settings.
Launch Conditions	Allows you to set conditions on the target computer that must be met for installation to continue.

12. From the **View** menu, choose **User Interface**.

13. Add a **Read Me** dialog box to the End folder.

14. Drag the **Read Me** dialog box up the list, so that it is displayed before the **Finished** dialog box.

15. Set the **ReadmeFile** property to *install_folder*\Democode\Mod10\ Readme.rtf.

    To set this property, follow these steps:

    a. Click **(Browse)** from the ReadmeFile Property menu.

    b. Double-click **Web Application Folder**.

    c. Click **Add File**.

    d. Browse to *install_folder*\Democode\Mod10.

    e. Double-click **Readme.rtf**.

    f. Click **OK**.

Build the Web Setup project

16. In Solution Explorer, right-click **SetupDemo** and choose **Build**.

17. Open Windows Explorer and browse to *install_folder*\Democode\Mod10\WebSetupDemo\SetupDemo\Debug

Copy and test the ASP.NET Web application deployment

18. Double-click **SetupDemo.msi** to run the installer package and install the new Web application.

    Point out the dialog boxes that are provided automatically by the setup project, along with the Readme file that displays when setup is complete.

19. Open Microsoft Internet Explorer and browse to:

    ```
    http://localhost/SetupDemo/DataSetView.aspx
    ```

20. Verify that the Web page works by changing the radio buttons or the drop-down list box.

Show the deployed files

21. In Windows Explorer, browse to C:\Inetpub\wwwroot\SetupDemo.

Remove the ASP.NET Web application

22. Open the **Add/Remove Programs** Control Panel and show that SetupDemo is listed as an installed program.

23. Uninstall the Web application.

Lesson: Maintaining a Deployed ASP.NET Web Application

- **Updating ASP.NET Web Applications**
- **Deploying Shared Assemblies**
- **Practice: Viewing and Using Shared Assemblies**

Introduction

After you deploy an ASP.NET Web application, it is often necessary to update files in the Web application. In this lesson, you will learn how to maintain a Web application by updating files.

Lesson objectives

After completing this lesson, you will be able to:

- Explain how to update ASP.NET Web applications.
- Explain how to deploy shared assemblies by using the global assembly cache.

Updating ASP.NET Web Applications

- **To update ASP.NET Web applications, copy new files to the Web server**
- **Output cache maintains existing sessions**
- **Updating assemblies:**
    - ASP.NET creates a shadow copy of the existing assembly file and locks the shadow copy
    - ASP.NET Fulfills existing requests with the current assembly file
    - ASP.NET Loads the new assembly file
    - ASP.NET Fulfills new requests with the updated assembly file

Introduction

Occasionally you will need to upgrade ASP.NET Web applications that you have already deployed to a Web server. Typically, ASP.NET Web applications are upgraded to:

- Apply bug fixes that will remedy the problems that exist with your Web application.
- Provide enhancements for the Web application's existing features.
- Provide the Web application with new features or capabilities.

Update ASP.NET Web applications by copying files

You can update ASP.NET Web applications by copying the new files to the directory, thereby overwriting the existing files. When the next user connects to your Web application, they receive the most up-to-date files. Unlike earlier versions of ASP, updating an ASP.NET Web application does not require you to stop and restart IIS.

Output cache maintains existing sessions

If you enable page output caching for the Web Forms in the ASP.NET Web application, users will continue to receive the older versions of the Web pages until the cache expires. After the cached Web pages expire, the users will then receive an updated version of that Web page.

Updating Assemblies

Unlike IIS under ASP, which loaded a component into memory and locked it on disk until the Web application (or IIS) was shutdown, ASP.NET first makes a shadow copy of each assembly file and then loads and locks that shadow file, instead of loading and locking the original assembly file. ASP.NET then monitors the original assemblies for changes. If updates are detected, ASP.NET fulfills any existing Web page requests with the current copy of the assembly file, and it then loads the new assembly file and fulfills the new Web page requests by using the updated assembly. This method of updating assemblies allows you to easily update any private assembly file that is used by your Web application without having to shut down the Web server, even temporarily.

Deploying Shared Assemblies

- **Install shared assemblies in the global assembly cache**
  - The global assembly cache is located in the
    Windows_directory\Assembly, where *Windows_directory* is the
    operating system folder
- **Before deploying, create a strong name for the shared assembly
  using the sn.exe command-line tool**
- **Install shared assemblies in the global assembly cache using:**
  - Windows Installer 2.0
  - gacutil.exe
  - Windows Explorer
- **Strongly named assemblies contain versioning information
  allowing two or more versions of the same assembly to be used
  side-by-side**

Introduction

Every computer that has the.NET Framework installed also has a computer-wide code cache that is called the global assembly cache. To share an assembly among multiple ASP.NET Web applications that are on the same Web server, without having multiple copies of that assembly file (one for each ASP.NET Web application), you must install the assembly file in the global assembly cache.

What is the global assembly cache?

The global assembly cache is a physical location on the Web server that contains shared assemblies. When the common language runtime needs to find an assembly, it first looks for the assembly in the same directory as the executable for the application (the bin folder for Web applications). If the assembly is not there, the runtime then looks for the assembly in the global assembly cache, which is located in the *Windows_Directory*/assembly folder (where *Windows_Directory* is the operating system folder).

Tip When you open the folder in Windows Explorer, all of the assemblies appear to be in this folder. However, each assembly resides in its own subdirectory, which is hidden from the user. The global assembly cache maintains a database of each assembly, its version, and its physical location.

Deploying shared assemblies

When using an assembly file that will be shared amongst multiple Web applications, you must place the assembly file in the global assembly cache. There are several ways to install an assembly into the global assembly cache:

- Windows Explorer

  The .NET Framework installs a shell extension that lets you simply drag the strongly named assemblies into the global assembly cache from any Windows folder. The global assembly cache automatically creates the hidden subdirectory and updates the database with the version information of that assembly.

- gacutil.exe

  This command-line utility lets you add assemblies to and remove assemblies from the global assembly cache, and it also allows you to list the contents of the global assembly cache in a command prompt. Gacutil.exe is installed when you install the .NET Framework, and it is located in the c:*WinDir*\Microsoft.NET\Framework*version* folder, where *WinDir* is the operating system folder and *version* is the .NET Framework version number.

  Tip You can run the gacutil.exe command-line utility from the Visual Studio .NET command prompt. To start the Visual Studio .NET command prompt: click **Start**, point to **All Programs**, then **Microsoft Visual Studio .NET**, then **Visual Studio .NET Tools**, and finally, **Visual Studio .NET Command Prompt**.

- Windows Installer file

  When you create a new Web Setup project, and the associated Windows Installer file, you can also include shared assemblies in the Windows Installer file. The Windows Installer file will then place the assemblies in the global assembly cache on the Web server.

Note Before you can deploy a shared assembly file in a global assembly cache, the shared assembly file must be strongly named. To strongly name a shared assembly file, use the **sn.exe** command-line tool. For more information about strongly named shared assemblies, see "Creating and Using Strong-Named Assemblies" in the Visual Studio .NET documentation.

Deployment and Assembly Versioning

Strongly named assemblies contain versioning information. The versioning information allows two or more versions of the same shared assembly file to be used side-by-side.

Note For more information on shared assemblies, the global assembly cache, and versioning, see the MSDN article, ".NET Framework: Building, Packaging, Deploying, and Administering Applications and Types—Part 2," in the Visual Studio .NET documentation.

Practice: Viewing and Using Shared Assemblies

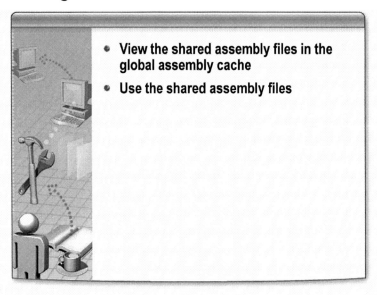

Introduction

In this practice, you will see how ASP.NET uses the global assembly cache to find components that are referenced by a Web application.

You will be using a very simple ASP.NET Web application to test the global assembly cache. The Web application contains a single Web Form with only two controls, a Web custom control that displays a grid on the Web page, and a **Label** control. There is a single event handler in the Web application; it is the **Click** event handler for the Web custom control.

When the Web Custom Control is clicked, the **Label** control displays the row and column number for the cell that was clicked. The Web Custom control also calls an assembly that multiplies the row number and column number.

The two assemblies that are referenced in this Web application are WebControlFireEvents.dll and Multiply.dll.

Viewing and using shared assemblies

1. Using Windows Explorer or the **gacutil.exe /l** command, determine which assemblies are in the global assembly cache. Write your answer below:

   _____

2. Open Internet Explorer and browse to the following URL:

   `http://localhost/upg/Mod10-GAC`

3. Click on a cell in the grid and verify that the cell background changes and that the **Label** control displays the correct information.

4. Leave the Web browser open and open Windows Explorer.

5. In Windows Explorer, browse to the following directory:

   `install_folder\Practices\Mod10\GAC\bin`

6. Delete the WebControlFireEvents.dll file.

7. In the open Web browser window, click the **Refresh** button.

8. When prompted to resend the information, click **Retry**.

   What happens? Why?

   _____

   _____

9. Again, while leaving the Web browser window open, switch to the Windows Explorer window.

10. Delete the Multiply.dll file.

11. In the open Web browser window, click the **Refresh** button.

12. When prompted to resend the information, click **Retry**.

   What happens? Why?

   _____

   _____

Lab 10: Deploying an ASP.NET Web Application

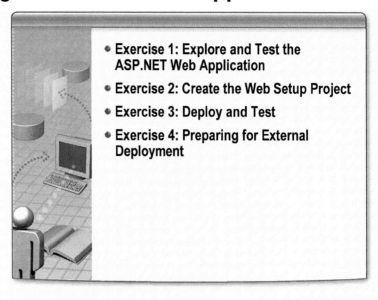

Objectives

After completing this lab, you will be able to:

- Deploy an ASP.NET Web application by using a Web Setup project.
- Customize the installation of an ASP.NET Web application.
- Update the existing files on a deployed ASP.NET Web application.

Note This lab focuses on the concepts in this module and as a result may not comply with Microsoft security recommendations. For instance, this lab uses an ASP.NET Web application that allows users to upload and execute .msi files on the Web server.

Prerequisites

Before working on this lab, you must have knowledge about the different methods that can be used to deploy an ASP.NET Web application.

Estimated time to complete this lab: 60 minutes

Exercise 0
Lab Setup

To complete this lab, you must complete the following steps.

▶ Build the XML Web service

In the following steps, you will build a project on your computer. This project is an XML Web service that will be called by a Web application.

1. In Windows Explorer, browse to the following directory:

   ```
   install_folder\Labfiles\Lab10\GetTemp
   ```

2. Double-click **lab10-GetTemp.sln**.

3. Visual Studio .NET opens the lab10-GetTemp solution.

4. In Solution Explorer, right-click **Lab10-GetTemp** and choose **Build**. If you see the **Save File As** dialog box, which will ask if you want to save the solution file, click **Save**, and then click **Yes**.

5. Close Visual Studio .NET.

▶ Register the converter.dll component

In the following steps, you will register an assembly so that it can be used by a Web application.

1. From a command prompt, go to the *install_folder*\Labfiles\Lab10*language*\ Starter folder and type the following command:

   ```
   regsvr32 converter.dll
   ```

2. When the **RegSvr32** dialog box is displayed, click **OK**.

Exercise 1
Explore and Test the ASP.NET Web Application

In this exercise, you will prepare an ASP.NET Web application for deployment.

Scenario

You will be deploying a Web application that includes references to a COM component and to a Web service. Before deploying the Web application, you will test it to verify that it works properly, and you will confirm the Web application's security settings.

▶ **Open the Lab10 Solution**

1. In Visual Studio .NET, from the **File** menu, click **Open Solution**.

2. In the Open Solution window, in the shortcut list, click **My Projects**.

3. Expand the **Labfiles**, **Lab10**, *language*, and **Starter** folders.

4. Select **Lab10-*xy*.sln**, where *xy* is either CS or VB, and then click **Open**.

▶ **Explore the Solution**

1. In Solution Explorer, expand the **References** and **Web References** folders.

   Note that a DLL file named Converter is one of the components in the list.

   In the Web References folder, what is the Web Reference proxy called?

   _____

   What is the Web Reference URL for the referenced Web service?

   _____

2. In Solution Explorer, double-click the **Web.config** file.

   What kind of security is implemented in this file? What are the effective access rights to the default.aspx page?

   _____

   _____

▶ **Set IIS Security Settings**

1. From the **Start** menu, right-click **My Computer**, and then choose **Manage**.

2. In the **Computer Management** console, expand **Services and Applications**, expand **Internet Information Services**, expand **Web Sites**, expand **Default Web Site**, and then expand **upg**.

3. Right-click **lab10-cs** or **lab10-vb** and then click **Properties**.

4. On the **Directory Security** tab, in the **Anonymous access and authentication control** box, click **Edit**.

5. Clear the **Anonymous access** and **Basic authentication** check boxes, and then click to enable **Integrated Windows authentication**.

6. Click **OK**, click **OK** again, and then close the IIS console.

▶ **Test the Web Application**

In the following steps, you will test the Web application to ensure that it is working properly on your computer before deploying it.

1. In **Solution Explorer**, expand **Web References**, and then right-click **localhost** and choose **Update Web Reference**.

2. In **Solution Explorer**, right-click **default.aspx** and choose **Build and Browse**.

   The Web browser window opens, and you are redirected to the Login.aspx page.

3. This logon Web page uses a table in the Northwind database to store and retrieve user names and the corresponding hashed passwords.

4. In the Login Web Form, enter **someone** for a user name and **Secret1** for a password, and then click the **Log In** button.

   You are redirected to the originally requested Web page, default.aspx. This Web page accepts a U.S.-based Postal Code for input and returns the average daily temperature for the area corresponding to the specified U.S.-based Postal Code.

5. Enter **98052** in the Postal Code text box, and then click **Get Temperature!**

   The Web page returns a temperature in both Fahrenheit and Celsius. The Fahrenheit temperature is returned from the **GetTemp** XML Web service that the Web project references. The Web Form then passes the Fahrenheit temperature to the **Converter.dll**, which returns the temperature in Celsius.

Exercise 2
Create the Web Setup Project

In this exercise, you will add a Web Setup project to the existing Lab10-*xy* solution. You will then configure the Web Setup project by adding custom actions and a custom user interface (UI).

Scenario

Although you can create a Web Setup project in its own solution, you can simplify the creation and customization of the project by adding it to the same solution as the Web application that you are deploying.

▶ **Create the Web Setup project**

1. In Solution Explorer, right-click **Solution 'lab10-*language*'**, point to **Add**, and then click **New Project**.

2. In the **Add New Project** dialog box, perform the following steps:

   a. In the **Project Types** list, click **Setup and Deployment Projects**.

   b. In the **Templates** list, click **Web Setup Project**.

   c. In the **Name** text box, type **DeployLab10**

   d. In the **Location** text box, set the path to *install_folder*\Labfiles\Lab10\.

   e. Click **OK**.

   The new Web Setup project is added to the solution and the File System window is displayed.

3. Using the Properties window for the Web Application folder, answer the following questions:

   What is the name of the virtual directory that will be created?

   _____

   What is the default Web page?

   _____

   Can you set specific authentication settings for the virtual directory? What security settings can you make?

   _____

▶ **Configure the Web Setup project output**

In the following steps, you will select the files that will be installed when the Web Setup project is executed.

1. In the left pane of the File System window, right-click the **Web Application Folder**, point to **Add**, and then click **Project Output**.

2. In the **Add Project Output Group** dialog box, select both **Primary output** and **Content Files**, and then click **OK**.

   A warning dialog box displays. Why?

   _____

   _____

   _____

3. Click **OK** to close the warning dialog box.

   What are the dependencies that were added to the Web Setup project? Are the dependencies needed?

   _____

   _____

▶ **Add UI elements**

You want to ensure that the users of your Web Setup project read and agree to a licensing agreement. In the following steps, you will add the UI for a licensing agreement.

1. In Solution Explorer, right-click the **DeployLab10** project, point to **View**, and then click **User Interface**.

2. Add a dialog box to the **Start** process that requires users to read and agree to a license agreement:

   a. Right-click **Start** and choose **Add Dialog**.

   b. Click **License Agreement**, and then click **OK**.

   c. Drag the **License Agreement** dialog up in the list, so that it will display after the Welcome screen, but before the Installation Address.

What other types of dialog boxes can you add to the setup process?

_____

_____

_____

3. Set the **LicenseFile** property for the License Agreement dialog box to License.rtf.

    To set this property, follow these steps:

    a. Click **(Browse)** from the **LicenseFile** Property menu.

    b. Double-click **Web Application Folder**.

    c. Click the **Add File** button.

    d. Browse to the _install_folder_\Labfiles\Lab10_language_\Starter folder.

    e. Click License.rtf, and then click **Open**.

    f. Click **OK**.

    Tip   You can create your own license document by using any Rich Text file editor, such as Microsoft WordPad.

▶ **Add a Custom Action**

Because you cannot change IIS security settings directly by using the Web Setup project, you need to add a custom action to the installation that runs a script file. The script file uses the adsutil.vbs tool, which is provided with IIS, to configure IIS virtual directories.

1. In Solution Explorer, right-click the **DeployLab10** project, point to **View**, and then click **Custom Actions**.

2. In the Install folder, add a custom action that runs the configure.vbs script file.

    The configure.vbs file is the in the Web Application folder:

    a. Right-click **Install** and choose **Add Custom Action**.

    b. In the **Look in** drop-down list, choose **Web Application Folder**.

    c. Click **Add File**.

    d. Click **configure.vbs**, and then click **Open**.

    e. Click **OK**.

        Configure.vbs is added under the Install folder.

Exercise 3
Deploy and Test

In this exercise, you will test the Web Setup project, correct any errors, and then deploy the Web Setup project to a different computer.

Scenario

Before deploying the Web Setup project, you can run the installation from within Visual Studio .NET to verify that everything runs properly.

▶ **Install the new Web application**

1. In Solution Explorer, right-click **DeployLab10** and then choose **Build**.

    Visual Studio .NET builds the project.

2. In Solution Explorer, right-click **DeployLab10** and then choose **Install**.

    What happens?

    _____

    What is the second screen that displays?

    _____

3. Proceed through the setup process until it completes.

4. When setup completes, click **Close**.

5. Open Internet Explorer and browse to the following URL:

    `http://localhost/DeployLab10`

    What happens?

    _____

    Why do you not need to specify a file in the URL?

    _____

6. Log on using a user name of **someone** and a password of **Secret1**.

7. In default.aspx, enter a U.S. Postal Code of **98052** and verify that the Web page is returned without errors.

▶ **Verify security settings**

In the following steps, you will verify that the authentication settings in IIS were properly configured during installation.

1. From the **Start** menu, right-click **My Computer**, and then choose **Manage**.

2. In the **Computer Management** console, expand **Services and Applications**, expand **Internet Information Services**, expand **Web Sites**, and then expand **Default Web Site**.

3. Right-click **DeployLab10** and then click **Properties**.

4. On the **Directory Security** tab, in the **Anonymous access and authentication control** box, click **Edit**.

   What access permissions are granted to this Web application?

   _____

5. Click **Cancel**, click **Cancel** again, and then close the **Computer Management** console.

▶ **Uninstall the Web application**

1. Using the Add/Remove Programs control panel, remove the DeployLab10 Web application.

2. After uninstallation is complete, open Internet Explorer and browse to the following URL:

   ```
   http://localhost/DeployLab10
   ```

   What happens?

   _____

▶ **Register the converter.dll component**

> **Note**   When you uninstall a Web application that references a COM component, the uninstall process unregisters the COM component. To continue working with that component, you need to re-register it.

1. From a command prompt, go to the *install_folder*\Labfiles\Lab10*language*\ Starter folder and type the following command:

   ```
   regsvr32 converter.dll
   ```

2. When the **RegSvr32** dialog box is displayed, click **OK**.

Exercise 4
Preparing for External Deployment

In this exercise, you will deploy the Web application to another server that is in the classroom. You will then decide on the tasks that are required to deploy the Web application to a server that is outside of the classroom.

In this exercise, you will use a Web application that allows you to upload and install Windows Installer files on the Instructor computer. In a real-world deployment situation, you would not use a Web application to transfer and install Windows Installer files. The Web application associated with this lab has been provided to simplify deployment within a controlled classroom environment.

▶ Change Web Setup project properties

Because every student will be deploying a similar Web project on the Instructor computer, you need to make a few changes to your Setup project to ensure uniqueness in the classroom.

1. In Visual Studio .NET, in Solution Explorer, right-click **DeployLab10**, point to **View**, and then choose **File System**.

2. In the File System window, select **Web Application Folder**.

3. In the Properties window, change the **VirtualDirectory** property to **Deploy_Name**, where *Name* is the name of your computer.

   For example, if your computer name is **Lima**, the virtual directory will be named **Deploy_Lima**.

4. In Solution Explorer, select the **DeployLab10** project.

5. In the Properties window, click the property field for **ProductCode**, and then click the ellipsis (...) in the property field.

6. In the **Product Code** dialog box, click **New Code**, and then click **OK**.

7. In the Properties window, click the property field for **UpgradeCode**, and then click the ellipsis (...) in the property field.

8. In the **Upgrade Code** dialog box, click **New Code**, and then click **OK**.

▶ Update the script

You must also update the script that the Web Setup project runs so that it will properly configure the virtual directory.

1. In Windows Explorer, browse to the following path:

   `install_folder\Labfiles\Lab10\VB\Starter`

   or

   `install_folder\Labfiles\Lab10\CS\Starter`

2. Right-click **configure.vbs** and then choose **Edit**.

   The configure.vbs script file opens in Microsoft Notepad.

3. Change each occurrence of **DeployLab10** to **Deploy_***Name*, where *Name* is the name of your computer.

4. Save the script as **new_configure.vbs** and then close Notepad.

▶ **Update the custom action and UI**

You will now update the Web Setup project to use the new script file. You will also remove the License Agreement from the UI.

1. In Visual Studio .NET, in Solution Explorer, right-click **DeployLab10**, point to **View**, and then click **Custom Actions**.

2. Remove the **configure.vbs** custom action from the Install folder.

3. Add the **new_configure.vbs** custom action to the Install folder.

4. In Visual Studio .NET, in Solution Explorer, right-click **DeployLab10**, point to **View**, and then click **User Interface**.

5. Remove the **License Agreement** from the Start folder.

▶ **Build and deploy**

In the following steps, you will deploy your Web application on the Instructor computer. To deploy on the Instructor computer, you will use a Web application on the Instructor computer. This Web application allows you to upload the MSI file and then install it.

1. In Solution Explorer, right-click **DeployLab10**, and then choose **Build**.

2. In Windows Explorer, browse to the following location:

```
install_folder\Labfiles\Lab10\DeployLab10\Debug
```

3. Rename **DeployLab10.msi** to **Deploy***Name***.msi**, where *Name* is the name of your computer.

4. In Internet Explorer, browse to the following URL:

```
http://London/upg/WebUpload
```

5. If you are prompted for a username and password, type **Instructor** for the username and **P@ssw0rd** for the password, and then click **OK**.

6. On the Web Form, click **Browse**, and then navigate to the Deploy*Name*.msi file.

7. Select the file, and then click **Open**.

8. In the Web Form, click **Submit**.

   You will see a confirmation that the upload completed successfully, and the **Install** button becomes enabled.

9. Click **Install**.

   The Web Form installs your uploaded Web Application on the Instructor computer. You may need to wait one or two minutes for installation to complete before continuing with the following steps.

▶ **Test the Web application**

In the following steps, you will test your installation.

1. When installation is complete, browse to the following address in Internet Explorer:

```
http://London/Deploy_Name
```

(where *Name* is the name of your server).

What happens when this location is opened?

_____

2. In the Login Web Form, enter **someone** for a user name and **Secret1** for a password, and then click the **Log In** button.

What happens?

_____

3. Enter **98052** in the **Your U.S. Postal Code** text box, and then click **Get Temperature!**

What happens? Why? What do you need to do to fix this?

_____

_____

_____

4. Close Internet Explorer.

▶ **Fix and update**

In the following steps, you will update the Web application so that it runs properly on the Instructor computer. You will update necessary files and re-test the Web application.

1. In Visual Studio .NET, in Solution Explorer, expand the **lab10-cs** or **lab10-vb** project, expand **Web References**, and then select **localhost**.

2. In the Properties window for the localhost folder, change the **Web Reference URL** property from **http://localhost/upg/...** to **http://***servername***/upg/...**, where *servername* is the name of your computer.

3. In Solution Explorer, right-click the **lab10-cs** or **lab10-vb** project and choose **Build**.

4. In Windows Explorer, browse to the following path:

```
install_folder\Labfiles\Lab10\VB\Starter\Bin
```

or

```
install_folder\Labfiles\Lab10\CS\Starter\Bin
```

5. Right-click **lab10-cs.dll** or **lab10-vb.dll**, and then choose **Copy**.

6. In the address bar, type **\\London\c$\Inetpub\wwwroot\Deploy_*Name***, where *Name* is the name of your server, and then press ENTER.

   This action opens the folder of your deployed Web application on the Instructor computer.

7. From the **Edit** menu, choose **Paste**.

8. In the **Confirm File Replace** dialog box, click **Yes**.

9. On your computer, open Internet Explorer and browse to the following address:

```
http://London/Deploy_Name
```

   (where *Name* is the name of your server).

10. Verify that the deployed Web application now works properly.

▶ **Deploying Web application externally**

Although the deployment of your Web application was successful in the classroom, there are at least three changes that must be made to the Web application before it can be deployed on a server that does not have the classroom setup.

What are the issues to be addressed before deploying your ASP.NET Web application externally, and what do you need to do to fix each of these issues, in either the original Web application or the Web Setup project?

1. _____

   _____

   _____

   _____

2. _____

_____

_____

_____

3. _____

_____

_____

_____

Course Evaluation

Your evaluation of this course will help Microsoft understand the quality of your learning experience.

To complete a course evaluation, go to http://www.CourseSurvey.com.

Microsoft will keep your evaluation strictly confidential and will use your responses to improve your future learning experience.

msdn training

Appendix A: Accessing XML Data

Contents

Microsoft

Overview

- ● **XML in Microsoft .NET**
- ● **Displaying XML Data on a Web Form**
- ● **XML and the DataSet Object**

Introduction

Accessing Extensible Markup Language (XML) data in a Microsoft® ASP.NET Web application is easier than accessing XML data in Active Server Pages (ASP) Web applications. To access XML data in ASP Web applications, you used Microsoft XML Core Services (MSXML) 4.0. To access XML data in ASP.NET Web applications, you will use XML classes in the Microsoft .NET Framework.

In this module, you will learn how to read, write, and display XML data in an ASP.NET Web application by using the XML classes in the .NET Framework.

Note   The code samples in this module are provided in both Microsoft Visual Basic® .NET and C#.

Objectives

After completing this module, you will be able to:

- ■ Explain the XML classes in the .NET Framework that are used for accessing XML data in ASP.NET Web applications.

- ■ Display XML data on a Web Form by using the **Xml** server control and by using the Extensible Stylesheet Language Transformation (XSLT) style sheets.

- ■ Read and write XML data by using a **Dataset** object.

Lesson: XML in Microsoft .NET

- What Is XML?
- Multimedia: Overview of Business Problems Solved by Using XML
- Programming with XML in ASP.NET Web Applications
- Demonstration: Using the .NET Framework XML Classes

Introduction

When working with XML data in ASP, you used the Microsoft XML Core Services 4.0 (MSXML) to access XML data. When working with XML data in ASP.NET, you can use the XML classes in the .NET Framework to access XML data. In this lesson, you will learn the difference between using the XML Parser and the XML classes in the .NET Framework.

Lesson objectives

After completing this lesson, you will be able to:

- Define XML.
- Explain the parts of a XML document.
- Explain the .NET Framework XML classes.
- Describe how the XML classes in the .NET Framework simplify accessing XML data in an ASP.NET Web application.

What Is XML?

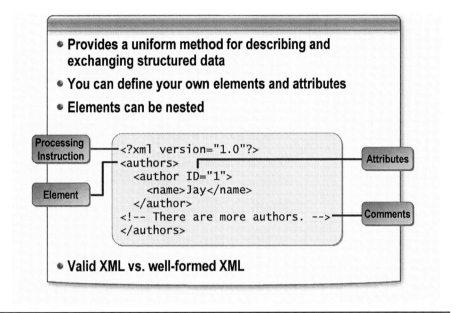

- **Provides a uniform method for describing and exchanging structured data**
- **You can define your own elements and attributes**
- **Elements can be nested**

Processing Instruction

Element

Attributes

Comments

```
<?xml version="1.0"?>
<authors>
   <author ID="1">
      <name>Jay</name>
   </author>
   <!-- There are more authors. -->
</authors>
```

- **Valid XML vs. well-formed XML**

Introduction

XML is the universal format that is used for describing and exchanging structured documents and data on the Internet. XML is a subset of the Standard Generalized Markup Language (SGML), and it is defined by the World Wide Web Consortium (W3C), thereby ensuring that the structured data will be uniform and independent of Web applications or vendors.

Unlike Hypertext Markup Language (HTML), which is primarily used to control the display and appearance of data, XML is used to define the structure and data types of the data itself. For example, you might define XML to declare pieces of data, such as the price, tax, shipping address, billing address, and so on, for a purchase order. The advantage of using XML over HTML is that XML separates the user interface (UI) from the structured data. This separation of data from presentation, the UI, enables the integration of data from diverse sources.

Contents of an XML document

XML documents contain tags that assign meaning to the content of the document. Unlike HTML, these tags are defined by the programmer. Such tags allow programmers to find the data that they need within the XML document. The contents of an XML document include:

- Processing instructions
- Elements
- Attributes
- Comments

Processing instructions

The XML processing instruction (PI) provides a way for an XML document to contain command information that is used by the XML processor or by applications. You can include one or more PIs in an XML document.

A PI begins with a left angle bracket followed by a question mark. A PI then ends with a question mark followed by a right angle bracket. There are two parts of a processing instruction; the first part, called the PITarget, is the name of the application that will process the instruction and the second part is the actual text of the instruction, as shown in the following example:

```
<?PITarget PIData ?>
```

In the following code example, a processing instruction sends a simple SQL query to an application that is called MyDbApp:

```
<?MyDbApp SELECT * FROM orders ?>
```

Elements

An element is a container for data and for other elements. An element consists of a start tag and a closing tag. The syntax of an element is as follows:

```
<ElementName>ElementContent</ElementName>
```

The following are the rules for how elements must be formed:

- Element names cannot contain white space.

- Element names cannot start with a number or a punctuation mark.

- Element names cannot start with xml or any case variants.

- Element names must start after the left angle bracket, with no space intervening.

- The element name is case-sensitive and therefore, the element name case of the start tag and the closing tag must be the same.

- An XML document must contain at least one element, called the root element or the document element. The processor will consider the first element that it finds as the root element. All subsequent elements are contained within that root element.

- All elements that follow the root element must be nested within the root element.

- The nesting of elements cannot overlap.

- An element that lacks content can consist of a single closing tag, unless it is the root element.

- The root element must consist of a start tag and a closing tag, even if the root element has no content.

The following is a code example of a portion of an XML document containing a root element and nested child elements:

```
<Contacts>
  <contact>
      <name></name>
      <address></address>
      <telephone></telephone>
  </contact>
</Contacts>
```

Attributes

Any element can contain attributes. Attributes define data that belongs to a single element. The following rules apply to attributes:

- Attributes may be located in start tags or in the processing instructions.

- An attribute consists of a name and a value assignment.

- Successive attribute names are separated by a space.

- You can use a particular attribute name only once in an element.

- You can reuse a particular attribute name between elements.

- An attribute name cannot contain a space.

- To assign a value to an attribute name, use an equal sign, followed by an expression that is enclosed in single or double quotes.

The following is an example an element containing several attributes:

```
<contact name="Paul West" address="507 - 20th Ave. E.,
    Seattle, WA" phone="(206) 555-0100" />
```

Comments

Comments are optional and are generally provided to clarify the structure of the XML document to the user viewing the XML file. Comments are created using the <!-- and --> tags, as shown in the following example:

```
<!-- This is a comment -->
```

Well-formed XML vs. Valid XML

A well-formed XML document conforms to specifications that are listed in the W3C Recommendation for XML 1.0. XML is valid if its vocabulary conforms to a set of requirements that are listed in its corresponding schema. In XML, a schema is a description of an XML document, and it is used to ensure that XML documents are written in a specific format that enables data exchange and retrieval.

There are three types of schemas that can be used for validating an XML document, as shown in the following table.

Type of schema	Description
Document Type Definition (DTD)	DTD is the original validation method that is described in W3C XML Recommendation version 1.0. XML Schema Definition (XSD) superceded the DTD. DTDs are not based on XML.
XML-Data Reduced (XDR schema)	XDR is an interim schema technology that was developed by Microsoft. While XDR is similar to XSD, XDR schemas are written in XML.
XML Schema Definition language (XSD)	XSD is the W3C recommendation for validating XML schemas. XSD replaces both DTDs and XDR schemas. XSD schemas are written in XML.

XSD is the most commonly used schema in the .NET Framework.

Do not confuse well-formed XML with valid XML. A well-formed XML document is one that meets all W3C requirements for an XML document. A valid XML document is one that meets the additional requirements for structure and data types, as defined in a schema document created by one or more parties by using that data. All XML documents must be well-formed; however, not all XML documents are validated by using a schema.

Practice

This practice will test your ability to discover and correct common problems in XML documents. You will use Microsoft Notepad to edit an XML file and use Microsoft Internet Explorer, and its built-in XML parser, to check your work.

1. Double-click the *Install_Folder***Practices\AppendixA\Customers.xml** file to open it in Internet Explorer.

   The file fails to load and an error is displayed.

2. Open Notepad.

3. Drag the Customers.xml file onto the Notepad window.

   The XML file displays in Notepad.

4. Correct any errors that you find, and then save the file. Double-click the file to open it again in Internet Explorer.

5. Continue to edit and save changes in Notepad until the XML file opens properly in Internet Explorer.

Multimedia: Overview of Business Problems Solved by Using XML

Introduction

In this animation, you will learn about the business problems that are often encountered by companies that share data, particularly those that conduct business over the Internet.

The animation begins with a brief presentation of how data flows between different companies. Click the **ZOOM IN** button in the lower-right corner of the animation. The animation then expands the featured company, Northwind Traders, and the button changes to read **OVERVIEW**.

You can move between the overview and the zoomed-in view at any time. At the bottom of the animation is a slider button that makes each portion of the process active, thereby showing interactions between Northwind Traders and its suppliers (which are to the left) and its customers (which are to the right). You can click the **more** buttons that are next to each application or component to display explanations of that application or component.

Doing business over the Internet brings together different companies that each use various operating systems. Although the concept of doing business over the Internet is relatively recent, many companies have a lot of time and money invested in the various operating systems that they have been using. Integrating data with your company's existing systems and with the systems of your business partners is one of the major problems facing programmers today.

Integrating disparate applications

For companies to share data, the data must be available to the various applications that are running on different operating systems. For applications to exchange data, the data must be structured so that the different applications can use it. Some data is stored in hierarchical systems, including XML documents. Other data is stored in relational databases, such as Microsoft SQL Server™ databases, or stored in an unstructured way, such as in flat files.

Translating between data formats

Companies that use the Internet confront many issues, including the following:

- Different XML grammars.

  XML files can be in a variety of grammars, such as a grammar that uses only elements, or a grammar that uses both elements and attributes. Companies can solve this type of data transformation problem by using templates that provide standardization of the grammar.

- Generating XML from data that is in another format.

  Business data exists in many different formats, including EDIFACT, ANSI X12, XML, comma-separated value (CSV) files, tab-separated files, and so on. Companies can solve data-generation problems by providing a standard structure for the data that all of the applications can use.

- Validating data structures.

  One of the main advantages of using XML in applications is that XML provides a way for applications to share data. However, because data can come from so many different sources, there must be a way to verify that the data is valid. Companies can verify data by using validating tools, such as schemas, which are standard across applications and data types.

Searching for and querying data

When data is available from a variety of sources and in a variety of formats, it can be difficult to find the precise data that an application requires. The issues involved in finding precise data include the following:

- Searching for specific items in data.

  Applications not only use data in different formats, but they also use data that is in different structures. Some data is stored in hierarchical structures, some in relational structures, and some data is stored in no structure at all, but merely as text. You must have a way to navigate the structure, or the lack of structure, of the data container.

- Summarizing, combining, and correlating data.

  After you locate the data that you want, you will need to act on it. For example, you may want to prepare reports or generate lists for shipping or accounting. You can merge, or combine, data from multiple sources into a single, consistent format that you can then process, edit, or manipulate to solve specific business problems. The data format that the .NET Framework was designed to work with is XML.

By using XML in the .NET Framework, you can filter data to minimize excess information so that you can focus on the specific data that is relevant to the current business problem.

Manipulating data

After you manipulate the data, you must also have a structure in which to display it. Manipulation issues include the following:

- Transforming data from XML into another format.

    You might need to transform data that is in one XML grammar into another XML grammar, if the elements and attributes of the application that you work with differ from the XML structure of the data that you consume. Also, if you work with a Web application, you might need to transform data in structured XML documents into HTML documents that you can then display on a Web site. You might also need to print out the data, for example, in Adobe Acrobat Portable Document Format (PDF) files.

- Changing the structure of a document.

    You might need to add elements or nodes to a document in XML format, or add or delete elements or attributes.

Programming with XML in ASP.NET Web Applications

> **.NET Framework XML Classes**
>
> - System.Xml.XmlReader
> - System.Xml.XmlWriter
> - System.Xml.XmlDataDocument
> - System.Web.UI.WebControls.Xml
> - System.Xml.XPath.XPathNavigator
> - System.Xml.Xsl.XmlTransform
> - System.Xml.Schema.XmlSchema
> - System.Xml.XmlValidatingReader

Introduction

If you have used XML in your ASP Web applications, you are familiar with using the MSXML 4.0. Although you can continue to use MSXML in your ASP.NET Web application, the .NET Framework provides new classes that simplify working with XML data.

The MSXML 4.0 functionality differs from XML classes in the .NET Framework in that MSXML is targeted for an operating environment that uses Component Object Model (COM) objects, MSXML 4.0 does not use managed code, and it has built-in support for the Simple API for XML (SAX).

Integrating XML in ASP.NET Web applications

The XML classes in the .NET Framework provide a set of classes that enable you to work with XML data.

The following table describes the XML classes that are in the .NET Framework.

Task	Class	Description
Reading XML	**System.Xml.XmlReader**	The **XmlReader** class provides forward-only, read-only access to a stream of XML data. **XmlReader** is an abstract class, and cannot be instantiated directly.
Writing XML	**System.Xml.XmlWriter**	The **XmlWriter** class represents a writer that provides a fast, non-cached, forward-only means of generating streams or files that contain XML data. **XmlWriter** is an abstract class, and cannot be instantiated directly.
Displaying XML as relational data	**System.Xml.XmlDataDocument**	The **XmlDataDocument** class allows structured data to be stored, retrieved, and manipulated through the **DataSet** class. The **DataSet** class provides a relational view of the loaded XML data. Any changes made to the **XmlDataDocument** are reflected in the **DataSet** and vice versa.
Displaying XML documents	**System.Web.UI.WebControls.Xml** (The **Xml** server control)	You can use the **Xml** server control to display an XML document, with or without the results of an XSLT transformation, on a Web Form.
Navigating XML documents with XML Path Language (XPath) queries	**XPathNavigator**	You use the **XPathNavigator** object to create an in-memory, navigable representation of the XML data.
XSLT transformations	**System.Xml.Xsl.XslTransform**	The **XslTransform** class transforms XML data into a different format or structure by using an XSLT stylesheet.
Building and manipulating XML schemas	**System.Xml.Schema.XmlSchema**	The **XmlSchema** class loads and edits an XML schema.
Validating XML schemas	**System.Xml.XmlValidatingReader**	The **XmlValidatingReader** class represents a reader that provides DTD, XDR schema, and XSD schema validation.

Demonstration: Using the .NET Framework XML Classes

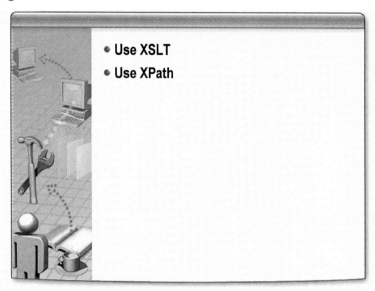

- • Use XSLT
- • Use XPath

Introduction

In this demonstration, you will learn how to use the .NET Framework XML classes in an ASP.NET Web Form.

▶ **To run the demonstration**

1. In Microsoft Visual Studio® .NET, from the **File** menu, click **Open Solution**.

2. In the Open Solution window, in the shortcut list, click **My Projects**.

3. Expand the **Democode**, **Appendix A**, *language*, and **XMLObjects** folders.

4. Select **XMLObjects-*xy*.sln**, where *xy* is either CS or VB, and then click **Open**.

Open WebForm1

5. Open WebForm1.aspx and notice the main UI components: a **Label** control, a large text box that will display the raw XML data, a **PlaceHolder** control, and two buttons.

6. Build and browse WebForm1.aspx. The text box displays the contents of the XML file.

   At this stage, the code for each of the **Button** control's **Click** event is not enabled, so the **Button** controls do nothing.

7. Open the code-behind file for WebForm1.aspx and view the **Page_Load** event handler.

   Notice that no .NET XML objects are used in the **Page_Load** event handler. Although the .NET XML objects are useful for most XML applications, other objects may be more useful or provide better performance.

Use XSLT

8. In the code-behind file for WebForm1.aspx, find the **btnXSLT_Click** event handler.

   The code for this event handler is in a comment block within a region.

9. Uncomment the code in the region and notice what each line does.

10. Build and browse WebForm1.aspx.

11. Click the **XSLT** button.

Use XPath

12. Return to the code-behind file for WebForm1.aspx.

13. In the **btnCalc_Click** event handler, expand the region and uncomment the code.

14. Build and browse WebForm1.aspx.

15. Click the **Calculate** button, and compare the results with your expected results.

16. (Optional). Add an additional manager.

   a. Edit the Employees(E).xml file so that one additional employee has a value of **True** for the **Manager** element.

   b. Build and browse WebForm1.aspx.

   c. Click **Calculate**.

   d. Verify that a third **TextBox** is added to the page.

Lesson: Displaying XML Data on a Web Form

* **The Xml Server Control**
* **How to Load XML Data and XSLT Style Sheets into the Xml Server Control**
* **Practice: Using the Xml Server Control**

Introduction

Although MSXML 4.0 can be used to read and create XML documents, it is difficult to use MSMXL 4.0 for displaying XML data on a Web page. In ASP.NET, you can use the **Xml** server control to display XML data on a Web Form, and to apply an XSLT style sheet to that data.

Lesson objectives

After completing this lesson, you will be able to:

- Read XML data or an **XmlDocument** object into an **Xml** server control.
- Use an XSLT style sheet to change the output format of XML data.

The Xml Server Control

* Can be used to display contents of an XML document
* Can use XSLT files to format the content of the XML document

```
<asp:Xml id="Xml1"
  Document="XmlDocument object to display"
  DocumentContent="String of XML"
  DocumentSource="Path to XML Document"
  Transform="XslTransform object"
  TransformSource="Path to XSL Document"
  runat="server"/>
```

Introduction

If you open an XML document in Internet Explorer or another Web browser that is capable of reading XML, the data is usually displayed exactly as it appears in the XML document, including all of the element tags, attributes, and processing instructions.

If you want to customize the display of XML data in a Web Form, you need to format the XML data with HTML tags, such as the **<TABLE>** and **<P>** tags. You must also provide instructions to the ASP.NET Web application for how the data from the XML file fits into these tags. For example, you specify whether each element in the XML file should be displayed as a table row, a member of a bulleted list, and so on.

Extensible Style Sheet Language Transformation

One way to provide the instructions for displaying XML data is to use XSLT. You must first create an XSLT file, and then apply the XSLT file to the XML data file. Applying an XSLT file to a XML file produces a new file with the XML information formatted according to the XSLT file.

When to use the XML server control

You can use the **Xml** server control to display an XML document, with or without XSLT, on a Web Form. The XML output appears on the Web page at the location of the **Xml** server control.

Note The **Xml** Server control is designed to work in **FlowLayout** mode so that other server controls will dynamically change position depending on the size of the XML document that is displayed. When designing a Web Form to use the **Xml** Server control, set the **pageLayout** property for the Web Form to **FlowLayout**.

How to Load XML Data and XSLT Style Sheets into the Xml Server Control

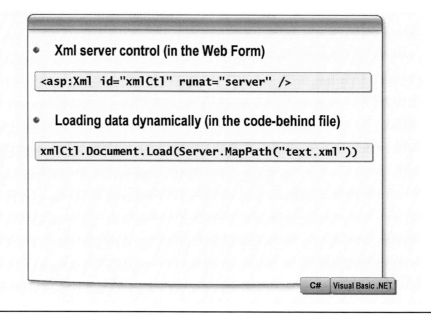

Introduction

Before loading and saving XML data into a Web application, you need to add the **Xml** server control to the Web Form, in the location where you want the XML data to appear.

To add an Xml server control to a Web Form

There are two ways to add an **Xml** server control to a Web Form:

- Drag an **Xml** server control from the **Web Forms** tab of the Toolbox onto the Design view, as shown in the following illustration.

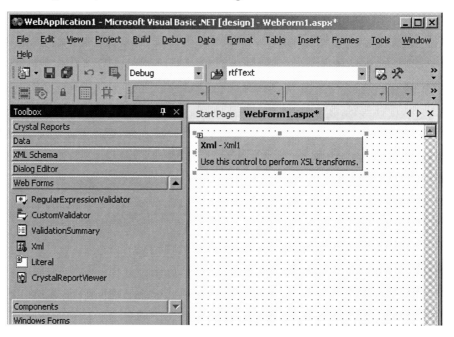

- To add an **Xml** server control programmatically, in HTML view, add the following line of code:

```
<asp:Xml id="xmlCtl" runat="server" />
```

To load XML data into the Xml server control

There are three ways to load XML data into a Web application. You can:

- Provide a path to an external XML document by using the **DocumentSource** property.

- Load an XML document as an object and then pass it to the **Xml** server control using the **Load** method, and then assigning the XML document to the **Document** property of the **Xml** server control.

- Include the XML content inline, between the opening and closing tags of the **Xml** server control.

To provide a path to an external XML document

To provide a path to an external XML document, perform the following steps:

1. Set the **DocumentSource** property of the **Xml** server control to the path of the XML source document.

2. The XML document will be written directly to the output stream, unless you also specify the **TransformSource** property.

   TransformSource must be a valid XSLT document, which will be used to transform the XML document before its contents are written to the output stream. The following code example shows how to refer to the source document and the XSLT document, both of which exist in the same virtual directory as the Web Form:

```
<body>
    <h3>XML Example</h3>
    <form runat="server">
        <asp:Xml id="xml1" DocumentSource="MySource.xml"
            TransformSource="MyStyle.xsl" runat="server" />
    </form>
</body>
```

To load an XML document as an object and then pass it to the control

To load an XML document as an object and then pass it to the control, perform the following steps:

1. On the **View** menu, click **Code**. In the Code Editor, find the **Page_Load** event handler.

   > **Note** You can add this code in any appropriate event handler. In this example, the **Xml** server control will display XML data when the Web Form loads.

2. Add code to load the XML source document, and then assign the source to the **Document** property of the **Xml** server control.

   In the following code example, the **Xml** server control is named Xml1:

   Visual Basic .NET

   ```
   Private Sub Page_Load(ByVal sender As System.Object, _
       ByVal e As System.EventArgs) Handles MyBase.Load
       Dim xmlDoc As System.Xml.XmlDocument = _
           New System.Xml.XmlDocument()
       xmlDoc.Load(Server.MapPath("MySource.xml"))
       Dim xslTran As System.Xml.Xsl.XslTransform = _
           New System.Xml.Xsl.XslTransform()
       xslTran.Load(Server.MapPath("MyStyle.xsl"))
       Xml1.Document = xmlDoc
       Xml1.Transform = xslTran
   End Sub
   ```

   C#

   ```
   private void Page_Load(object sender, System.EventArgs e)
   {
       System.Xml.XmlDocument xmlDoc = new
           System.Xml.XmlDocument();
       xmlDoc.Load(Server.MapPath("MySource.xml"));
       System.Xml.Xsl.XslTransform xslTran = new
           System.Xml.Xsl.XslTransform();
       xslTran.Load(Server.MapPath("MyStyle.xsl"));
       Xml1.Document = xmlDoc;
       Xml1.Transform = xslTran;
   }
   ```

To include the XML content inline

To include the XML content inline, perform the following steps:

1. In HTML view, find the **<asp:Xml>** and **</asp:Xml>** tags.

2. Add your XML code between these two tags.

   For example:

```
<asp:Xml TransformSource="MyStyle.xsl" runat="server">
    <clients>
        <name>Frank Miller</name>
        <name>Judy Lew</name>
    </clients>
</asp:Xml>
```

Practice: Using the Xml Server Control

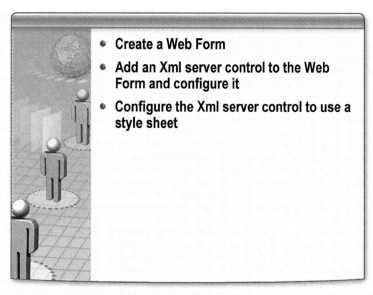

Introduction

In this practice, you will learn how to use the **Xml** server control to display XML data.

▶ **To run this practice**

Open the solution

1. In Visual Studio .NET, from the **File** menu, click **Open Solution**.

2. In the Open Solution window, in the shortcut list, click **My Projects**.

3. Expand the **Practices**, **Appendix A**, *language*, and **XMLServerControl** folders.

4. Select **XMLServerControl-*xy*.sln**, where *xy* is either CS or VB, and then click **Open**.

Create a Web Form

5. In the Visual Basic .NET or C# project, create a new Web Form.

Add an Xml server control and configure the Xml server control

6. From the Toolbox, drag an **Xml** server control onto the Web Form.

7. Set the **DocumentSource** property of the **Xml** server control to the PubTitlesData.xml file.

8. Build and browse the Web Form.

   This is the default view of the data as set by the **Xml** server control. The default view of the data is unformatted.

Configure the Xml server control to use a style sheet

9. Set the **TransformSource** property of the **Xml** server control to the PubTitles.xsl file.

10. Build and browse the Web Form again.

    This is the view of the data as set by the **PubTitles.xsl** style sheet.

Lesson: XML and the DataSet Object

- **Using XML with DataSet Objects**
- **Demonstration: Reading and Writing XML Data to and from a DataSet**

Introduction

One way to use XML data in an ASP.NET Web application is to read the data into a **DataSet** object. After the data is in a **DataSet** object, that data can then be displayed just as any other **DataSet** object.

Lesson objectives

After completing this lesson, you will be able to:

- Read XML data into a **DataSet** object.
- Write **DataSet** data into an XML file.

Using XML with DataSet Objects

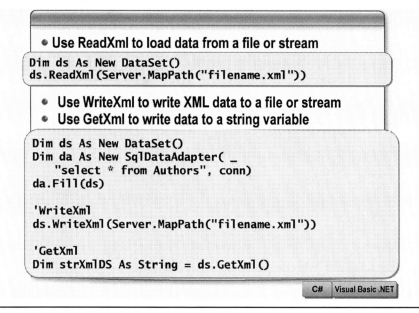

- **Use ReadXml to load data from a file or stream**

```
Dim ds As New DataSet()
ds.ReadXml(Server.MapPath("filename.xml"))
```

- **Use WriteXml to write XML data to a file or stream**
- **Use GetXml to write data to a string variable**

```
Dim ds As New DataSet()
Dim da As New SqlDataAdapter( _
    "select * from Authors", conn)
da.Fill(ds)

'WriteXml
ds.WriteXml(Server.MapPath("filename.xml"))

'GetXml
Dim strXmlDS As String = ds.GetXml()
```

C#   Visual Basic .NET

Introduction

Although the **Xml** server control provides a simple way to display XML data, the usefulness of the control is relatively limited. If, for example, you want users to be able to manipulate the data or alter the view of the data, you need to use a more powerful alternative, the **DataSet** object. The .NET Framework provides the **DataSet** object for handling data from a wide variety of sources, including XML documents.

The contents of a **DataSet** object can be created from an XML stream or document. You can also write XML data from the **DataSet** object to a stream or file. In addition to reading and writing the XML data, you can also use the **DataSet** object to read and create XML schema documents.

Note For more information about the **DataSet** object, see Module 4, "Accessing Database Data Using Microsoft ADO.NET," in Course 2640, *Upgrading Web Development Skills from ASP to Microsoft ASP.NET*; Course 2389, *Programming with ADO.NET*; or Course 2663, *Programming with XML in the Microsoft .NET Framework*.

The ReadXML method

To fill a **DataSet** object with data from a XML file, you use the **ReadXml** method of the **DataSet** object. The **ReadXml** method reads from a file, a stream, or an **XmlReader**.

The **ReadXml** method reads the contents of the XML stream or document and then loads the **DataSet** with that data. **ReadXml** also creates the relational schema of the **DataSet**, depending on the **XmlReadMode** that is specified and whether a relational schema already exists.

The following code example shows how to fill a **DataSet** with XML data:

Visual Basic .NET

```
Dim ds As New DataSet()
ds.ReadXml(Server.MapPath("filename.xml"))
```

C#

```
DataSet ds = new DataSet();
ds.ReadXml(Server.MapPath("filename.xml"));
```

Note   The **Server.MapPath** method returns the physical file path, which corresponds to the specified virtual path on the Web server.

The WriteXML method

To write a **DataSet** to a file, stream, or **XmlWriter**, you use the **WriteXml** method. The first parameter you pass to **WriteXml** is the destination of the XML output. For example, you can pass a string containing a file name, a **System.IO.TextWriter** object, and so on. You can also pass an optional second parameter of an **XmlWriteMode** to then specify how the XML output is to be written.

The following code example read data from an existing SQL Server database into a **DataSet** object, and then saves that data as an XML file:

Visual Basic .NET

```
Dim ds As New DataSet()
Dim da As New SqlDataAdapter("select * from Authors", conn)
da.Fill(ds)
ds.WriteXml(Server.MapPath("filename.xml"))
```

C#

```
DataSet ds = new DataSet();
SqlDataAdapter da = new SqlDataAdapter
  ("select * from Authors", conn);
da.Fill(ds);
ds.WriteXml(Server.MapPath("filename.xml"));
```

GetXML

The XML representation of the **DataSet** can be written to a file, a stream, an **XmlWriter**, or to a string. These choices provide great flexibility for how you transport the XML representation of the **DataSet**. For example, to obtain the XML representation of the **DataSet** as a string, use the **GetXml** method, as shown in the following code example:

Visual Basic .NET

```
Dim strXmlDS As String = ds.GetXml()
```

C#

```
string strXmlDS = ds.GetXml();
```

GetXml returns the XML representation of the **DataSet** without schema information. To write the schema information from the **DataSet** (as XML schema) to a string, use **GetXmlSchema**.

Demonstration: Reading and Writing XML Data to and from a DataSet

* Reading XML data
* Writing XML data

Introduction

In this demonstration, you will see how to read and write XML to and from a **DataSet**.

▶ **To run the demonstration**

1. In Visual Studio .NET, from the **File** menu, click **Open Solution**.

2. In the Open Solution window, in the shortcut list, click **My Projects**.

3. Expand the **Democode**, **Appendix A**, *language*, and **XMLDataSet** folders.

4. Select **XMLDataSet-*xy*.sln**, where *xy* is either CS or VB, and then click **Open**.

Reading XML data

5. Open the Books.xml and Employees.xml files in Visual Studio .NET.

   These files contain the data that will be displayed in the demonstration. Both files are simple XML files with a few elements.

6. Build and browse the DisplayXML.aspx page.

7. In the text box, click **Books.xml**, and then click **Load**.

8. In the text box, click **Employees.xml**, and then click **Load**.

9. Open the code-behind file, DisplayXML.aspx.vb or DisplayXML.aspx.cs, in Visual Studio .NET.

10. In the **cmdLoad_Click** event handler, show the code that reads an XML file into a **DataSet** and that then binds the **DataGrid** to the **DataSet**.

Note The **DataGrid** can only handle one level of elements in an XML file.

If there is too much nesting of elements, the data will not be displayed. You can demonstrate excessive nesting by adding an author element to the book elements in the Books.xml file:

```
<book>
  ...
  <author>
      <firstname>Jay</firstname>
      <lastname>Bird</lastname>
  </author>
</book>
```

11. Build and browse the DisplayXML.aspx page.

    The data is not displayed due to excessive nesting.

Writing XML data

12. Build and browse the SaveAsXML.aspx page.

    The **DataGrid** displays the **DataSet** data that will be saved into an XML file.

13. Click **Save as XML**, and then click the **View XML** hyperlink.

    This is the XML data that was created from the **DataSet**.

14. Open the code-behind file for SaveAsXml.aspx.

    There is a function called **CreateDataSet** that builds the **DataSet** from a SQL Server database.

15. To create an XML file, show the code in the **cmdSave_Click** event handler that calls the **WriteXml** method of the **DataSet**.

16. To create an XSD schema file, show the code in the **cmdSchema_Click** event handler that calls the **WriteXmlSchema** method of the **DataSet**.

msdn training

Appendix B: Improving Microsoft ASP.NET Web Application Performance Using Caching

Contents

Microsoft®

Overview

- ● **Using the Cache Object**
- ● **Using ASP.NET Output Caching**

Introduction

You can improve the performance of a Microsoft® ASP.NET Web application by using the caching features of ASP.NET. To improve the performance of an ASP.NET Web application, you can set up the **Cache** object and the output cache. Setting up the **Cache** object and the output cache optimizes the response times for an ASP.NET Web application.

Note The code samples in this module are provided in both Microsoft Visual Basic® .NET and C#.

Objectives

After completing this module, you will be able to:

- Use the **Cache** object to store information.
- Use ASP.NET output caching to store Web pages and Web page fragments.

Lesson: Using the Cache Object

- ● What Is the Cache Object?
- ● Advantages of Using the Cache Object
- ● Using the Cache Object
- ● Removing Information from the Cache Object
- ● Demonstration: Using the Cache Object

Introduction

One of most effective ways to increase the performance of an ASP.NET Web application is to use the ASP.NET **Cache** object. The **Cache** object allows you to place information in server memory so that they can be quickly retrieved. However, loading too much information into the **Cache** object can slow down server response times by reducing the available memory on the server.

In this lesson, you will learn how to set up the **Cache** object to optimize the response times for an ASP.NET Web application.

Lesson objectives

After completing this lesson, you will be able to:

- ■ Explain what a **Cache** object is.
- ■ Explain the advantages and disadvantages of using a **Cache** object.
- ■ Use a **Cache** object to store and retrieve information that is used by ASP.NET Web applications.
- ■ Remove items from a **Cache** object after a period of time, or when the item changes, to limit memory use.

What Is the Cache Object?

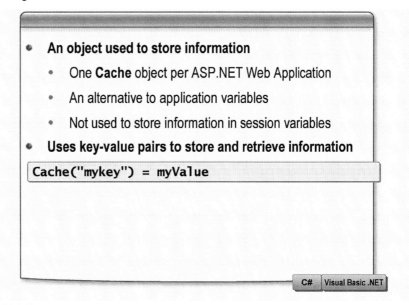

Introduction

An issue that you will encounter when building high-performance ASP.NET Web applications is the need to avoid duplication. A **Cache** object allows you to cache, or store, information in memory the first time that they are requested, and then use the cached copy for later requests. Using the cached copy allows you to avoid recreating information that satisfied a previous request, particularly information that demands significant processor time on the server every time it is created.

In addition to caching individual items, such as computational results in the **Cache** object, ASP.NET offers an output cache that can be used for storing Web pages and user controls. The **Cache** object and the output cache are distinct objects with unique roles and properties.

An object used to store information

ASP.NET provides a full-featured cache engine that can be used to store and retrieve pieces of information. The **Cache** object has no information about the content of the items it contains. The **Cache** object merely holds a reference to those pieces of information and provides a process for tracking their dependencies and setting expiration policies.

The **Cache** object also provides a method to pass values between pages that are in the same Web application. The **Cache** methods implement automatic locking; therefore, it is safe for values to be accessed concurrently from more than one page.

How the Cache object works

The process for using the **Cache** object is:

1. A Web page requests an item that has been identified as being stored in the **Cache** object.

2. ASP.NET checks the **Cache** object and uses the cached version, if it is available.

3. If a cached version is not available, ASP.NET recreates the item, uses that item, and then stores that item in the **Cache** object for future use.

One Cache object per Web application

ASP.NET creates a single **Cache** object for each Web application. The items that are stored in the **Cache** object are unique to the Web application and cannot be accessed by other Web applications that are running on the same Web server or on other servers. As a result, the use of the **Cache** object to increase Web application performance is not scalable above the single Web application level.

The lifetime of the cache is the same as the lifetime of the Web application. When the Web application is restarted, the cache is then recreated.

Storing variables

The **Cache** object can be used to store information that could also be stored in application variables. Rather than recreating the value each time you use it, a single cached value can be accessed by any page in the Web application.

The **Cache** object cannot be used to store information that is found in session variables. Session variables can be stored in cookies, the page Uniform Resource Locator (URL), or the hidden **ViewState** control.

Note For more information about application and session variables, see Module 5, "Managing State in a Microsoft ASP.NET Web Application," in Course 2640, *Upgrading Web Development Skills from ASP to Microsoft ASP.NET.*

Uses key-value pairs

The **Cache** object uses key-value pairs to store and retrieve information. The *key* is the cache key string that is used to reference the information. The *value* is the information to be cached. In the simplest scenario, placing information in the cache and retrieving it is exactly like adding information to a dictionary.

To add information into a **Cache** object:

Visual Basic .NET

```
Cache("mykey") = myValue
```

C#

```
Cache["mykey"] = myValue;
```

To retrieve an item from a **Cache** object:

Visual Basic .NET

```
myValue = Cache("myKey")
```

C#

```
myValue = Cache["myKey"];
```

Advantages of Using the Cache Object

- **Faster than creating a new object for each request**
- **Supports internal locking**
- **Automatic cache resource management**
- **Supports callback functions**
- **Supports removal based on dependencies**

Introduction	The **Cache** object provides a simple dictionary interface that allows you to easily insert values and then retrieve them later. Using the **Cache** object to store values has several advantages.
Faster than creating a new object for each request	An item that is stored in memory can be retrieved much more quickly than it can be rebuilt. For example, a **DataSet** filled with data from a computer running Microsoft SQL Server™ must reconnect to the SQL Server for each page request. Placing the **DataSet** in the **Cache** object provides much more rapid access to that data.
Supports internal locking	The **Cache** object provides automatic lock management on items that are in the cache; therefore, concurrent requests for an item cannot modify the object. Automatic lock management protects in-process transactions when items are being updated.
Automatically manages cache resources	ASP.NET automatically removes items from the cache on a regular schedule. This automatic removal is an improvement over earlier cache versions requiring the developer to manage cache resources manually.
Supports callback functions	Callback functions are code that runs when an item is removed from the cache. For example, you can use a callback function to place the newest version of an object in cache as soon as the old version of an object is removed.
Supports removal based on dependencies	If an item in a cache has a dependency on another cached item or a file, you can set the **Cache** object to remove that item when the dependency meets certain requirements. For example, if you store data from an Extensible Markup Language (XML) file in the cache, you can remove the cached data when the XML document changes.

Using the Cache Object

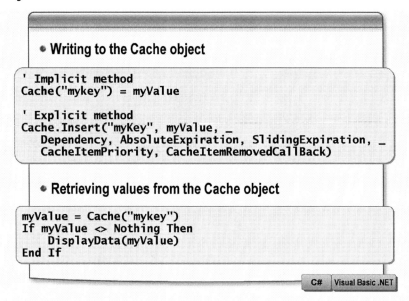

Introduction

To use the **Cache** object, you use key-value pairs to store and retrieve information. The *key* is the **Cache** object's key string that is used to reference the information. The *value* is the information to be cached.

Writing to the Cache object

You can write an item into a **Cache** object implicitly, as shown in the following code:

Visual Basic .NET

```
Cache("mykey") = myValue
```

C#

```
Cache["mykey"] = myValue;
```

You can also supply parameters, such as a time limit for storage in the **Cache** object, when inserting an item into the **Cache** object. The following code shows the explicit **Insert** method with parameters:

Visual Basic .NET

```
Cache.Insert("myKey", myValue, _
    Dependency, AbsoluteExpiration, SlidingExpiration, _
    CacheItemPriority, CacheItemRemovedCallBack)
```

C#

```
Cache.Insert("myKey", myValue,
    Dependency, AbsoluteExpiration, SlidingExpiration,
    CacheItemPriority, CacheItemRemovedCallBack);
```

Retrieving values from the Cache object

Retrieving values from the **Cache** object is equally simple in that you only need to provide the correct key to receive the value.

The following code uses the key **myKey** to retrieve the value **myValue** and then displays **myValue**, if it is not empty:

```vb
Visual Basic .NET

myValue = Cache("mykey")
If myValue <> Nothing Then
    DisplayData(myValue)
End If
```

```csharp
C#

myValue = Cache["mykey"];
if (myValue != null)
    DisplayData(myValue);
```

Removing Information from the Cache Object

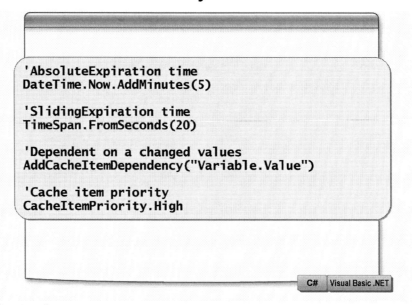

```
'AbsoluteExpiration time
DateTime.Now.AddMinutes(5)

'SlidingExpiration time
TimeSpan.FromSeconds(20)

'Dependent on a changed values
AddCacheItemDependency("Variable.Value")

'Cache item priority
CacheItemPriority.High
```

Introduction

The ASP.NET **Cache** object is designed to ensure that it does not use too much of the Web server's memory. As a result, the **Cache** object automatically removes the least-used information when available memory becomes limited. You can influence how the **Cache** object saves and removes information by defining time limits, dependencies, and priorities for information that is in the **Cache** object.

Information in the **Cache** object is removed as soon as a dependency or time limit is triggered. Attempts to retrieve the removed information will return a **null** value unless the information is added to the **Cache** object again.

AbsoluteExpiration

You can define the maximum absolute lifetime for information in the **Cache** object by using the **AbsoluteExpiration** parameter. This parameter is a **DateTime** type parameter that allows you to specify the time at which the information will expire.

The following code example specifies that **myValue** be removed from the **Cache** object exactly five minutes after it is created:

Visual Basic .NET

```
Cache.Insert("myKey", myValue, Nothing, _
  DateTime.Now.AddMinutes(5), Nothing)
```

C#

```
Cache.Insert("myKey", myValue, null, _
  DateTime.Now.AddMinutes(5), Cache.NoSlidingExpiration);
```

SlidingExpiration

You can define the maximum relative lifetime for information in the **Cache** object by using the **SlidingExpiration** parameter. The **SlidingExpiration** parameter is a **TimeSpan** type parameter that allows you to specify the time interval between when the cached information was last accessed and when the object expires.

The following code example specifies that **myValue** be removed from the **Cache** object exactly 20 seconds after it is last accessed:

Visual Basic .NET

```
Cache.Insert("myKey", myValue, Nothing, _
  Nothing, TimeSpan.FromSeconds(20))
```

C#

```
Cache.Insert("myKey", myValue, null, _
  null, TimeSpan.FromSeconds(20));
```

Dependencies

There are times when you want information to be removed from the **Cache** object because supporting information, such as a file, has changed. ASP.NET allows you to define the validity of cached information, based on file dependencies or other cached information. Dependencies based on external files and directories are referred to as file dependencies, whereas dependencies that are based on other cached information are referred to as key dependencies. If a dependency changes, the cached information is invalidated and removed from the **Cache** object.

The following code example specifies that **myValue** be removed from the **Cache** object when the myDoc.xml file changes:

Visual Basic .NET

```
Cache.Insert("myKey", myValue, _
  new CacheDependency(Server.MapPath("myDoc.xml")))
```

C#

```
Cache.Insert("myKey", myValue, new
CacheDependency(Server.MapPath("myDoc.xml")));
```

Cache item priority

When the Web server runs low on memory, the **Cache** object selectively removes information to free up system memory. Information that you assign higher priority values to are less likely to be removed from the cache, whereas the information to which you assign lower priority values are more likely to be removed.

The following code example specifies that **myValue** has a high priority and should be one of the last information pieces removed from the **Cache** object when the server memory becomes limited:

Visual Basic .NET

```
Cache.Insert("myKey", myValue, Nothing, Nothing, _
  Nothing, CacheItemPriority.High, onRemove)
```

C#

```
Cache.Insert("myKey", myValue, null, null,
Cache.NoSlidingExpiration, CacheItemPriority.High, onRemove);
```

Example of setting the parameters in Cache.Insert

The following code inserts a value for **MyBook** into the **Cache** object with a number of parameter arguments. The following dependency or timeout event that occurs first will be the dependency or timeout event that removes the information from the **Cache** object:

- Remove the information five minutes after being stored.

- Remove the information 30 seconds after the latest access.

- Remove the information if the Books.xml file changes.

- Make the priority of the information high so that it is removed last if Web server resources become limited.

- When the information is removed from the **Cache** object, the callback function **onRemove** runs.

The following sample code inserts a value for **MyBook** into the **Cache** object with a number of parameter arguments:

Visual Basic .NET

```
Cache.Insert("MyBook.CurrentBook", CurrentBook, _
  new CacheDependency(Server.MapPath("Books.xml")), _
  DateTime.Now.AddMinutes(5), _
  TimeSpan.FromSeconds(30), _
  CacheItemPriority.High, onRemove)
```

C#

```
Cache.Insert("MyBook.CurrentBook", CurrentBook,
  new CacheDependency(Server.MapPath("Books.xml")),
  DateTime.Now.AddMinutes(5),
  TimeSpan.FromSeconds(30),
  CacheItemPriority.High, onRemove);
```

Demonstration: Using the Cache Object

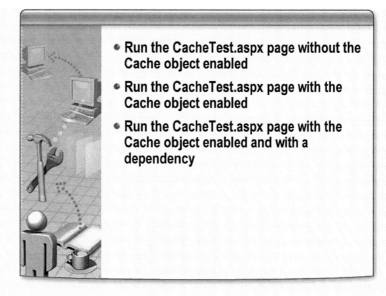

- Run the CacheTest.aspx page without the Cache object enabled
- Run the CacheTest.aspx page with the Cache object enabled
- Run the CacheTest.aspx page with the Cache object enabled and with a dependency

Introduction

In this demonstration, you will see how to use the **Cache** object with a **DataGrid**.

All files for this demonstration are in the Cache.sln solution file, which is in either the Democode\AppendixB\VB or Democode\AppendixB\CS folder.

▶ **To run the demonstration**

Run without caching

1. Open the CacheTest.aspx page.

2. Show the code-behind file.

   Point out that the **DataSet** reads an XML file and that the **DataGrid** is filled with the XML file.

3. Set the CacheTest.aspx page as the start page for the project, and then click the **Run** button to browse to the page in Microsoft Internet Explorer.

   Note   Because of feature differences between the built-in browser in Microsoft Visual Studio® .NET and Internet Explorer, it is important to use Internet Explorer for this demonstration.

Enable caching

4. In CacheTest.aspx.vb or CacheTest.aspx.cs, comment out the lines that are marked with the following comment in both the **Page_Load** and the **dgXML_PageIndexChanged** event handler:

```
Visual Basic .NET

'comment this line for caching
```

```
C#

//comment this line for caching
```

5. Uncomment all of the remaining code in both the **Page_Load** and **dgXML_PageIndexChanged** event handlers.

    Explain how this additional code creates a new cache key, **dsCache**, which places the **DataSet** object **dsXML** in the cache and sets the absolute expiration time at two minutes.

6. Click **Start** to build the CacheTest.aspx page and view it in Internet Explorer.

    Verify that the **DataGrid** is populated with the XML data and that the paging feature works.

Test the caching

7. Leave Internet Explorer open, and in Visual Studio .NET, open the pubs.xml file.

8. Change the title of the first book that is listed to a title that the students can easily detect, and then save the pubs.xml file.

9. In Internet Explorer, switch to Page 1 of the **DataGrid**.

    If you are already viewing Page 1, switch to another page and then go back to Page 1.

10. Show the students that the title of the first book listed did not change because the information is coming from cache.

11. Switch to another page, wait at least two minutes, and then switch back to the Page 1.

    The **DataGrid** will now display the new title for the first book.

12. Close Internet Explorer.

Add a dependency

13. Open the CacheTest.aspx.vb or the CacheTest.aspx.cs page.

14. For both of the Cache.Insert lines of code in the CacheTest.aspx.vb or CacheTest.aspx.cs pages, add a dependency on the pubs.xml file.

    Your code should look like the following:

    Visual Basic .NET

    ```
    Cache.Insert("dsCache", dsXML, New _
        System.Web.Caching.CacheDependency _
        (Server.MapPath("pubs.xml")), _
        DateTime.Now.AddMinutes(1), Nothing)
    ```

    C#

    ```
    Cache.Insert("dsCache", dsXML, new
        System.Web.Caching.CacheDependency
        (Server.MapPath("pubs.xml")),
        DateTime.Now.AddMinutes(1), Cache.NoSlidingExpiration);
    ```

15. Right-click the **CacheDemo** project in Solution Explorer and click **Build**.

16. Right-click **CacheTest.aspx**, and then click **Browse With…**.

17. In the **Browse With** dialog box, click **Microsoft Internet Explorer**, and then click **Browse**.

18. Click **Start** to build the CacheTest.aspx page and view it in Internet Explorer.

19. Leave Internet Explorer open, and in Visual Studio .NET, open the pubs.xml file.

20. Change the title of the first book listed to a title that the students can easily detect. Save the pubs.xml file.

21. In Internet Explorer, switch to Page 1 of the **DataGrid**.

    If you are already viewing Page 1, switch to another page and then go back to Page 1.

22. Show the students that the information in the **DataGrid** changes to reflect the change that was made in the pubs.xml file, because the cache is dependent on that file.

Lesson: Using ASP.NET Output Caching

- Multimedia: Output Caching
- Output Cache Types
- How to Use Page Output Caches
- Demonstration: Page Output Caching
- How to Use Fragment Caching

Introduction

One factor developers that must consider in creating high-performance Web applications is the need for minimizing the response time to page requests. By storing a page, or parts of a page, in memory the first time that they are requested, and then using that stored page, or parts of that page, for later requests, you can avoid the processing time that is required to recreate the page.

In this lesson, you will learn how to set up the output cache to minimize page response times for a Web application.

Lesson objectives

After completing this lesson, you will be able to:

- Explain why you would use output caching.
- Explain the different output cache types.
- Use page output caching.
- Use page fragment caching.

Multimedia: Output Caching

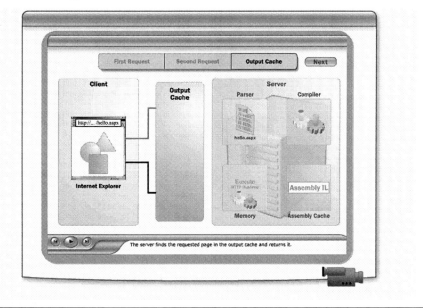

Introduction

In this animation, you will see how the output caching affects server response times when an ASP.NET Web Form is requested more than once.

Output Cache Types

* Page caching
* Page fragment caching as a user control
* XML Web service caching

Introduction

ASP.NET provides page output caching, which allows you to store entire Web Forms and user controls in server memory. After the first request, the Web Form, user control, or XML Web service code is not executed; instead, the cached output is used to satisfy the request.

ASP.NET creates a single output cache for each Web server. The pages and page fragments that are stored in the output cache are unique to the Web server and cannot be accessed by other servers in a Web server farm. As a result, the use of the output cache to increase server performance is not scalable above the single Web server level.

Page caching

Page caching allows you to cache dynamic content. When a Web Form is requested for the first time, the page is compiled and cached in the output cache, and it is then available to serve the next request. This cached page is removed when the source file is changed or the cache timeout is reached.

Page fragment caching as a user control

Sometimes it is impractical to cache an entire page, because portions of the page may need to be dynamically created for each request. In these situations, it may be worthwhile for you to identify the objects or data that are associated with the page request that do not change often, and therefore do not require significant server resources to construct. After you identify these objects or data, you can isolate them from the rest of the page by creating them as user controls, and then caching the user controls with the page output cache.

An example of a page fragment that would be worthwhile to cache is a page header that contains static graphics, or a sidebar menu system.

XML Web service caching

XML Web services also support caching to increase response performance. In the **WebMethod** attribute, you add the **CacheDuration** property and set the value to the number of seconds that the results for the XML Web service method will remain in the output cache.

For example, the following code example places the results from the WebMethod **CachedInfo** into the output cache for five minutes:

```vbnet
Visual Basic .NET

<WebMethod(CacheDuration:=300)> _
Public Function CachedInfo() As String

   ...
End Function
```

```csharp
C#

[WebMethod(CacheDuration=300)]
public string CachedInfo()
{

   ...

}
```

Important   Creating an output cache for an application should be your final task in Web application development. Otherwise, when you debug your pages, you may get out-of-date pages that are stored in the output cache instead of getting new and modified pages.

How to Use Page Output Caches

- Cached content is generated from dynamic pages
- Entire Web page is available in cache
- Set cache duration in seconds
- Set the VaryByParam property to control the number of page variations in the cache

```
<%@ OutputCache Duration="900"
VaryByParam="None"%>
```

Introduction

ASP.NET provides page output caching, which allows you to store requested Web Forms in server memory. After the first request, the Web Form code is not executed; instead the cached output is used to satisfy the request.

Cached content from dynamic pages

To load a page into the output cache, you must add the **OutputCache** directive to the Web Form. The **OutputCache** directive includes two properties: a **Duration** property that sets the maximum storage time for the cached page in seconds, and a **VaryByParam** property that determines when a new copy of the page is created in the cache, based on parameters that are passed to the page.

Entire Web page is available in cache

Output caching allows requests for a particular page to be completed from the cache so that the code that initially creates the page does not have to be run on subsequent page requests. Using output caching to store your Web site's most frequently accessed pages can substantially reduce your Web server's page response time.

Set the cache duration

You can specify the cache timeout value for a page by setting the **OutputCache** page directive. For example, to cache an ASP.NET page for 15 minutes, add the following **OutputCache** page directive to the .aspx page:

```
<%@ OutputCache Duration="900" VaryByParam="None"%>
```

The unit of time for the **Duration** property is seconds. The default is 0 seconds, which means the response is not cached.

Set VaryByParam

The **VaryByParam** property is used to determine whether ASP.NET should create different versions of the cached page in situations in which page requests pass specific parameters. Setting the **VaryByParam** property to **"none"** means that only one version of the page will be cached. Setting the property to **"*"** means that any variation in page parameters will result in a new version of the page being cached. Identifying one or more parameters means that only changes to these parameters will result in new pages being cached.

For example, the following directive in an .aspx file sets an expiration of 60 seconds for the cached output of each dynamically generated page, and therefore, ASP.NET requires the creation of a new page in the output cache for each new **productID**:

```
<%@ OutputCache Duration="60" VaryByParam="productID"%>
```

Caution When you use the **OutputCache** directive, the **Duration** and **VaryByParam** attributes are required. If you do not include those attributes, a parser error occurs when the page is first requested. If you do not want to use the functionality that the **VaryByParam** attribute provides, you must set its value to "**none**".

Demonstration: Page Output Caching

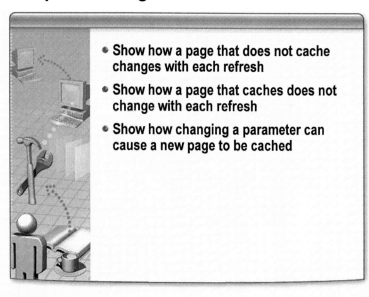

Introduction

In this demonstration, you will see how page output caching affects a user's experience. First, you will see a page running a clock function that does not cache. Next, you will see the same page with a 10-second output cache duration. Finally, you will see how changing the **VaryByParam** property controls the caching of different versions of that page.

All files for this demonstration are in the Cache.sln solution file, which is in either the Democode\AppendixB\VB or Democode\AppendixB\CS folder.

▶ **To run the demonstration**

Show how a page that does not cache changes with each refresh

1. In Visual Studio .NET, open the code behind file for the OutputCache.aspx page in the CacheDemo project.

2. Show the code that gets the current time and date, and then display the code in a **Label** control.

3. Build and browse the page.

4. Refresh the page several times consecutively to show that the seconds are changing.

Show how a page that caches does not change with each refresh

5. Add the following directive to the page, after the line of code that contains the page directive.

```
<%@ OutputCache Duration="10" VaryByParam="none"%>
```

6. Build and browse the page.

7. Reload the page several times consecutively to show that the seconds are changing only after a 10-second interval.

Show how changing a parameter can cause a new page to be cached

8. Open the OutputCacheVaryByParam.aspx page.

9. Show the **OutputCache** directive with the **VaryByParam** property.

10. Build and browse the page.

11. At the end of the URL, add the parameter **?Name=Someone**.

12. Show the effect on the output cache when changing the value of the **?Name=Someone** parameter to a **?Name=Someone2** parameter.

How to Use Fragment Caching

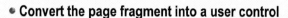

- Convert the page fragment into a user control
- Set the Duration and varyByParam properties

```
<%@ OutputCache Duration="120"
VaryByParam="None"%>
```

Introduction

To cache only parts of a page, you must isolate those parts from the rest of the page by placing them in a user control. You then cache the user control for a period of time that you specify, which is known as *fragment caching*.

Fragment caching allows you to separate the portions of a page—such as database queries, which take up valuable processor time—from the rest of the page. With fragment caching, you can choose to allow only the parts of the page that require fewer server resources, or the parts of a page that must be created with every request, to be generated dynamically for each request.

Items that are good candidates for fragment caching include headers, footers, and drop-down lists that are used by multiple pages.

Convert fragment to a user control

After you identify the parts of the page that you want to cache, you must create user controls that encapsulate each one of those fragments.

Note For more information on creating user controls, see Module 2, "Developing a Microsoft ASP.NET Web Application User Interface," in Course 2640, *Upgrading Web Development Skills from ASP to Microsoft ASP.NET*.

Set the Duration and VaryByParam properties

You set the caching policies for the user controls, such as the duration and the number of variations stored, the same way that you set page output caching policies. You set these caching policies declaratively, by using the **OutputCache** directive.

For example, if you include the following directive at the top of a user control file, a version of the user control is stored in the output cache for two minutes, and only one version of the user control will be cached:

```
<%@ OutputCache Duration="120" VaryByParam="none"%>
```

Job Aid: Migrating ASP Web Applications to Microsoft ASP.NET

This job aid is intended to help track the changes that must be made when migrating Active Server Pages (ASP) Web applications to Microsoft® ASP.NET.

Page Extension

☐ Update the page extension from **.asp** to **.aspx**.

Page Directives

☐ Position the language directive with the @ **Page** directive.

☐ Position all of the page directives at the beginning of the .aspx file.

Page Structure

☐ Use only one language per Web page.

☐ Declare functions and global variables inside a **<script>** block.

☐ Replace Microsoft Visual InterDev® design-time controls with Web controls.

☐ Replace Render Functions (code mixed with HTML) with calls to **Response.Write** or custom Web controls.

Functions

☐ Explicitly declare by reference (**ByRef**) arguments. By Value (**ByVal**) is now the default.

Methods

☐ Add parentheses to all of the method calls, even to the method calls that do not take parameters.

☐ Explicitly reference default method properties.

☐ Update the method calls that return multiple values from one-based to zero-based.

Variables

☐ Declare all variables; **Option Explicit** is now the default.

☐ Replace **Let** and **Set** with **MyObject1 = MyObject2**.

☐ Replace the **VARIANT** data type with primitive data types or the **Object** data type.

☐ Declare all date and time data types as **Date**, or as the common language runtime **DateTime** type.

☐ Replace **Date()** with **DateTime.Now** to get the current date.

Validation

☐ Add **RegularExpression** validation controls to all of the string inputs that come from users.

☐ Replace existing validation code with Web Validation controls.

Error Handling

☐ Change to structured exception handling:
   Try... (start methods),
   Catch... (collect and handle errors),
   Finally... (close connections, and release resources).

COM Interop

☐ Select the appropriate setting for your COM objects.

COM object Type/Method	ASP.NET Setting/Procedures
Custom STA (Components marked as "Apartment")	Use **aspcompat="true"** and early binding.
Custom MTA (ATL or custom COM components marked as "Both" or "Free")	Do not use **aspcompat="true";** use early binding.
Intrinsic objects (accessed through **ObjectContext**)	Use **aspcompat="true"**and early binding.
OnStartPage, OnEndPage	Use **aspcompat="true"** and **Server.CreateObject(Type).**

ADO

☐ Leave Microsoft ActiveX® Direct Objects (ADO) alone, if possible.

☐ Upgrade data access to Microsoft ADO.NET for:
- Disconnected operations.
- **DataSets** that are supporting data-bound controls.
- **DataReaders** that are supporting data-bound controls.

☐ Use ADO commands or **Recordsets** to fill ADO.NET **DataSet** objects.

Application Configuration

☐ Add an XML Web.config file, containing the following sections, to each new ASP.NET Web application.

Field	Contents
<authentication>	Authentication support.
<pages>	Page-specific settings.
<sesssionState>	Session state settings.

☐ Set the **Authentication** option for ASP.NET Web Forms.

Option	Description
Microsoft Windows® authentication	Use Windows authentication.
Forms-based authentication	Use cookie-based, custom logon forms.
Microsoft .NET Passport SSI	Use external Microsoft .NET Passport single sign-in service (SSI).
None	No authentication is performed.

☐ Set the **Session State** option for ASP.NET session state storage.

ASP.NET cannot share state variables that are stored in ASP **Session** or **Application** objects.

Option	Description
Inproc	Stored locally on the server, similar to ASP.
StateServer	Stored in a state service, processed locally or remotely.
SqlServer	Stored in a Microsoft SQL Server™ database.
Off	Session state is disabled.

 training

Appendix D: Review Game

Contents

Microsoft®

Overview

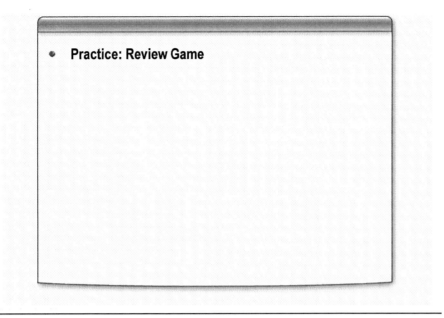

- **Practice: Review Game**

Introduction

Throughout Course 2640, *Upgrading Web Development Skills from ASP to Microsoft ASP.NET,* you learned many of the skills that are needed to develop, secure, test, and deploy a complete Microsoft® ASP.NET Web application. You also learned how Microsoft Visual Studio® .NET can significantly reduce Web application development time by simplifying the development process.

In this appendix, you will have the opportunity to apply your new knowledge in the practice, which is an interactive review game.

Practice: Review Game

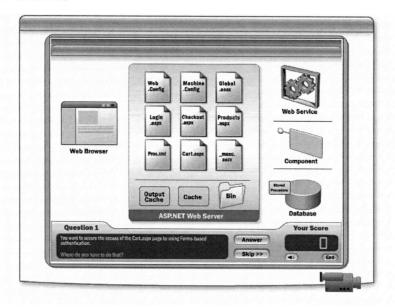

Overview

In this practice, you will run an interactive review game to test your understanding of the concepts and procedures that were presented throughout this course. The game is self-paced and can be run multiple times.

As you progress through the game, you will find that the questions become more technical and more difficult, building on previous questions. Therefore, it is important to understand the answer to the current question fully before proceeding to the next question.

▶ **To run this practice**

Open the file *install_folder*\Practices\AppendixD\StarterScreen.htm in Microsoft Internet Explorer.

When you run the game for the first time, you will see a welcome screen in which you choose whether to play the game in Microsoft Visual Basic® .NET or C#. After selecting a programming language, you will see a graphical representation of a Microsoft ASP.NET Web application. The illustration includes icons that represent many of the major components of an ASP.NET Web application.

The questions are displayed automatically in the bottom-left corner of the game. Each question has three parts to it.

Part 1

The first part of the question requires you to select the appropriate icon on the screen, based on the question displayed. After you select the correct icon, a code window appears.

Part 2

The code window is the second part of the question. In this code window, you will add the necessary code to complete the task that is stated in the question. To enter code in the code window, click any placeholder (represented by three dashes, ---), and then type your code. Your code will appear as you type.

When you think you have entered the correct code, click **Verify**. If you have any errors, the game engine points to the areas of code that are incorrect.

Tip   You can drag the error pointers away from the code to help you read the code more clearly.

You will then need to click the incorrect areas and correct the code.

Tip   If you do not know the answer, click **Answer**. The correct code will be supplied in the code window.

Part 3

After you have the correct code, click **Continue**. The third part of the question is a brief animation that shows which components are affected by the changes that you made. A pop-up window provides an explanation of the animation. You can control the animation by using the navigation buttons (Play/Pause, Forward, Back, and Skip), which are located in the pop-up window.

The game engine then returns to the initial screen and displays a new question for you to answer.

Scoring

There are 20 questions in the game.

Every question in Part 1 is worth 5 points; every incorrect guess subtracts 1 point from that initial 5 points. If you continue to guess after 5 incorrect answers, you will not earn any points, but you will not lose any more points from your total score.

Every question in Part 2 is worth 10 points; every incorrect guess subtracts 2 points from that initial 10 points. If you continue to guess after 5 incorrect answers, you will not earn any points, but you will not lose any more points from your total score.

In Parts 1 and 2, if you skip a question or ask for the answer, you will not earn any points for that question.

Part 3 is an explanation and animation of what you have changed; therefore, no points are awarded for this part of the game.

At the end of the game, you receive a **Game Over** message that displays your final score.

Notes

Notes

Notes

Notes

Notes

Notes

Notes

Notes

Notes

Notes

Notes

Notes